LOUIS'
CHILDREN

LOUIS' CHILDREN

American Jazz Singers

by Leslie Gourse

 Quill

In memory of

HARRY ANDREW GOURSE, who used to sing

"Marta, Rambling Rose of the Wildwood"

Grateful acknowledgment is made for permission to reprint the following excerpts from:

Dinosaurs in the Morning (Lippincott). Copyright © 1960 by Whitney Balliett, Jr. Originally in *The New Yorker*.

Reviews on Mabel Mercer and Frank Sinatra. Copyright © 1982 by Whitney Balliett, Jr. Originally in *The New Yorker*.

Of Minnie the Moocher and Me by Cab Calloway. Copyright © 1976 by Cab Calloway (Thomas Y. Crowell). Reprinted by permission of Harper & Row, Publishers, Inc.

Brother Ray by Ray Charles and David Ritz. Copyright © 1978 by Ray Charles and David Ritz. A Dial Press Book. Reprinted by permission of Doubleday & Company, Inc.

Billie's Blues by John Chilton. Copyright © 1975 by John Chilton. Reprinted by permission of Stein & Day Publishers and Quartet Books Ltd. (London).

This For Remembrance by Rosemary Clooney and Raymond Strait. Copyright © 1977, 1979 by Rosemary Clooney. Reprinted by permission of Berkley Publishing Group.

I Had the Craziest Dream by Helen Forrest with Bill Libby. Copyright © 1982 by Helen Forrest and Bill Libby. Reprinted by permission of Coward, McCann & Geoghegan, Inc.

An article by Ralph Gleason in the *New York Post*. Copyright © 1966 by the *New York Post*. Reprinted by permission.

Lady Sings the Blues by Billie Holiday with William Dufty. Copyright © 1956 by Eleanora Fagan and William F. Dufty. Reprinted by permission of Doubleday & Company, Inc.

"Louis Armstrong—A Self-Portrait," an interview by Richard Meryman. Copyright © 1966 by Time, Inc. Reprinted by permission of Richard Meryman and the Eakins Press Foundation.

Articles published in *The New York Times*. Copyright © 1953, 1957, 1968, 1974, 1977, and 1982, by The New York Times Company. Reprinted by permission.

Great Singers by Kurt Pahlens. Copyright © 1973 by W. H. Allen & Co., Ltd. English translation by Oliver Coburn. Reprinted by permission of Stein & Day Publishers and W. H. Allen and Co., Ltd. (London).

Early Jazz by Gunther Schuller. Copyright © 1968 by Oxford University Press. Reprinted by permission of Oxford University Press.

Jazz Dance by Marshall and Jean Sterns. Copyright © 1968 by Jean Sterns. Copyright © by Jean Stearns and Estate of Marshall Stearns 1964, 1966. Reprinted by permission of Macmillan Publishing Co., Inc.

His Eye Is On the Sparrow by Ethel Waters and Charles Samuels. Copyright 1951 by Ethel Waters and Charles Samuels. Copyright © renewed 1979 by Executor of the Estate of Ethel Waters and Charles Samuels. Reprinted by permission of Doubleday & Company, Inc.

Grateful acknowledgment is made for permission to reprint excerpts from the lyrics of:

"Ain't Misbehavin'" by Thomas Waller & Harry Brooks & Andy Razaf. Copyright 1929 by Mills Music, Inc. Copyright Renewed, Waller's interest controlled by Chappel & Co., Inc. (Intersong Music, Publisher) for the U.S.A.

Library of Congress Cataloging in Publication Data

Gourse, Leslie.
  Louis' children.

  Bibliography: p.
  Includes index.
  1. Jazz music—United States.   2..Singers—United States—Biography.   I. Armstrong, Louis, 1900–1971.
  II. Title.
  ML3508.G68   1984b   784.5[B]   83-13991
  ISBN 0-688-02241-3
  ISBN 0-688-02243-X (pbk.)

Printed in the United States of America

First Quill Edition

1 2 3 4 5 6 7 8 9 10

BOOK DESIGN BY ROBERT FREESE

Contents

Part III: Singers on Their Own

Acknowledgments

Special thanks to the musicians who gave their time to make this book possible. They include Joe Williams, Norman Simmons, Patti Bown, Eddie Chamblee, Billy Mitchell, Janet Lawson, Dizzy Gillespie, Thelma Carpenter, Annie Ross, Joe Muranyi, Danny Barker. And a hundred others. Thanks, too, to Gerri Wayne, formerly with Local 802, American Federation of Musicians; Footlight Records; George Simon; Ed Eckstine; David Chertok; Joy Harris; Jo Mangiaracina, CBS Records; Ray Ross; Dan Morgenstern; Barbara Mack; Al Feilich, BMI; Mrs. Eddie Jefferson; Mrs. Nat "King" Cole; and many others in the music business.

"I hear Louis Armstrong in all of those singers, even in Billie Holiday."—EDDIE HEYWOOD, JR., who can remember sitting in as an adolescent as the replacement for his father, also a pianist, to accompany Bessie Smith in a southern performance.

PART I

Prelude

In the beginning were the gospel singers and the blues singers: Ida Cox, Mamie Smith, Victoria Spivey, Blue Lou Barker, and especially Ma Rainey's protégée, Bessie Smith, perhaps the most powerful and popular of all, and a legion of others in the countryside and the cities, the North and the South, and wandering in between. And they helped to beget Louis Armstrong. And then everyone knew Louis. . . .

And Ethel Waters and Fats Waller drew some inspiration from the blues singers, too, and from musical theater, vaudeville and the music of the Europeans. And from Louis Armstrong. All of them helped to beget Valaida Snow, Mae Alix, Una Mae Carlisle, Sophie Tucker, Al Jolson, Alberta Hunter, Adelaide Hall, Jabbo Smith, and all the others who sprang from the temples of the blues and begat Bing Crosby, Mildred Bailey, Fred Astaire . . . and a long list of singers.

Find some of their names at the end of this book . . . a representative list of some bluesy-jazz, jazz and jazz-influenced singers, all part of the jazz idiom, which has been evolving through the century and never defined, except for its underlying swing. Some of the blues and musical-theater singers of the 1920s bridged the gap into the big-band era of the thirties and

11

forties, while others went Hollywood, or pop, or Fusion. Some of yesterday's innovative jazz is today's popular music; little of today's Free Jazz or Fusion Jazz sounds like the vernacular idiom that jazz started out to be in the early days of the century, when jazz was called ragtime.

CHAPTER 1

Cousin Joe
of New Orleans

The feeling of the blues is necessary for the singing of jazz. And there is no way to say where the blues ends and jazz begins.—DIZZY GILLESPIE

Every musician agrees that Louis Armstrong created modern jazz by the way he played his horn and sang. He took all the musics that he heard in New Orleans, fused and embellished them. And he became the first jazz singer—the one that everybody from Bing Crosby to Jon Hendricks, Tony Bennett and Betty Carter looks to as the Master. Of course, Armstrong heard the blues. To tell the story of the evolution of jazz singing, I set out to find out all the influences Louis Armstrong had taken in as a child and teenager. Dizzy Gillespie directed me to the Old Quarter of New Orleans. He said, "Talk to Danny Barker," a jazz and blues guitarist and singer, "and Cousin Joe," a blues singer, composer and pianist. "Ask anybody in the Old Quarter where they are. Anybody will know." Cousin Joe and Danny Barker would have heard people whom Armstrong had heard singing and playing. Joe and Danny, although several years younger than Armstrong, were among his musical precursors. Armstrong began modern jazz where the music of his New Orleans contemporaries left off.

But before I got to New Orleans, Cousin Joe arrived in New York City on a freezing night, with red silk shirts, custom-made suits and a Gibson L5 guitar. He always carries it along in case he wants to compose a new blues. He performs with a piano. "But I tape a song with my guitar, and then I play it over and over until I get it right. I picked up everything I know," he said. He was going into Tramps, *the* blues club in New York, for a long winter's gig.

Pleasant Joseph (his real name) has clung to an old blues style of singing for his whole career. A witty lyricist, a hip entertainer into the 1980s and an admirer of Armstrong, Cousin Joe never felt inclined to leave his roots or the folk art that surrounded Armstrong, too, as a child. Cousin Joe talked about what it felt like to grow up and drift into the musical life of New Orleans.

He was born in 1907, seven years after Armstrong, and didn't meet him until he was a world-renowned musician home for a gig at the Page Hotel. But Joe had known right along that Louis had spent time in the Colored Waifs' Home for Boys, and that he had come out "playing like nobody else. Some of the best musicians you ever heard came out of the Milne* home. Peter Davis had taught him to play horn there. And when he came out of Milne, he really upset people. Nobody ever heard a tone like that before." Neither Cousin Joe nor anyone else knows for sure "where Louis got it"; people believe that Armstrong simply made up his style. It was a mischievous thing to do, blow on the changes (musicians' slang for improvising on the chord structure of tunes); that's what Louis Armstrong was all about. Mischief is what landed him into the waifs' home. When he came out, the mischief was still in him but getting vented through the music from then on. Cousin Joe knew a good thing when he heard it; he started singing that way pretty quickly: the blues with jazz feeling, improvisations.

A sense of mischief led Cousin Joe to become a musician, too. He had a stable if impoverished family life but shared with Armstrong the background ambience of the Old Quarter and Basin Street's Storyville, the lure of the music and red-light district pleasures, and a desperate need to flee the grim prospects for a poor black child in the South. By the time I met Cousin Joe, his flight had been

* Another name sometimes used to refer to the home.

successful for many years. His story was archetypal for a blues singer—at one time as ubiquitous as rock bands. Furthermore, his work had spanned the entire history of jazz as well as helped spawn it.

At Tramps, Cousin Joe listened to Michael Barnett, a young blues guitarist playing in a trio, warming up the audience. Cousin Joe was particularly thrilled with the way "that young white boy can really play the blues. I've never heard any white boy play that good," he said. But the audience wasn't clapping loudly enough for Joe's pleasure. So he yelled at everyone, "Clap! Clap! What's the matter with you? Sitting on your hands!" then he turned around and said, "I'm terrible. Ha-ha-ha."

He ordered a glass of white wine and took it with him to the stage, where he found someone's coat and mittens lying across the keyboard. "Well, first let's get this off. Who does this belong to?" He looked at the band. No one volunteered, so Joe simply laid the winter clothes down at the back of the stage. "It's getting in the way of the keyboard," he said, unruffled. He picked up the microphone, couldn't hear himself loudly enough and called out to the sound tech, "Let's put a little more juice on the loose." There didn't seem to be any difference in the sound level when he pronounced himself satisfied and enveloped the audience with a mock-evil cackle—an upbeat version of The Shadow's "heh-heh-heh." But his ear is much sharper than almost anyone's.

And the man whom *Down Beat* magazine said had put wit into the blues, the way Big Joe Turner was known for making them jump up, began his gig with a laughing audience. Cousin Joe had a vital voice; sometimes, despite his age, still a very pretty, lyrical voice. He sang for a long time, then took a break to talk to the audience. "Lay it on my trio. They in this spaceship, clean out of sight." The white wine came in as a prop. He took a drink, "put a little more juice on the loose," sprinkled his hair with a few drops and told a couple of nutty jokes. "Fellow down in Louisiana gets some money, wants to buy some real estate and asks the Man, 'What can I buy for five hundred dollars?' The Man say, 'You standing in it.' Ha-ha! Heh-heh-heh! Heh-heh-heh!" And a few more. The accent is Deep South, but you can get all the words, while his charming delivery makes you laugh. This is a down-home blues singer with pizzazz.

More songs, and after an hour and a half the audience saw that this hospitable southerner had given a longer set than most New Yorkers were used to.

"When I came to New York, I had to have my own songs. They said to me, 'Do you have your own material?' I said, 'No, but I will have.' I came back the next day with it. Sometimes I used to sit in the back at recording dates, writing the lyrics while I was waiting to go on. I can sing my lyrics to any twelve-bar blues. It's just the lyrics, that's what counts. The lyrics are more important for me. I don't know how to write no music. I wouldn't know a note if it was as big as you are. I'm a lyrickist," he confided between gigs, lounging around his borrowed apartment in New York, in plain pajamas, robe and fraying slippers, watching soap operas on TV, whiling away the nonworking hours. "If you get different lyrics, that's your tune. I get professional royalties, and royalties for the lyrics."

He has written and co-written a long list of blues songs full of fun in their titles: "Lightning Struck the Poor House and Tore My Kingdom Down"; "My Tight Woman" ("I couldn't get a nickel out of her," he explained); and "Old Man Blues":

"Whatchya gonna do, old man, when another year rolls around, I've been a good old racehorse, now I'm broken down. From twenty to thirty, if a man lives right, it's twice in the morning and twice at night. From thirty to forty, if a man lives right, it's once in the morning and once at night. From forty to fifty, if a man lives right, it's either once in the morning or once at night. From fifty to sixty, if he's still inclined, You don't have to worry, because it's just on his mind. Ha-ha."

He has a quick ear, perfect pitch and a driving rhythm that never lets up. He can play ukelele, guitar and piano; he has even played bass. When he sings a ballad, he becomes more of a commercial jazz singer, reminiscent of Louis Armstrong, with a prettier voice. But it's not a spot he likes to linger in; the blues is his idiom. With it, he has managed to avoid working for most of his life, he said.

He was born in Wallace, Louisiana, forty miles from New Orleans. "Country, farmland, sugarcane, rice fields. In winter when it was cold, you cut the sugarcane. In summer you grassed the rice. My mother and father moved to New Orleans when I was two. In summers and on vacations, my father sent me to my aunt in Wallace. She would send her four sons and me out to cut sugarcane and grass rice.

"You can't wear no shoes in the rice water. There's snakes in the water. On land there's red ants. They eat you up. Some people get killed from an allergy to fire ants. We had to get to the rice at five A.M., and by noon you get off. You cut sugarcane from sunrise to sunset. I didn't like the cane because it was so cold. And what I didn't like about grassing the rice was them snakes.

"The only man who could wear boots in the rice fields was the foreman. He was as black as a brand-new Ford with no whitewall tires. If you saw the rice moving"—Cousin Joe made his hand shimmy through the air—"it was a big black water moccasin. The foreman had a hickory stick. He was a crack shot. He didn't never miss. He could break their backs, pick them up and throw them away. Then we'd get back in the water. I got tired of that.

"During winter, as far as you could see, it was sugarcane. I was trying to light a fire to get warm one early morning. The foreman, he was an old white geezer on a horse, he kept telling me to put the fire out, because fire spreads fast through a cane field. He called me 'boy.' They still do it some places, but not very much, because it ain't practical. He told me, if I was cold I should sit on his horse until the sun came up. But I threw down my knife and said, 'No, sir, I'm going home. I've never sat on a horse in my life.' I walked miles back to my aunt's house. I was age twelve. And I told my aunt Martha I had quit. She said, 'The rest of my boys are out there.' I said, 'Yeah, but they've been doing that since they were born.'

"Then I went to the gambling house that night. I found a rusty nickel by the step. I had learned how to play cards in my daddy's barbershop in New Orleans. My cousins, named Zeno, ran the gambling house. Two of the baddest cats in that part of town. They said it was 'okay' for me to come in, even though I was too young. In there one cat had won a home gambling, done broke everybody in the place. But I had learned the games since I was ten years old. That cat saw my nickel and said, 'Well, I don't want to see you with that.' I won my bus fare back home with that nickel.

"I told my daddy, I don't want to go back there anymore. So I went to Joseph A. Craig Junior High School and was promoted to MacDonald Thirty-five High School, but I quit to help take care of my mother and sister. My father had a job in Baton Rouge by then and helped build Louisiana State University and the Capitol building.

"I was eighteen when I left school. In grammar school I was too small to play football and was not tall enough for basketball, so I learned how to pitch baseball in the sandlot. I won five silver cups as a pitcher and bought me a dollar-seventy-five ukelele and started fooling with it. I could always sing and whistle, too. It was sort of a complementary instrument, the ukelele, in those days, just a rhythm instrument, like the guitar till they started picking the single strings. So I just sang the blues; I didn't know nothing else except some gospel and spirituals.

"I got my inspiration from the Baptist Church. My grandmother took me to church two, three, four times a week. I was sixteen before I saw a movie, but I was singing gospel in church when I was six. A child prodigy. I had to stand up on one of those big old high benches, because people couldn't see where the voice was coming from. There was no piano or tambourine or choir in those days. People just clapped their hands and sang. Some of the most melodious things you ever heard, some of the most gorgeousest voices came out of the Baptist Church.

"The minister told me that I had to join the church or get out. I used to get some collection money for singing. He said that I would have to sing for nothing if I didn't join. So I got out. But that's where I got the idea to go into music later. That's where the blues originated, in the Baptist Church.

"When I grew up, I bought a six-string guitar for seven dollars and fifty cents. I only could play on the last four strings, not the two bass strings on the top, that fine part where they bust your eardrums. Danny Barker, who was raised up with me, played all six of them strings. He taught me how to play all six eventually. But for a while, I had a band and didn't know how to tune my own guitar.

"Saturday nights, I used to play my ukelele for fifty cents at fish fries and all I could eat and drink. I just had me a ball. Nobody actually did inspire me. I just had Gawd-given talent. But when I started listening to phonograph records, I heard the famous women blues singers: Bessie Smith was the greatest. From what I heard her and Ida Cox doing, I got the idea to write my own lyrics.

"Where my daddy was living at, in Baton Rouge, there was a piano in the rooming-house parlor. I started fooling around with it when he was at work. By me being a guitar player, knowing the simple chord changes, I could do the same thing on the piano. The main thing that caused me to play piano was a band I had at the Famous Door at Conti and Bourbon for thirteen years. My piano player was Alton Purnell; his brother, Theodore, played sax and clarinet; I played the guitar, all six strings. I bought me a Gibson and a big old amplifier and pushed a button with my foot.

"During the Second World War, I was getting ready to play one night, when Alton Purnell called me to say he was in Chicago. He had gone there with a woman, who was a madam, with white and black girls, in the days when you couldn't walk down the same side of the street with a white woman. Purnell had gone up there on a holiday with her. I played the piano that night. When he came back, I said, 'Now, you get yourself another job. You ain't my friend if you gonna mess up my living.' I went across the street to the Absinthe Bar, singing alone and playing piano. I stayed there six years. I've been alone ever since.

"As a young man, I was considered as kind of on the handsome side. I had a lot of girls kind of take care of me when I was about eighteen till thirty, maybe older. I was a pimp, in other words, coming down to the nitty-gritty. I was married when I was eighteen to a sixteen-year-old girl. We stayed together for nine months and then were separated eighteen years. I got a job shining shoes in a white barbershop. I had one girlfriend, high yaller, with a white police sergeant for a client. She gave me her money and said, 'You don't have to be smelling feet no more.'

"Another one had a black mother and an Italian father; she was in charge of a pastry department and wore a pure white UR-MINE jacket. She would spend the weekend with me. I was young then and could last a long time. I got off work at six P.M., and her husband got off at seven P.M. She had me come by for that hour. Isn't that something?

"I learned how to change heels on shoes from a one-legged shoemaker. I would bring my ukelele to work. On Saturdays people would come to pick up shoes; me and the one-legged guy would harmonize, me with the ukelele. One day in walked 'Hats and Coats' and 'Green,' the two tapdancingest cats you ever seen. We nicknamed them. They said, 'You ain't got no business cutting up your hands.' We went hustling all over town. Afterwards we used to go to a place called Entertainer—a black-and-tan place, with white whores and black men. That place paid off. We used to stop there and settle up the money after the night's work.

"My first real big gig was in a club called the Gypsy Tea Room. I made ten dollars a week; started to earn a real living. I met Eva

Soule, a waitress, there. She was older than me, with three kids. She earned about ten dollars a night with tips. I helped her raise her kids for seventeen years. My stepdaughter is over fifty now. When I go to see her, she still wants to know what I've brought her. She still costs me money.

"When I was living with Eva Soule, I had about forty-five suits. I was one of the best-dressed men. I bought suits to match my cars. Once I had a lemon-yellow plaid suit to match my car. Ha-ha-ha. Later on I got married to Irene C. Joseph. We have been married for thirty-one years. Actually we didn't get married right away. We lived together twenty years. Then she decided: What's wrong with getting married? Now we've been married eleven years legal.

"After the Gypsy Tea Room, I went to work at the King Fish Club named for Huey Long on Ursuline and Decatur for a dollar-a-night pay and a big old coffee can. I passed it around and made the money. I had to take a cab home so the white boys wouldn't take my money. Then the white boys in that neighborhood near the water were terrible. And these cabdrivers took a liking to me.

"Then we come to the Major Job. At the Famous Door. I was the first black band to play. I played one half hour; a white band of Mexicans played for one half hour. The boss, Mr. Hippolyte Guinly, told me, 'I don't know how you're going to like playing with them, and I don't know how they're going to like playing with you, but nobody can understand what they're saying anyway, so you just try it.' That was before the bands were all mixed up the way they are now, black and white together.

"I've played and recorded with the best. My records are in the jazz institute at Tulane University. I've been to all the major jazz festivals. The big one in The Hague, Holland, in 1973. I've played every country in Europe three or four times a year. I've played with Dizzy. In a way, I was aware from the start of getting some respect for being a musician, because musicians were the first to integrate. But I went into music ... well, I never wanted to work, period. I never wanted to be anything but a musician."

It was similar to the way that Armstrong, living in the same milieu, felt in the boys' home when he began playing cornet, "married the music," and took it further than anyone who had played before him.

CHAPTER 2

Louis Armstrong: "Everyone's Pops"

"And you're sure lookin' FLY IN THE SU-MMER-TAAM," Eddie Jefferson sang on a WBGO record broadcast from Newark, New Jersey. A New York City restaurant piped the tune into the room's nether reaches one Sunday in 1981. For sure, it was the late Eddie Jefferson, a mainstream bebopper and storyteller with a soft, swinging style full of movement—a drawl here, a nasal whine there—who was enjoying a renaissance. The sound reached other brunchers, too, who had heard thousands of jazz songs, perhaps even by Eddie Jefferson, over the last sixty years. Jazz has permeated our unconscious minds. Almost any American can recognize the voices of Louis Armstrong, Bing Crosby, Nat "King" Cole, Ella Fitzgerald, Billie Holiday, Frank Sinatra, Tony Bennett and others with lightning speed. Few Americans recognize the voices of any world leaders so readily, with the exceptions of F.D.R., Winston Churchill or the Kennedy brothers. Even to people who know little about the differences between jazz instrumentalists, two singers never sound alike.

It seems as if the music were always there—the surprise of the jazz rhythms, the idiosyncratic phrasings, enunciations, improvised melodies, characteristic tricks, textures and qualities of the singers' voices. They form the landscape of the American sound.

21

One can't imagine a time when Armstrong's style of singing didn't exist. Americans abroad stop in their tracks for a familiar jazz song on someone's tape or radio, or for a foreign band trying to emulate American swing.

But it wasn't until the 1920s that modern jazz singing began. Louis Armstrong was singing in Chicago, blending all the musics he had heard as a child in New Orleans and making them swing, just the way he played his horn. By now the story of this American folk hero has become a popular legend. He was born on July 4, 1900, in a back-alley slum in New Orleans. One New Year's Eve, celebrating with three other kids, with whom he sang tenor in a street quartet, he fired a gun that belonged to one of his many stepfathers—and landed for a stretch in the Colored Waifs' Home for Boys. He came out "blowing sounds that no one had ever heard before," said Danny Barker.

Growing up, Armstrong heard Kid Ory, Jelly Roll Morton, Bunk Johnson and perhaps even Buddy Bolden, a legendary, rough-sounding horn player at the turn of the century in Storyville, the red-light district of New Orleans' French Quarter. Armstrong heard Dixieland, Indian chants, the gospel and the blues that the prostitutes sang on the streets, bending the notes, about how their men had mistreated them. Louis saw beauty in the girls and heard it in their music. He listened to the music of carnivals and minstrel shows. He had heard about the voodoo music of priestess Marie Laveau at Congo Square, once a slave market; one source says his maternal grandfather had played drums for Marie Laveau.

Armstrong heard scat singing, songs without words, the "monkeyshine singing," as Danny Barker said it was once called, of the Cajuns, descendants of the Arcadian French, in the bayous; and of the Creoles, a New Orleans blend of the French, Spanish and blacks. He heard dirgeful processions of military bands going to the cemeteries and the up-tempo return trips, with the drums playing in two—an early jazz beat with the laid-back sound "of Europeans clapping," said New Orleans-born drummer Vernel Fournier. Armstrong's genius would take it further.

Danny Barker, who was born nine years after Louis, knows that Armstrong heard, and recorded with, some of his contemporaries: Bessie Smith, Bea Booze, Mamie Smith (who was older than Armstrong), Ida Cox, Victoria Spivey; and other blues and popular singers of the day: early black stars like Lizzie Miles, Willie Jackson and Nookie Johnson. Ethel Waters worked with Willie Jackson on the vaudeville circuit, while Bessie Smith took Nookie along on her tours. Armstrong heard Mary Mack, who with her husband, Billy Mack, toured on TOBA, the black vaudeville circuit. The acronym stood for Theater Owners' Booking Association, but blacks called it Tough on Black Asses. Armstrong also heard Virginia Liston, a singer of whom little is known, and Esther Bigeau, a headliner with TOBA, and others who played at the Lyric Theater in New Orleans or simply sang in the streets and joints.

Louis heard ragtime piano players, who got a chance to play all the notes in the chords. He started playing them, too, on his horn instead of just one note. *And he played notes that the chords suggested.* Musicians called his new technique "blowing on the changes." It means that Armstrong invented modern jazz on his horn. He also sang the way he played his horn. He not only bent the notes (that is, glided from one to another, as every black child in church and every gospel and blues singer does) for a deeper, more plaintive musicality; *he also sang two to eight notes for one, notes that the chords in a tune as it was written had suggested.* His style transposed from horn to voice made him the founder of modern jazz singing.

"So many people died of trying to imitate Louis, sticking their heads out of windows in a blizzard," rapped Danny Barker. "They died of choking, trying to get that raspy voice like Satchmo's. Before him, singers were categorized as coloraturas, tenors, lyric sopranos or basso profundos. There were the blues, opera, gospel, et cetera. But Armstrong said: a cat sings from his soul, with feeling. It didn't matter about the voice. The style was how he sang, in his phrasing. Most trumpet players were playing staccato. Louis Armstrong began playing legato and soaring on the notes with long phrases. He sang the same way. To see him in person was exhilarating. He scooped up everything he had ever heard in Storyville and everyplace else and put it together."

By 1919, Armstrong had played with Kid Ory's band, regarded as the best in New Orleans, and with Fate Marable's riverboat band, traveling up the Mississippi to St. Louis. In 1922 Armstrong accepted the invitation of Joe "King" Oliver, a New Orleans-born cornet player and bandleader, Louis' mentor and inspiration, to join the Oliver band as second cornetist in Chicago. (Down home, Oliver had provided Armstrong with a decent cornet and platefuls of his favorite food, red beans and rice. With his transcendent charm, Armstrong later translated the spirit of that soul food into closings for letters: "Red Beans and Ricely Yours, Louis Armstrong.")

Armstrong went to Chicago in revolutionary times for the music world.

The recording industry had been under way since about 1880, but by 1920 it was still tentative. Eubie Blake had recorded with Noble Sissle's band in 1917. However, the races remained segregated on records. Blacks recorded sporadically—and only on race labels meant to sell in black communities. A publicity gimmick launched blues singer Mamie Smith's race recording of "Crazy Blues." One morning, Harlem shopkeepers blared it from their storefronts. People stopped to listen on their way to work. In short order, word of mouth brought about hundreds of thousands of sales and started a new industry. Armstrong began recording in the 1920s, working with nonpareil blues singer Bessie Smith, with Alberta Hunter and others, as well as with Joe Oliver's band and Armstrong's own Hot Five and Hot Seven groups.

In 1922 the carbon microphone was invented. Singers who couldn't pass the test of the microphone, which picked up every flaw, failed in their careers; others who mastered the mike became stars.

Newly invented, the radio became ubiquitous and added to jazz's impact. In the 1930s the redoubtable jazz Establishment figure John Hammond heard a broadcast by Count Basie from a Kansas City club and quickly put Basie in touch with Willard Alexander, then an agent with Music Corporation of America. Alexander started booking Basie on his way to international stardom.

The inventions spread the music. Race records carried the music of the blacks—a gospel of the vernacular—to the musically impressionable and gifted. Churchgoing blacks may have regarded the blues as a stepchild of the gospel. But every musician in the 1920s and thereafter felt a shock of recognition at the sound of Armstrong.

Ray Charles wrote that one of his main joys in life as a blind, impoverished child in Greenville, Florida, was listening to Armstrong on a jukebox. Billie Holiday wrote about the thrill of hearing him on records in a whorehouse in her Baltimore neighborhood. She also listened to Bessie Smith and Ethel Waters—two other influential singers who recorded in the era.

Fats Waller, a great Harlem stride pianist, entertainer and composer, became friends with Armstrong in the 1920s, when he first worked in New York with Fletcher Henderson's band. Waller had a light, straight style derived from musical theater. But in his recordings one hears many of Louis' licks (musical phrases) and improvised, throwaway lines. Waller liked to end a tune with sly comments about rascals, jampots, or about how one never knew—such touches—to the chagrin of Victor Records but the delight of his fans. He sang duets with girl singers, for whom he played piano, and entranced audiences with his shtick: "I'm saving my love for you . . . for you . . . for you," looking around the room, tossing a "for you" to each pretty girl. (Later Louis Armstrong would sing duets with great comedic-romantic flair with Velma Middleton and his own group, the All-Stars, and then, by the time he had received worldwide ovations as "Ambassador Armstrong," he made some especially popular recordings with Ella Fitzgerald.)

Sophie Tucker, a formidable and powerful blues shouter, heard the music of the black singers in vaudeville on records and in the black clubs of New York. Al Jolson, who had been influenced early by blues singers, minstrels and Jewish liturgical singers, heard Armstrong in the 1920s. By the 1930s Bing Crosby, who had been hearing jazz, including Armstrong, in the black clubs since the mid-1920s and who said he was influenced by Jolson, began making films with Armstrong. Fred Astaire, a Crosby admirer, was given songs to deliver in his own jazz-influenced style in films, too. The swing of the black singers infiltrated the styles of those early white singers, who knew a hip sound when they heard it.

In 1928 Louis Armstrong made an extraordinary vocal and instrumental recording of "West End Blues." The musingly scatted and hummed vocal version had the dreamy beauty of a reverie—a perfect jazz song because of Louis' spontaneity and flirtatious, carefree spirit. The song fits alto saxophonist Charlie Parker's glib definition of jazz as "a happiness blues." (Few musicians have ever agreed upon a definition of jazz. But Louis invented the style that made him sound as if he wrote the songs on the spur of the moment—the hallmark of much of his singing and the goal of every jazz singer.) "West End Blues" sounded just as spontaneous when he recorded it again at a slower tempo in the 1950s.

Technically Armstrong was childless, except for one son that he and his last wife, Lucille, adopted. But all musicians and singers call him "Pops" and cite him as one of their first and most enduring inspirations. Gunther Schuller wrote that Armstrong's greatness lay in his light, open, airy elegance of tone, the easy swing of the beat, the subtle and varied repertory of vibratos and shakes, a superior choice of notes, and phrasing. Subsequent musicians have kept elaborating upon Armstrong's inventions. But it was his treatment of the chords that made musicians who came after him his spiritual children.

Many books have been written about the varied prejazz musics of New Orleans. Field songs, work songs and ragtime had their roots in African music, particularly the traditional West African call-and-response music with drums and voice. There's no question that jazz evolved because of the everlasting miracle of the musical genius of the black race, from the blend of African with European music.

As New Orleans grew to be a major port city, it became a musical melting pot crucial to jazz development. Slaves from all parts of Africa scattered throughout the city with their diverse cultures and musics, blending them together and with European harmonies. Voodoo ceremonies, though outlawed for a while, became popular public performances. Latin influences from the Caribbean worked their way into the music. Military bands attracted the blacks, too, who formed secret societies. Each society had its own band, adopting Western instruments for funerals. Blacks played not only for the preservation of their souls but to make their mark in a musical way on the larger, white culture.

Barred from most pursuits, with black male children forbidden to learn to read and write on pain of execution, blacks channeled their creative energies into music. They carried on the African tradition of oral expression by singing their messages, histories and stories. The blues, which followed the call-and-response pattern of West African rites, often sounded exactly like gospel songs. But the blues had secular subjects and blue (flatted third and seventh) notes, with a half cry derived from the field holler, colored by European harmonies, in a twelve-bar form usually, or more rarely in an eight- or a sixteen-bar or related forms. The long lines made story-telling graceful. More important, the blues turned gospel-group praises into a cry of secular individuality: I am, therefore I sing a song of myself. The blues stand at the heart of jazz singing, as its emotional *raison d'être*.

In the reported memories of some southern blacks, the age of the great blues singers began as far back as the Civil War and flowered by 1900. The popularity of the blues ebbed by the 1930s, when the slow, mournful narratives about bone-searing woes tired a postwar public. Its fancy turned to swing. The blues singers' talents for storytelling in the vernacular carried over to enliven the more up-beat music. Stories came from musical theater, vaudeville and the black experience. At one time prohibited from speaking their own African languages, the slaves had developed an English vernacu-lar, partly from lack of schooling, partly to please their owners and partly to speak a secret language. Blacks became masters of the pithy, earthy phrase. LeRoi Jones in *Blues People* traced some idiosyncrasies of the black vernacular to the construction of Afri-can languages lingering in the immigrants' speech. Black English today still carries a remnant of that conciseness and musicality. Dashes of motherwit provide the spice. (A respected, college-edu-cated black jazz singer and lyricist, stopping in New York for a few weeks during the especially freezing winter of 1982, described his misery to a friend: "New York said: 'I'm tired of this hot-ass weather, give me some Yukon!, Now it's Yukon like a mother out there, baby!'" You can sing it.)

For some books on the early music of black Americans, see the list at the end of this book. Experts have written about African roots, black folk music, blues singers—most notably Bessie Smith, with special appeal for blacks as her queenly entourage toured the coun-try. Though especially popular in the South, she followed her records to northern theaters, where young jazz hopefuls—most of them black but Mel Torme in Chicago among them, too—plunked their pennies down to hear her. And she sometimes found herself the darling of white society in her raucous visits to its drawing rooms in the North.

Marshall Stearns has written a jazz history, *The Story of Jazz*, with chapters on the blues, ragtime, minstrel singing and gospel. Leroy Ostransky has traced the development of jazz in New Orleans, Kansas City, Chicago and New York, four jazz capitals of the United States, in *Jazz City*. Leroi Jones has explored the warp of the black culture and the woof of the music intimately in *Blues People*. Biographies of early jazz stars—Fats Waller, Cab Calloway, Duke Ellington and Ethel Waters among them—give a panorama of the first jazz scenes. One of the best biographies is *Louis Armstrong, a Self-Portrait*, edited by Richard Meryman who published the interview in *Life* magazine, April 15, 1966. Following are excerpts from an Eakins Press reprint that give the flavor of Armstrong, his era and attitudes:

—"When I got my first job in New Orleans playing in a honky tonk—Matranga's at Franklin and Perdido—I was 17, and it was same as Carnegie Hall to me. Yeah. Night I made my debut, I thought I was somebody. I took 15 cents home and I give it to my mother, and my sister woke up out of a sound sleep, say, 'Huh, blowing your brains out for 15 cents.' I wanted to kill her. Finally I got raised up to $1.25 a night—top money, man."

—"The time of those riverboats, we'd just put in to New Orleans and on the levee was a cat named Jack Teagarden wanting to meet me. . . . There ain't going to be another Jack Teagarden. Never was loud. He loved mechanical things, electronics. Go into his room, you liable to get shocked on wires. He was from Texas, but it was always, 'You a spade, I'm an ofay. We got the same soul. Let's blow'—and that's the way it was. He kept all his sad moments, his grievances to himself. But I could tell his whole heart, his life coming out of that horn. And it was all good."

—"Between trips on the boat, I'd go up on the top deck with the mellophone player, David Jones, and he'd teach me about reading music—how to divide, like two four time, six eight time, had me count different exercises. 'Course I'd always had that voody voody there to play the jazz. We'd just go to a department store and get one of them copies. The man who could read take the lead, and we had it from there."

—"All those years that trumpet comes before everything—even before my wife Lucille. Had to be that way. I mean, I love her because she understand that."

—"I don't try to get out of nothing. All I want to do is live good or bad, just live. If you're dead, it's all over. If I get poor, I'll still be happy. Like I always say, it's better to be 'once was' than 'never was.' "

—"I sang some in Chicago, but it didn't get big until New York when the arrangers like Gordon Jenkins made up the arrangements with me singing that chorus. I just went along with whatever they brought for me. Everybody liked the singing and I never was trying to prove anything. Just wanted to give a good show."

—"Jazz is all the same—isn't anything new. At one time they were calling it levee camp music, then in my day it was ragtime. When I got up north I commenced to hear about jazz, Chicago style, Dixieland, swing. All refinements of what we played in New Orleans. But every time they change the name, they got a bigger check. And all these different kinds of fantastic music you hear today . . . used to hear that way back in the old sanctified churches where the sisters used to shout till their petticoats fell down. . . . Now a lot of stars picking up the old records, and phrasing from them, and making hits. Ain't a trumpet player alive that don't play a little something I used to play. Makes them feel like they're getting hot or something. Real Negroid. That's all right. Makes me feel good."

And the books on jazz will tell you, too, that by the 1920s, because of Louis Armstrong the singers had begun trying to sound like horns instead of the horn players trying to sound like voices. And Armstrong was king.

Henderson's musicians laughed at Armstrong's odd shoes—"cop's" shoes, someone called them—until Armstrong played. Then everybody wanted to dress like a hayseed, as Louis did. By 1932 he played London's Palladium for the first time. In the thirties he began making movies. In 1947 he formed his All-Stars, the group he would perform with for the rest of his life.

Some of the funnier onstage vignettes in jazz happened because of the chemistry between Armstrong and his bandsinger, Velma Middleton, his professional soul sister. From the first bars of "That's My Desire": "To spend one night with you, in our old rendezvous and reminisce with you . . . ," she used exactly his phrasing. Her voice wasn't the prettiest in the world. But it was strong and reliable. She had absorbed his concept completely to enhance his performance. When he chimed in, gravel-voiced: "Mmmmmm, that's my desire," she gave the response: "Mine, too."

> HE: Hmmmmmmmm, we'll sip a little glass of wine . . .
> SHE: A little Mission Bell . . .
> HE: I'll feel the touch of your chops all wrapped up amongst mine—to hear you whisper low—doggone it's time to go . . . (*And a little sound of horses' hooves, courtesy of the drummer*)
> HE: That's my desire.
> SHE: Though you've found someone new . . .
> HE: Babababababababa . . .

After Velma died of a stroke on a tour of Africa, Armstrong was never able to fill her spot again to his satisfaction. But another jazz superstar, Ella Fitzgerald, became wildly famous for her duets with Armstrong; she with her ecstatic soprano, he with a voice described by one critic as the mating call of a piece of sandpaper. All those vibrant high Cs and upper-register straining that he did with his horn, repeated when he sang, increasingly took their toll on his voice. He recorded thousands of tunes and sang them in performances countless more times. Naturally his voice deteriorated; his vocal cords must have turned into giant nodes. But the raspier his voice became, the more popular his records.

One of the most inconsequential tunes, he thought at first, was "Hello, Dolly." Arvel Shaw, Armstrong's bassist in the All-Stars, recalls the group was playing a Chicago club, probably in 1963, when "Kapp Records called us to New York City. . . . They gave us the sheet music to 'Hello, Dolly.' Louis looked at it and said, 'What's this?' He hated it. 'You mean you brought us all the way from Chicago to play this?' But we did it. Later the All-Stars went on tours of one-nighters, stopping on many college campuses. Everyplace we went, they asked us for 'Hello, Dolly.' Finally, when it happened in Nebraska, Louis turned around and asked me, 'What's that?' I said, 'Remember?' He didn't. We had to send to New York for the music and relearn it. It became one of his biggest hits."

Armstrong sang it everywhere to crowds who demanded it for the rest of his life. He rebuffed criticism that he had sold out, gone pop, commercial. He defended his aesthetics, improvising each time he delivered the tune to the public he loved to please, saying he was onstage in the interests of entertainment.

He recorded "Mack the Knife" with some inkling of its destiny. He thought that disk jockeys would plug it on radio. But he didn't predict the smash hit it would become. He made one version for release by Columbia and at the same recording session sang a duet with Lotte Lenya, widow of Kurt Weill, whom Louis had known for many years. He gave the unique record to Miss Lenya.

"It was a great tune and a perfect vehicle for Louis, because of its construction and story. He liked substance in his tunes," said Arvel Shaw.

He swears that Armstrong's reported feud with the beboppers was a publicity stunt. Bebop musicians who evolved from Louis began, to put it simply, to play more notes than he had done, to discover new harmonies and dissonances, polyphonies and polyrhythms. Among the most inventive beboppers were Charlie Parker, alto saxophonist; Dizzy Gillespie and Miles Davis, trumpeters; tenor saxophonist Dexter Gordon; Thelonious Monk and Bud Powell, pianists. They had a profound effect on other instrumentalists and, of course, the singers.

Taking their cue from Louis' innovations, beboppers improvised solos based on chord suggestions taken from the blues and the standards. By improvising, they wrote thousands of new tunes, hundreds from the chords of "I Got Rhythm" alone, to build a vast jazz repertoire. Increasingly singers tried to emulate all kinds of horns—trombones, trumpets, flutes—and other instruments, sometimes with lyrics, sometimes by scatting. Most singers felt flattered when they found themselves compared with the horns they most resembled in sound. Some singers wrote still more new tunes by improvising from suggestions and improvisations of the instrumentalists.

Louis Armstrong reportedly accused the beboppers of ruining jazz. The beboppers believed in his deep antipathy despite Arvel Shaw's denial.

Says Shaw: "The All-Stars did a bebop parody of the Yale song, which we thought was kind of humorous. But Louis didn't speak ill of other musicians. He said that some bebop swung and had a good feeling. Some of Parker. He loved Lester Young. He loved some of Dizzy's work. There was some bad Dixieland that Armstrong hated."

In proportion to the debt that musicians and American music owe to Armstrong, the public has given spotty recognition to his legacy. Danny Barker said he suggested erecting an Armstrong statue on the site of the old Congo Square in New Orleans. A group of jazz musicians, including Benny Carter and Clark Terry, organized the statue fund. "At the last moment, somebody reminded these idiots down here [in New Orleans] that I had suggested the statue," said Barker. "So I was asked to speak eight minutes at the unveiling. . . . I . . . exclaimed that serious students should listen to his natural speech style, his immense humor, and compare it with the way popular music sounded before Armstrong . . . put it all together. . . . Later at a cocktail party [a well-known jazz concert producer] told me, 'You know, Danny, I never thought or realized seriously that Armstrong contribution . . .' "

Musicians who knew Armstrong have stressed his charm, his sense of humor, his tolerance of racial prejudice, and his kindness. "If they didn't let him in the front door, he went in the back door," one musician remembered. "It was the only place to eat in town, so he didn't care. People called him an 'Uncle Tom,' but he had to eat, and he got through. He joked all the while; he called everybody 'Gate.' "

One of the NASA *Voyager* spacecraft, carrying a smorgasbord of American culture, holds twenty-seven different pieces of music, including one jazz tune, "Melancholy Blues," performed by Louis Armstrong—perhaps as an extra inducement to the Martians to invade us.

People remember Louis Armstrong primarily as a gifted entertainer. But his genius still holds younger jazz musicians in thrall and influences their approaches, no matter what their personal styles are. Dave Frishberg, a boîte jazz singer and composer, recounting his influences recently, ended: "And Louis! I listen to him all day, all night. He's my hero for musical energy. It's much too stylized for me to sing that way, but he opened my eyes to the musicality of what he's doing. He really brings life to the music. "

CHAPTER 3

The Eloquent
Ethel Waters

Ethel Waters was already attracting some attention, singing in a bluesy style with musical-theater overtones, when Louis Armstrong arrived in Chicago. His innovations would affect her, too. And she would influence a whole generation of singers. "Ella [Fitzgerald], Billie [Holiday], Sarah [Vaughan]—they all come from Ethel Waters." Mahalia Jackson said it. By the mid-1920s to the 1930s, everybody, from Billie Holiday in Baltimore to Thelma Carpenter in Brooklyn, was listening to Waters' records.

"Ethel Waters was the first singer I ever heard," said Thelma Carpenter, a 1940s big-band singer, who was born in 1922. Thelma, all her life "a pretty little brown-skinned girl," as she has called herself, won first prize at age twelve in the Wednesday night amateur contests run at the Apollo Theater in Harlem. Hundreds of teenagers around New York, including Thelma, Etta Jones, Ella Fitzgerald and Sarah Vaughan, tried for the Apollo prize. Thelma sang "Stormy Weather" exactly as she had heard Ethel Waters do it on the radio.

"I shed real tears. They said, 'That child's strange.' People thought I was a midget because I sang 'Love Is the Thing,' 'Love for Sale,' 'Lost in the Stars,' heavy shit, man, as a kid."

Thelma loved Waters' enunciation. Almost every singer, unique among all the musicians, says the words are more important than the music. Of what exactly is a jazz singer or a jazz-influenced singer made? Of phrasing, intonation, pronunciation, enunciation, choice of material, improvisation, rhythm, and an independent imagination that allows a singer to challenge, answer and lead the instruments; in short, of countless little touches that make up the total sound and style of a singer. One such touch is "Chin-a," not "Chi-nah," according to the phrasing of a much later blues, jazz and pop singer, Joe Williams. Another jazz touch came from Waters in a lyric saying she was afraid that *Dinah might* get up and leave her: She sang "Dynamite," not "Dinah (space) might." Ethel Waters dealt with syllables and words as if they were her private cache of diamonds.

She could sing the Queen's English, though it's doubtful she could read much of it; she couldn't read music. She could hit the high notes like a silver spoon ringing on a crystal glass, at the beat of her choice. Her natural soprano could drop quickly to a rich contralto. And she phrased with feeling: "Every night I shake with fright, because my Dynamite [pause] change-her-mind about me [run together]. But ... if Dinah ... [she lay back on the beat]."

"We knew that she had a beautiful voice. But most of all she was a great delineator of song," said Thelma Carpenter. To demonstrate, Miss Carpenter imitated Miss Waters' drawn-out style on a lyric exaggeratedly. "You sing out, but you're delineating, painting the picture. She would be acting it. When she sang, 'to plough,' she was ploughing. Or when she sang, 'gay,' she was gay. 'Sing and play,' she was singing and playing. 'Sailing by' "—and as Miss Carpenter sang the words, you could feel the wind making the sail billow and the boat glide. Although her voice has always been lower and rougher, with a smaller range than Ethel Waters', Miss Carpenter had the right feeling for the original's phrasing. "That attracted me. You always knew exactly what she meant. She put all of herself into it. I called Ethel Waters 'Momsy.' I was allowed to stay backstage and watch her.

"She was a great admirer of Bessie Smith and Mamie Smith," Thelma said, though Waters herself wrote in her autobiography that she had never had Bessie's "loud approach" and had a low, sweet style instead. But she said that Louis Armstrong influenced her in the choruses on some recordings. "She heard Louis in herself, the way I hear her in me," said Thelma. "And of course she had two careers. She sang some dirty songs for some audiences. 'My Handy Man Ain't Handy No More.' All kinds of stuff like that. Alberta Hunter [a blues singer popular at the same time, and again half a century later] does it, too."

In her "other career," Waters recorded songs bawdier than the standards most people remember her for. Waters told several interviewers that she had disliked singing the double-entendre songs. When she tried to duck them, audiences called out: "Oh, come on, Ethel, get hot," she said. "Audiences didn't come up to Harlem to go to church. I wanted to sing decent things, but they wouldn't let me. They didn't even know I could."

She much preferred acting to singing. After opening to critical acclaim as Hagar in *Mamba's Daughters*, a Broadway play, she told a reporter on the *New York Evening Post*, "Now, don't mention anything I've ever done on the musical-comedy stage in the same breath with Hagar. It's easy to go along with a song. You pick up on the lyrics or some special strain in the music, and it carries you on. But this straight acting is different. You're out there on your own. You've got to BE the character—no matter what kind it is— and STAY with that character." She also said that she could only act characters with whom she could identify because of some life experience—the same method she used for interpreting a lyric.

Though Waters told the press she hated singing, Thelma Carpenter didn't believe it. Ethel Waters said nothing of the kind in her autobiography. Perhaps she meant that she disliked only the double-entendre songs, but not her great hits: "Stormy Weather," "Dinah," "Supper Time," to name a few. She wrote of her passionate regard for "Stormy Weather," expressive of her tumultuous marriage to Eddie Matthews—and for "Supper Time," about the widow of a lynching victim.

Once as she sang "Supper Time" at the Apollo, a man in the gallery started to snicker. She stopped singing and snapped: "I wouldn't laugh at this, buddy, if I were you. The white folks are still lynching our people down South. And they'll keep on doing it till you and your kind learn what it's all about." Before she had known if she would be allowed to sing "Supper Time" in a show, she hoped for approval, thinking it would allow her to tell "about my people . . . I knew I would be singing for all my people."

Of "Stormy Weather" she wrote: "It was the perfect expression of my mood, and I found release in singing it each evening. When I got out there in the middle of the Cotton Club, I was telling the things I couldn't frame in words. I was singing the story of my misery and confusion, of the misunderstandings in my life I couldn't straighten out, the story of the wrongs and outrages done to me by people I had loved and trusted.... Only those who have been hurt deeply can understand what pain is, or humiliation.... I sang 'Stormy Weather' from the depth of the private hell in which I was being crushed and suffocated."

She did associate singing with the hardest times in her life. She had as woeful a childhood as anyone ever did in America. Record books say she was born illegitimately on October 31, 1896, in Chester, Pennsylvania, to a twelve-year-old girl, Louisa Anderson, who had been raped by John Wesley Waters. Thelma Carpenter thinks Ethel Waters was actually a few years older than she admitted. She wrote of her sordid beginnings in nearby Philadelphia's red-light district in her autobiography, *His Eye Is on the Sparrow*. The nightmarish details seemed to have no relationship whatsoever to the bell-clear, pretty and feminine voice with a subtly lusty undertone. The little growls that she inserted into some of her most stylish songs were surprising—filled with fun and delight. And she did like her own voice, calling it "sweet and bell-like. On a clear night, you could hear me five blocks away."

She learned songs by hearing them a couple of times; then she simply opened her mouth and sang. All black children can sing, musicians say. That's not true. Some of the worst singing I've ever heard has been done by blacks in nonmusical jobs. Still, the gorgeous, joyous song raised in churches all day every Sunday offers relief from the grinding hardships of Spartan lives in barren landscapes. But some black children, Ethel Waters among them, have sung better than nearly anybody. She had plenty to try to compensate herself for by singing. Her mother was cold: "I worked hard to win her affection. I gave her servant-like devotion, but I couldn't get close. Her answer to everything I did was: 'I borned you! I borned you!' Sometimes I think this big size of mine has prevented me from becoming a human being. Nobody's protective instinct ever seems to be aroused by a huge girl. I was eager to feel sheltered and have people like me. I was hungry for a kind word. When it didn't come, I cried inwardly, but, being myself, I also began to build up my defenses...."

Her grandmother, Sally Anderson, a maid, took Ethel along on jobs, sang to her—mostly hymns—and raised her as a Catholic. Ethel christened her autobiography with the title of a hymn that her grandmother used to sing and which Sally Anderson on her deathbed asked Ethel to sing. But it was primarily as a sophisticate that Waters made her mark on song. In hundreds of other singers, especially the big-band singers who followed her, you could hear the legacy.

"She had no heroes," said Thelma Carpenter. "Certain things she said she was imitating. But on the whole, she was out there as an original and thought no one could do it better than she could."

In Philadelphia she heard vaudeville singers Butterbeans and Susie, a husband-and-wife team; the Whitman Sisters, a popular act; Charles Anderson, a female impersonator who did the "St. Louis Blues" and inspired Waters to get permission to do it, too. In the 1930s she referred admiringly to Marie Lloyd. "Marie Lloyd Memories, Parts 1 and 2" was a 1933 recording made in England by music-hall pantomime star Alice Lloyd, born in 1880. She and her sister, Grace, toured the United States successfully in 1907. Alice Lloyd sang, "The nearer the bone, the sweeter the meat"—a familiar American blues line. The English music hall borrowed tunes from the United States and had a constant cultural exchange with American entertainers. Waters might have seen the Lloyds on tour. But not much is known of Ethel Waters' early taste and influences beyond her grandmother's affection and religiosity.

Thelma Carpenter's account of Ethel Waters' personal life digressed from published accounts. Varied sources say she was married at age twelve, then again at age eighteen to Merritt Purnsley, then to Eddie Matthews, and finally to Eddie Mallory, a horn player, who once worked in a Cab Calloway band. Ethel arranged for Mallory to perform with her. However, Thelma believed that Waters had only one legal husband: Eddie Matthews—"pretty Eddie, a little man but nice-looking," who did some gambling and otherwise did not work. Waters probably never divorced him.

In her autobiography she told of going through a wedding ceremony with a youngster named Buddy when she was thirteen, but she hadn't signed the marriage license herself. Since she was underage, Buddy had taken another girl with him to sign. Waters never mentioned marrying Purnsley, though at one point she used his last name. Eddie Matthews was her legal husband, she wrote. She never commented on her legal status with Eddie Mallory.

"Men were very important to her," Thelma remembered. "She was famous for keeping men. They were all hustlers." Thelma pointed out that Bessie Smith and Sophie Tucker had the same kinds of relationships with men. "Ethel Waters was always buying men Cadillacs and giving them money. One time we were on the East Side. She saw some mink coats and said, 'Every mink on Seventh Avenue [in Harlem] I bought.' What she meant was that the men to whom she had given cars and money had bought mink coats for women. The men used Ethel. With her background, she wouldn't have known how to handle a so-called square.

"If it's you that's paying him, he's really a paid servant. And you can do what you want to. I remember one time I was with Ethel and Eddie Matthews at a theater. She bought the tickets. I said, 'Why doesn't he buy?' She said, 'What do you expect from a paid servant?' She was a difficult woman. But in her world she had to protect herself."

In her autobiography Ethel Waters never mentioned her friendship with Thelma Carpenter—or with anyone else. But after Waters died, Thelma said that she and Eddie Matthews had a long telephone conversation about Ethel. "And he told me that when he had met her, he had said to himself, 'I've got to stop wearing drawers with holes in them.' He knew when they were breaking up. When she used to sing 'Stormy Weather,' she would always cry. He noticed one day she wasn't crying. That's how he knew she had another man: Eddie Mallory." Actually Waters may not have met Mallory until a bit later. But it's true that "Stormy Weather" reminded her of Matthews. And Mallory came along soon afterward, by 1936. Did Eddie Matthews love Ethel Waters? "What kind of love could you have if you're living off a woman?" asked Thelma.

But Ethel Waters was alert and "street smart," said Thelma. She remembered a night when she and Waters were leaving a theater, where Waters was playing in *The Member of the Wedding*. "We passed the Coliseum, which was being built then. Somehow it reminded her of Germany in the 1930s. She had been there and thought it was so decadent; it disturbed her so much that she had wanted to get out of there. That's how the Coliseum struck her."

Another time, Thelma said that Waters was walking to her hotel after a performance and saw some homosexuals kissing each other. She hadn't liked it. But she quickly reminded herself: "What am I making fun of them for? I haven't got anybody."

She did have some good friends who were men. Thelma said she personally saw letters "filled with 'my dears,' " written to Ethel by "the great [Giovanni] Martinelli." Other prominent show people, writers and even European nobility cared about her.

She was less well-informed by intuition about handling clothes and money. Newspapers reported that she favored dark clothes and dreary shoes. But Thelma summed up: "She had no sense of style. I loved the way she would wear a housecoat with a mink coat. I would pick out clothes for her to wear in public. She had the most beautiful feet and legs in the world.

"And she was broke on and off all her life. As soon as she got money, she gave it to men." Some, Ethel Waters wrote, simply robbed her. "She walked around with thousands of dollars in her pocketbook. It goes back to the old days of not being acquainted with banks and taxes. She got robbed by friends because she didn't believe in banks," said Thelma.

Waters was known to ride the buses up to her property near 116th Street in Harlem. Late one night she rode home alone with thousands of dollars in her pocketbook, "a stately woman wearing diamonds like crazy," Thelma said. (Ethel wrote of wearing diamond rings for protection. If she hit somebody with them, they hurt, rather like brass knuckles, especially because she packed a mean punch.) "And not a soul, not a living ass, in the streets. But in her mind, all's well with the world. Out of the shadows comes this guy. 'Hello,' he says. 'I'm going to rob you.' 'Why me?' she says. She kept walking and talking. 'I'm old enough to be your mother, son.' He stayed with her. She said, 'I'm not afraid, because he won't let you.' 'Who?' the man asked. This was before she got religion. She said, 'Jesus.' 'But he isn't with you,' the fellow said. She said, 'But he is.' The fellow ran away. Just ran. She later told us: he didn't know the real thing when he saw it."

She became at times enormously fat and said it was "just plain evil—her way of being punished after she got religion." She was very jealous of Lena Horne and raised the devil on the set of *Cabin in the Sky,* a film with an all-black cast including Lena, a story that Waters confirmed in her autobiography, although she didn't say she was jealous of Lena Horne.

Thelma remembered being in a shower in a Washington, D.C., hotel room as part of the road company of *Pippin* in September 1977, when she heard something about Ethel Waters on TV. "I ran out and saw her picture on the screen. That night I asked my stage manager to let me make the announcement that she had died."

Ethel Waters' first job was as a chambermaid for about four dollars a week. But she kept an eye on the show people coming and going in the hotel where she worked, and practiced little routines before the mirrors. One night she wandered into an amateur contest in Philadelphia, won it and attracted the attention of two friends. They began managing her career and booked her into a Baltimore club for twenty-five dollars a week. But they gave her only about nine dollars of it. She went on her own, a vaudeville singer on the TOBA circuit. Eventually she arrived in Harlem.

She worked for years in Edmond Johnson's Cellar at 132nd Street and Fifth Avenue, which was known as a place in which people usually worked on their way down the ladder. But Ethel's singing was very popular. She liked Johnson personally and built a solid reputation that drew audiences to the club. She herself first saw Sophie Tucker at the Alhambra; later Tucker reportedly paid to study Ethel's delivery, though Sophie's own work sounded closer to Bessie Smith's genre. In the early twenties, too, Ethel did some haunting blues records with Fletcher Henderson's band and others. Piano player Lou Henley helped her learn standard tunes and characterizations. Eventually she replaced Florence Mills at the Plantation Club on Fiftieth Street and Broadway. Then Waters' fortunes began rising.

From the Plantation Club, she was invited to sing in Paris. But she refused. "I was dumb about traveling and didn't want to go," she said. "I asked five hundred dollars a week, knowing that would be too high. They took Josephine Baker instead. She was just an end girl and could mug. But she went great with my stuff. When I went to Europe in 1928 to have a wartlike growth taken off my vocal cord, they said, 'You so much resemble Josephine Bak-errrrr! Do you know her?'

"Did I know her? She was me!"

Eventually she starred in Lew Leslie's *Blackbirds* in 1930; *Rhapsodies in Black* in 1931; and in 1932 she burlesqued Josephine Bak-errrrr in *As Thousands Cheer*. But the rolled *r* was purrrrrrrre Waters. Hear it on a 1933 Brunswick recording of "Don't Blame Me," with Jimmy Dorsey on alto sax, Tommy Dorsey on trombone, Bunny Berigan and Sterling Bose on trumpets and Victor Young conducting. Throughout the twenties, her salary rose from $175 to $1,250 a week and kept going upward.

After Mamie Smith's success with "Crazy Blues" in 1920, Columbia signed Mary Stafford, billed as a black Kate Smith, then Edith Wilson. A small company called Arto signed Lucille Hegamin, a popular vaudevillian. The black-owned Black Swan recording company headed by Harry C. Pace and W. C. Handy signed Ethel Waters, who had done a little work with an obscure label called Cardinal. More than two hundred black women singers made records in the 1920s: among them Bessie Smith, Ma Rainey, Ida Cox, Mary Dixon, Susie Edwards, Sippie Wallace—mostly blues singers who worked primarily in the South. None had Ethel Waters' immaculate enunciation or versatility.

A national audience discovered her when she recorded "Dinah" in 1925, but knew nothing of her pitiful beginnings. Eventually Ashton Stevens of the *Chicago Herald & Examiner,* hearing her on tour, wrote: "A new star is discovered on State Street. Ethel Waters is the greatest artist of her race and generation." She had another fine record with "Shake That Thing." And in 1933 at Harlem's Cotton Club, backed by Duke Ellington's orchestra, she sang "Stormy Weather," a highlight of her career. Then came "Supper Time." Amoco sponsored her on a radio show. Irving Berlin, hearing her either at the Cotton Club or on radio, cast her in *As Thousands Cheer."* She became the first black since comedian Bert Williams to star in an all-white Broadway production.

She recorded for Columbia and Decca. Supposedly her records were not as carefully produced as they could have been and, of course, not equal to the woman singing in person. There is never any substitute for an artist in live performance. After 1930 the blues singers recorded a relative handful of songs. To Europe went singers like Adelaide Hall, who cited Florence Mills as an even bigger influence on her singing than Ethel Waters was, and who married an Englishman, Alberta Hunter, Valaida Snow, Zaidee Jackson, and Ada Smith, better known as "Bricktop," who would become a club owner in Paris and Rome. But Waters' legacy on records is arresting, with all the clarity and the poignancy for which she was famous. The vitality of her pretty face when she was Sweet Mama Stringbean is missing, of course.

Billie Holiday made her debut on records for Columbia in the mid-1930s, joining Waters, Armstrong, Bessie Smith and Mildred

Bailey to give the cue to the new wave of singers attracted by the swing of jazz and the popularity of the big bands.

Waters' eloquence, however, took her on another route, to films and legitimate theater, which, for her, from childhood, must have represented the American jackpot. Occasionally, she reappeared in clubs and concert halls as a singer. Oddly, for one appearance she received dreadful reviews; the critic hated the way she left the tunes as they were written and improvised her own harmonies. She might have been flirting with bebop. But she emphasized a career of straight film and theatrical successes in *The Sound and the Fury, Pinky, Mamba's Daughters* and *The Member of the Wedding*—and as *Beulah* on TV.

"I'd rather act," she explained.

CHAPTER 4

ℬing ...and, of Course, Fred Astaire... and Bobby McFerrin

The singer is Rudy Vallee, but for voice control, it's Bing Cros-beeeee.

—TAJ MAHAL

Dave Frishberg, jazz pianist, accompanist and composer, born in St. Paul, Minnesota, on March 23, 1933, grew up loving Bing Crosby. Really loving the voice. Crosby had become a big star a couple of years before Frishberg was born. "The best singer we've ever produced for our music," said Frishberg about Crosby. "Also Fred Astaire; [composer-record producer-singer] Johnny Mercer; Louis Jordan [a rhythm-and-blues singer]—I very much love them. And Billie Holiday. They weren't into virtuoso perform-ances; they were into putting the material across. Of all of them, Crosby had the best sound, the best rhythm and the best way of making a lyric live."

It's worth debating. Crosby built a megacareer on his voice. Frishberg has felt his own aesthetics came to a great extent from listening to Crosby. Not Frishberg's sound, which has more in com-mon with Bob Dorough, a breathy, pulsating, rhythmic stylist. But Frishberg sings without bending notes or scatting or trying to sound like an instrument. "I'm pretty austere about keeping to the

43

melody. Let the song do the work," he said. It comes close to sounding like an analysis of Crosby's style.

"Bing was the champ. I never heard anyone handle rhythm as beautifully as he did. He had perfect vocal delivery; he sang in tune. He did acrobatic things with his voice, but you never felt he was reaching for a musical effect.

"I met him at the Concord Pavilion in California a month before he died. I couldn't believe it! I was going to open a show for him by singing six songs. It was like meeting Babe Ruth and being out in the field with him at the same time. So I did my show. Bing shook my hand, complimented me and went onstage. He did thirty minutes of a show. Then the sound system failed. This fantastically expensive system went dead in the middle of his forty-minute medley of hits. I watched a frantic scene backstage. The crew was looking for the source of the electrical failure. They were shouting and screaming. But Bing stood onstage and said nothing and did nothing. The audience waited good-naturedly for fifteen minutes. He said a few things to some ringside people. They laughed a little. Someone backstage said that if it had been another singer, he would have been on a plane on his way out of town by then. But Bing didn't show one little bit of temperament. He finished to a giant ovation.

"He came offstage and said, 'What the fuck happened?'

"Oh, the best sound system in the world, they explained; they didn't know why it happened.

"I said to him, 'Well, that can't be the first time it happened.'

"He said, 'It never happened before in my life.'

"That was his last American appearance. He played in England and then died in Spain on a golf course. To me, Bing, Johnny Mercer and Fred Astaire were the first white jazz singers. They sang with the black influence and not in blackface. They brought jazz singing to us as an art."

Bing with his European influence came out and sang it straight, with quality, as the thing itself, not a parody or hype.

In 1977 he told the press that he preferred making records to any other part of show business. In stores specializing in old records, the bins overflow with Bing's records. Music about Christmas, shillelaghs, homes on the range, as well as standard love ballads. Bing alone, Bing and Jolson, Bing and Astaire, Bing and Judy, Bing and Satchmo, Bing and the Dixieland bands, Bing and Frank,

Bing and Rosie on "That Traveling Two-Beat"—the old-fashioned beat that New Orleans-born drummer Vernel Fournier, who still plays "in two" sometimes even in New York, has described as "the earthiest, with a certain amount of freedom and happiness. Dixie's a happy music to make you forget the remorse you feel, for example, coming home from the funeral."

That beat suited Crosby. He broke attendance records at the Paramount Theater in 1931 when he was twenty-seven, earning four thousand to seven thousand dollars a week. After the beboppers came along in the 1940s, he said he was confused by what had happened to the music. But he never dropped out of the ranks of that show-business elite known internationally by first names alone.

He sang popular jazz; you can hear it in his easy swing and his phrasing. He lacked great depth of feeling; his voice had, sometimes, a set and monotonous sound. Hoagy Carmichael, the pop- and jazz-influenced singer-pianist-composer, and Fred Astaire have more feeling in their idiosyncratic singing with their voices so inferior to Bing's relentlessly warm, deep tone. To some extent because he just sang and sang and sang, Crosby became a victim of overexposure, responding to public demand. So the sound of sameness as time went on. But he could swing, especially when the feeling was supposed to be offhand, as, for example, in "In the Cool, Cool, Cool of the Evening," which Bing recorded with Sinatra. Sinatra's voice is brash and harsh compared with Bing's mellow, sensuous tone and subtly accented phrasing that achieves a devil-may-care feeling. Bing's swing nestles in his understatement, a kind of pulse related to the bass, while Sinatra has more of the blare of a trombone.

When Bing sang "Blue Room," you could hear jazz influence in his unexpected phrasing; he accented *"blue"* instead of *"room."* He caught you with subtle improvisations, particularly fine on upbeat tunes. If a song were sentimental, his no-frills approach saved it from corniness. He interpreted "Cheek to Cheek" as effortless swing with pauses and emphases that made him the most political of singers—a real vote-getter, as Armstrong was. Bing sang, "I love to go out fishing, in a river or a creek ... ," substituting "crick" for "creek." One homey touch made a lyric his own, offhand love song. Even if he wasn't singing, "I love you," it was implicit in the tone.

He could sing about love and passion and God and complex holidays and passing seasons with such glib control that he marked popular music with a touch of Robert Browning: "God's in his heaven/All's right with the world." With his confident swing from jazz, he sounded in his element singing with Satchmo.

Born in Tacoma, Washington, raised in Spokane, Crosby had a family that liked music. His parents brought a phonograph and a piano into the house; his brother, Ted, built a crystal set and gave Bing access to popular music played in Seattle. He had an uncle with a strong Irish tenor. And Bing heard the Peerless Quartet, old-time singers Henry Burr, Harry Lauder and John McCormack.

As a boy, Harry Lillis Crosby (his Christian name) went around singing and humming; in his early teens he found a job at Spokane's Auditorium Theater on the vaudeville circuit, where he heard Gallagher and Shean, Eddie Cantor, Al Jolson and George White's *Scandals*.

In college he became friends with Al Rinker, a singer and brother of singer Mildred Bailey. With Rinker, Bing formed a five-piece band, the Musicaladers, in which nobody could read music. Bing never did learn to read it. So he, as drummer and vocalist, and Al, the bandleader, went to a local record store and learned by ear from Paul Whiteman, Fred Waring, the Cotton Pickers, the Memphis Five and the Mound City Blue Blowers. Eventually Bing decided to try his luck as a singer, particularly because he was earning more money from gigs around town than from his part-time job as a prelaw student with a lawyer in town. He quit college and drove to Los Angeles with Rinker. They went to Mildred, who was singing in a speakeasy. She got them an audition with some vaudeville producers, who hired Bing and Al as a singing duo for a show. One revue led to another. Audiences found them delightful, with Bing's voice offset by Rinker's more jazzy cadences.

Bing got a call from the Paul Whiteman office, inviting the boys to an interview. Bing thought it was a joke. But Mildred encouraged them to keep the date. Crosby and Rinker made a hit with Whiteman for a while. Eventually, for sophisticated New York audiences Whiteman teamed the boys up with Harry Barris, dubbing the trio the Rhythm Boys. They pleased crowds, even if they frequently displeased Whiteman—partly because Crosby liked to drink, raise hell and flaunt indifferent attitudes about such things as curtain time.

But in his Whiteman days, Crosby learned a great deal, associat-

ing with the legendary horn player Bix Beiderbecke and Red
McKenzie, an especially fine singer. And in California Bing met
Hoagy Carmichael and made a record of Carmichael's "Stardust."
In Chicago when Crosby and Rinker first joined Whiteman, they
heard Louis Armstrong. Crosby was a jazz fan from his earliest
professional days.

When the Rhythm Boys left Whiteman and went on their own
into the Cocoanut Grove in Los Angeles, Bing emerged as a romantic solo. Some biographers say that, at about this time, Bing, who
had been nicknamed "Binge" for his drinking scrapes with the law,
began to "get religion," becoming ambitious about making money
and conscientious about holding on to it. Harry Barris hit his
stride as a composer at the Grove. Bing sang Barris' tunes, "I Sur-
render, Dear" and "Wrap Your Troubles in Dreams." The dancing
crowd stood still to hear him. Bing began improvising to sound
more like a soft, laid-back string bass, some biographers say.

Still in his early twenties, he married Dixie Lee, a starlet and a
complicated woman with whom the equally complex Crosby had a
long, unhappy marriage. During this period, too, he left the
Rhythm Boys to strike out on his own, managed by one of his brothers in a way, some biographers tell us, that ruffled the feelings of his
former partners.

By November 1931 Crosby was singing four or five shows a day
at New York's Paramount Theater. Afterward he went to hear
other musicians. He was seen in the crowd at Harlem's Cotton Club
for Cab Calloway's opening night.

Bing got worn out at the Paramount from checking out the local
talent while perpetually showing off his own; his marathon party-
ing didn't help. One report says he lost his voice from overuse. A
doctor prescribed absolute silence to get rid of the nodes and warts
on his vocal cords. He had never had any formal breathing lessons
to speak of, had never run scales. So the strain made his vocal cords
look knock-kneed instead of parallel. Here's an extreme caricature
of what are actually little warts on smooth, glistening, thickened
cords.

like this: nodes

instead of this: no nodes

But his voice came back—if indeed he ever lost it. Stories conflict about Bing's reported bout with nodes; one biography says Crosby was drinking and had missed radio performances prior to his hit at the Paramount. In any case, he recovered from his difficulty. As the years passed, his drinking became less of a problem, while his wife became an alcoholic.

His career simply went on forever. After his Paramount success, he made his first feature film, *The Big Broadcast of 1932*. In 1933 Chesterfield cigarettes gave him a radio contract. He won an Academy Award for *Going My Way* and was nominated for *The Bells of St. Mary's* (and much later for *The Country Girl*). By 1940 he started the *Road* movies with Bob Hope, beginning with Singapore, on to Zanzibar and Morocco, *ad infinitum*. By 1940, too, he had many imitators. Perry Como unabashedly copied Crosby and had the vocal equipment to do a first-rate job of it.

Along the way, his marriage ran out of steam. He and Dixie Lee had been married briefly when she announced plans for a divorce. Bing made a good friend but an incompatible husband for her, she said. Biographers say that Dixie disliked Crosby's remoteness; he preferred to stay out at night with his cronies and increasingly pursued a sportsman's life—an interest his wife didn't share; his work took him away from home for protracted times. When Dixie Lee tried to divorce him, Crosby, a devout Catholic, flew to Mexico to dissuade her. He succeeded; the marriage lasted, but the couple and their four sons never found happiness together. Wife of one of the richest entertainers in the world, an unhappy Dixie Lee died in her early forties of cancer.

Several biographers have tried to unravel the complexities of Crosby's personal life. He has been depicted as ruthlessly ambitious, cold and distant, a sportsman, golfer, and entertainer first and a husband and a father last, a man burdened with an ailing, antipathetic wife—until he married aspiring actress Kathryn Grant.

But he built a seamless public reputation as an unruffled onstage personality, a good sport and a leading man that carried him along when his style of singing went out of vogue. The voice overrode jokes and mimicry. He seduced a mass audience with his average range, conversational ease and unique tone, as Nat "King" Cole would also do.

. . . and, of Course, Astaire

In the late 1950s Jonah Jones, the trumpeter, got a call to make a television special with dancer Barrie Chase and Fred Astaire. Jones had been working on Manhattan's Upper East Side at the Embers, a glowy supper club with the piano directly overlooking the roast beef and scotches. Jones had also made several records for Capitol. Things were going pretty well. One of the tunes was "St. James Infirmary." When Fred Astaire heard it, he "flipped," he told jazz historian Marshall Stearns, and "began to block out in [his] mind the dance steps to go along with [Jones'] playing and singing of the number." Astaire contacted Jonah Jones for a TV date.

Jones, who feels he hit his stride at the Embers in 1955, said Astaire's call surprised him. "He had retired like. But I was very happy to hear from him. He came to see me in a club and said, 'I've listened to your music, and that's the kind of beat I like. Do you think you're ready to do a special?' "

The show won nine awards. "Afterwards I landed on *The Perry Como Show*. I got TV, records and everything going because of that," Jones recalled.

His own mightiest influence had been Louis Armstrong. The beat that Astaire liked came from that. Jones had traveled in a Sunday-school band with forty kids from his hometown, Louisville, Kentucky, to stay at Chicago's YMCA. Chaperones took them to the Vendome Theater to hear Erskine Tate's band starring Louis in the pit.

"Louis stood up and started blowing. Oh, he sounded so good. He sounded better than on records. I probably would have put down the horn, if it hadn't been for that. I didn't care nothing about anybody but Louis," Jones recalled.

"From the beginning, I didn't know what I was doing [in the Sunday-school band]. I just did what they told me. I don't know where I picked up my style, but I had picked it up by the time I joined Cab Calloway in 1946. I had already been playing with Stuff Smith and Horace Henderson; I met Roy Eldridge [another great horn player] with the Henderson band."

All that cast a spell over Fred Astaire. He had started singing in films in the 1930s. From the beginning, he did "the straight melody and sang something sensible, with a good beat; he has good jazz feeling," Jones summed up. Astaire can't remember which singers might have influenced him by the 1930s. Certainly Bing Crosby for one.

"But," Astaire reflected in retirement, "I just sang it the way they presented it to me. Nobody told me what to do. There was nobody that I heard do it before me. I just did it. I didn't design it; I didn't say, 'I'll do it this way.' And sometimes it didn't come the same way twice."

Well, that's jazz.

In all likelihood he developed a jazz feeling for singing from his dancing, which Bill Robinson, the legendary tap dancer, called "eccentric." He meant that Astaire didn't belong to any genre except of his own creation. Other dancers in the 1930s concurred that Astaire's dancing style couldn't be pigeonholed. Charles "Honi" Coles, a much younger tap dancer, believes that Astaire may have observed and derived style in the twenties and thirties from Nick Castle, who did choreography for Hollywood; and Billy Pierce, who had his own studio; and Buddy Bradley, who became a tap dancer and choreographer in England; as well as dancers and teachers who passed through Ned Wayburn's New York school. Astaire studied tap-dancing with Wayburn, who did choreography for Klaw and Erlanger, Ziegfeld, the Shuberts and vaudeville acts. Honi Coles said that Astaire "sold body motion,"* while choreographer Cholly Atkins added: "He's a descriptive dancer who works painstakingly with his musical accompaniment; he was the first to dance to programme music, describing every note in the dance."† In short, he was a stylist who wrote that he always tried to avoid repeating anything in dance that he had done before. Singing was only a short step away. And the rhythm of his body combined with his conversational style of acting to instruct him in phrasing a fluid and kinetic song.

Astaire said, "Mel Torme is always complimenting me about my jazz singing, but I'm not a jazz singer. I didn't think that much about what I did as a singer. I was in the middle of the jazz era. Irving Berlin, Cole Porter, Gershwin, Johnny Mercer wrote songs

* From *Jazz Dance,* by Marshall and Jean Stearns
† Ibid.

especially for me and liked the way I did them. I liked them all. I might say, 'I don't think I can sing that,' occasionally, but when I said I would do it, I did it. Eventually I would do what was written. I used to learn it, and then I performed. You don't always get all tense about it. If you do, you don't get any result. I never lost any sleep about it, I can tell you that.

"I always tried to keep to the melody. I liked to do it the way it was written. But that's in the past. The early days. I thought it was very important to get the words across. That doesn't exist today. You hear a lot of smeary stuff, and you have to say, 'What the deuce is the name of that one? What's that?'

"I wasn't crazy about the way I sang. I knew I was getting a song across, but I wasn't a singer or a vocalist."

"Did you practice singing every day the way you did your dancing?" he was asked.

"Oh, no! I just did it."

With an immediately identifiable sound and a swing in the light voice. There were prettier voices. But the stamp of Astaire's style on a song enlivened the lyrics and swept audiences along with him. If you liked the light way he walked, you liked the way he tapped tapped tapped at the words and made a song come tumbling out. Most of the artistry lay in his phrasing, which was as unpredictable as the mercurial rhythm of his taps. On "Night and Day" from the sound track of an early film, Astaire stretched out the word "night," then hurriedly sang the following words: "and day"; in the context of the film's story, he was anxiously trying to keep the woman he was singing to by his side. He didn't want her to say good night. He purposely used the artifice of high style—a fast phrase followed by a slow, drawn-out one, and nothing on the beat—to get his desire across to her. He made it sound arresting and debonair, a sexual understatement. If he couldn't really sing, if he didn't even seem particularly interested in making love, he could be one of the classiest jazz acts in films by sleight of voice: "Night and day—day and niiight—day—and night." His *esprit de phrase* painted the picture of a twenty-four-hour passion. When he sang of raindrops, he slowed the tempo down to the speed of dripping raindrops. The "drip . . . drip . . . drip. . . of the raindrops" became the embodiment of nature and, with the smoothly swinging accompaniment, implied the nature of jazz.

Years after Astaire sang in films, Mel Torme fashioned whole medleys around Astaire's style, calling Astaire his idol and a very great jazz singer. Betty Carter, a purist, nods her head "yes" when you call Astaire a jazz singer. Bing Crosby, too, admired Astaire's singing. Crosby wrote a paean to it on the jacket of "Attitude Dancing," an old United Artists album by Astaire:

"One day somebody asked Fred Astaire just what kind of dancer I was. Fred replied, 'He dances about as well as I can sing.' . . . I have always considered this high praise. Fred has a remarkable ear for intonation, a great sense of rhythm, and what is more important, he has great style. . . . Style is a matter of delivery, phrasing, pace emphasis, but most of all presence . . . qualities Fred has in abundance. . . ."

On records the sound of his tapping feet heightened his delivery of a lyric. The singing was a part of his whole image, so chic that he made jazz singing seem as respectable as light opera in a country that still regarded other jazz musicians as folk artists.

By the 1930s Fred Astaire had married a Back Bay aristocrat; his sister married an English lord; their mother, the wife of a brewer, had impressed upon the children that they stemmed from one of Omaha, Nebraska's best families. By the 1930s, too, the sophisticated jazz improvisations that stemmed from Louis Armstrong had become part of Fred Astaire's persona. In Astaire jazz had already begun traveling in "High High High High High So-Ci-Uh-Ty" (as Armstrong later would sing it in Newport).

. . . and Bobby McFerrin

Astaire's style influenced one of the most unusual singers in the country: Bobby McFerrin.

By 1981 jazz critics began talking about scat singer McFerrin for his art-jazz work in performances in the Kool Jazz Festival. Jon Hendricks, rejuvenating his bebop singing group, hired McFerrin to tour for a while. In 1982 McFerrin appeared in a festival concert showcasing some exciting young jazz musicians. The concert was dubbed Young Lions of Jazz. As slender as an adolescent, in his early thirties, McFerrin arrived onstage with no visible instrument, a little guy in purple-colored pants, and sang a straight, solemn tune called "Nigerian Sunset" while conga player Daniel Ponce drummed an anxious tocsin. If Astaire can sound like raindrops, McFerrin, with inspiration also drawn from nature, can sound like a monsoon. Then McFerrin sang a Free Jazz tune, which he had written, in a trio made up of a bassist, a trumpeter and himself. The audience roared for the little guy in purple pants who played himself as if he were a horn, even fingering the air as if it were a horn. (Behop-influenced singers often affect that mannerism when trying to sound like horns.) McFerrin sang in a beautiful, high tenor, soaring to soprano, flutelike notes, then plummeted to the baritone register and plucked himself as if he were a bass, while playing conga on his chest—a most eccentric and innovative jazz singer.

Born in 1952 in New York, McFerrin started school in a Juilliard class for musically gifted children. His mother taught music; his father sang opera. They quickly spotted their son's talent. His first album, a mélange of ballads and scat tunes, came out on the Elektra Musician label in 1982. It gave intimations of McFerrin's wit, versatility and oddity even though it included no a cappella tunes, exactly what he hoped to become known for in jazz concerts one day.

He put a stop to talk about a dearth of good young jazz singers. In the 1960s and 1970s, it looked as if nobody were coming along to replace the old guard who had climbed to fame before rock eclipsed jazz; jazz singing was hard work with small pay. In the early eighties, critics began noting exciting young singers; Bobby McFerrin counted among the few.

A college graduate with a degree in composing and arranging, he played keyboard until 1977. Then he auditioned for a singing job, got it, knew that he wanted to sing forever and began learning a tune a day. His whole life changed at that time, he said; he became more confident, free, fulfilled. He has named an eclectic variety of major influences, probably one of the most unusual groups that any jazz singer ever concocted:

"Keith Jarrett, a pianist—he just walks onstage, sits down and plays piano. That's where I get the image of walking out onstage and singing a cappella. Charles Ives, the composer, whose work is full of life and nature. And Fred Astaire; there's just no one like him. The joy that he imbued his work with! He influenced my singing just by his dancing. The way he jumps around on furniture and makes things fly through the air. It's not so much his singing but the rhythmic thing he did with his feet," said McFerrin, who lives in San Francisco with his wife and child, teaches vocal improvisation and believes deeply in jazz education. "I like that as much as anything."

In short, McFerrin doesn't sound and certainly doesn't dance like Astaire, but feels a kinship with Astaire's unique élan and eccentricities. Both Astaire and McFerrin go out on a limb alone.

CHAPTER 5

Cab

Begin with exuberant scatting, then call "Minnie the Moocher." And that's how Cab Calloway, who co-wrote that song, launched himself with his ebullient personality at the Cotton Club in 1931, to international fame.

The comedic singing may spring to mind first when you think of Calloway. But he wore two hats musically—singer and bandleader. He began as a bandleader in the 1920s during Chicago's heyday as the country's jazz mecca. By the 1930s, and especially in the 1940s, Calloway employed magnificent musicians. Chu Berry, Dizzy Gillespie, Jonah Jones, Tyree Glenn, Ike Quebec, Hilton Jefferson, Illinois Jacquet, Paul Webster, Doc Cheatham, Leroy Maxey, Benny Payne, Milt Hinton, Danny Barker and Cozy Cole passed through his bands. Lena Horne and June Richmond sang with him. He discovered Pearl Bailey in the forties. As a singer, he also wore two hats—one of the ribald comic who charmed audiences, one of the master of every pop, jazz and blues trick in the book, with a rich, loud tenor voice that captivated other singers from Billy Eckstine to Billy De Wolfe. They studied him. The Calloway tenor was so robust that it qualified as a borderline baritone. In his biography *Of Minnie the Moocher and Me*, it's estimated that he grossed over nine

55

million dollars in his career. At the time the book was published, he was sixty-nine years old.

"And in semi-retirement," he wrote. "I still go out on the road occasionally, singing at hotels and resorts and nightclubs. I don't do it much, but I have to do it sometimes. It's been my life, and I can't stop entertaining just like that. I've slowed down, but I can't come to a full stop."

In 1982 at age seventy-five, Cab Calloway decided to "sit in" one night with some younger musicians (cats merely in their fifties) at Sweet Basil, a Greenwich Village jazz club. That year Calloway had been appearing at the Red Parrot, where audiences appreciated vintage jazz more than the Village crowds. The night he decided to sit in,* he had been in the Village anyway to see *One Mo' Time*, about New Orleans blues, at the Village Gate. So he did not have to go very far to sit in, even though the by now rare practice of sitting in, like the even rarer practice of jamming,† takes him a much further distance in time. (The musicians' union ended the tradition of jamming because musicians didn't get paid. But jamming used to be one of the main ways that young musicians learned to sing and play their instruments. Musicians have always gotten a kick out of sitting in or jamming whenever the chance occurs.)

Nearly fifty years ago, when jamming was a routine part of a jazz musician's life, Cab Calloway took over a Chicago band, the Alabamians, and brought it to New York City. It bombed at the Savoy Ballroom in Harlem. But the audience loved Cab's bandleading style. Soon he was leading another band, the Missourians from Kansas City, and starring at the Cotton Club, invited there by the Mafia as vacation replacement for Duke Ellington. Calloway renamed his group the Cotton Club Band, then Cab Calloway's band, and took it around the country and to Europe. By the end of the big-band era, when finances forced him to close down, he could look back on some of the greatest personnel lists in the history of jazz bands.

"I had one of the finest-sounding bands in the country, and I was singing out front. Yessuh," said Cabell Calloway III the other day,

---

* Sitting in: when a musician joins a group officially playing in a club and plays informally for a number or two, without pay.

† Jamming: when several musicians get together and play for a long time for an audience, without pay.

tucked away in the quiet, shady living room of his suburban West-chester County house. His smile was still rakish—an intimation of the dash that a young, flamboyant Calloway exuded in an oversized white zoot suit, tails flying through the air. You can still see him in the vintage film, *Stormy Weather.* "Just to have those guys playing was a thrill. Every time I got in front of that band, it was a knock-me-out. I had a lot of arrangements done for me. Then I adjusted to the band music and put a vocal in the middle."

Calloway fidgeted in his chair, walked around the living room, went to fetch a newspaper, signed a check for his wife, Nuffie, and sat down to fidget in the chair again. Very light-skinned, with an uninhibited Latin-lover smile (Billy Eckstine later imitated it but it came out looking like Clark Gable's), Cab Calloway can radiate energy.

In the 1930s the rhumba attracted him; it made him move, put him in the groove—and whatever other corny, megahip term you might dream up to describe him in pallid imitation of the way he used to talk. He was the master of overkill in hip language as well as in his clothing and rollicking performances, with a lock of black hair falling in his eyes. Television audiences remember him mostly for his manic renditions of novelty tunes and hyped and hokey blues, his swoops around the octaves, his growls and falsetto yowl-ings, and perhaps most of all for his individualistic scat words, "Hi-de-ho," which he invented in a Cotton Club performance. "I forgot the lyrics," he explained. He exaggerated every nuance of the straight, romantic balladeers, blues and pop singers. Other showmen-bandleaders inspired some of his antics, he has said. Through it all, Cab Calloway has kept a rich voice, barely deepened in his seventies.

"He was great, still in fine voice," said one of the younger cats with whom Calloway sat in at Sweet Basil. The younger musician knew how to play "Minnie" to accompany Calloway. "You know that one?" Calloway asked incredulously and was touched to find out that everyone did.

Born in Rochester, New York, in 1907, Calloway moved to Balti-more at about age ten and studied singing for four years. He had been singing in the Methodist Church choir; his mother played the organ.

"The family knew right away I was going to sing instead of play an instrument," he said. "They wanted me to be a lyric tenor. But I used to sing in nightclubs in Baltimore. I was singing jazz." And the smile flashed on. It glowed as exhibitionistically as the sun on the green grass in the ordinary suburban setting outside his doors —a setting he achieved as laboriously as any man ever achieved comfort. "My singing teacher, she knew it. She'd tell me, 'You've been singing jazz.' She could tell from the lessons."

He went the route that gave vent to his personality. "I was a hustler, ha-ha-ha," he said. "With everything that implies." Gambling. Pimping. All things he documented in his autobiography. "Ha-ha-ha. I made it.

"I had a little five-piece band when I was still in high school in 1926, '27. I was the drummer." Although his father was a lawyer and his mother a teacher, the Calloway family was "average poor," with just enough food and heat in the house and the rent paid. His father died at around age thirty-five—"I don't know what from," Cab said. In Cab's autobiography his father appears to have been hospitalized briefly for mental illness; he died in the hospital. Cab hustled newspapers on street corners, helped with the horses at the track—a Calloway passion—and shined shoes. When his mother remarried, he kept hustling to add to the family income and sneaked in jazz gigs at night. That money went to his mother, too.

His elder sister, Blanche, in the cast of a show called *Plantation Days,* became the first professional singer in the family. She tried to discourage Cab by talking about the hardships of show business. But he persisted. So she got him a job in the show, which took him to Chicago, ostensibly to study at Crane College and later to go to law school. "But I got involved in the shows. I had to make a living," he said. "Blanche got me a job in the Dreamland Café, later the Sunset Café, then the Plantation Club across the street. I really wanted to do music. I never wanted to become a lawyer, except to please my family."

He heard the whole gamut of musicians who passed through Chicago in the late twenties and thirties: Louis Armstrong, Earl Hines, Erskine Tate, Dave Peyton, Reuben Reeves and Sammy Stewart, who had the orchestra at the Metropolitan Theater in Chicago. He mentioned the instrumentalists first. He also heard Ethel Waters, Bessie Smith, Adelaide Hall. Hall was a New Yorker with a fine, low voice, who went to live in London and came back to the United States singing "Streets of London" as if it were her native and best-beloved city, her American accent gone but her debt to

Mills and Waters still obvious. Cab also heard scores of other singers on the vaudeville circuit and pop singers around Chicago. "But they didn't influence me. I just liked them. I patterned myself after no one. I was like myself," he said.

In his autobiography he wrote that he listened to Louis Armstrong pretty closely. "Louis' favorite songs at that time were things like 'Muskrat Ramble,' 'Gut Bucket Blues' and 'Oriental Strut.' All of the songs he did were full of fire and rhythm, and he was scat singing even then. I suppose that Louis was one of the main influences in my career. Later on I began to scat sing in the Cotton Club with all of the hi-de-ho-ing. Louis first got me freed up from straight lyrics to try scatting."

Cab's first big band, the Alabamians, bombed at the Savoy Ballroom in Harlem, because the band gave customers an old-fashioned combination of Dixieland and 1920s Chicago swing. "Dipsy-doodle Midwest music," Calloway called it. "I broke up the band. That's when Louis Armstrong got me into the review *Hot Chocolates*. We had met when he was playing with his band at the Sunset; I was singing there at the same time. Fats Waller wrote all the music for *Hot Chocolates* but wasn't in it." Cab went in as replacement for the juvenile lead and sang 'Ain't Misbehavin.' I did it pretty legit. I didn't stylize it at all. When I did stylize things, I used all my own tricks. I didn't get them from anybody."

He played for the audience's eyes, not just their ears. "I'd just go out there and move. Make people feel good and happy. That's what I always attempted to do. Some singers in a nightclub say they can't stand people smoking. I say that if you go out there, attract their attention, entertain them and keep them satisfied, they won't smoke. That's what I attempt to do. I was always very at ease onstage. No nerves beforehand.

"Financially it wasn't too bad," he said. The smile flashed. He didn't mention the ups and downs after the demise of his band. But when the money was good, it was very, very good—$200,000 a year, Calloway said in his autobiography.

During opening night at the Cotton Club, scores of celebrities watched him. Bing Crosby was so charmed that he arranged for Cab to headline at the Paramount with him. A radio network hired Calloway to do a nationwide show. That made him one of the first blacks to break the network color barrier. "I had good management from Irving Mills," he said, "after I got to the Cotton Club." Cab and Mills wrote "Minnie the Moocher" together, as soon as they saw Cab's hi-de-ho had won the public's fancy.

Critics recall Calloway's band of the 1940s more than the one of the '30s, because of the later band's illustrious personnel. Dizzy Gillespie played in it. And in the lore of the jazz world, Cab and Dizzy had a musical feud going on. Dizzy was playing more modern music than Calloway wanted. Dizzy also occasionally threw spitballs on the bandstand. One hit Calloway one night. After the show he fired Dizzy. Not until years later did he find out that someone else in the band, not Dizzy, had thrown the spitball that night.

Musicians lionized all Cab's bands because of the security the boss offered—August and Christmas Week off with pay, a fair employment practice unheard of for musicians in those days and still a rarity in the music business.

"They deserved it. So I just gave it to them," Cab said. "It didn't hurt me financially. We were making a lot of money. There was always work. It was a steady job."

Calloway played theaters rather than clubs in every town. "There were loads of one-night stands, one month or two months at a time, every night a different place. How did I keep my voice going?" He looked up at the ceiling.

His daughter, Chris, a slender, freckle-faced singer and actress, walked into the sedately furnished living room. She was wearing a visored cap embellished with silver wings and a brightly colored shirt, reminiscent of her father's penchant for costumes. "Look at him looking up," she said. "God must have had something to do with his voice."

She slipped into a chair across from her father and explained to him that NBC would let her take two weeks' vacation from her soap opera, *The Doctors,* so that she could play a couple of gigs with Cab at the Concord Hotel in New York State and in Beverly, Massachusetts. Road jobs. Cab Calloway has been on the road for nearly a decade with Chris, the third of five daughters, and the firstborn with his third wife, Nuffie. Another daughter, Lael, has also worked with Cab.

Chris was asked: "What was the first music you remember hearing?"

Cab chuckled and smiled at her. "Isn't that the damnedest question?" It had stymied him.

But she remembered nursery rhymes, French and country songs, and "Christmas music, because my mother is real big on Christmas music." Her mother promoted annual family Christmas pageants in the living room. That made "Daddy" and Chris laugh a lot. Hi-de-ho met ho-ho-ho, and the marriage lasted thirty-six years. Actually he and his high-school sweetheart, parents of a daughter, were never legally married. But he always maintained a paternal relationship with his eldest daughter and counted her mother, his first love, as his first wife. His second wife, with whom he adopted a retarded daughter, threw so many roadblocks in the way of his getting a divorce to marry Nuffie that Chris and Lael were born before their parents could untangle the finances and legalities. Cabella, a fifth girl for Cab, was the last child born. But by 1982 all the grandchildren were boys. Nuffie and Cab met in 1942 and married in 1949.

Chris remembered some of the ups and downs in her father's career. "There was a period when he was the half-time entertainment for the Harlem Globetrotters. I was about fourteen. He was going out there with just a piano on a gymnasium floor. That's not a glamour trip. That's hard times. That just impressed me so much. He had folks singing hi-de-hi-de-hi-de-ho. He was terrific."

Calloway talked about those days with a great deal of heart. After his band broke up in 1947, and he went from $200,000 a year to no bookings, he waited three years to get a break again, as Sportin' Life in *Porgy and Bess*. With that hit over, he went to a small combo and then to the Globetrotters. He had always loved basketball anyway and, in his autobiography, recalled his work at half-time:

"It was a ball, me just swinging and swaying with my hair flopping down on my forehead and my arms stretched out, singing my heart out. There's no feeling like that for me in the world. I don't care what the setting is, you put me in front of a mike, with a little instrumental support and a crowd, and I will perform. I love it." By 1967 he had another hit, *Hello, Dolly*, with Pearl Bailey. But though her father's fame remained, Chris saw the instability of an entertainer's life, even an illustrious one, at close range.

"Two years ago," she said, "I did a bus and truck show with *Eubie* on the road. That dispelled any notion of glamour. Athens, Ohio; Des Moines. The old Keith and RKO theaters. I think my father played those at one time. And universities and civic centers. You have trouble keeping your clothes neat, and you have trouble keeping your brain neat. It's a separate reality. You don't know where you are, where you've been, where you're going. It's scary. And hard work. You get off a bus and want to take a shower, and instead you have to face thirty-two hundred people who've just come in off their track. Either you want to do it, or you don't, my father has taught me. And if you do, shut up and do it. That's how you're going to earn your living."

Chris married for the second time in her early twenties to "a dynamic actor, Rupert Crosse," with whom she had a son, Osaze. Rupert, who was nominated for an Oscar for a role in the film *The Reivers,* died of cancer in 1973. Osaze was nine months old. Chris has not remarried.

After her husband died, "Dad said, 'Hey, come work with me.' That's when we created another relationship. I get along with him as a daughter and as a performer. Two very different things. We did two shows a night, six nights a week. You come offstage and have those things in common. I absorbed his professionalism."

Pacing the floor, Cab said, "I taught her to respect an audience and work to the audience. The singing, that takes care of itself. She watched me."

Chris: "You come off the bandstand and talk about the set. That's where we created this bond. Also I saw some of the raunchier aspects of road life. Out there, he can't pull the father bit with me. But when he comes home, he becomes my father again. I've seen him wishing he were the playboy of the Western world. The road is the road. You do what you have to to keep yourself amused. Up to eight years ago, he would go out to a place with me and hang out. Now he doesn't have the strength anymore, so he hangs around the room, watching TV. On the road Daddy and I just have a real, open musicians' habit," said Chris. "We communicate through the music. There's camaraderie, even if it's only on the surface. It's enough to get you through Des Moines.

"He taught me how to handle an audience, rehearse a band, deal with management. Not because he said: 'Do this.' But I watched him. He *did* say: 'Always take your contract with you to the job. Always check your music and parts before you leave the house. Always check your music before you leave the gig. Don't ever leave the bass book in Atlantic City. You can lose ten thousand dollars' worth of music.' I got traditions of that era from him. My style and interpretation, I got on my own or developed through my studies.

"Daddy also taught me: you give everything to your audience, or there's no point in your being there. Dad says it's not an ego thing. It's not entourage or camaraderie. It's a job. You're a fortunate person doing what you love."

PART II

Big-Band Era

CHAPTER 6

The Big-Band Singers: Introduction

By the 1930s New York and Kansas City eclipsed Chicago as jazz capitals of the country. And by the 1940s there was a brain drain of musical talent from Kansas City to New York City. But for one decade, a small area of Kansas City bounded on one side by Twelfth Street (for which the "Twelfth Street Rag" was named) became a magnet for jazz musicians. Hundreds of clubs opened in town. A corrupt political machine kept the liquor flowing during Prohibition. Well-heeled, high-living midwesterners on vacation, gamblers and varied gangsters flocked to the paradise of the Kansas saloons and gambling houses where management threw in some music, reckoning it as part of the overhead. In the long run, only the music survived the era.

Count Basie arrived from Red Bank, New Jersey. After a few years of scuffling, he formed his own band. Bandleader Andy Kirk had his Clouds of Joy. Others came and went. Yesterday's horn player became tomorrow's leader, and vice versa. Bands needed singers for the hot, swinging music of the nights. Pha (pronounced Fay) Terrell was one of the best-known balladeers, singing with Kirk. Blues shouter Joe Turner and Jimmy Rushing had stamina and volume equal to the challenge of the lifestyle and new band sounds. With the end of the Pendergast machine and Prohibition,

Kansas City lost its importance in the region's economy. So the clubs closed. Without work, the big-band musicians moved on.

But not before jazz Establishment figure John Hammond heard the Basie band broadcasting from a Kansas club and alerted Willard Alexander. Hammond and Alexander went to Kansas City and signed Basie with his singer, Jimmy Rushing. Big Joe Turner went out as a solo to sing in New York's Café Society and became a star on his own, acquiring, through the decades, backup groups with amplified instruments of the rock and rhythm-and-blues age.

Many musicians found work in Harlem, in Fifty-second Street clubs, in Greenwich Village spots and even in Upper East Side clubs with snob appeal. Finished with a war and coming out of the Depression, people wanted to dance. So each hotel had its trademark band. Musicians wanted to work with the big bands in the hotel rooms. Radio broadcast the bands live by what were known as "remotes." When the bands hit the road for their inevitable one-night stands, the fans from radioland turned out in droves to dance.

Young singers, who had listened to Louis Armstrong, Ethel Waters and Bessie Smith on records, found jobs with the bands in New York City. Early in the era, Billie Holiday arrived in New York, enthralled musicians and audiences, and began recording. The most exciting stylist since Waters, Billie became standard-bearer for a new generation of singers.

On the road, bands also scouted local talent. Basie found Helen Humes, with her forever youthful quality, singing at a midwestern dance. Artie Shaw found Helen Forrest in a Washington, D.C., club. Blues and ballad singers, jazz and jazz-influenced popular singers latched on to the swing bands and adapted their styles to the band arrangements.

Singers in the Apollo Theater's Wednesday night amateur contests won one-week engagements with leading bands; sometimes steady jobs developed. Ella Fitzgerald went with Chick Webb. Sarah Vaughan went with Billy Eckstine in Earl Hines' band, then with Eckstine's early bebop band. Anita O'Day went with Gene Krupa. Ivie Anderson, Joya Sherrill, Betty Roche and Herb Jeffries sang with Duke Ellington and Jeffries sang with Hines, too. Frances Wayne, clearly influenced by Ethel Waters, sang with Woody Herman; Doris Day with Les Brown. Martha Tilton and

Peggy Lee became Goodman bandsingers. Dave Lambert worked with Charlie Barnet and recorded, in duets with Buddy Stewart, with Gene Krupa's band. And Stewart sang with Claude Thornhill.

Johnny Mercer sang with Bob Crosby on radio; Rosemary Clooney with Tony Pastor; June Richmond with Andy Kirk and Jimmy Dorsey. Chris Connor and June Christy became Stan Kenton's bandsingers. Bob Eberly and Helen O'Connell starred with Jimmy Dorsey. Glenn Miller's orchestra had Ray Eberle, Bob's brother. Kay Starr, a jazz singer in her early days, played with Joe Venuti, a legendary nut and fine jazz violinist, and with Charlie Barnet. Lena Horne sang with Barnet, too. Frank Sinatra and Jo Stafford starred with Tommy Dorsey. Hundreds more singers began careers.

The era died out in the late 1940s, foundering on money—the costs of transporting bands and the dance taxes paid by the big halls during World War II. Musicians came back from the war to find their bands dispersed. The small-combo era had started. Nat "King" Cole's trio became popular in the early forties, after a rocky beginning in the late thirties. Some bandsingers went on to better days artistically and financially after they left the bands. Doris Day went Hollywood and pop. So did Lena Horne for a long time. Ella Fitzgerald and Sarah Vaughan became popular jazz superstars on their own, maturing in the bebop era, which clearly instructed them. Jazz-influenced pop singer Jo Stafford spent years perfecting her work in clubs and on records.

While it lasted, the big-band era served as a singers' boot camp. Many leaders handed arrangements to singers, no matter what their preferences or strong points, and required them to fit in with the group. Most big-band musicians, including the singers, suffered with low pay and rotten living conditions. Black musicians were segregated and harassed in towns they passed through. Girl singers were courted by the locals or by the boys in the bands. "Courted" is not really the word; "hit on," musicians' slang, reflects the spirit better. And the job never ended. A band went immediately from one gig to another, sometimes hundreds of miles away, with musicians driven by memories of even leaner days with no work at all. Singers and musicians sat on buses interminably and disembarked to hurry onstage. In hot weather they found themselves booked in the South; in cold weather they played the North. Everyone missed meals and sleep and a bed for the night. And "those days" for menstruating women meant nothing to bus drivers, who couldn't alter schedules and stop to help out with hygiene problems.

One has the impression that the big-band buses, trucks and cars riding around the lonesome roads were like time capsules or desert outposts; anything could happen with people cooped up together for long periods of time. There were flare-ups and quick exits from the personnel lists of the bands. Doris Day quit Les Brown to get married—and went home to the band when the marriage fell apart. The band was a family sometimes, with all the undercover passions that family life implies. Some bandsingers married musicians or bandleaders. Romances could end in chaos, with a singer leaving a band. And since familiarity can breed anything, sometimes a good love story happened.

The grueling conditions made professionals of the young female starlets and male heartthrobs. As the years from 1930 to 1945 passed, the styles of these musicians influenced the evolving art of jazz singing.

CHAPTER 7

The Kansas City Singers: Little Jimmy Rushing, Big Joe Turner and Pha Terrell

"Tell Them Little Jimmy Rushing, He's Been Here and Gone"

Little Jimmy Rushing was five feet tall and five feet wide. He didn't drink much, didn't smoke and didn't gamble. He sang the arias of the underdog with a swing, with Basie's band in Kansas City, at the same time that Fred Astaire was absorbing the beat for his high-style repertoire.

Pianist-accompanist Patti Bown remembered some good times with Rushing toward the end of his life in New York City. "I was hired to be a rehearsal pianist for Jimmy Rushing at Colpix Records. We were up there, rehearsing, when in walked Otto Preminger. He said with his heavy German accent: 'You're the shortest, fattest man I ever met.' Jimmy said: 'And you're the tallest, baldest man I ever met.' They laughed for ten minutes, fascinated with each other. They had never met before."

Patti, who is ample herself, recalled the logistics of taxi travel with Jimmy. "When he got in the back seat, I had to get in the front seat. He loved to barbecue in the spring on Long Island. He carried all that weight. And he walked proudly, like the cock of the walk. Like Marshal Rommel. He had a deep voice, and he was quick with words. Just the sound of his voice could make you laugh. You'd laugh to death. And then try to get the song right."

James Andrew Rushing was born on August 26, 1905, in Oklahoma City. From there he made his way to California to play piano in whorehouses. He did some ballad singing in a lyric, high tenor voice while he played. Attracted by the jazz scene in Kansas City, he went to sing with Walter Page's Blue Devils, one of the bands popular there at the time. William "Count" Basie, free-lancing around town, joined the Blue Devils, too, and became friends with Jimmy Rushing. After about a year, they joined Bennie Moten's band. Moten died. The steam ran out of the group. It took about six months for Basie to put a band together and book it into the Reno Club with Jimmy Rushing singing ballads. In those days men were usually hired to sing the ballads, while women did the blues. But when Willard Alexander signed Basie to the Music Corporation of America, management decided that Jimmy Rushing should sing the blues.

"So when we went down South," Buck Clayton remembered, "Rushing featured them more. He must have listened to Bessie Smith and probably Louis Armstrong, but he didn't try to sound like them. Basie was unknown in the South. So we recorded, with Rushing singing the blues. We shipped our records ahead of us. And that really saved the band. The vocal attracted the attention."

By the time the band reached New York, Rushing had a following. The Basie band, expanded from nine to thirteen pieces, had its troubles at first in the Big Apple, playing out of key with musicians who couldn't read music, historians say. Accustomed to head arrangements, the Basie musicians couldn't cope with a sudden expansion of the band's personnel.

But they stuck with it. Buck Clayton remembers that the band still numbered thirteen musicians, including Rushing, when it went to work at the Famous Door on Fifty-second Street. Each musician earned about a hundred dollars a week, far more than the Kansas City salaries. Fifty-second Street had many clubs—all as small as stables. (In fact, one was named Kelly's Stables, though probably not in honor of its size.) And all those clubs welcomed black musicians. For the first time, Jimmy Rushing sang "Mr. Five by Five" at the Famous Door. He also wailed his plaintive, warm and lyrical signature line: "Tell them Little Jimmy Rushing, he's been here and gone." He appealed to all audiences. The band hit its stride.

He wrote some of his hit songs while he was with Basie and had great comic appeal, too. In a film clip owned by David Chertok, a jazz-film collector with an impressive archive, Rushing dozed off on the bandstand with a saxophone in his mouth and dreamed of asking his pretty ex-girlfriend to take him back, promising to diet. He was succeeding with her beautifully, until Basie shook him awake. In another film, in which Rushing made a cameo appearance incidental to the story, he stole the show, negotiating his incongruously huge girth around a dance floor, wearing a blank expression on his moon face.

On the road Rushing was not a jolly barrel of laughs. Everyone on the Basie bus, called the Blue Goose, would shoot craps and lose money gladly to stay in the game and keep from going crazy on the long hauls. But Jimmy Rushing held back.

"He was tight with money," Clayton recalled. "One trick Rush could do. If you asked him for a dollar, and he had a hundred and fifty dollars in his pocket, in all kinds of denominations, he could reach right in and get the dollar. He wouldn't bring out any fives or tens. He was conservative. He lived a quiet life, even on the road. The most he did was eat ribs, barbecue. He didn't hang out with us much. We'd go looking for different places, but he'd go home. Maybe he figured he was too big to get around with the rest of us. He was very shy. And he was married when I met him. He got divorced, then married again."

Another musician remembered that Rushing told a story about his mind wandering to food congenitally, while other matters excited the rest of the band. The others gambled in the towns they played and sometimes lost in fixed games. So the musicians devised a code word for anyone to use if he spotted a fix. The word was "eggs."

One night as Basie was gambling, Jimmy Rushing became restless or bored or hungry. He said to Basie: "When you finish up here, let's go get some ham and eggs." "EGGS!" Basie yelled—and nearly blew the cover.

Clayton stayed with Basie for seven years, then went into the Army in 1943. When he got back, Rushing was out of the band, too. "I think it had been cut back to six pieces for financial reasons at the time," Clayton said. So stately, lean Buck Clayton and Little Jimmy Rushing, probably the fattest man in jazz, did some collaborating. Clayton arranged a record of numbers by the old blues singers Bessie and Mamie Smith for Rushing. "I wrote what he told me he wanted. He told me the songs and the keys that he wanted. I arranged them. Simple. That's all it really is," said Clayton.

Rushing started his own band to play clubs in New York, including the Savoy Ballroom in Harlem. He made many records arranged by Clayton and others, and went to Australia with Eddie Condon, Vic Dickenson and Clayton. Later, even jazz singer Bob Dorough, who has a soft voice and a driven, insistently rhythmic style, and who specializes in intimate boîte songs for sophisticated audiences, said that Little Jimmy Rushing influenced him despite the great disparity in their backgrounds and approaches. Joe Williams paid close attention to Rushing, Williams' predecessor with the Basie band. Dave Frishberg, a boîte singer and composer and pianist, names Rushing as a favorite.

When he was in his sixties, Little Jimmy Rushing became sick with cancer. And the unthinkable happened to him; he went down to about 125 pounds. He died in 1972. Three months later, his wife died.

"A Loving Proposition": Big Joe Turner

In his seventieth year, Big Joe Turner, last of the great blues shouters, packed crowds into Tramps, the New York City blues club, as he had filled the clubs in Kansas City fifty years earlier. He hunkered down at the club bar quietly. Over 235 pounds by most estimates, he had once weighed about 350, his friends, pianist Jay McShann and songwriter "Doc" Pomus, have estimated. Reportedly very ill with diabetes, Big Joe was sipping Tabs with his third wife, who is white and has a Texas accent. His broad face was unlined and calm as he waited for ten o'clock.

He used crutches to make his way to the bandstand. His lower body, stiffened by arthritis, floated through the air as his powerful arms did all the work. On the bandstand he sloughed off the crutches and picked up the mike. A vital, joyful baritone with a combination southern and midwestern twang bounded from the man to reach every corner of the long, dark room. The unsteady walk never signaled a quavering voice.

"He was a big influence on me," remembered Joe Williams, the eminent blues, jazz and pop singer of a later era. "He was the first blues singer that I heard where I could understand the words he was saying."

Big Joe Turner analyzed his fifty-year career—remarkable longevity for any singer. "Before me, most people sang slow blues. I put a beat to it. It's a jumper blues," he said.

Born on May 18, 1911, in Kansas City, Turner was among the first musicians on the music scene there. Not long ago, Bruce Ricker, a midwestern lawyer, left his job to make a film, *The Last of the Blue Devils,* about those days, with Big Joe wailing a blues again, unwieldy but standing without crutches. He was back where he had come from.

Jay McShann reminisced that one of his first impressions of the Kansas City music scene was Joe Turner's robust voice. "It was so exciting I couldn't go to sleep for fear I'd miss something," said McShann. "Big Joe would get up and sing for forty minutes. I never heard anything like it before."

Turner's beginnings were simple. As a child he heard gospel music in church. But he got his real music education in the streets.

"I learned from two street singers with a harp [harmonica] and guitar. I used to follow them around. Then I earned fifty cents a day leading a blind man around with his guitar, singing with him, when I was twelve. I listened to some records, folk, blues and pop songs—so long ago I don't remember which ones anymore. I didn't get my first singing job until I was twenty-one. Until then I sold papers, had a horse and wagon and sold junk."

Big Joe had no special glamour, beauty or obvious drive. But there was his energy—and a piano in the hallway of the house where he lived. He practiced blues songs, "improvising the words," he said, while he was a peddler. And he liked to listen to his brother-in-law, a piano player, in the Sunset nightclub.

"I heard him play. That did it," Turner said. It was not just his rich voice or his articulation that made him a star, he thought. Nor was it the influence of any great blues singer before him. He never heard Bessie Smith or Leadbelly.

"I owe my success to my creativity," said Turner. "I write most of my songs. I feel my creativity. It's an excitement. I enjoy it. I'm very sure of it. I like to write catchy words, good expressions, with a meaning to tell a story. My inspiration was my experience, the different expressions I heard people use, what they say and do. And I always loved music. It was a gift. It's one of the things that's the most fun in the world. I've been doing this all my life," he summed up.

Although music was a financially risky life, the insecurity never affected his singing. "I always sang 'up,' even if I was down. I sing because I like to, whether I get paid or not. I put some spirit into it."

In the rough days of Kansas City, Big Joe Turner wrote songs about the spirit of his times. One of his most famous, "Cherry Red," dates back to the early thirties. With it, he always elicits a rousing ovation from audiences for the buoyancy of the music and the wit of the lyrics.

"Runny here, pretty mama," Joe sang seductively at Tramps. "Sit down on your daddy's knee. I want you to tell everybody, how you been sending me. Well, if that's your secret, you better keep it to yourself. 'Cause if you tell me, I might tell somebody else. I ain't never been in love, hope I never will. 'Cause a loving proposition is going to get somebody killed. Well, you can take me, pretty mama, jump me in your big brass bed, I want you to eagle rock me, baby, till my face turns ... CHERRY REEEEEED. I want you to boogie my boogie-woogie, till my face turns CHEEEEEERY REEEEED!"

"That's the end of it," he said, reciting the lyrics for me as a way of explaining them.

"What was the inspiration for that one?" I asked.

"I was in Kansas City, working at the Backbiter's nightclub on Independence Avenue and Troost. Back in those days, they had big brass beds. I took it from that." A sweet, innocent smile lit up his face. "And from my own experience."

"It's a charming song," I said, "and a rough one."

"Yeah," he agreed, nodding; the smile spread all over his face.

Joe Turner, composer of such tunes as "Roll 'Em Pete," "Piney Brown Blues," "Lucille," never learned to read or write a note, and probably not much English either, say some musicians. But he has held sophisticated audiences in thrall with music with the flavor of a frontier society.

At age sixty he moved to Los Angeles, having long ago left Kansas City to travel around the world, moving to New York in the 1980s. Then he was as much of a star at Tramps as he had been years before during a five-year gig at Café Society, the first racially integrated downtown club in town. He recorded with Count Basie and Sonny Stitt and never felt himself handicapped for one moment by not being able to read or write. No one surpassed him in his genre. He said no younger blues singers had caught his ear the way he caught theirs. (Though perhaps he had simply never crossed paths with Pearl Murray, a blues singer in Houston, Texas, who once owned a club in Manhattan.)

Pha Terrell

Andy Kirk, who worked for a while as a letter carrier, had early music lessons in Denver public schools with Paul Whiteman's father around 1910. "A good school system," Kirk said. In his eighties, attractive, witty, and wearing a fluorescent, pink-colored shirt, neat suit and preppy tie, he recalled touring the Southwest, and, by the 1930s, starring with his own band in Kansas City. With him he had singers June Richmond, Henry Wells, whom the critics loved, and pianist Mary Lou Williams. And Pha Terrell, whom critics did not like. But musicians have always had their own preferences and ideals.

When Harry Truman was a judge in the era of the Pendergast political machine, Pha Terrell was a slightly known singer and dancer in a club where he was also the bouncer, a short man with strong, muscular arms. Somebody told Kirk that Terrell was a fine singer.

"So I went by to see him," Kirk recalled. "He sang 'Lullaby of the Leaves.' That impressed me. I asked him if he had ever thought of a singing career. He said no. I asked him if he would like to go on the road with me. He said yes."

Kirk's band, which played waltzes at country-club dances as well as jazz, had record sales of sixteen thousand to eighteen thousand copies—nice figures—with Vocalion, the race-records label for Brunswick. Brunswick's boss, Jack Kapp, then started the Decca label in New York City, and wanted Kirk's band to do some jazz. Kirk said he wanted Pha Terrell to do a ballad. Kapp said, "Why?

How come when you fellas get going, you always want to do what the white boys are doing?" "No," Kirk said, "I've been doing ballads before I met you." Kirk's band recorded Fletcher Henderson's theme song, "Christopher Columbus," and, apropos the ballad, got Kapp to compromise with "Until the Real Thing Comes Along." Kapp heard it "and didn't think much about it," Kirk recalled. "But I *knew*. We had eighty-six thousand sales. When I went back to Jack Kapp to do jazz, he said, 'Poor Butterfly.' "

Pha Terrell emoted. Critics called him "unctuous" and criticized his histrionic falsetto. But musicians remember that audiences loved him; he could really sell a song. "There was no bigger hit than 'Until the Real Thing Comes Along' for a long time," Buck Clayton remembered. "The ladies carried on, passed out like they did for Frank Sinatra. Pha was a dapper kind of guy, wore nice clothes. He wasn't big but strong. And a nice person."

Kirk remembers one night when the band was playing in Durham, South Carolina, in the late thirties and early forties at a segregated black dance, with whites from Duke University and North Carolina State in the balcony. Terrell was singing on a bandstand about four feet off the floor. A young man, a head taller than Terrell, stood at the edge of the stand. The man may not have liked Terrell's looks—something like that, Kirk recalled. As Terrell was singing, the man tried to shove the microphone into Terrell's face. But Pha had a good grip on the mike. It held still. After the first chorus, Terrell moved back. Kirk pulled the mike back from the edge of the bandstand. Terrell took it forward again to do the last sixteen bars of the song.

"Afterwards he leaned down," Kirk recalled, "and must have said something. So the guy jumped up on the stage to meet his death. Pha flattened him. The audience yelled: 'More! More!' He didn't bother anybody, unless you bothered him."

Eventually Terrell left the band, sensing the era was changing, from big bands to small groups, and settled in California, working in intimate clubs. Divorced, he bought a two-family house and brought his mother from Kansas City to live in California. Kirk's band went into the Orpheum Theater for an engagement. On the last night, Kirk invited Terrell and actress Hattie McDaniel to play with him.

"Afterwards, he took us out to his house for dinner. He was doing fine. That was in July 1942," Kirk remembered. "In September, he was dead. He had been a tough little guy. So when he got some pains in his back, he didn't pay attention and take care of it. It was a kidney infection."

He left about fifty recorded songs. In the mid-1940s, Joe Williams, then making a name for himself in the Midwest, sang with some Terrell influence with Kirk's band. Williams had recalled audiences going "Aaaaaaaahhhhhhh" when Terrell sang. Billy Eckstine, struggling as a singer when Terrell was enjoying his heyday, liked Terrell's crowd-pleasing work, too.

CHAPTER 8

"There Was No Middle Ground with Billie Holiday"

"Originality should be the highest goal ... without it, art or anything else stagnates and eventually degenerates,"* said Lester Young, who played tenor saxophone as languidly as Billie Holiday sang.

Unlike Young, who could sing the praises of his soft-toned, articulately original music, Billie Holiday reacted instinctively, stunned by artistic criticism and racial persecution. She and Lester Young were musical "soul mates," one of the finest teams in jazz. And they were kindred spirits in despondency. Both drank themselves to death in the late 1950s. But Billie's excesses were not the source of her misery. She emerged from a childhood of crushing abuse, armed only with a potent voice and a slender memory of an affectionate grandmother, and found that a great number of people disliked her singing style. It was not commercial. The world abused her, too, as a black and as a woman. So she tranquilized herself with drugs against the memories and the ongoing brutal experiences. Eventually she switched from heroin to alcohol, which gave her cirrhosis of the liver. Weakened by alcoholism, she died of a kidney infection at age forty-four.

Much of what was written about her is inaccurate, her friends

* From *Billie's Blues,* by John Chilton.

have said. She beclouded her own autobiography to make it commercial. Furthermore, she didn't come under close scrutiny as a cult figure and a musical innovator until after her death. Bobby Tucker, her good friend and accompanist in the late 1940s, before and after she served a jail sentence for drugs, has discounted the veracity of her autobiography with its attention-getting opening paragraph: "Mom and Dad were just a couple of kids when they got married. He was eighteen, she was fifteen, and I was three." Tucker himself intuitively preferred not to ask questions about the truth.

John Chilton wrote *Billie's Blues,* a postmortem biography as accurate as anything published about her personal life. Friends and acquaintances have shed some light on aspects of Miss Holiday, called Lady Day or simply Lady by her friends, a title conferred by Lester "Prez" Young. (She in turn gave him his title, "President of the Tenor Saxophone.")

In her autobiography, not Chilton's work, Billie said that her mother left Baltimore to find work in the North. Billie, a young girl at the time, stayed in the care of an aunt and vicious cousins who abused her. An affectionate grandmother died in Billie's arms. Eventually her mother, Sadie Fagan, returned to Baltimore and took Billie to live with her. The father, Clarence Holiday, a guitarist, had been long gone from the scene, leaving Sadie and Eleonora (Billie's real name) to fend for themselves. Billie took her stage name from Billie Dove, an actress.

She began her métier by cleaning the steps of a local whorehouse, and as payment, she listened to the house's records of Bessie Smith and Louis Armstrong. Other sources say Billie worked in the house as a prostitute. As a child, she had already been raped by a neighbor and sent to jail for his crime, accused of enticing him. Her mother remarried a dockworker briefly. But he was killed in an accident on the job. Probably traumatized and bereft, Sadie never remarried. Then that elusive, or in any case inconsistent, mother left for the North again.

Billie followed but didn't join Sadie right away. Billie tried her luck for a while as a maid and then as a prostitute. When she and her mother met again, Sadie maintained an exploitative attitude toward Billie, perceiving the teenager in part as a meal ticket, according to Billie's autobiography. Billie occasionally importuned Clarence Holiday for money at stage doors—to his chagrin. Billie grew to be a tall, stately teenager, and for a while weighed about two hundred pounds. Finally, desperate for money, with her mother sick in bed, Billie looked for work as a dancer in a Harlem club, she said. She danced pathetically, then started to sing. That was how she got her first paying job as a singer, Billie reported, though Chilton's book said musicians remembered her singing professionally at joints around New York City before the Harlem gig.

Billie began attracting attention right away. John Hammond, with a great eye and ear for talent, discovered her at another club and pushed for record dates. She was booked at the Apollo Theater. John Chilton wrote of her stage presence: "The sight of this tall, buxom, beautiful girl with the exquisite coloring was enough to make any neck swivel. On looks alone, Billie was potential star material, but her voice was her greatest asset, for she sang in a style that was new to the world."

Clarence Holiday did not agree at first. He disliked her style, predicted her failure unless she changed it, and tried to deny his paternity because it interfered with the impression he was trying to make on young women. (He had remarried and also taken on a mistress, with whom he had children.) He did not evince any pride in Billie until she was rebooked at the Apollo. She in turn called herself Billie Halliday, until her father's attitude toward her softened. He died, a relatively young man, of pneumonia in 1937, a virtual stranger to Billie, just as her musical reputation began to spread. He never survived to see his existence as a musician become a mere footnote to his daughter's major influence on jazz.

Billie continued making records and gigging in clubs. In 1939 she sang at the Onyx Club, one of many Fifty-second Street joints in full swing then, possibly the one where Sylvia Syms, then a young, hopeful singer, stood outside on the sidewalk, transfixed by Lady's music.

"I listened to everybody and knew who I wanted to sing like when I heard Lady," said Sylvia. "She was the first one who made sense to me. She had an innate animal sense of what she was singing. Others I listened to so I could learn what not to do. Lady was intelligent, articulate, feelingful. She understood far more than anyone would think she could. She was not an intellectual. She wasn't educated. But Billie had a wit. It was unbelievable."

Bobby Tucker, Billy Eckstine's accompanist since Tucker left Billie in the late 1940s, recalls a night when Billie and Eckstine were bantering. Billie said to him, "You're a real pretty mother-fucker, but you ain't as pretty as Buck Clayton." At the time Buck Clayton, with gray-green eyes, was "the prettiest man anyone ever met," Sylvia Syms said. And many years later, teaching at Hunter College, he was still very attractive. But Billy Eckstine, whom Billie was teasing, was nationally known as a formidably handsome singer.

"Billie loved to laugh," said Sylvia Syms. "She doesn't sound sad to me, not at all. She was really a wild-looking girl in those days, sexy, tall. That was before her arms looked bad. She was very endowed, not heavy and very stylish."

Syms added that she supplied Billie, nine years her senior and her idol, with a gardenia to wear behind her ear. The flower became Billie's insignia.

"I didn't preconceive it," says Sylvia. "I didn't sit hours all night and dream up ways to make her look better. She was stoned one night in the dressing room and burned a hunk out of her hair with a hot comb. We couldn't find anything to hang on her head. A hole so big! The checkroom girls used to sell favors—nuts, stuffed animals, anything to make a couple of bucks. So I got a few gardenias and wired them together. It was easy to pin on her because of the wires in the stems.

"I heard living in her music. I heard the most music in her music of any singer. She had a purity of intention. There are a lot of scat singers. But she never deviated from her sentences. And somehow she brought into view a proper picture of what she was feeling musically, articulately.

"Billie sang the blues. She migrated to guys who treated her like hell and didn't want anything to do with her. So she sang 'Billie's Blues' and 'Traveling Light' about traveling without a man again. These were the things she knew best. Without even trying, she knew everything. She could swing the blues. And I think she improvised so beautifully because she never knew the tune and played within the changes that the guys were playing, too.

"I was a young and floundering kid, but, from listening to her, I realized that the goal was (a) to relate things you're telling to people who are listening to you, and (b) not to lose sight of your story and what it means to you."

Billie alternated at the Onyx with Leo Watson, the fastest scat singer in the world, and his Spirits of Rhythm, a bill which must have made extremely engaging entertainment. By 1938 Billie traveled with the Basie band.

"Billie's pitch was in such a key that the trumpet player had to play high or low for her," Buck Clayton remembered about the months when a young, plump Lady worked with Basie. "Normally 'Body and Soul' was played in middle range, but with her you had to play high or low. If it were in the key of B flat, Billie would sing it in F. And it was hard to play for her. She changed the original key; sometimes I would have to play it so high that the trumpet would screech. So then I would have to play it low. There was no middle ground with Billie.

"I would keep watching her mouth to see if she were fixing to close it. Then I'd fill in and play two or three notes until she was ready to sing again. Then I cooled it. That was the best way to play with Billie. I had more fun playing with her than with any of the others in the Basie band. More than with Helen Humes second and Jimmy Rushing third.

"She liked sharp-looking guys who were pimps. They tried to take her money, her royalty checks. I don't think until her last marriage [to Louis McKay] that she found someone not trying to get her money. The others would take it and beat her up. Every time she got paid, she had to give her money to her 'old man,' whoever he was at the time. Not Freddie Greene [Basie's guitarist since the thirties, with whom she had a brief affair]. Although he was a nice-looking guy, he wasn't slick. He wasn't married at the time they had an affair. He was the only one in the band that she cared about in that way. With Lester Young [whose small-toned horn playing along with Billie's singing sounded like a musical expression of the same soul] she would go places. People thought they were having an affair, but it was just a friendship based on the music. Billie and I were just friends, too," added Buck, a slender, exceptionally handsome black man with a long, aquiline nose and cheeks sculpted into rivulets. A narrow-brimmed tweed hat can put the finishing touch on his resemblance to Rex Harrison.

Bobby Tucker: "I told Billie that I could line up a platoon of men in front of her and, blindfolded, she could pick out the two lemons." Tucker, who worked with Billie during her relationship with John Levy, thought Levy could have qualified easily as two lemons all by himself. Levy, a clubowner in New York, met Billie soon after her release from prison in the late 1940s on drug charges. Billie wrote in her autobiography, *Lady Sings the Blues,* that Levy bullied and probably fleeced her on the pretext of helping her, giving her presents but no cash from her earnings for several years. And, she wrote, he appeared to have gotten her arrested for possession of opium at a time when she wasn't using drugs.

That happened about ten years after she had endeared herself, drug free except for a taste for marijuana, to other young musicians traveling with Basie.

Clayton: "She would shoot craps on the bus and be one of the boys and do things to help pass the time, so we wouldn't go crazy."

One day in 1938, Clayton went to work and found that Billie had suddenly left the band. He isn't exactly sure what happened: a never-explained disagreement with Basie that had some connection to money, Billie's moodiness and inconsistency. Although Basie and the band loved her improvisation, she did have an odd Sound, without commercial appeal because of the unusual timbre of her voice and the relaxed phrasing—so slow and drawled, with a subtle vibrato. The very thing that she was most famous for—laying back on the beat—caused her the most grief commercially. But she sang melodies with a whole lot of notes that she put in so deftly you would never know how she did it. Her style, despite her laid-back attitude toward professional work habits, may have rescued her from oblivion.

(As a foil and comparison, consider Lena Horne, Billie's opposite number. Lena Horne spent many years learning from her husband, the late Lenny Hayton, and all the marvelous musicians he associated with and introduced her to. She became a wonderful soul singer. In her one-woman show on Broadway in the early 1980s, preceded by her tour with Tony Bennett, Lena Horne sometimes sang *ahead* of the beat. The trick gave her songs runaway excitement and drive; commercial socko at the box office. The accountants are still trying to catch up.)

After Billie left Basie (who usually called her "William," according to Chilton), Basie said about her: "Billie is a marvelous artist, who remains unappreciated by the world at large."

He suggested that her pride and belief in her music made artistic and racial shocks all the more difficult for her to absorb. Her days with Basie may have been among the most carefree in her complex life. On the Basie bus, the Blue Goose, she had traveled with her special friends: Prez, Buck, trumpeter Hot Lips Page and Freddie Greene. If they had been traveling light, they had done it together.

She quickly joined Artie Shaw and faced difficulties as the first black singer on the road with a white band. (June Richmond sang with Jimmy Dorsey in the thirties; Lena Horne briefly with Charlie Barnet; and Ella Fitzgerald recorded a few tunes with Benny Goodman's band for Victor. Ethel Waters worked with white musicians, too, and Fats Waller with Lee Wiley. But not on the road.) With Shaw, Billie had the support of her well-intentioned, complicated bandleader. He helped her face down some ugly incidents with hotels, restaurants, club and ballroom owners. However, in St. Louis, Shaw deferred to a ballroom promoter who insisted that Shaw hire a white singer with a commercial sound. Helen Forrest, whom Shaw had heard sing months earlier in Washington, got the job for the ballads, while Billie kept the blues. She was "too artistic" to have enough of the common touch, as well as too light-skinned to be considered truly black by some businessmen and too dark to be accorded whatever politeness a white singer could command. For Helen Forrest the road offered a blessed improvement over her difficult childhood, with some seaminess reminiscent of Billie's. For Billie the road offered, sadly, more of the same.

Back in New York City, Shaw's band moved into the Lincoln Hotel's ballroom. Management forbade Billie to mingle with the customers as white musicians did. One version said she had to sit alone in a little room, waiting for her turn to sing while the band played or drank at the bar. Helen Forrest remembered that she and Billie stirred up controversy by sharing a ringside table, waiting to sing.

In short, Billie had to deal with the principle of "Every Tub." The lyrics, supplied by bebopper Jon Hendricks in the 1950s to a Basie tune, say that every tub stands on its own feet, a metaphor for every black standing his or her ground, an "every man for himself" philosophy, in the face of racial prejudice—and incidentally a universal metaphor for man's fate to stand alone and up for himself.

After quitting Shaw, Billie went to work for Barney Josephson at Café Society Downtown, the Sheridan Square club in Greenwich Village, where black and white patrons mingled freely in the audience. Billie gained self-confidence as a performer. Josephson attributed her improved attitude to his evenhanded race policy.

▲ Louis Armstrong was generally regarded as the greatest inspiration for the jazz singers. "Armstrong said: a cat sings from his soul, with feeling," recalls Danny Barker, New Orleans jazz guitarist. Photograph taken October 1955. (*CBS Records*)

▼ Louis Armstrong at the piano with his Hot Five, one of his early groups. (*CBS Records*)

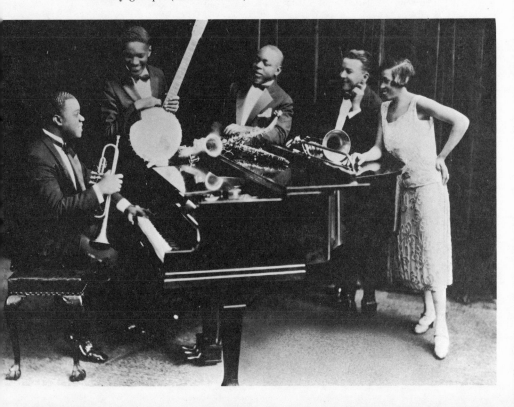

▲ Mildred Bailey, one of the first and greatest bandsingers, became famous with the Paul Whiteman band in the late 1920s. She started the year singing "Moaning Low" at $75 a week and ended earning $1,250. A close friend remembers Mildred's passions for food, clothes and jewelry. Victimized by her own excesses, Mildred had nothing when she died—except for the legacy of her records. Photographs probably taken in the 1940s. (*CBS Records*)

◄ Lee Wiley may have been the first singer to do albums devoted to one composer's work, as Ella Fitzgerald would do later with special success. (*CBS Records*)

► Far less influential as a singer than Louis Armstrong but especially entertaining was the brilliant composer Thomas Wright "Fats" Waller. To make quick money for alimony to his first wife, he often sold compositions for pittances. Copyrights for twenty-eight years of royalties on "Ain't Misbehavin'" and "Black and Blue?" went for $500 in 1929. Jabbo Smith remembers after-show parties with Fats jamming at hotels. "Fats wasn't singing the blues; he was fat and happy, a jovial guy. You could hear his spirit through his songs. He was a spendthrift and had a lot of girls. All musicians have a lot of girls always there. They always want to get under the light with that cat. What can you do? What's a mother to do?" Photograph from about 1943. (*CBS Records*)

▲ Cladys "Jabbo" Smith rivaled Louis Armstrong in popularity as a singer and trumpet player in the 1920s. "We had battles in Chicago. Armstrong was the seasoned man, while I was the kid," Jabbo remembers. He began by singing gospel and blues in his contralto days in the Jenkins orphanage in Charleston, South Carolina, where he added to the home's coffers by going on the road with a touring band of kid musicians. Photograph taken about 1982. (*Nancy Elliott*)

▲ Al Jolson studied the music of the blacks and came away with a driving beat to fire the lusty vibrato in his voice. His primary influence was the liturgical music of the synagogue—his emotional wellspring. And the excitement of his syncopation, phrasing and dynamic deep voice made him one of the most influential entertainers for decades. (*Joe Franklin*)

▲ Adelaide Hall, who credits Florence Mills as being the major influence on her singing in Harlem in the 1920s, married an Englishman, went to live in London, and after a show-stopping performance was introduced to the Queen. As a young woman, "Addie" was called a blues singer, but later in life she sang ballads with a marked English accent. Photographs taken in 1980. (*Leslie Gourse*)

"I had one of the finest-sounding bands in the country, and I was singing out front. Yessuh," Cab Calloway III reminisced. His family wanted him to be a lyric tenor, but he was singing jazz in Baltimore clubs. His singing teacher detected his early instinct for "hi-de-ho" and told him, "You've been singing jazz." (*Cab Calloway*)

◄ Little Jimmy Rushing, five feet tall and five feet wide, sang the arias of the underdog with a swing with Count Basie's band. An early photograph, probably from the 1930s. (*CBS Records*)

► Big Joe Turner, a powerful blues singer and an earthy lyricist, sang in the 1930s in the heyday of Kansas City jazz. Turner didn't need a microphone. (*Nancy Elliott*)

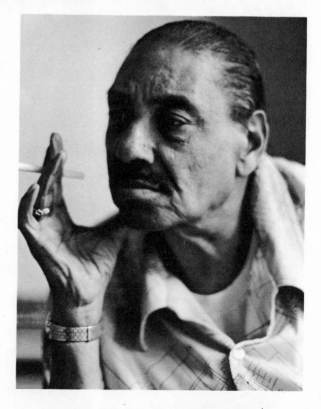

▲ Johnny Mercer, *left*, and Hoagy Carmichael, *second from left*, won Oscars in 1951 for the song "Cool, Cool, Cool of the Evening." Mercer, one of the founders of Capitol Records, influenced the careers of such singers as Jo Stafford and Nat "King" Cole. Carmichael, a jazz-influenced pop singer, pianist and composer, is more fondly remembered for "Stardust." Donald O'Connor, dancer, *second from right*; Franz Waxman, *right*. (*The Institute of Jazz Studies, Rutgers University*)

▶ Nellie Lutcher became a Capitol recording star in the mid-1940s. Just before she became famous, Johnny Mercer played her record for Barney Josephson of Café Society. Josephson hired her for about $200 a week and paid her plane fare from California. She had been working for $20 a night in a club that could barely make its payroll. By the time she got to New York, her record had been released. "She was a hit! My God! She was famous, making $3,000 a week," Josephson recalled. "Then she comes to me. I didn't have to publicize her. After ten weeks, I gave her a little something extra—$1,000—and say how pleased I am. She flips it back and says she doesn't want it." "You didn't know I would have a hit record. You're entitled to make money on me. The great place I was working in folded with [me] working in it. Besides, I never knew of a white man who gave anything he didn't have to to a colored person," she said. Josephson made her take the money. She asked if she could return the next year for $1,000 instead of her normal $3,000—and did.

▲ Benny Goodman, singing, and
Frank Sinatra, playing clarinet.
(*The Institute of Jazz Studies,
Rutgers University*)

▶ Frank Sinatra, superstar.
"When he sang about 'Violets for
Your Furs,' you could almost see
the sleet for miles," says singer
Anne Marie Moss, one of the le-
gions of singers whom he in-
fluenced. (*The Institute of Jazz
Studies, Rutgers University*)

"A singer had full view of the door and could see her people ushered to prominent tables. So the singer feels better and sings better. In addition, her boss gives her a song to sing. 'Strange Fruit' by Lewis Allen. That was his songwriting name. Abel Meeropol was his real name. Abel and his wife, Anne, adopted the children of Julius and Ethel Rosenberg, Michael and Robbie Meeropol. But I knew him as Allen. He showed me the music and lyrics. I don't know music, but I like the lyrics. I'm a left guy. 'What do you want to do with it?' I said. 'It would be great if you could get Billie Holiday to sing it.' 'Okay, stick around. When Billie comes in, I'll get her to listen.' Billie said, 'What do you want me to do with that?' I said, 'Be great if you did it. Great song.' 'Okay, if you want me to sing, I'll sing it.' She did—and became internationally famous for that song. It gave her status as a black singer with a brain, a mind, an awareness, something to say. Though Billie was apolitical. Not a fighter."

Josephson also retold the story of Billie's "Moon over Manhattan," when she was part of Café Society's show with three acts. "The first two acts were bands. If their instruments permitted it, the musicians would come down on the floor near the audience. The singer was told to do three songs and go off and take bows. Billie was told to do that and to honor all her encore calls, too; if she had one or five, to do them all.

"We had one little dressing room. Everybody came in there, disrobed and put on their evening gowns. One night, Billie comes in, slips her gown on and goes out to do the show." (She was fairly high on marijuana, Josephson recalled, too; although he didn't permit marijuana in the club, he knew that she sometimes took a taxi for a turn around town and smoked.) "She sings with one little spotlight on her face in this black room. Afterwards, the applause is coming. She turns around and does like this." Mr. Josephson turned around and mimicked a woman throwing up her dress and showing her bare ass to moon the audience. "She did that. She was high and uninhibited. I went backstage and said to her, 'What are you doing?'

"She said, 'Fuck 'em.'

"I said, 'What happened?'

"She said, 'Don't bother me.'

"I couldn't get anything out of her. But I can guess what had happened. She must have overheard somebody say something.

Somebody in the audience must have made a remark about black performers and a mixed audience. That kind of thing went on all the time. So many of these musicians and singers don't have the words. They can't express themselves with words. So Billie told them: 'You can kiss my black ass.' That's what she was saying. No, I didn't fire her. Of course I didn't fire her."

Billie often got into wild fights with club owners who disliked her odd Sound. (Not Josephson.) They yelled at her to sing faster and louder or get out. She told them to sing their way, and she would sing her way. She got out, never peaceably.

Call Billie's work a monotone with a bounce, or a dreamy reverie, or a lazing conversation. Call her Sound the greatest nonclassical vocalizing on records, as John Hammond did. The overwhelming charm of her small Sound has the effect of bombast. She achieved an arresting catch of laughter in her voice with her staccato notes, Whitney Balliett explained. In her last years, these notes became a mechanical and melancholy imitation. Her style hinted at her private confusions; her Sound became a patina. But in the young Lady's song, there was an indefatigability. The nearly tone-deaf can carry her haunting Sound in their memories long after the music has stopped.

By 1943 Billie rued never having won a *Down Beat* poll. She watched disconsolately as other singers, who imitated her, won instead. But in 1943 jazz critics voted her the winner in a Critics' Choice poll. Billie trounced Ella Fitzgerald by 23 to 4 and Mildred Bailey by 23 to 15. A 1950 *Down Beat* review called her Lady Yesterday. Then the same magazine relieved the sting by giving her an award in 1954 as "one of the all-time great vocalists in jazz."

She also had enough prestige that she was polled to pick her favorite young singers. In 1946 she picked Perry Como and Jo Stafford. Another time she selected a group including Etta Jones—to Etta's everlasting joy. "You always think your idol doesn't even hear you," she said.

By that time Billie was deeply involved with drugs. She married and lived briefly with Jimmy Monroe, the ne'er-do-well younger brother of New York City club owner Clark Monroe. When Buck Clayton saw her again, in California, years after she left Basie, Billie was using drugs. "She was clean when she left Basie. When I saw her again, she was . . . messed up." Billie said that she started using drugs with Jimmy Monroe to give them something in common and hold their shaky marriage together.

By the late 1940s, she was constantly embattled by the law, primarily because of drugs and then, too, because of her increasing unreliability about dates. In 1947 she spent time at the Federal Reformatory for Women at Alderson, West Virginia. In her autobiography she related her grim experiences in prison with a Dostoyevskian attention to detail that conveyed a sense of her crushing depression. She did not sing a note there. Afterward, when she performed, she wore her trademark gardenia less often.

Divorced from Jimmy Monroe by the 1950s, she married Louis McKay, her second and last husband. Not only Buck Clayton but other musicians who knew the couple say that McKay loved Billie. Though Bobby Tucker has mused that Billie may have cared only about Jimmy Monroe and an even earlier love, Bobby Henderson, one of her first piano accompanists, a married man. She wrote about him without using his name in her autobiography: "It was the first time I was ever wooed, courted, chased after. He made me feel like a woman. He was patient, loving; he knew what I was scared about, and he knew how to smooth my fear away." Whomever Billie preferred of all her men, Big Nick Nicholas, a veritable honeydripper of a singer himself, who was playing tenor saxophone at a regular gig in an uptown club, recalled that Billie and McKay would drop by to listen to Big Nick's sweet brand of music. Billie seemed happy, laughing; she was still good-looking. McKay, who was quiet, appeared to care about her. Ray Ross, a veteran photographer on New York's scene, said that McKay tried to get Billie clean of all drugs.

"But she was too far gone by that time," Ross added, for McKay to do much good.

Even so, for many years she was often able to keep up appearances. In the late 1950s, not long before she died, she was filmed for a CBS-TV show, *The Sound of Jazz*, singing "Fine and Mellow" in a group including Mal Waldron, her last accompanist, on piano, Lester Young on tenor saxophone, and the legendary drummer Jo Jones on drums. Billie was a beauty—with high forehead, hair backswept into a chignon, eyes alight and keenly fixed on Lester Young; she sang his licks exactly as he blew her words. Clearly engulfed in his sound, she paid little attention to the other musicians.

Not long after that, pianist Patti Bown, who met Billie in her last years, recalled seeing the insides of Billie's arms. "They looked like punch boards, with scar tissue all around. Some scars are permanent. It breaks your heart to look at it, especially because you know it's some kind of self-abuse. Your heart goes out." New to New York, young Patti, who had worshiped Billie from afar and written a tune for her, was also taken aback by Billie's profanity in the dressing room. Patti couldn't bring herself to talk about the song. "One time I saw her wearing a leopard coat, taking a walk with her dog in Central Park. She looked so bad, so sad. At Town Hall she gave a concert. It was horrible. She could barely make it to the concert. Those were the hardest years."

Billie's story is not about a singer and her men, nor her women, nor any of the appetites for which she became infamous. If the right man could have fixed all the problems that assailed Billie Holiday from the start, then Louis McKay might have provided the remedy, despite their tumultuous ménage in which Billie got physically bruised sometimes. But no one person could ever provide the reason or antidote for Billie's short, fast life. Eventually she and McKay separated. Essentially alone, she lived out her last, degenerating years singing with a combat-weary, battle-scarred voice. Some fans have said that by the 1950s she sang with more maturity and feeling because of her experiences. Others have perceived her, at best, as dispirited. The odd Sound became even odder—the high voice eerily and artificially pitched instead of buoyant. Still, it mesmerized.

Mal Waldron, her last accompanist from 1957 to 1959, recalled those downhill years. She liked to cook for a lot of people and "set fantastically good meals before them, but wouldn't eat anything herself. She said: 'The cook only samples the food in the kitchen but doesn't eat her own food.' " She always had a drink in her hand, he said, "except on the bandstand." And although only in her early forties, she talked about her death, telling Waldron that she didn't want to be buried underground because she wouldn't be able to breathe. "She wanted to have her ashes spread over the ground from a plane," he recalled. He also remembered her laughing at his jokes with quite a lot of energy left, even in those grim days.

In the New York City hospital where she died, he visited her. So did a Czechoslovakian woman named Alice who helped Billie care for herself in her final years in a West Side apartment. So did clarinetist Tony Scott. Chilton's biography said that Louis McKay visited often. But Mal Waldron never saw him there. Nor did Billie ever mention that McKay visited.

Billie Holiday died on a Sunday. Patti Bown, who was living on Christopher Street in Greenwich Village, recalled: "One faggot kept playing 'Gloomy Sunday' over and over again."

Billie was buried next to her mother in St. Raymond's Cemetery in the Bronx. Eventually Louis McKay put a marker on the grave.

It had been a terrible fight all the way for a slightly armed woman. She had the stamina to withstand the rigors for a little while. But a legion of protégées has seen her reanimated.

As soon as they heard her records or saw her in live performances, scores of singers singled her out as their ideal: Dinah Washington, Anita O'Day, Etta Jones, Ernestine Anderson, Sylvia Syms, Helen Merrill, Sarah Vaughan and Carmen McRae, to name a few, owe more to Billie than to anyone else—all of them Billie's children as well as Louis Armstrong's.

CHAPTER 9

Tales of Big-Band-Era Singers

Other singers, known mostly as bandsingers, also led dramatic lives.

Mildred Bailey, one of the first and greatest, was, in a word, gross. If, as they say, inside every fat person a thin one is struggling to get free, Mildred's other persona resided totally in her lovely voice, with which she charmed the public, Bing Crosby, Paul Whiteman and, last but not least, her well-liked, slender husband, swing bandleader Red Norvo.

Mildred Rinker, Al Rinker's older sister, was born in 1907 in Tekoa, Washington, to a mother who was part Coeur d'Alene Indian, and an Irish father. Mildred's mother could play classical and ragtime piano; no one knew where she learned or even how she heard ragtime in those preradio days. But she taught Mildred and Al how to play. Mildred grew up near Spokane, Washington, and began singing for pay in her teens behind the music counter of a Seattle dime store, plugging tunes for ten dollars a week. She also worked in a local nightspot called Charlie Dale's Cabaret. Briefly she married a man named Bailey and kept his name after she divorced him. In about 1925 she set out to try her luck in Los Angeles. Several Rinker brothers went into the music business, but only Mildred attained critical fame as a première diva of jazz.

Her brother Al and Bing Crosby drove to Los Angeles to see her sing in a speakeasy. She sang such tunes as "Oh, Daddy Blues," "Ace in the Hole," "Sweet Mama, Where Did You Stay Last Night?" She helped the boys get their first job as a duo and gave them a room in her house, which she shared with her second husband, a bootlegger named Benny Stafford. Barry Ulanov later quoted Crosby in *The Incredible Crosby*: "She had a lot to do with my style; we sang so much together." Her singing had clarity, wonderful enunciation, swing, fine phrasing, good intonation—and a pretty sound, all of which influenced many singers of her generation.

In California with the Rhythm Boys, Al Rinker invited Paul Whiteman and other musicians to Mildred's house in Hollywood Hills. When the party got going, she sang "Sleepy Time Gal." Whiteman hired her on the spot to sing on his radio show, beginning with "Moaning Low," at $75 a week. Before a year ended, she was earning $1,250 a week. She became Whiteman's first girl bandsinger and was probably the first female singer with a band. She had a particular success with the tune "Rockin' Chair," reaffirming Whiteman's celebrity.

She married the band's xylophonist, Red Norvo, and joined him when he started his own band. The public called them "Mr. and Mrs. Swing"; she called him Norvox.

According to Sally Venuti, one of Mildred's best friends and once the wife of the colorful jazz violinist Joe Venuti, Mildred met Norvo in 1929 when she joined Whiteman's band. The two couples lived together in a duplex on Long Island, Sally recalled. Mildred, who loved black underwear, used to sit around in her bra, panties and a corset.

One day she and Joe Venuti were sitting at the piano, both in their underwear, "and yelled at Red and me to get dressed better. There they were, half naked," Sally remembered. "Once, we drove to upstate New York. We had an Italian dinner. Millie was doing her thing. A carful of kids flashed lights on Joe and Millie. Millie mooned them. Joe did a figure eight on the car. They didn't care. They were uninhibited."

The Bailey-Norvo ménage was a wild place, according to most tales. Once Mildred got angry at Norvo for staying away from home for two nights with Benny Goodman on a fishing trip. When Norvo came home, she waited a day and, in the middle of a dinner party, went into a closet, got his Cavanaugh hat and tossed it into the fire-place. Then he threw something of hers. Finally there was a bad fire in the house. The argument ended in hysterics. "A battling couple," says Dick Phipps, a manager and producer for educational radio at a station based in Columbia, South Carolina, and a friend of Norvo's. "Red said that their fights should have been written up in *Ring* magazine," said Phipps.

But Norvo "was convinced that she was a genius," wrote Bucklin Moon in liner notes for a Columbia Records re-release of Bailey's work. In 1982 Norvo worked with Phipps on rebroadcasting thirteen of Mildred's half-hour CBS programs done originally in 1944. Norvo did three-minute commentaries at the start of each show.

Some sources say that Mildred Bailey earned a reputation as a difficult person in a profession where difficult people are generally accepted as *comme il faut*. But pianist Teddy Wilson, who worked as a studio musician with her, has said that she was a pleasure. Sally Venuti concurs. Anyway, Mildred was clearly a howl to be around. She and Joe Venuti had historic meals—three lunches at a sitting, through which they hollered and laughed.

One day, upset about a spat with Norvo, Mildred showed up for a recording date. There was no lead sheet. She verbally abused someone so outrageously that he had to go into a control room, according to Dick Phipps. Finally Mildred walked up to Teddy Wilson, who was noodling, then went into the control room, apologized and did the tune in about sixteen takes, crying all the time. "The rage would pass," said Phipps, "and there would be laughter and tears."

The marriage eventually broke up. "It probably just got to be too much," Phipps said. "Red might have just wanted a normal life with kids. When he married Eve [Shorty Rogers' sister] he got cooled down and more relaxed." But even after the divorce, he and Mildred worked together, remaining friends. "Eve and the kids went to Mildred's farm, and Mildred adored Red and Eve's red-headed child. But a son died in a gun accident. A year later Eve died."

Norvo preferred not to talk about his former wife and relied upon Mildred's friends to recall her. "Mildred's life was a very sad and a very happy one. There was no other state of mind for her, and she traveled from sadness to delight by the shortest route ever discovered. She was lonesome, and she was not beautiful," wrote Irving Townsend in liner notes for an album. "But she loved her dogs and what friends she had as a child loves a kitten—so much that she almost smothered them with affection. . . ."

Mildred weighed about two hundred pounds and was short, with small feet and ankles. She felt her size prevented her from causing a greater stir with the public. She was "resentful that she was not a commercial success," wrote John Hammond. But her resentment didn't deter her from eating. She developed diabetes, which caused many later physical ailments. She called herself a "food, clothes and jewelry degenerate," recalled Sally Venuti, who went on many shopping and eating expeditions with Mildred. "She loved food and clothes. Oh, God, and she was a barrelhouse lady; she knew everything that was going on around her."

She loved to go to clubs with other musicians, trumpeter Jimmy Maxwell, pianists Hazel Scott and Mary Lou Williams among them. She saw Billie Holiday and Ella Fitzgerald at the start of their careers. She may have tipped off John Hammond about Billie, according to some sources—a version of Mildred's reaction to Billie that doesn't jibe with the report that she was jealous of Billie's talent. Her friends think the jealousy was very unlikely. But supposedly Mildred was so jealous of Billie's formidable gifts that she hired Billie's mother and gossiped to everyone about what a terrible cook and a lazy maid she was.

Mildred was well aware that friends and musicians considered her one of the greatest, most influential singers. Bucklin Moon wrote that she could give validity and dignity to trite material, and "where respect was due, it was granted, without fanfare, by a subtle, warm overtone in the voice or by a gesture . . . swinging lightly and politely and a joy forever."

She sounded as if she were influenced by Ethel Waters. Other singers believed that, though Sally Venuti said that Mildred didn't learn from anyone—unless it was from the blues singers. "She liked to listen to Deep South records," said Sally. "She had a deep understanding of everything southern and loved the blues singers." Otherwise she was an originator, Sally added.

"If she got the reputation for being difficult," said Red Norvo, "it was because women were not supposed to set tempos in those days. And she did." He also added that she didn't emulate Ethel Waters.

But the fat little girl never overcame whatever internal parasites plagued her spirit. "Mildred was given to towering rages born of almost continual frustrations," wrote John Hammond in liner notes for an album that sells for close to a hundred dollars in a New York City record collector's shop. And Bucklin Moon wrote: "Her overweight was the result of something closely akin to gluttony.... A truly comic sight was watching her walking down the street with her brace of dachshunds ... one of her favorite dishes was spaghetti, and she could and did eat most men under the table."

Weeping with sentimentality, Sally Venuti also recalled Mildred's conspicuous generosity. "She would give away her clothes and jewelry." As a result, though she earned thousands, she had nothing when she died, victimized by her own excesses.

By the late 1940s, in bad health, she retired to a New York State farm with her dogs, a parrot and a rooster, and worked only sporadically. She played Café Society Downtown and entertained friends in a ground-floor apartment on East Thirty-first Street—with fried chicken, served with talk, tears and curses. By Thanksgiving 1951, as she finished a nightclub date in Detroit, she collapsed. She was taken all the way to St. Francis Hospital in Poughkeepsie, New York. Supposedly she had been on a strict diet. But arranger Ralph Burns reportedly went with her to such places as Chinatown and watched her eat and eat. She died in Poughkeepsie on December 12, 1951, "of hardening of the arteries, malfunctioning liver, a weakened heart and a variety of ailments. She destroyed herself," wrote Bucklin Moon. Word came out that various entertainers—among them Bing Crosby, Frank Sinatra and Jimmy Van Heusen, perhaps even Alec Wilder—had paid her medical bills.

One of Mildred Bailey's closest friends was Lee Wiley, who was three eighths Cherokee Indian. Lee, who also left home in her teens, appealed to the same audiences Mildred Bailey did.

Stories of her childhood and probably the childhood itself were confused. One report is that when her parents split up, Lee and a sister or two went to live with the mother, while a brother went with the father.

Born in Oklahoma in 1915, Lee Wiley sang on the radio in Tulsa, then in St. Louis, then went on to Chicago and New York. Her publicists said she was directly descended from a Cherokee princess and an English missionary. At fifteen the pretty blond singer, showing no physical traces of her lineage, starred on network radio soon after arriving in New York. From there she moved to the Paul Whiteman program. She did far more radio than band work.

Musically her instincts led her to wonderful music: the sophisticated tunes of Irving Berlin and Vincent Youmans, Cole Porter, George Gershwin, Rodgers and Hart, and Harold Arlen; she recorded their work for Schirmer, RCA and Columbia in the thirties, forties and fifties. In the early seventies, she made a record for Monmouth-Evergreen. She may have been the first singer to do albums devoted to one composer's work as early as the 1930s. In those years, she also recorded with Fats Waller.

A stylist and lyric delineator in the Ethel Waters tradition, Wiley exuded confident femininity. She could hit high notes easily, could even swing when humming. "Find Me a Primitive Man," she sang, and the horn ("wa-wa-wa") echoed her vocal sound, emanating from her lines.

To give an inkling of her taste, her repertoire included "I Got Lost in His Arms," "Heat Wave," and—amazingly, for a pretty blond seductress—"Supper Time," one of the diamonds in Ethel Waters' crown, originally a black woman's song about her man who was lynched and wouldn't come home for supper ever again.

By the late thirties, Wiley sang in musician-club owner Eddie Condon's circles, and in the forties toured with bandleader Jess Stacy, her husband from 1943 to 1948. Later she married Nat Tischenkel, a druggist who had a store in the Astor Hotel, where Lee lived after she divorced Stacy. The marriage to Tischenkel appeared to have been satisfactory.

A fine-looking woman, she dressed fashionably—"a chic, sleek, slim chick, next to the short, squat Mildred," said Dick Phipps. "But the disparity didn't mar their friendship." Lee lived a relatively quiet life, friendly with a square crowd—business people, money people," said Phipps. "She was Fifth Avenue, not barrelhouse." She died of cancer in New York City in 1975. By then only fans from the thirties and forties remembered her enthusiastically.

Dainty Isn't Fragile: Helen Forrest

She was always as dainty as a fairy-tale princess, diminutive in height, with tiny feet, even though men recalled her as well rounded. "Voluptuous," said George Simon, a big-band expert. In 1942 and 1943 she won *Down Beat* and *Metronome* polls as the number one female singer in the country. With a suitably turned-up nose (from plastic surgery, before it was commonly done) she had been in the running for years before she won polls, as she moved from Artie Shaw's band to Benny Goodman's to Harry James'. Forty years later she was still singing very well. Nothing in her light step and clear green eyes suggested that she had survived a childhood nearly as miserable as Billie Holiday's.

Named Helen Fogel, Helen couldn't remember her father, who died of influenza when she was an infant. Her mother blamed her for the man's death. How she made the connection always remained a mystery. Only "a colored cop" in her Atlantic City neighborhood, Helen wrote in her autobiography *I Had the Craziest Dream,* had a kind word to encourage her. He kept saying that Helen would amount to something special.

Helen moved with her mother and brother from Atlantic City to Brooklyn, where her mother got remarried, to a housepainter nicknamed "Fiegy." He supplemented the family income by incorporating a whorehouse into the apartment.

Helen studied piano in the afternoons after high school. But one afternoon she went home to find the business going full blast. Another day Fiegy accosted her in the kitchen and told her to have sex with him. Everybody else in the house did, he reasoned. They wrangled. She scratched him with a knife and ran to her piano teacher's apartment. The teacher suggested that Helen tell her mother. But Helen had already warned her about Fiegy's advances; her mother didn't care. So the piano teacher took Helen in to live with her family, discovered her singing talent, which outshone her piano playing, and encouraged her to become a singer.

In school Helen had the highest soprano and got parts in school productions, which took her out of classes. One brother, a tenor sax player with his own band, cajoled her into singing with him for a danceathon contest in Atlantic City. At age sixteen she quit high school and haunted music publishers' offices to learn the latest songs. Someone told her to audition for a club on Fifth Avenue. She got the job, sang on the air, changing her name to Forrest minutes before the broadcast. Station WNEW offered her a singing job. Then bandleader Mark Warnow hired her to be "Bonnie Blue" for the CBS *Blue Velvet Hour.*

"For a year as Bonnie Blue, I had to go in and out a secret entrance so I would seem mysterious. I thought it was crazy. That's how it was in those days," she said.

She was fired from that job when she refused to sing a ballad in an up tempo. Afterward, she marked well, nobody seemed to notice that a new girl was singing with a different voice under the name of Bonnie Blue. Some lean days passed until her musician brother invited her to Washington, D.C., for a brief gig. It stretched into a permanent job at a club called the Madrillon patronized by politicos.

A childhood friend from Atlantic City, Ziggy Elman, told Artie Shaw to go hear Helen. Shaw offered her a job with his band. But she turned it down, because she felt tied to Washington. Her mother, who had finally separated from Fiegy, was living with Helen again. She had a boyfriend, too; Al Spieldock, a drummer, who walked her home after gigs. Shaw told her to send him a demonstration tape if she changed her mind.

Benny Goodman went to hear her, too, and walked out on her performance. "He said that I couldn't sing," she recalled. "Later I worked for him for two years. A very hard man to work for. He doesn't know you're there."

Eventually ready to make the break with Washington, she sent a demo to Shaw; he told her to meet him in St. Louis. Billie Holiday, a few years older than Helen, was already traveling with the Shaw band and kindly urged the bandleader to get some arrangements together for Helen. In Helen's candid autobiography, she wrote of Billie, the pioneer black singer with a white band in the late 1930s: "The prejudice was everywhere, not just in the Lincoln Hotel in New York but everyplace. Billie said, 'Finding a place to sleep, finding a place to eat, even just finding a place to go to the bathroom is a mess.' It was so much easier for me just because I was white. I envied her singing, if not her life. . . . If my childhood was hard, hers was harder. 'Lady Day' was a lady with a lot of dignity, but the white audiences saw only her color and didn't hear her singing."

For Helen the band represented virtual nirvana, overriding many of her early difficulties. She spent a year with Shaw, then two years with Goodman, by which time she was attracting attention as one of the best big-band singers—many of whom didn't consider themselves jazz singers but scored nevertheless in the jazz polls.

Helen has written in her book: "I started out copying Mildred Bailey and Ella Fitzgerald and picked up a bit of Billie. Mildred listened to Bessie Smith and Ethel Waters and the great black blues singers of the early days and was the first white woman to sing like a black blues singer. She married Red Norvo, the great jazz vibist, and developed a distinct style of phrasing with his band. Billie probably had the purest jazz phrasing of any singer. Neither had great range. Ella, of course, has a pure, rich sound and a great range. . . . I don't compare myself to them. . . . I was . . . born out of the big bands and with a background of swing music and show tunes, and I had to find my own way with a song. . . ."

She added in conversation: "I don't really listen to anybody, because if I learn a song from a record, I imitate it. That's no good. So I have to get a piano player and let him teach me the tune and do it my own way. I've been called a jazz singer so many times. I don't agree. It's a compliment. It puts me in a class with Ella Fitzgerald, the greatest jazz singer. I listened to her and to Mildred Bailey from the time I was about twelve to fourteen. I was more influenced by the vocalists than the musicians, except for Harry James. Harry was the most important thing in my life; the biggest, deepest love of my life."

It was not love at first sight for Miss Forrest. She auditioned for James successfully and stipulated that she wanted band arrangements built around her; she wanted to sing a whole song and even the verse, if it was good, leading into the song. "I wanted to start with the band and finish with the band," she said. "Not just sing a chorus in the middle of an instrumental as all the band singers were doing then." Harry James agreed. The new technique set a standard for all the bands and launched both Helen and James to greater fame. She sang whole songs, including verses, on two of her five biggest hits, "I Don't Want to Walk Without You, Baby" and "I Had the Craziest Dream"—gold records in the days of 78 rpms. She made three other gold records, "But Not for Me," "I've Heard That Song Before" and "He's My Guy." She did many recordings with Goodman and James.

She had never had real singing lessons and barely read music. But instinctively she mastered "phrasing, quality, feeling and the enunciation—the diction. I had listened to Artie play clarinet. His quality in his phrasing rubbed off. And then with Benny, I got into more of a swing style, even though I did heavy ballads with him— 'More Than You Know,' 'The Man I Love.' " Although fans liked her swing with Goodman, she disliked the records she made with him. "My phrasing and sound got into my final slot with Harry. I think I was almost copying his phrasing and feeling, following my heart." Her affection for Harry James fed her respect for his schmaltzy music; her respect for his music fed her affection for him, she recalled. And she blossomed in the popularity polls.

All singers with excellent enunciation acquire it through feeling, she explained. No matter where a singer comes from, no matter what the regional accent or language difficulty, no matter how little schooling in the background, a good singer hurdles the language barriers, propelled by a feeling for the lyrics to enunciate and infuse them with style. The difference between the singing and conversational styles of some leading singers is wondrous.

She was still learning when she went on the road with Shaw. But her instinctive musicianship garnered fans right away. Once they mobbed her as she came out of the stage door at Loew's State on Broadway. She was wearing a new Persian lamb coat with a collar fastened by a twirled rope with two balls on each end. Two fans grabbed the rope from each side, trying to snatch the balls as souvenirs, and tugged so hard they nearly choked her to death. That happened before she became a poll winner.

She had a more fallible instinct about men.

A virgin on the road with Artie Shaw's band, she kept ducking invitations for romance with musicians. When she was on furlough from the band, she married that protective drummer, Al Spieldock, who lived back in Baltimore. She spent a wedding night with him and flew to meet the band the next day, shielded in an abstract way by her new wedding band. But she and her husband had sporadic rendezvous. Their lifestyles diverged. He left music, became a photographer; she became a star. By the time she joined Harry James' band and fell in love with the leader, she and her husband had the emotional intimacy of distant acquaintances.

She fell so headlong in love with James that, forty years later, she still recalled a night when they lay together in a dark New York hotel room. She was married to Spieldock at the time, James to singer Louise Tobin, when the lovers saw a red flash go off on the fire escape. At the time they imagined the light to be a photographer's infrared bulb. But they never saw a photograph of that tryst. Neither was sued for adultery.

James, whom Miss Forrest recalled as "not the most faithful of men," was a king of the one-night stands, sexually as well as musically. Still, she hoped to marry him. Spieldock categorically refused to give Helen a divorce until he picked the moment to sue her for desertion, he told her; he didn't want her to make a mistake by marrying Harry James. Although Helen called Spieldock "the sweetest man who ever lived," she added, "he's the reason I didn't marry Harry." She had desperately wanted to marry James—"though it could have ended in a clash or murder," she reflected. James divorced Louise Tobin. Spieldock finally divorced Helen a year after Harry James married Betty Grable, then the nation's number one pinup girl.

Helen surmised that James was unfaithful to Grable, too, because while married to her, he made a proposition to Helen. Even so, Helen held on to her memory of her two-year romance. On his wedding night to Grable, Helen, in a trance, nearly jumped from a window ledge. But the boys in the James band pulled her back from danger. A few months later she quit Harry James' band. Still, she ended her autobiography by saying about the totality of her life: "There are nights never to be forgotten. Like when a red light flashes in a hotel room when you are in the arms of your lover."

Buffeted by varying illnesses, from gallstones, to benign uterine tumors, to a lingering hearing problem in the aftermath of childhood scarlet fever, and even to a mild stroke, Helen couldn't easily recall the exact dates of her later marriages. She married actor Paul Hogan, who was jealous of her nonexistent lovers on the road and financially dependent upon her earnings. Afterward she married Charles Feinman, the father of her child, Michael, who uses the name Forrest. Michael was born when she was forty-three. "The only way I can remember the marriage dates is by the year I bought such and such a home. It was a stormy marriage and a stormy divorce. We married in 1959, separated in 1963. Anyway the late fifties to the early sixties. I've blocked it out. The terrible things I block out." She had thought she was settling into a domestic routine with Feinman, a manufacturer of falsies. But he insisted that she keep working, even with an infant son, and always introduced her as Helen Forrest, the singer, not as Mrs. Feinman. That marriage fell flat. And she got no alimony.

When she left behind the $250-a-week paycheck with the James band, she began working as a solo for $2,500 a week and more. New York critics gave her rave reviews as a send-off. When she filled a Honolulu club to overflowing, the Mafia offered to stake her to her own club. A club owner in the Midwest called his place La Tête

Rouge (The Redhead) for her. She had dyed her dark hair red; later she bleached it very blond and cut it short and feathery—a style that heightened her dainty air.

But by the 1960s rock blitzed her career, which didn't pick up until the 1970s. She bagan singing in supper clubs again, themselves back in fashion—Marty's in New York City, for example, and Hopper's. She toured with Tex Beneke's nostalgia package. Not only had bebop jazz come back into favor by the late 1970s, but bebop's predecessor, the big band, drew audiences again. In 1982 Helen had some income from money that she had begun investing rather "late in the game," she said. "Not enough to keep me if I live to be a hundred, not enough for BMWs." But she was supporting herself and helping her son, she said.

By the time her autobiography was published, one of her brothers had died; the others were "around someplace. One lived in Florida," she said. Her mother, for whom Helen became the sole support, had died. Helen wrote that she took care of her mother because she thought a good Jewish girl was obliged to do that, though her mother had never stopped trying to plant seeds of self-doubt into the former Miss Fogel. Mother advised Helen to sleep with a film producer to launch a star's career in films. Miss Forrest refrained—but not without the afterthought that her mother might have had the germ of an idea (or at any rate a germ.)

Jo Stafford: A Voice Like Chocolate Mousse

Of the white singers, only one—Jo Stafford—impressed me much. She had a silky quality to her voice, which I liked; there was something haunting about her style—From *Brother Ray*, Ray Charles' autobiography.

The critics didn't agree with Charles. They called Miss Stafford's voice cold when she starred as lead singer with Tommy Dorsey's quartet, the Pied Pipers, and even when she soloed as the band's ballad singer from 1939 to 1942. But years later she struck the critics differently. John Wilson in *The New York Times* reviewed her record *Broadway's Best,* after she switched from Capitol to Columbia Records in the 1950s, saying: "Jo Stafford has recently burgeoned into a fully rounded singer with a mastery of her art which qualifies her to be mentioned in the same breath with [Mildred] Bailey and [Ella] Fitzgerald.... [The album] offers an excellent sampling of her ability to bring an added dimension even to familiar and well-worn material. The warmth and color with which her intelligently controlled, open style of singing dresses up such an overdone number as 'Embraceable You' breathes new life into this fine song. Her rich, full-throated way with 'Come Rain or Come Shine' gives this Johnny Mercer-Harold Arlen tune the rendition it has been waiting for since it turned up in 'St. Louis Woman.' Her approach is invariably direct and understanding whether she is doing 'Dancing in the Dark,' 'Night and Day,' 'They Say It's Wonderful!,' 'My Romance,' 'All the Things You Are' or even—a supreme test—'September Song,' in which for once the shade of Walter Huston does not seem to be hovering in the background, waiting to step in and demonstrate how it should be sung." Wilson wound up by saying Miss Stafford knew how to achieve effective, artistic balance between the demands of her singer's training and the material she sang.

Miss Stafford herself was puzzled by the early charge that her voice was cold. "But I heard the comment made enough,"she said, "by more than one person. So I thought there might be something in it. But you can't evaluate yourself, because you're doing the best you can." She tried to analyze herself. She had been a group singer, joining her older sisters, Pauline and Christine, to form the Stafford Sisters trio in California. After that Jo went into the Pied Pipers as the lead singer. "Group singing is a very disciplined affair. You can't go off on your own and improvise when you're leading a group. You do what's on the paper, just as if you were leading a trumpet section. So the discipline may be too much for a soloist. Subconsciously I may have still been a group singer. As time went on, "the more I worked as a soloist, I could be freer."

Born in 1917, Jo was raised in California and was singing, her sisters said, before she could remember that she was singing. By the time she was ten or eleven, her mother used to get furious with her for listening to remote broadcasts from ballrooms at night.

"My first was Louis Armstrong, who used to play in Sebastian's Cotton Club in Culver City, a great big ballroom. I wouldn't go to sleep until the broadcast was over, and I had to get up and go to school in the mornings. Then I listened to Glen Gray's Casa Loma Orchestra in the early 1930s. It was broadcast from the East—a

Camel cigarettes program. Then the whole world changed for me when I heard Benny Goodman's sax section in about 1935 or '36. I was a big Ellington fan in high school. A whole bunch of us, my group, the glee club members and the musicians, pooled five cents each and bought a record of 'Sophisticated Lady.' Early in the mornings, before classes, we got together in a tent in Long Beach and listened to the record." After an earthquake hit Long Beach, California, in 1933, she finished high school in classroom tents. "I was pretty well immersed in music all my life, influenced certainly by Ella, with enormous respect for her time and ability to improvise."

Still in her midteens when her family trio split up, Jo sang with an octet, the Pied Pipers. Alice King of the King Sisters heard the Pipers and told her boyfriend, Paul Weston. Yvonne King told her boyfriend, Axel Stordahl. Both men worked as arrangers for Tommy Dorsey. When Dorsey played the Palomar Ballroom in Los Angeles, he called for the group to audition for him and hired it to sing on a half-hour sponsored radio show. The job lasted two months. Then Dorsey let them go, most likely because he couldn't afford eight extra singers. The Pied Pipers then became "eight people on their uppers," Miss Stafford remembered. After four members dropped out of the group, she got a prepaid call from Chicago.

"I didn't know anyone in Chicago. I couldn't imagine who was calling me. But it was free, so why not call back?" she said. It was Tommy Dorsey, saying he could use a quartet, not an octet, and asking the smaller group to join him at the Palmer House in Chicago in December 1939.

The Pied Pipers stayed with Dorsey for almost three years. During that time, Sinatra joined, too. "One of the best of all time, with a unique sound. The first time I heard him, I knew it," she recalled. "Before him, everyone tried to sound like Crosby. But no one has sounded like Sinatra before or since. And he has a great respect for music. He had the discipline to fit in with the Pied Pipers, too. Male solo singers can't usually fit into a group."

With Dorsey the Pied Pipers sang many up-tempo and ballad arrangements by Sy Oliver. Then Jo Stafford took over the solo ballad work. Johnny Mercer, who was founding Capitol Records, recruiting some of the best musicians to record on the West Coast, signed Peggy Lee, Martha Tilton, Margaret Whiting, Nat "King" Cole. When Jo was still singing with Dorsey, Mercer told her that, if she left the band, he wanted to sign a contract with her. Eventually she did sign and became a special favorite of the armed forces.

"A lot of the kids in the war wrote me letters, talking about my haunting quality. They said it made them homesick—and happy to be unhappy. They could identify with it. It made them lonesome for their girlfriends," she said.

I said that I had heard a blueness, a tinge of unhappiness, not a coldness, that I thought was very expressive in the 1940s. Had she herself become happier as time went by?

"Well, actually, I did," she said. First, she had fallen under the influence of Johnny Mercer. "One of the most joyous things was to hear him sing. He taught me about the lightness and humor in jazz. And there's nothing like a happy marriage and a couple of great kids to make you feel good. I've never intellectualized my singing." She married arranger Paul Weston in 1952, a year after she left Capitol Records and signed with Columbia. "All the Things You Are," one of the songs that John Wilson praised in Jo's interpretation, is the Westons' song ("one of the best harmonically, melodically, ever written," she said).

The big-band years on the road with Tommy Dorsey never depressed her. "Music was no decision for me. It was just always there and what I wanted to do. So I just went through transitions from group to solo work. I've had a steady life and consider myself lucky. Sure I was traveling on the road, but what do you know? you're so young." She was twenty-one when the Pied Pipers followed her lead with Dorsey. One time they spent two months at the Astor Hotel Roof in New York City—the longest the band ever stayed in one spot. "So I know all about the road. I thought it was fun. Musicians were fun. They have the best sense of humor. They're kind, gentle men; we lived like a family and laughed constantly. We had running gags; say one word and the whole bus fell down. I got dreadfully tired—but I learned a lot from Tommy, a great teacher, and from all the musicians. I was surrounded by some of the best in the world."

Not long ago her son, Tim Weston, a guitarist who had been traveling with Diana Ross to Atlantic City, Lake Tahoe and England, came home complaining about six weeks on the road. "It was a drag," he said.

"I said, 'Twerp. Think of three years.' "

His sister, Amy, a singer in her midtwenties, was starting to get gigs in Los Angeles clubs in the mini-regeneration of the Jazz Age in the early 1980s, while Mom and Pop ran a mail-order business, Corinthian Records, the Westons' small record company from which they reissued their own records.

"I sued Columbia for something or other, and as part of the settlement, I got my masters back. So Paul and I have issued fifteen of our albums so far. And we're doing quite well. There's a radio station here, KMPC, a big one, which has just gone all big band," she said the other day in a voice that, even coast to coast by phone, sounded as dark and smooth as chocolate mousse.

That Cat from the Carlyle Talks About Ivie Anderson

That cat from the Carlyle, Bobby Short, with the sort of palaver that boîtes can spawn, opened a talk on Ivie Anderson at St. Peter's Lutheran Church in New York City. The church is an angular and spacious building with the minimalist design of a hip art gallery.

Short had heard Ivie Anderson on the radio numerous times but didn't see her until 1937, when a vaudeville theater, The Tower in Kansas City, showed the film *Hit Parade*. Duke Ellington's band featured its girl singer, Ivie Anderson, doing "I've Got to Be a Rug Cutter," a swinging ballad.

An orphan who grew up with the first name of Mary in convents, Ivie set out for New York in her midteens and became a Cotton Club chorus girl and second lead singer. "Throughout her career, she was always a kind of second something," Short said. "Never a star like Ethel Waters." She moved around quite a bit and worked in some South Side nightclubs in Chicago. Earl Hines hired her; then Duke Ellington decided he wanted a nice-looking girl bandsinger. He considered Mae Alix, a beautiful New Yorker known for her version of "Big Butter and Egg Man." But she was too light-skinned to travel with his band. Ivie was hired, in 1931, for her darker complexion. "Those days are gone forever, thank God," said Short.

She set out on the road, going from rickety to glamorous hotels, with a bunch of "ruffians," as Duke's drummer, the late Sonny Greer, characterized the Ellington band. Ivie had sharp little features, never wore much makeup, and always dressed in white to look angelic, chic, "above it all."

Watching Waters at the Cotton Club, Ivie had learned a great deal. So her clean delivery caught the attention of many other singers; her voice unfurled like a beautifully colored silk ribbon with a lot of vibrato.

"You're as good a singer as you sing your consonants. Without them, the words just don't end," said Short. "And Ivie had superb diction—a great jazz singer with a marvelous sense of the blues. I hope it rubbed off on me."

In their vaudeville performances, the Ellington band dressed to the nines. Ivie's energetic style and fashion sense brought the band's image into focus. In vaudeville it was very important to be a very classy-looking act. Short said: "Blossom Seeley doused her whole set in Shalimar to give the audience a big whiff"—probably the most expensive prop in the history of vaudeville.

Sonny Greer had special rapport with Ivie. In performance he talked to her with his drums; she answered him back. They stopped shows. After she left the orchestra, Ellington asked Greer to continue his drum conversations with Duke's other fine bandsingers, Joya Sherrill and Betty Roche. But Greer said, "Oh, no, that was Ivie's thing. Now that she's gone, it's all over."

She recorded Ellington's "Ebony Rhapsody," "A Lonely Coed," and introduced many Ellington songs. Although "Stormy Weather" had already been appropriated for the era by Ethel Waters, Ivie brought audiences to tears with it, Duke Ellington wrote in *Music Is My Mistress*. In the early forties, she had a hit with "I've Got It Bad and That Ain't Good." She did all her most important work with Ellington in the thirties and forties.

But Ivie was handicapped by a severe case of asthma and sometimes suffered attacks while she was waiting to perform. Sonny Greer suffered watching her. It must have been with a sense of relief that she retired, at about age forty-five, in 1946. She married a man named Bart Neil, settled on the West Coast, and opened Ivie's Chicken Shack, with which she and her husband prospered.

Occasionally, she did singing dates on the West Coast or in Chicago. Once she and Bobby Short went to jail together to entertain some prisoners. Ivie's prison repertoire included preachy songs that started out: "Now, listen girls . . ."

One is tempted to say that the stories of happy bandsingers are all alike. Unfortunately, Ivie Anderson's happy story was cut short. She died young, in 1949.

PART III

Singers on Their Own

CHAPTER 10

Singers' Camaraderie: Thelma Carpenter, Etta Jones and Helen Merrill

Some singers handed down their tricks, befriended, admired and knew each other's business. Thelma Carpenter, a protégée of Ethel Waters', remet Etta Jones, whose musical idol was Billie Holiday, at a theater where Etta Jones was playing in 1982. Years earlier Etta Jones and Helen Merrill, another of Billie's children, had been buddies, too, when they sang with Earl Hines' band.

Thelma Carpenter: "You Get Used to Seeing Diamonds"

At age five Thelma Carpenter, born in 1922, wrote a letter to a New York City radio station to say she wanted to sing. She first performed on kids' shows on radio, singing Ethel Waters tunes like "Lazy Bones," learned from records. "I was introduced as a little coon shouter. Of course, they used to call Sophie Tucker that, too," she recalls. "Not that she was on the shows with me. Baby Rose Marie was, though."

Thelma's grandmother had insisted that Thelma's mother drop all notions of becoming a professional dancer. But Thelma's mother let Thelma, age twelve, enter a Wednesday night amateur contest at the Apollo, as Ella Fitzgerald, Sarah Vaughan, Carmen McRae and others would do later. Thelma won first prize, which meant a week's gig as a girl singer with Duke Ellington's band. Afterward her mother forced her to retire until she finished high school.

On graduation day she popped out of Brooklyn and into Gray's Drugstore on Broadway in Manhattan, where she had gone many times "to commiserate with people about: will anything ever happen to me? Even at age twelve, I used to do that." A pretty girl with chiseled features, she ordered the obligatory soda. A man she had never seen before told her that jazz pianist Teddy Wilson was leaving Benny Goodman's band to start his own. Wilson was looking for a girl singer.

Thelma said, "He'll take Billie Holiday."

"No," the man said. "They want someone young."

Thelma agreed to go with him to Columbia's recording studios. She met Mildred Bailey, who interrupted her recording session to call her producer, John Hammond. Hammond listened to Thelma sing "Embraceable You" and helped her get the Wilson job. "It used to happen like that," Thelma said.

She sang with Teddy Wilson for about a year. Wilson recalled how the pretty teenager used to show up for work with her mother as chaperone. One day Coleman Hawkins came back from Europe as World War II was starting; he was playing at Kelly's Stables on Fifty-second Street. "I just went there and auditioned for him," Thelma remembered. "He thought I was the cutest thing. I went to work for him the next night. Teddy found out through the grapevine."

Thelma recalled that she had pulled off that trick because Wilson had hired another girl, Jean Eldridge. Then he had two band-singers with a similar approach. "Wilson was getting religion. When he hired Jean, I said to myself, 'Hey, you had better look around.' He didn't need two girls who sang somewhat alike. I was street-wise, second-guessed him and cut out. Luckily I got another gig right away. The same thing happened with clubs. You would leave one, go to another next door, and your following would follow."

She spent a year with Coleman Hawkins, then went out on her own, working in Greenwich Village at Ernie's Three Ring Circus, then at Kelly's Stables again. When Helen Humes was leaving the Basie band, Basie went to Kelly's to hear Thelma and hired her for a two-year gig in the early 1940s. With him she went into the Blue

Room of the Lincoln Hotel, a big-band bastion on Eighth Avenue between Forty-fourth and Forty-fifth streets in Manhattan. She recorded little with Basie's band, then went to her true milieu: the Upper East Side.

Julius Monk was putting on the shows at Le Ruban Bleu at Fifty-sixth Street and Fifth Avenue. Comedians Irwin Corey and Imogene Coca and singer Maxine Sullivan, an Ella Fitzgerald sound-alike on early recordings in the late thirties, also worked there. Bill Robinson spotted Thelma for a part in *Memphis Bound* with Billy Daniels and "a great jazz singer named Anna Robinson, who died young not long after that," Thelma recalled. The show closed after a short run. Thelma auditioned for *Inside U.S.A.*, starring Bea Lillie and Jack Haley, eventually got the part and later went into the Capitol Theater during a very hot summer. "I stayed there sixteen weeks. It was air-conditioned and known as a place to go to sleep in. From there I went back to the Ruban Bleu. And here is a ghost story:

"Imogene Coca was there again. One night, she and I were sitting backstage when a girl, who looked so filthy, a hippie in advanced stages, came to this really chic chic chic club and sent word back that she would like to speak with me. I said, 'Please come in,' because my mother had taught me you don't know when you're entertaining angels. But this girl was really raunchy. Everybody laughed at me. She said to me, 'Pretend you know me.' In the dressing room they kidded: 'Anyone can know Thelma.' The girl went on:

" 'Eddie Cantor is looking for a singer, and tomorrow night his daughter is coming to hear you sing.' I thought she was some nut. Eddie Cantor wasn't going to have a black girl. Of course, Ethel Waters had had a show on radio for Amoco. But still. Anyway I said okay. Sure enough, Marilyn Cantor and others came the next night. She told me her father was coming to town; she would bring him to hear me. I never saw the raunchy girl again. Marilyn said she had never heard of such a girl. She certainly didn't look like someone whom Marilyn would talk with. Anyway I got signed up for the Cantor radio show.

"They told me I would have to keep it a secret because they were going to have other auditions. And they didn't know how it would be taken. So I kept my mouth shut for six months. One day I bumped into Kay Arman on the street. She said, 'Guess what?' She

was getting the Cantor job. I said, 'Great.' But I got the job for the
'45 and '46 seasons." The gig gave her national exposure as nothing
else before had done. She had recorded "He's Funny That Way" on
the back of Coleman Hawkins' classic, "Body and Soul." With
Basie she did "I Didn't Know About You." Because it was released
after she left the Basie band, she said, "To be evil, the record company didn't put my name on it." She had previously done a few
recordings with the Wilson band, which she remembered fondly for
its sound. It was criticized because it played subtle swing, unlike
the other black bands. Thelma's jazz conception added to the gen-
teel Wilson sound. "Teddy Wilson swung," she said. "Always that
prejudice shit."

She had recollections of prejudice cutting all kinds of ways—
against Wilson for sounding un-black and against Count Basie for
simply being black. Before the band's opening at the Lincoln Hotel,
Basie heard that the management didn't really want a black band
there because of a fear that the black musicians would fool around.
"So Basie told the guys to play their music, go upstairs and get out
of sight. They wore gorgeous clothes for the opening. It turned out
that the management liked us very much. They turned out to be
very good friends of mine."

Partly because she was beautiful, with such a very pretty voice,
her life after the bands took her into society. In the 1940s, at the
chic Blue Angel club in the East Fifties, she played for "terribly
rich people who invited me onto their yachts. Show business was
still divided into black and white. But all I met were rich people,
who took you under their wing. It was heady. Thrilling to have Mrs.
Vanderbilt, the czarina of society, a little old lady, watch you sing.
So you get a little spoiled. You get used to seeing diamonds.

"I met some wonderful people. I played the Borscht Circuit and
met Sondra Berle, Milton's mother. In the Griswold Hotel in New
London, Connecticut, I did an all-Gershwin program. Barbara
Walters was there with her mother. I saw a redheaded woman crying at a table as I sang "Love Walked In." Someone introduced me
to the woman afterwards. It was George Gershwin's mother, Rose.
He had died. I leaned towards Gershwin quite a bit.

"Oh, I met some wonderful people. I was a pretty little brown-
skinned girl and intelligent. If you had done your homework correctly and read some books, from *Silas Marner* to Thomas Wolfe, if

you could carry your own load, it didn't matter too much if you were Chinese or yellow or green or brown."

Immersed in that lifestyle, Thelma never married, in part, she said, because she disliked the relationship she had seen between her mother and father, who divorced when she was a child. "If that was how marriage was, I didn't want it for myself," she said. "So I never got married. But I did light housekeeping and heavy rooming." One roommate was "a very rich man," with whom she had a daughter who doesn't use Thelma's last name and calls Thelma, who is four feet eleven, "Shorty." The daughter, in 1983, calls her mother that nickname primarily by telephone, having left home at age eighteen "to live with a forty-five-year-old man," Thelma said. "She dabbles at things—and goes off and writes or calls, but she's a private person. She calls me. I say, 'Where are you?' She says, 'I'm in the hills of Tuscany.' It's painful for me. Nothing's ever bothered me like that. That's the only thing that's ever really bothered me. Otherwise it was a fabulous life.

"You have to live now, of course."

By 1982 there was less splash and less money. She tried to continue along the Waters route, acting in a road company of *Pippin;* in Movies of the Week; in *Love, American Style* and *Love Boat.* Small roles, not singing parts. In private she could still delineate a song off the cuff and sell it, syllable for syllable, sensibly and movingly to an informal audience. And she remained a raving beauty. People who had never seen her before stared at her pretty face. People who had not seen her in years gossiped after chance meetings about her time-resistant beauty. She was living quietly on the Upper West Side of Manhattan, on little money. She owned a pair of tiny-sized gray suede boots with filigree-patterned, black leather trim, which she had kept in perfect condition for decades.

Etta Jones: The Oneyaluv, Oneya Oneya Oneyaluv

Etta Jones was sitting around backstage at Symphony Space, waiting to go on with a trio including Houston Person, the saxophone player who has accompanied her for many years. Houston was so big that Etta, who was tall and rounded, looked diminutive next to him. Chic in a black satin pantsuit with white satin trim, she was excited to hear that Thelma Carpenter was sitting in the audience. Etta kept peeking around a curtain to try to see Thelma, talking matter-of-factly about herself all the while.

"Billie Holiday is my favorite singer. Then Thelma Carpenter," she said. "When I was nine years old, I was living in a place where a woman in the front of the house had the record 'Fine and Mellow.' She would put it on. I had heard Basie, Erskine Hawkins and Sister Tharpe—all that. But the first time that music really dawned on me was when I heard Billie Holiday's 'Fine and Mellow.' "

Born in Aiken, South Carolina, on November 25, 1928, Etta came to New York at age three with her mother and elder sister. Etta, nicknamed "Delores" by an aunt who simply favored it, sang around the house. "My sister used to tell Mama to make me shut up. I said she (my sister) would have to pay to come to hear me one day."

When she was fifteen, she decided to try out at the Apollo amateur contest. But she looked into the audience, saw all those faces, felt her knees knocking and started in the wrong key. People booed her. Doc Wheeler, the emcee, told the audience to give her a chance. But they kept booing.

"I was ready to faint. I was shy and didn't have that pushy thing. And I was in the Apollo," which was to blacks what the Palace was to whites.

Joe Medlin, a singer with Buddy Johnson's band at the Apollo that night, told her to wait until everybody left. "He must have heard something. Buddy's sister, Ella, who sang with the band, had left because she was pregnant. They were looking for a vocalist. I waited to sing with Buddy playing piano. That was Wednesday night. On Friday I left to go on the road. They taught me music in the bus. 'Listen, you come in here.' They didn't have to teach me the lyrics too much, because I knew them from the jukebox.

"I left Buddy when his sister came back about a year later. Little groups and trios were coming in then [in 1945]. Billie Holiday was working across the street and came to hear me. Later Bobby Tucker [Billie's piano player] told me that she had liked me. He showed me a story where she was asked to comment on up-and-coming singers. She named me. I was surprised. In those days I probably sounded like her. At first you don't have your own style; you sound like the one that you adore."

Around that time, writer and record producer Leonard Feather

got Etta her first recording date to do "Salty Papa" and "Evil
Gal"—tunes that Dinah Washington, working with Lionel Hampton in the forties, did at about the same time. Dinah had four days
off in Washington when Etta was working with the Johnson band.
Dinah loaned Etta a false-hair bun and gave her a couple of
gowns—a typical Dinah Washington gesture, which it was typical
also of Etta to remember appreciatively.

It was getting closer to the time that Etta had to go onstage at
Symphony Space. She got up for a minute and said quietly, seemingly without nerves, "Let me see how I get on this stage. I don't
like to be fumbling around. Takes too much time."

She found the stairs leading to the stage, then came back to sit
around a while longer. "After the Onyx Club, I did some things on
my own and went with the Harlemaires. I played brushes; we sang
harmony. In 1948 I went with J. C. Heard's group. Then I went
with Earl Hines for a couple of years. When I was with him, he had
Art Blakey, Benny Green, Jonah Jones, Tommy Potter, Aaron
Sachs—and Helen Merrill. Helen did several weeks with us in California because she came out to be with her husband, Aaron Sachs;
she took her baby along with us.

"Helen and I sang together: 'It's So Nice to Have a Man Around
the House.' She would sing four bars, then I would come in. At the
end we were supposed to sing in harmony. But we would start
laughing. Couldn't do it. The harmony is so corny. It's like barbershop harmony. Helen always was advanced and wanted to sing
flatted fifths. Earl said he was going to fire us: 'This is a business.
This is not funny.' But I could hear her voice going vibrato in her
stomach, and I would laugh. We would turn our backs on each
other and still feel each other trembling. Ha-ha-ha. We couldn't
do it. Ha-ha-ha. We would just break up. I don't believe we ever
sang it."

Eventually Earl broke up the band; Etta took a day job for "a
few minutes," then got the chance to do a record: "Don't Go to
Strangers" on the Prestige label. She had a gold record.

When it was time for her to go onstage, she stood up and suddenly realized: "I have to go to the bathroom. No, I won't go. I just
always have to go to the bathroom."

"You had better go," I said because she seemed so serious
about it.

"No, but this time I really have to go. But it will go away as soon as I get onstage. I don't know why. I guess my mind is thinking of other things out there. I can't think of anything else."

Out there, she had a unique little yodel in some of her songs. She did "Don't Misunderstand," then a medley, including the tune—with which she spent quite a while—about how it is when the "oneyaluv, oneya oneya oneyaluv" belongs to somebody else. A highly stylized singer, she's far more forceful, more socko than Billie. (Anybody would be.) All of Etta's push lies in her voice. Musicians say she simply "sings her ass off." Then she did an uncanny imitation of Billie. The audience roared with laughter and clapped wildly. (Zi-zi-zi, Billie lives! Billie lives!)

"I don't know how I did it," Etta said later. "I don't know. How did I do it? Uh, I don't know how. I just don't know. I just enjoy singing. The lyric is what I like. I make mistakes, forget the words, but I hate to. Houston talks to me onstage: 'Why did you do that?' I like up-tempo songs, but not too fast. I want you to understand what I'm saying. I hate it when you can't understand the words. And I don't like nonsense music. The ones with two words: Get up and jump down. I like a song that says something.

"I don't want to sound prudish, but songs that throw me into bed at the drop of a hat—I don't like them. I like: '[It's no good unless he's with you] All the Way.' I like 'By the Time I Get to Phoenix.' That suggests to me that he tried and told her it just wasn't working out; he finally got up the courage to try something else. I like to sing 'Don't Misunderstand.' Houston says it's a one-night stand, but I hear it as love. Heuston says, 'No no,' but I hear they're in love. Old standards are the best."

Some old friends—people she had known for so long that they still called her Delores—came milling backstage. Literally over a dozen people milling to get to her. Etta wondered aloud if she could go out into the audience to say hello to Thelma Carpenter, but decided she shouldn't do it right after performing. She peeked around a curtain again. Thelma Carpenter, in a form-fitting, pale blue denim jump suit, a straw hat, redolent of fine perfume, parted the curtains and embraced Etta.

"Do you hear you in me?" Etta asked. "My idol. I hear it."

Thelma said, "I hear Billie in you the way I hear Ethel in me."

"I hear you in me, too," Etta insisted.

Thelma can imitate Ethel Waters exactly because she used to rehearse for her "and let her sit down," she said. And Etta can mimic

Dinah and Carmen and Billie and Ella Fitzgerald, too. And the most obvious lineages were from Ethel to Thelma, and also from Ethel to Billie, and from Billie to Etta Jones.

Helen Merrill: "Bebop Sounded Normal"

She sings down a halftone from the written note in a tune, then again down another halftone on another note, then up a halftone from another written note. That's how Helen Merrill on record gains control of you and handles your heart and soul with a melody. She did it instinctively to make the music "interesting," she said. She has always been interesting to look at, too, with Miss-America-from-the-Cornbelt features. She has a keyed-up though soft and dreamy way of talking. Talking about the past gets her keyed up; it had its spacy, difficult moments. She dressed very well in 1982. A tailored, camel's hair pantsuit emphasized how blond and petite she is. At one time she was so "absentminded" about clothes that "Dinah Washington used to reprimand me for going onstage with oxfords," she recalled. "I was painfully shy. I came out of a background that created that."

She was born on July 21, 1934, in Manhattan to parents of Yugoslavian background. Her mother sang in the house—twelve-tone singing from the fishermen's isle of Krk. "So all those bebop things sounded normal to me. Bartók sounds familiar to me, because it came out of folk music."

Her mother, she said, was unhappy in the United States. When she sang, she expressed her emotions. Helen absorbed her mother's musical influence but went a different route in life without guidance from immigrant parents who were basically too naïve to guide a hip American child in a singing career. Helen had to make decisions on her own. Complicating matters, the family went to the Seventh-Day Adventists' Church. "To go near a nightclub was unthinkable," she said.

As an adolescent, Helen went to record stores and listened to blues singer Muddy Waters, to Big Joe Turner and Billy Eckstine, particularly the last's blues hit "Jelly Jelly" with Earl Hines. And Billie Holiday; and Jo Stafford—"I loved her sound and intonation. They were people I had never heard of, but my tastes were broad."

With a special interest in art, she went to the High School of Industrial Arts, which offered no music courses. "I tried to get into the High School of Music and Art, but I had no formal background, no lessons." She tried to take piano lessons but had no piano at home, only a cardboard keyboard. In her teens she began hanging around musicians' rehearsal studios—in particular the Nola Studios on Broadway in midtown. The Nola family didn't mind kids hanging around. Woody Herman's band, Boyd Raeburn and small groups played there.

"Once in a while, we'd get together a kid group. Then I would do some singing. I landed myself a concert, sitting in. A musician called Bill Triglia worked in Nyack on weekends. So I worked there. And when I was fifteen, I worked at the Eight Forty Five Club. What nerve I had! It was in the Bronx. There was Helen Milcetic on the marquee. That was me.

"You've got to be persistent. You've got to really be a pain in the neck. People see you around and give you a hand because they know you're a kid, and you have a driving force. They help you with it, once they hear you can sing. Musicians are kind.

"Miles Davis, Charlie Parker, Bud Powell, Al Haig, Oscar Pettiford and Red Rodney [all jazz instrumentalists] played there. All part of that era. Ira Gitler [jazz writer and entrepreneur] used to be hanging around there, too. Oh, it was marvelous. So much talent around. Something had to rub off on you. Musicians are very protective and spiritual. Teddy Wilson said about Billie: she was fine when she was protected by musicians. But when she got into other company, the drugs began. Babs Gonzalez [an early bebop singer] was hanging around, too; Roy Haynes, the drummer; Betty Carter. None of us became rich singing jazz music. We all had very rough lives. I don't know why I stuck it out. But this is what I do.

"In the late forties and early fifties, jazz music was definitely a 'drink whiskey' music. People didn't want to listen to bebop and cool music. The school of chord changes. We came out of that; the heritage line of Monk, 'Bird' [Charlie Parker], Diz and Bud Powell. Because there wasn't a lot of work, we formed an elitist group and closed everybody else out. We spent all our time trying to figure out new chord changes, improvising on them, on 'All the Things You Are' and 'Round Midnight.' We would take the chord structure, change it and call it by another name.

"It was the only way to get approval for your talent in the late forties and fifties. So we had an incredible school in those days. It was a vehicle to express a lot of emotions, not a commercial art form. I was accepted, though I was raw material, because my singing was different. I was protected by Oscar Pettiford and Charlie Parker. They saw me traveling on some original road and were supportive. Parker would ask me to sit in all the time; he understood the talent and the desperation. That's the Charlie Parker that people don't talk about. Billie Holiday was very generous, too, in her own way with her encouragement.

"Most of the important things that happened to me happened through black musicians. I always used the musicians I wanted to on record dates. I got a lot of flak. On TV I was considered weird because I used black musicians. I was considered just too different, a jazz person who worked with integrated groups. It had nothing to do with altruism. They're just simply good. I love talent and just like to share musical experiences.

"Eventually I sang with Mingus. He had a Rolls-Royce and a chauffeur's cap. In the fifties he thought it was risky to be seen driving a Rolls-Royce with a blond woman in the front seat. So he made me get in the back seat so we wouldn't get arrested. I worked with him in Detroit with Teddy Charles, the vibraphone player. The owner of the club had about all he could take, and pulled me hard and said, 'How can you sing with a nigger on the stand?' There was some language that I've blocked out. I'm very haughty and superior to this person. I never did tell Charlie. He was accustomed to hurt feelings. Blacks expect stupidity from white people and are on their guard.

"In the late forties and fifties, very few blacks and whites worked together. I got blackballed from TV because of the race situation. It's that blunt. There were days when we toured the South, and I had to realize with my eyes that kind of prejudice. The musicians went to black hotels. Miles couldn't go to the bathroom where they would let me use the bathroom. He said, 'Those are your people.' Today that sounds ridiculous. Still, it's a sensitive issue. But in music, you choose people for their ability.

"Had I been black, it would have been easier. A white woman musician heard a record of mine with Clifford Brown and Oscar Pettiford; Quincy Jones had done the arrangements. The white woman musician thought it was a black chick. When she saw it was a blond, white chick, she said, it changed her attitude toward the music. That singing moved her. She would have preferred it was a black person, because white people are not supposed to be soulful. Black people, too, think you're not supposed to be soulful if you're white.

"But my feelings come from a universal bank of feelings about people."

In 1951, when she was seventeen, she married and had a son with musician Aaron Sachs. "The marriage was a disaster," Helen summed up. But in 1953 the marriage did take her on the road to join Sachs in California, where he was playing with Earl Hines. Earl Hines hired her. So she and Etta Jones got to sing their ill-fated duet "It's So Nice to Have a Man Around the House," whose harmonies made them hysterical onstage. "That's when it all started for me," said Helen. "All my daydreams had stopped between '51 and '53, because I had to take care of my child. But Earl's valet babysat. So I was on the road for a while. After my divorce I stayed unmarried for a long time. I was always so fearful after that," she said, because her early experience of marriage had disappointed her.

"Musically, Etta Jones came out of the Billie Holiday tradition. And I can guess what was most important to Billie, as it was to all of us. Her phrasing. So few singers have really good phrasing. Hers was fantastic. Every singer should listen to Billie for that. She's the singer who influenced us all. She got the most out of her limited vocal equipment because of her phrasing and musicianship. It was intuitive and uncanny what she got from behind the words. You felt feelings beyond the lyrics. And so many notes in her songs. With her ears and musicianship, she could take the melody and change it to fit her vocal equipment—with the greatest musicality. You can't teach that instinct. That's all your own. You can help people to be in touch with their feelings, so they can sing a song with their own instrument. Then it all has to go together. Phrasing, words, music, storyline have to be related. Holding a note, emphasis on a word have to have not only musical but emotional meaning. It's like speaking. Singing has to touch you in some universal sense, move you, or else it's meaningless; you could just as well listen to a machine creating sounds."

Helen sang and recorded with excellent, active musicians. But in part because there wasn't enough work in the United States, and in part because her early marriage jolted her, she went to live in Italy and Paris. She became very well known in Europe and eventually in Japan, where she toured many times. In Paris she worked with the late Don Byas, with drummer Kenny Clarke and others among the best expatriate and European jazz musicians of the 1950s (and she still does). In the early sixties, she returned to New York—just in time for rock's coronation. The Beatles came to town.

"It was dark. Nothing was happening," she recalled. "There wasn't anyplace to work. I was very disappointed and moved in with my sister. My son [Alan Merrill, now a rock musician] went to live with Aaron for a short while. Then I made a record. Things started to change a little. But I had to go back to work. That meant Europe and Japan. So Alan and I went back on the road." Working back in Sweden, she was asked by a young singer: "How did you get that job?" "It took about twenty-four years," Helen answered. In Brazil she won an award. "I was floating around," she reminisced. "It gave me the good fortune to work with the best musicians in all the countries."

In Japan she met a newsman who was in charge of a news bureau for United Press International (UPI). In 1967 they got married. Returning to New York, where her husband became an executive with UPI, she began her own production company, Spicewood Enterprises, recording Roland Hanna, Tommy Flanagan, others—and herself. Her first production, with John Lewis of The Modern Jazz Quartet, was nominated for a Grammy. "It was nerve-wracking to be in the booth and then on the record, too. However, the freedom my own record company presents to me is worth more than any promises a record company can't keep." On one of her own records, you can hear this especially creative singer doing "What Is This Thing Called Love?" with everything flatted. Musicians like her work. "But it has been taken so much further by Betty Carter," Helen said demurely.

(Later for Free Jazz singer Betty Carter, whose work *is* also much later—that is, musically complex—though she started out long before.)

CHAPTER 11

Beyond the Vibrato: The Cutting Edge of Billy Eckstine, Heartthrob

On my way up to his hotel suite in Washington, D.C., where he was starring at the redoubtable Blues Alley, I called first and woke him up.

"How do you take your coffee?" I said.

"With milk and ginger ale on the side."

"Ha-ha."

"YOU KNOW WHAT I MEAN."

Of course, the first thing I noticed when Billy Eckstine opened the door was the perfect crescent of a widely smiling mouth under a neat moustache. One musician had told me that Eckstine is irreverent. Another said that Eckstine has a raunchy sense of humor. But none of that streak evidenced itself at first blush that day. Quickly the smile disappeared; the expression turned dour. And the man occasionally injected into the conversation the soft-voiced remark: "I don't mean to sound caustic."

There's an intensity to Billy Eckstine. It smolders. In performance it has fired his delivery. Other singers, who came after "B," as his friends call him, sang the same type of love songs. Arthur Prysock has a deep, scratchy voice—a throat full of hot coals and a lot of vibrato that smooths out to hit a high note softly. Funkier than Eckstine's, Prysock's voice has the matinee idol's resonance, too—

and a manner to go with it. (Recently after a set of love ballads, which he delivered with gravelly passion, I asked him politely if I could interview him for a book. In reply he tickled me under my left arm. Later, by telephone, he summed up his musical *modus operandi:* "Lyrics are the most important thing to singers, or should be; otherwise they're not singers. And lyrics always mean Woman to me. Always. I've built a whole career out of singing to Woman. I get the same feeling when singing any ballad. It's always Love. I'm trying to hit the ear, the eye, the brain—and wherever it goes after that, so that a woman feels good. I always wanted to be a singer. And Billy Eckstine was always the one who moved me." Prysock had hits with "Blue Velvet" and "I Worry About You" in the fifties and sixties. Another Eckstine protégé has been Johnny Hartman, a ballad singer and great recording artist with a beautiful, deep voice, too, and a friendly manner. Hartman won a Grammy nomination in 1981 for a gorgeous album of love ballads. Al Hibbler, who is blind, sings on the Eckstine axis. Pop singer Perry Como, who was so laid back, and Tony Martin, who was so fervent, had impassioned female fans. But none of them seduced a nation more than Eckstine did in the 1940s and 1950s.

His son, Ed, a businessman in the Quincy Jones office in Los Angeles, said that from the start his father refused to take the role of the suitcase carrier in films or sing the blues primarily. "His attitude was: 'I don't carry my own goddam suitcases.' He was intensely patriotic to his own values. For that I respect him. He had several strikes against him; he was born black, he was handsome, and he was driven and made bitter by the times he lived in, climbing the ladder of success as a ballad singer. Why would anyone want his daughter to love Billy Eckstine instead of a white singer like Frank Sinatra?"

Arranger Jerry Valentine, who became friends with Eckstine when they worked together in Earl Hines' band in the 1940s, tells of an incident in Boston. The musicians were playing in a remodeled opera house when someone in the audience cast a racial slur. "It ended up in a big fight because of Billy. He fought back. He had a very bad temper. If something can erupt, it will, if he doesn't feel something's right. He has always been very tough. You end up being rough, if you weren't in the first place," Valentine said, in the difficult world of show business.

Eckstine's intensity always had a cutting edge.

In conversation he can do a diatribe against labels. "I never thought I was a ballad or blues or jazz singer," he said, sitting in his hotel suite, waiting for show time at night. He was wearing a bathrobe, from which emanated very long, slender, blue-veined ankles and feet—the kind meant for black silk stockings, shiny shoes and a tuxedo. One show-business manager, Armando del Rivero, retains the image of Eckstine, always classy in a tuxedo, gallant with a joke, or a peck on the cheek to encourage Chita Rivera when they appeared in a show together. "It's a lie that I didn't like the blues," Eckstine continued. "How could I not like it? It's a good form of music, with pathos. Hell, I wrote 'Jelly Jelly' [a huge hit for him with Earl Hines' orchestra in the 1940s]. It's been going for fifty years. Bebop. Another label. I don't like labels. Stevie Wonder [whom everyone calls a "pop" musician] is potentially one of the people who'll carry on in the tradition of great black musical talents. He's a very intelligent writer and singer. His music is intelligent. He's jazz, not pop. Rock is jazz. He's the best. Labels have done more to destroy good talent. In his 'Sir Duke,' there's a little improvisation that's pure jazz. I hate labels."

His expression was deadpan with a hint of glower. He had just recovered from an attack of one of his headaches—"a migraine," he called it, while son Ed called his father's problem "cluster headaches." "Scary headaches," Ed added. "I've seen them when they get very intense and he's been on the verge of blowing his brains out. They can last from five minutes to five hours over a period of six weeks to a year. His left eye tears; the face begins to disfigure. And the doctors don't know what causes them." Eckstine has performed with them.

In the 1930s when he was singing with Earl Hines, Eckstine had a high, straightforward voice and style. But by the 1940s it became deep, agile and enriched with persistent vibrato. Women swooned over him, the first black singer to break through the color line as a heartthrob—a veritable black Gable. Calloway had gone bounding and flying through on comedy, though he had the potential for seduction. Eckstine insisted on the seduction. Pushing it, he became the first black to sign with MGM Records. By the late 1940s and early 1950s, he was a top record star, given first-rate songs to sing. Billie Holiday, even with John Hammond and Milt Gabler pushing her, got second-raters: "Easy Living," "What a Little Moonlight

Can Do," songs that nobody else was singing. But Eckstine got "My Foolish Heart."

"He sold records," explained Bobby Tucker, Eckstine's piano accompanist since 1949.

"Since they started telling me about vibrato," Eckstine said, "I didn't know what they were talking about. I don't have any idea how it came about. It's the way I hear the melodic line, I guess; the way I want to sound. I try to be direct in my performance. If it has been sexy, I didn't do it that way on purpose. I was just thinking about the music. Vibrato doesn't make a damn thing. It's not sexy on purpose. It just comes out that way. Straight tones are very easy to do. Same thing as playing on the horn. If you want to use vibrato, do it. It's the way you personalize. But thank God for the image of me as a heartthrob. It fed me and my family."

Eckstine was born in Pittsburgh, went to Washington, D.C., to go to college, and ended up playing in the Howard Theater there instead. He grew up musically in the big-band era and turned professional at about the time the beboppers came forward from the back benches.

"I heard instrumentalists. They inspired me more than the singers," he said. "Among the singers my inspirations have been Pha Terrell; he used to come through Pittsburgh. I met him through Mary Lou Williams when I was just starting to sing around the clubs there. He was strong and slender, with a very warm voice and a lot of feeling. He had romantic appeal and influenced me somewhat. You're influenced, if you like something. Cab Calloway was my main inspiration. And then, when I started singing melodically, it was Paul Robeson."

He and his two sisters received some music lessons on the piano; he came by a few breathing lessons for playing trombone and even a little trumpet—but never any singing lessons. He simply started singing in the Holy Cross Episcopalian church choir in Pittsburgh, then in the clubs and eventually in Washington when he was supposed to be in college. But he won an amateur show and started working with musicians in the Tommy Miles band in the thirties along with Tyree Glenn, Trummy Young and Jimmy Mundy, who did arranging for Benny Goodman. Although Eckstine appreciated the music, he didn't plan a career as a singer, he said, because he didn't really know how to plan one.

"I was leery. Not sure of myself," he said.

From Washington he went home to Pittsburgh and little clubs there again, then Buffalo, then Detroit. Budd Johnson, a horn player in Earl Hines' band, passed through Detroit and stayed with Eckstine one night. Hearing him sing, Johnson told him to go to Chicago. Eckstine hesitated, shy. Johnson brought Earl Hines to hear Eckstine. And Billy quickly joined Hines, from whom he learned stagecraft. "No way I could put my finger on exactly what Hines did," said Eckstine. "I simply watched him. He's a master showman. I learned technical aspects by asking about things as they confronted me. Budd Johnson, Willie Randall and Jerry Valentine, a great trombone player and arranger, gave me a knowledge of the basics. Singing is nothing but talking. And I knew enunciation. You learn things through experience. I was always interested in the musical aspects. I improvised from the chords as I went along."

He talked acerbically, except when delivering opinions on the state of the music in the hands of the critics, who supply labels and then ask why everything is happening; then he talked acidly. "Music just progressed from its primitive singers up. The first part was communication in the cotton fields, when people wanted to keep secrets about what was on their minds. Jazz is communication. It's a person telling someone else his happiness or sadness or what's happening with him."

Does Billy Eckstine express his feelings when he sings lyrics? Or writes them? Son Ed Eckstine thinks his father is a very emotional singer. But Billy said, " 'Jelly Jelly' was written in twelve minutes. That was a case of necessity. We had time left on a recording date to do another number. The man in the recording session asked us, 'Do you have a blues?' We had half an hour left. So Earl Hines and the band got this little head arrangement of a twelve-bar blues. Then all we had to do was write the lyrics. So I went outside and wrote them. I don't know what inspired me. Nothing that was going on in my personal life."

Once he firmly established himself as a star, MGM gave him "My Foolish Heart" to sing. "It was a good song. I looked at the lyric and melodic line and told the story. That's the way I felt it. I don't mean to be caustic about it when I say I don't say this bar is going to mean this and that bar is going to feel that way. I played what I was feeling. So many feelings instruct you. You try to read the lyric and marry it to the melodic line. I believe in the song, if it's believable. I don't have any favorite song. Anything that is good and musical, something that's harmonically good. It's a marriage between the lyric and the music; I don't sing a lyric if I don't like it. A song like 'Feelings' is a bad lyric and a bad song."

"Hmmmmmm, 'Feelings,' " I said, singing the one word. "I can't remember it."

"Good! I wish I couldn't. I like a song that says something. Not novelties. 'Mule Train.' I couldn't do that. It was great for what Frankie Laine did. I couldn't do it. Neither could Frankie sing with vibrato. That's my thing.

"I didn't feel 'My Foolish Heart.' I was given a great lyric and great music, and I married them and tried to cover the song for MGM at the time. But if you have fifty songs, you can't change feelings from a ballad to up tempo just like that. You'd look like a puppet."

"So it's an exterior showmanship?" (Sarah Vaughan has said that sometimes her mind wanders to a shopping list when she is performing.)

"I guess so. It's your business. It's the way you sell yourself. The techniques come with experience. And fundamentally it's a part of you, the way you play or sing a thing. That's why there are so many different styles. There are so many good versions of 'Body and Soul.' Coleman Hawkins is the one who got over. But Clifford Brown is good, too. Art Tatum's version I enjoy. Baby, I was influenced by anybody who played good. Charlie Parker, Earl Hines, Budd Johnson, Dizzy Gillespie, Charlie Christian, Wes Montgomery, Freddie Hubbard. The beboppers were my era, new and a step beyond. We generally called it progressive jazz. Music was becoming more intelligent."

In 1944 he formed a band and sang vocals with it. Personnel included Gene Ammons, Fats Navarro, Budd Johnson, John Malachi and Sarah Vaughan on her second band job after her stint with Earl Hines. She and Eckstine did famous duets together. And Art Blakey, Jerry Valentine, Charlie and Leo Parker, Miles Davis, Howard McGhee, Lucky Thompson, Dexter Gordon and Dizzy Gillespie. Eckstine played valve trombone, too, and concentrated more on the instrumentals than the vocals. But he had to break up the band because it went into big-time debt in 1947.

"It was a good band, ahead of its time. People said we were out of tune, because they didn't know what they were hearing. Now they're ready for us." (By 1982, when the so-called Free Jazz players and singers were still annoying part of the jazz public with dissonances, the public was eager for the sound of the beboppers. They were finally perceived as relatively mellow. But at one time, they irritated the swing-band leaders for whom they worked. Legend has it that Cab Calloway told Dizzy Gillespie to stop playing his "Chinese music.") The demise of Eckstine's band, which really had a clean, swift sound, allowed Eckstine to go out as a solo ballad singer and flash his Clark Gable smile at all the women in the audience without thinking about the musicians behind him. The voice was so full of life force that it sounded as if its source were located in his heart. With the trademark vibrato and with strings behind him, on records he sounded like *your* heart throbbing. If Cab Calloway's tenor was so robust that it came across as a borderline baritone, then Eckstine's baritone struck you as a basso profundo—the Paul Robeson of the boudoir.

There were women closer to Eckstine than the ones swooning in the audience. Eckstine and his first wife, June, divorced. Eckstine had a son, Billy, Jr., now a Pittsburgh fireman, with a woman whom Eckstine, Sr. "encountered along the road of life," said Ed Eckstine. How did Senior know for sure that Billy, Jr., was his son? "Because," Ed said, "he came out wearing a Mr. 'B' collar [the roll collar that Eckstine popularized] and singing 'I Apologize' [one of Eckstine's biggest hits]." In early 1953 Eckstine married model and actress Carol Drake, with whom he had four children. Ed, the oldest, could play guitar and bass, but preferred the business end of music; Guy, three years younger than Ed, played drums, but decided to study for a law degree at UCLA. "Drums are his first love," said Ed, "but he knows it's not always how good you are that gets you over. So he's getting the law degree. He's a smart little fucker." Then came Charlotte Carolle, called "CC," who in 1982 was a model and drama student and didn't want to sing. All the Eckstine children have been gifted with "pipes," said Ed, but opted not to perform. Except for the youngest, Gina, a singer, who has worked in supper clubs with her father. "She's going to be fine," Billy Eckstine said.

The Eckstines divorced in 1978, he said, talking about his personal life deadpan, monosyllabically, with an air that suggested that he was not open to chitchat. The divorce, said Ed, who waxed voluble about it, was acrimonious. Acrimonious rhymes with alimonious. Billy Eckstine moved from Los Angeles to Las Vegas, where he played a lot of golf, Eckstine's son said, labeling his father "a golf junkie," among other irreverent things. Billy Eckstine had always told his children that he believed in doing something all the way and doing it right, Ed recalled. And Eckstine has repeated that sentiment in an attempt to explain the wellspring of his intensity. Ed has always believed his father's lessons and couldn't reconcile them with the new family situation.

Reflecting on better days, Ed recalled how his father came home from spending forty weeks a year on the road and tried to make up for being away so much. When the family went out for dinner, "people kept coming up and saying how they remembered him from the good old days and the first times they shtupped their wives." Ed resented the lack of privacy. But he knew that anonymity would have meant that his father was bankrupt.

He liked his father's sense of humor, or irreverence; it kept things loose. "My father gave Richard Pryor his first gig outside New York. It was in the mid-1960s. Dad was going to do the chitlin circuit. Not really, but some black clubs in the East ('Filet of chitlin' circuit, Junior Mance dubbed them] with Quincy Jones and Redd Foxx. But Foxx couldn't go. My father used to keep an apartment in Harlem near the Apollo Theater since the 1940s. Mom was walking back to the apartment and saw a skinny guy on a street corner doing an incredible act about Super Nigger and Rumpelstiltskin. It was Pryor. She told Dad, who said, 'Great.' So Pryor went to audition and met Dad between shows. Dad was wearing a tuxedo and said to Pryor, 'Well, you're an ugly enough motherfucker, you'd better be funny.' I guess you have to have been there. But that loosened Pryor up. Oh, God, another time, one of my elder brothers [Billy Eckstine had two stepsons, Kenny, who writes poetry, and Oran, a promoter, from his ex-wife's first marriage] came home with some semblance of venereal disease. He tells Pop. Pop was smoking his pipe and reading the sports page. My brother says, 'I've got a dripping coming out of myself. I think I got it in a toilet.' Pop looked up and said, 'That's a hell of a place to be fucking.' He went back to what he was doing. Oh, the totality of events. That does bring a flutter to my heart."

On the road as he neared seventy, the smile intact, Billy Eckstine still got treated to demands for his biggest hits, "I Apologize," for one. At Blues Alley, the premier jazz club in Washington, Bobby Tucker noted: "Last night, someone yelled for 'Jelly Jelly.' She wasn't even born when he did it. She yelled all through it, too."

CHAPTER 12

The Instrumentalists Sing:
A Jazz Subculture

"When I was coming up," trumpet and flugelhorn player Clark Terry said, "all the players and singers, everyone was inspired by Louis Armstrong. Anyone who says anything else is telling a damn lie. He gave in to his improvisational feelings instrumentally and vocally. Anyone inspired by him would try to sing a little bit, too."

The instrumentalists may not always have had practiced delivery, but they had enough jazz feeling and charm to put on an entertaining performance. For charm is the essence of their business. They frequently have good voices and usually sound more improvisational than the jazz singers.

However lightly the instrumentalists take their jazz singing, they are fun to listen to. They remind you that the music is, as all the arts are, fun. Most instrumentalists have given at least one professional peep. The soft-voiced Mr. Gillespie does an unforgettable "Swing Low, Sweet Cadillac," with a seductively pitched tag line: "Body by Fisher." Catch him singing, dressed as a swami, on a rerun of *The Muppets*. Slam Stewart became famous for inventing a style of singing in unison with his bass, as he bowed it, humming so exactly what he was playing that he amplified his own sound, achieving an eerie, mechanical sound. Bassist Major Holley learned from him, singing in the same register as the bass, sounding like a voice from another galaxy. Clark Terry is another perfect example of this jazz-singing subculture.

Clark Terry Sings Something

"SING SOMETHING!" a robust club manager, Harry Whiting, bellowed at Clark Terry. His quintet had gotten halfway through the second set of a weeknight without Clark Terry singing something. Nothing. He was having a complication with his horn and had stepped back on the bandstand after pausing to shake something out of the pipes. Chris Woods, who has worked with Terry for twenty years, was playing a fast alto sax.

"Beg pardon?" Terry called back. He was dressed in a business suit and wire-rimmed glasses, with an animation to his neat features and trim figure. Busy executive image. "Something? Okay. ... I'm going to sing a song called 'Something.' " He blew a lick and sang out: "SOMETHING!" The audience tittered. He blew a few more notes very loud and sweet and sang again: "SOMETHING!" And a few more phrases on the horn: "SOME-THING!" And again, this time longer, louder and even more drawlingly, with the laryngitic black catch in the throat evident: "SOOOOOOOOMMMMMTHANG!" Right away again, with a relentless swing: "SOMETHING! SOMETHING!" It was a nice jazz song, a memorable musical moment, melodic, witty and never heard before.

Chris Woods sang "Something" solo. He and Terry sang a plain little bark of a duet: "Something!" The song wound up with one brash "Something" from Clark Terry, who sometimes ends a set by saying he is Bunk Johnson, a legendary old-time horn player, or Herb Alpert. But who knows if he will ever sing "Something" again? He said he never sang it before.

If jazz is improvisation, feeling and a rhythmical musical idiom, if it is syncopated music springing from the gospel that begat the blues, if it is harmonic and melodic music reflecting the varied and dynamic American people who have played, sung and developed jazz throughout the twentieth century, then Clark Terry is the quintessential jazz singer—filled with the lore and skill of jazz singing and able to communicate with fresh notes, sounds and lyrics. He sounds spontaneous, as if he were popping out of a cake.

After "SOMETHING," he did a little something on the flugel-horn, which the audience sat through sedately. Then he let fly a wail: "AAAAAAAI!" People were caught up; looked up, smiling, openmouthed. "I want a little girl to fall in love with me . . . I don't even care if she doesn't . . ." He whispered into Chris Woods' ear. Woods covered his mouth in mock, old-style comic fashion, signifying embarrassment. Terry carried on. "I want to reach down in my pocket and give her all my foreign currency. AaaaaaaaI want a little girl to fall in love with me!" The voice was rich, the words were quickly enunciated—but conversational. To the audience: "I'll tell you something more . . . I want a little girl to fall in love with me!" His knees jumped up and down like a little boy's at his first birthday party. Afterward, even the waitresses whooped it up, banging on the tables, clapping, shouting. When Clark Terry sings, it's recess time for propriety.

One of the jazz singers least known to the general public, Terry has billed himself as a trumpet player. But jazz musicians have long regarded him as one of the best singers. In 1982 he went on the Johnny Carson show without a horn and simply scatted—in SWEDISH, or in nonsense syllables with such a Swedish intonation that it sounded like the very language. His deft ear picked it up during years of playing in Sweden. He has a diffident attitude about his singing. "I sing when there's nothing else to do," he said. "It's exactly like playing an instrument. You sing like you play and vice versa."

As much as anyone, he captures the vocal expression of human emotions with his horn; in a concert where singers Joe Williams and Nancy Wilson were doing a little flirtation preliminary to singing, "Well, All Right, Okay, You Win," Clark Terry stood aside, watched Williams do a few diddleybop dance steps toward Wilson, and blew soft, cooing noises on his horn. "You can hardly be two people. You can have some moods, but basically you would be the same type of singer as you are an instrumentalist."

Inspired by a crowd's size one night, Terry announced: "Sometimes on weekends, the management lets us sing some risqué songs of the blues. Turn over your mother-in-law's picture." Together he and Chris Woods wailed Joe Turner's blues, "Cherry Red."

"Run here, pretty mama, ooooh, rock me in your big brass bed, run here, pretty mama, ooooh, rock me in your big brass bed. . . ." Then Woods took off with improvised lyrics: "You've got bad blood, mama, and I believe you need a shot. You've got bad blood, mama, and I believe you need a shot." It was loud and bawdy; the audience laughed hard. "This is a doctor talking to his patient. Now, turn over here, pretty mama, and let's see what else you've got."

Clark Terry took over: "My father was a jockey, and he sure taught me how to ride—oh, he sure did. My father was a jockey, and he sure taught me how to ride, ooooh, he sure did, ooooh, just sit right there in the middle and just rock it from side to side. Ooooooobeeee, I said [he made scat sounds] and she said, ooooooo! uh!" He swung some "whooooops." The audience chimed in with laughter; the noises became indescribable. Terry and Woods wailed on the horns again. It was the blues with a raunchy, joyous feeling—not suggestive, but the feeling of sex itself in sound. Which was funny somehow, maybe because it was displaced.

Where did Terry get those improvised lyrics? "I don't know," he said. "They could go back to the Honeydripper, Roosevelt Sykes [a blues singer] or to Mamie Smith, Bessie Smith or even to Ida Cox. Ida used to sing: 'See that spider crawling down the wall. He's going down there to get his ashes haul.' These old blues lyrics have been around a long time."

Then Terry and Chris Woods did some lip-twisting scatting— "shoobedoo" and "wiffleeewiggleee-wiggleeee-ibbblibbbibleeee"—not your everyday scatting. For a few seconds, it was funny until you realized that the two men were in perfect sync; they continued through five minutes of "ulgirlulgirl," etc. Critics call it Terry's mumbles, which parody the way people get to the Senate.

"Chris and I have been playing together for twenty years. We are in sync on our instruments. It's even easier for us vocally, because you don't have the problem of articulation. I don't have to think of the range of his instrument compared to mine. We call it noodling, on our instruments and when we sing. We try to complement each other rather than outblow each other. It has to be compatible.

"Anything played is basically heard as a voice. We've been teaching clinics on an itinerant basis at schools." (Terry and other jazz stars have been teaching, now that jazz education has become a regular course and even a degree program in many schools since the

1960s in the wake of the Equal Opportunity Act. Terry calls his course "The Interpretation of the Jazz Language.")

"We've found that the most successful way to teach improvisation and phrasing with an instrument is to make the kids sing first," said Terry. "Kids don't know phrasing. They play the round tones evenly, but it's not the interpretation of the jazz language, 'ooobeeeedoooah.' We teach them to give vent to emotions, 'oooooobeeeeeedoooooooaaaahhhhhhh,' and then pick up their instruments. And it's different from 'tooootooootoooootoooo.' And it's the jazz language. People have to give vent to their feelings and a state of abandon in jazz. No three people feel the same way. Improvisation can't be cloned. Feelings are very personal; different pulsations that a musician has are part of it. Maybe knowing how to articulate, manipulate and attack on instruments is an ally for scatting. Maybe it has to do with trumpet playing, for me.

"When a young person left home in my day, the requisite was to be able to bend a note, to go above and below a pitch and keep the pitch in mind. Classical teachers didn't teach correct tonguing for jazz, so we developed the doodle system for want of a better word, with a 'd' or a 't.' But it was the doodle system. Put a parenthesis around the 'e.' Doodl(e). That's the ghosted, swallowed area. If you play legitimately, you say 'tatatata.' We in jazz create 'deedle doodle doodle'—to get sounds the jazz musicians need." Terry gave a mesmerizing example of the doodl(e) system by making rubberband sounds with his mouth. First, he made the band expand, beginning at a middle register, going higher and higher, "pingping-ping-ping," until the band was pulled very tight, squealing a fast "pingpingpingping." Then he came bounding down, letting the band contract again: "Ping-ping-pong-pong-pohng-pohng-pohng. You see, it's not 'ooooo' up there; not 'ooo,' but 'eee' makes sense up there." He sang a high-pitched "eeee" with his eyes going up, looking up to find the natural habitat of "eeeee." Then he came down, singing a song of sounds which is uniquely Terry's: " 'Eeeeeeedleeeeedoooodleeadddddleoooodleeeshobeedoba.' You use certain vowels in certain areas. 'Aaaaaaa' is higher than 'oooooo.' Whatever fits the material. When it comes to scat singing, we teach young singers not to use the same syllables. Not 'oooodoooshibeeedooo' all the time. We teach them there are twenty-six letters. Use whatever the rhythm and tempo are suited for.

"Louis Armstrong was my main inspiration. As I became more

involved in music, Duke Ellington became my inspiration [Terry played with Ellington throughout the 1950s]. We took it in from him by osmosis; all the good things about him, we absorbed."

Terry was born in St. Louis, Missouri, on December 14, 1920, and sang first in the Baptist Church, his earliest memory of music. Then he played in a kids' band with makeshift instruments. "I made a trumpet out of a piece of garden hose and a kerosene funnel for a bell. That was the closest thing I could find to look like a trumpet. I got a real trumpet when I was thirteen or fourteen.

"I also grew up in a neighborhood of sanctified churches—'boooobchubaboonchibenboooonchili.' We little kids used to sit on the curbs and listen; we liked the rhythms and the way they indulged in their services. Of course, we didn't go inside because we were Baptists."

After high school and a stint in a Navy band, Terry played over the years with Lionel Hampton; Eddie "Cleanhead" Vinson, a blues singer; Charlie Ventura, Count Basie, and Quincy Jones as well as Duke Ellington. Then in the 1960s he joined Skitch Henderson's band for the *Tonight* show until Johnny Carson moved to Los Angeles. Since then Terry has had his own group featuring Chris Woods.

"What's important when I sing is intonation and communication. If you don't sing but one note, sing it on tune, and that's not always easy to do," he said. "As a jazz musician, you've got to have good pitch anyway. The voice is another instrument. You've got to use the voice all the time and keep it clear and open. I practice horn every day but not singing.

"I don't always know what I'm going to sing or play. It's not calculated. My inspiration comes sometimes from the environment and the material. Mistakes turn out well sometimes. You can spin off mistakes and make some of the most successful passages. It's like a boxer rebounding." He began throwing some punches into the air, varied combinations, a jab, a hook, a flurry of fists going one way, then a flurry another way. The first set of the night had loosed all his manic energy.

He feels some tunes are off limits to him. "You have to know yourself. I don't jump up and sing 'Stardust.' I choose material conducive to my delivery. I don't sing romantic ballads at all. Unless it's something like ... 'I've Got It Bad and That Ain't Good.' I wouldn't try to deliver with a basso profundo or a baritone. I just deliver. I'm not like Joe Williams and his polished big pipes. He could sing an aria. I'll do something like put two Ellington tunes together, 'Come Sunday' and 'Sophisticated Lady,' because the chord changes suggest each other. I'm a horn player. I'm not a singer really."

CHAPTER 13

Feeding the Maw with Tunes: From Leo Watson to Eddie Jefferson to Lorraine Feather

Pianist Jay McShann knew two tunes when he sat down to play at a college party. He earned a dollar and decided to learn more tunes. Singers usually begin learning the tunes as children, whether from jukeboxes, radio or records they keep playing. All jazz musicians must be able to step into a job in a short time and work with people they may never have seen before. So knowing the tunes is very important.

The jazz repertoire keeps growing. Jazz is a voracious consumer of tunes. Great American composers started writing the standards, which jazz musicians adopted for jazz. Then beboppers wrote hundreds of tunes from the chords of "I Got Rhythm" and other standards. "The chord changes are like the body. The melody is the clothing you hang on it," bebop lyricist Jon Hendricks has said. The chord changes in "What Is This Thing Called Love?" became "Hothouse"; "Whispering" became "Grooving High." Increasingly through the years, jazz musicians joined the list of great composers of American popular tunes. Billie Holiday wrote "God Bless the Child," "Don't Explain," "Billie's Blues"; Peggy Lee wrote many tunes; Ella Fitzgerald is credited with "A-Tisket, A-Tasket," her improv on a nursery rhyme. Eddie Jefferson and Jon Hendricks wrote lyrics for some of the best jazz instrumentals, turning them into commercial standards; tunes such as "Moody's Mood for Love" by Jefferson, one of the first and most sensuous jazz lyricists.

From Leo Watson to Eddie Jefferson to Lorraine Feather

In the 1930s a great scat singer named Leo Watson gained some notoriety, primarily among musicians. He sang all over the octaves; he skittered over the notes, tossed one out here, another one there, at breakneck speed, in nonsense syllables, a language of his own. Born in 1898 in Kansas City, he undoubtedly heard Louis Armstrong's scat lines on records and stretched the idiosyncratic idiom as far as it would go.

Leo played trombone, drums and tiple (a transitional instrument between banjo and guitar) with a small group called the Spirits of Rhythm. Jonah Jones recalled that most musicians weren't interested in the type of music that Watson's group and quite a few like it were playing, sometimes with washboards and kazoos, too; everyone wanted to work in the big bands.

"I don't know if you could call a tiple player a musician or not," Jones added. "I don't know about the reading ability. But if Watson could have played a horn, I'm sure he would have been good. He needed a trombone."

"He had one," I said, "but he lost it to the hock shop. That's what Leonard Feather once wrote about Watson."

"Yes, but he had so much talent in him; the only way he could get it out was with scat singing. He needed a trombone," said Jones.

Jones had recently seen a film on TV with a vignette of Leo Watson and the Spirits of Rhythm in the cast. "I saw that, and I stopped! That must go back to 1936. That's when I first met Leo at the Onyx Club on Fifty-second Street, when that street was great."

Leo used to say hello to Jonah by riffing his name: "Jonahjonah Jonahjonah . . . Jonah . . . dedeeahda . . . Jonahjonah."

"Short, built like an ox and strong-looking," in Jones' memory, and with an extremely big mouth, as Feather recalled, Watson emanated most of all a sense of great wildness. One night in the Onyx, something made him angry. Jones couldn't imagine what.

But Jones went away for a few minutes, then walked back into the club and found a big hole in the wall. "Who the hell did that?" Jones asked. He was told: " 'Leo.' He had put his fist right through a strong wall. It would tear your hand to pieces. Some kind of plaster. Otherwise Leo was beautiful. I didn't know the real bad part of his life."

His singing was so inventive that he caught the ear of Artie Shaw, with whom he did some brief solos on three 78-rpm records in 1937. Gene Krupa hired Leo of the lyrical syllables and the leaping lips to go on the road in 1938 and 1939. Leonard Feather wrote in *Esquire* magazine about how Leo lost that job after eight months: "It . . . happened on a train somewhere in the South. Leo, perhaps for want of a drum to play or a horn to blow, was amusing himself slashing a window shade. When the conductor tried to put a stop to this sabotage, Leo plunged his fist through the windowpane. He was removed from the train; that was the end of his tour with Gene Krupa." So Watson's big-band days were numbered long before the end of the era.

Back in New York, he broke a drummer's foot pedals four times in a Greenwich Village club where the musicians were alternating. Then Leo went to California. One night in a club, he got into a groove, abetted by marijuana, and kept drumming for over thirty minutes; he kept beating on a little drum as the police carried him out the door.

His records cannot be found in stores. You have to look in jazz-library archives or find a private collector. Leo made "Tutti Frutti" with Gene Krupa, on a Columbia LP called *Drummin' Man,* and "Jeepers Creepers." Leo's pronunciation of the word "hypnotizzzzze" came straight out of the lexxxxicon of Louis Armstrong.

"He was fly [fresh and innovative]," Dizzy Gillespie remembered. In the same era, Slim Gaillard, who sang for a while with bassist Slam Stewart, made a bigger splash with some original scat tunes. Gaillard's 1946 hit record "Cement Mixer Putty Putty" gave the country its first and only love affair with concrete. During a break in a recording session in California, he heard the putt-putt of a cement mixer in the street. That noise inspired him. Gaillard had had a previous hit in 1938 with "Flat Foot Floogey With the Floy Floy." Watson never became as famous as Gaillard.

For one thing, Leo was always high. Leonard Feather, who met Watson in the midforties in Los Angeles, reminisced: "He was the most disorganized man, professionally and personally, in every way." If the little bit of his wildly vital scat singing preserved on records is any indication of his personality, he never could hold still long enough to fit in anywhere, either into a big band or any strata of society. In the early forties, he was off the scene. Feather sent someone looking for Watson. After three months he was found in a Main Street restaurant, doubling as a porter and drummer.

Feather dubbed Watson "the James Joyce of jazz" and took him out of obscurity for a few days to record for Bob Thiele's Signature label. Feather played piano under the pseudonym of Jelly Roll Lipschitz for the dates as part of a quintet led by trombonist Vic Dickenson. On September 7, 1946, Watson recorded the funniest version of "Sonny Boy" anybody could imagine, growling riffs, scatting, singing odd phrases, such as "ship ahoy" to rhyme with "Sonny Boy," high and clear, wailing like a trombone. Feather said he arranged "Sonny Boy" for Leo because "the cornier the subject matter, the more ingeniously Leo could sublimate it." On this same record is a raucous, trombone-like solo by Watson, "The Snake Pit," weird and wonderful: "SNAKES SNAKES COBRAS BOA CON-STRICTORS BAAAAAAAAAAAAAH LALALALALALALA-LAUEEBIBO BABABABAB . . . WAH-WAH WOOOOOO."

After making this stab at resurrecting his career, Watson again lapsed into obscurity, disappearing, as Feather remembered, into a bar. In May 1950, Watson, fifty-two, died of viral pneumonia or, more to the point, self-neglect in Los Angeles General Hospital. Musicians' union officials, who had once spent a year looking for Watson, failed to locate any relatives. Watson may have had a wife and daughter. An indigent, he was buried in the Paradise Cemetery under the auspices of the Benevolent Variety Artists.

But not before he made an everlasting impression on several other singers—on a great and innovative bebopper, Joe Carroll, to name one, who sang scat duets with Dizzy Gillespie, and probably on Babs Gonzalez, an early, zany bebopper who had a forties group called Three Bips and a Bop. He wrote "Oop-pop-a-da" and "Low Pow" for Gillespie's tunes. "I think Babs' lyrics typify our music," said Dizzy Gillespie. "Like 'babadelidee.' Scat words. That's what the music sounds like." And, very important, Leo influenced Eddie Jefferson.

Born on August 3, 1918, in Pittsburgh, Eddie Jefferson was probably the first musician to write lyrics for existing jazz instrumentals, most notably "Moody's Mood for Love," a jazz standard based on "I'm in the Mood for Love."

Jefferson started as a tap dancer and scat singer. Although he swung hard, with a mellow, flexible voice, he could never outscat Watson. Watson advised Jefferson to do something else. Jefferson mulled over Watson's advice. Appearing as a tap dancer in Detroit with his partner, a tiny dancer named Irv Taylor, Eddie used to invite people to his hotel room to listen to records. Jefferson said that at one party Taylor, who would also sing some licks, improvised words to an instrumental. That gave Eddie the idea to write lyrics for the great horn solos. "You could still improvise but do it with lyrics," Jefferson told a reporter in the 1940s. One of the first tunes elected was "Moody's Mood for Love."

James Moody had been playing with Dizzy Gillespie's big band and small combo in the grueling road life of the late forties and early fifties. Moody got pretty tired and started to use a drink to get himself going, then two drinks, then more, until he had a bona fide drinking problem that was killing him. His mother persuaded him to visit his uncle, who lived in Paris in a nice apartment near the Place du Trocadéro, with a splendid view of the lights of the Eiffel Tower. Moody went for three weeks and stayed three years.

He dropped into Club St. Germain now and then. Someone asked him to visit Sweden to make records—"Cherokee," "Fools Rush In," and his first recording of "Moody's Mood for Love," which began selling in the United States. Eddie Jefferson loved the tune and decided to put lyrics to it.

Back in the United States, Moody started his own group. One day in Detroit, he recalled, "a cute little girl named Tiny came up to me and said: 'My old man has written some great lyrics to "Moody's Mood," and you're going to hear more about him.' She was talking about Eddie Jefferson, but I didn't know him at the time."

Later, Eddie Jefferson went looking for a gig as Moody's singer. It was the 1950s, an era of small combos featuring singers—a singer's paradise, as paradise goes in the jazz business. Eddie got the job, became road manager, too, and sang his own lyrics for Moody's jazz instrumentals and others. It was a sophisticated concept for the 1950s.

"Audiences looked at us," Moody remembered, "like we were crazy. But I dug what Eddie was doing." Lyrics for "Confirmation," alternate lyrics for "Pennies from Heaven," rechristened "Benny's from Heaven." This song was about a soldier who came home after three years to find his wife with a year-old baby named Benny, who, she claimed, came from heaven. But none of the neighbors remembered seeing Benny coming down. And Jefferson wrote many love songs.

But by the 1960s Moody had broken up his group for lack of money. Jefferson was out of a job. He had already run into bad luck. Although it had been his brainstorm to write lyrics for jazz instrumentals, another singer, King Pleasure, appropriated the lyrics to "Moody's Mood." King Pleasure heard Jefferson sing the tune at the Cotton Club in Cincinnati, brought the song to Harlem's Apollo Theater and recorded it for the Prestige label in 1952. He had a hit.

Dancer Ned Gravely found out what had happened and called the Prestige people's attention to Eddie Jefferson. Jefferson recorded other tunes for them in 1952, including the solo of "Body and Soul." But King Pleasure had a financial success with "Moody's Mood."

Living in Cambria Heights, Queens, Jefferson found occasional club gigs. He took a day job as manager of shipping and receiving for a men's clothing firm. On the road in Omaha, Nebraska, he had met a young woman named Pearl, whom he married. "He was very enthused about her," James Moody remembered. "They hit it off right from the start. She traveled with him for a good while." After Moody's group broke up, so did Eddie Jefferson's marriage.

But his influence in the music business began to grow. Another young singer heard "Moody's Mood" and became enchanted with the notion of lyrics for jazz solos. Jon Hendricks had been writing pop songs for such singers as Louis Jordan. " 'Moody's Mood for Love' opened up a whole world for me," Hendricks told *The New York Times.* "I was mesmerized . . . I thought [it] was so hip. You didn't have to stop at thirty-two bars [the usual number in a popular song]. You could keep going."

Hendricks, a minister's son, well read, well traveled, intensely introspective and worldly, had a college degree, a law-school background—and the courage and push to use his assets. He sought out Dave Lambert, an older bebop singer, with a track record in improv. Lambert had written vocal arrangements behind legendary bebop innovator Charlie Parker, who played more notes in more intricate and passionate saxophone solos than anyone had ever done. Lambert had also scatted with Gene Krupa's band in the 1940s. "He was a singer with gorgeous taste, timing and intonation," said Don Schlitten, a jazz record producer and an avid Lambert fan. Lambert's biggest commercial success would come with Hendricks.

They got together with Annie Ross, a British-born bop singer who wrote lyrics also—most notably "Twisted," for a Wardell Gray tune in the early fifties. She had a deft, high soprano and a compelling rhythmic sense. Lambert, Hendricks and Ross recorded lyrics, written by Hendricks, to some of Count Basie's repertoire, producing a hit LP, *Sing a Song of Basie,* for ABC Paramount. Launched by the record, the trio had four stellar years. Then little redheaded Annie Ross, with her ineffable jazz feeling, left the group.

Lambert and Hendricks continued to play with Yolande Bavan and Anne Marie Moss—fine beboppers. But the group petered out. In the mid-1960s, Dave Lambert was killed in an auto accident. Hendricks, outspokenly discouraged by the ascendancy of rock over jazz, took his family to London for a month and, warmly welcomed, stayed five years.

One of Hendricks' daughters, Michele, born in 1954, began singing bebop lyrics—"vocalese," the beboppers called it—with her father's act occasionally. She started at age seven, singing Daddy's lyrics to "Shiny Stockings," a Count Basie tune. "Michele was always very hip," Jon has said. As far as she knew, the jazz lyrics had always been there.

On the night of the first blackout in New York City, in the midst of a Jazz Depression of the 1960s, Eddie Jefferson and his nephew went to the Apollo Theater. Since they couldn't get back to Queens, his nephew took him to a friend's apartment nearby. The friend's sister, Yvonne, a slender, vivacious young woman with a gracious manner, came home from work, talking about walking down thirty flights of stairs.

"Introductions were made. Two or three days later, Eddie called," Yvonne reminisced. "Would I be interested in helping him entertain some out-of-town guests he had coming in? I did. A month later, he invited me for the same thing. After that, we started seeing each other on a regular basis. My sons from my first marriage, who were eight and nine, fell in love with Eddie. When I told them that

Eddie and I were considering getting married, they were very happy. 'You're marrying our friend?' they said."

In her early thirties, nearly twenty years younger than Eddie, she moved with her sons, her brother and her mother to a house in Cambria Heights, Queens.

"I guess he worked for a year after we were married. But Moody was regrouping. Eddie asked if I could cope with his traveling. I thought he should be doing that anyway. So he worked with Moody until the early 1970s."

Moody: "When I got a group back together, he introduced me to Yvonne. He really dug her. He dug women. We spent plenty of time girl watching. We would be sitting someplace, looking at women coming and going. Boy, look at that, he'd say. Or I would. We had different tastes. He liked buxom, big women. Heh-heh. Yeah. It was groovy. Yeah. Yeah. We could be sitting down and see someone come in. And we'd make eyes subtly at each other across a room and know which one of us she was for. Ha-ha-ha. Ha-ha-haha-hahahahahahahahaha.

"One cold Christmas Eve, we were driving someplace. And smoke was coming up from a chimney in a house we passed. And E. J. says: 'Now, in that house, they have finished the turkey, and she is saying to him'—and E. J.'s voice went up into that falsetto he used for the woman's part in 'Moody's Mood'—'You get in bed, darling, and I'll put the blueberry pie away.' Ha-ha-hahahahahahahahaha-haha.

"I could be in a car with twenty other people and not communicate at all. But Eddie and I could get in a car and have a ball going to a gig. We talked about love and music. We both enjoyed love, liked it and needed it. We didn't talk about the music too much. He might hear something and like it. Solos were like stories to him. He would listen; something would come to mind. He would sit up in a hotel room, eating cake, cookies and ice cream, and write. One time we split a chocolate cake in half and ate it and drank milk with it. Yeah. Yeah," said Moody, who has given up smoking, and occasionally drinking, but habitually spots pizza signs. "I would never say anything about what he wrote. The first thing that he thought of was usually right. I would usually like what he did anyway."

Yvonne: "Then Moody went to the West Coast, and Eddie gigged locally. It was rough. He was driving a cab."

He rued his financial straits, telling Yvonne, a personnel special-
ist in mental health, that she should have more than he could provide—a common dilemma with musicians and their families, who
often split up from the stress.

In the 1960s, too, Eddie became friends with the insomniac, complex but joke-loving horn player, Billy Mitchell. Billy has played
with many major bands and groups—and repaired pool tables during the lean days in the seventies when Eddie was driving a taxi.

"He wasn't depressed about driving a cab, and I wasn't depressed about pool tables. But we weren't jumping up and down
about it," said Billy.

"I can't really say when we first met," Billy reminisced in the
early eighties as we sat in his dining room adjoining the living
room, chewing sugar-free gum and smoking those herbal cigarettes
spiced only by pungent incense. His wife, Marjorie, was washing
the lunch dishes. "When we moved here about twenty years ago, he
was already living here." Billy and Eddie began teaching jazz at
Bennington College for a summer in the early seventies. Billy's
fondest memory of teaching was driving with Jefferson to and from
the job.

In the sixties and seventies, record producer Don Schlitten com-
piled a historical series for Prestige, including recordings Jefferson
made with Irv Taylor and James Moody originally for Riverside in
the fifties. Schlitten introduced Jefferson to Joe Fields of Muse
Records. Fields and Schlitten produced more Jefferson records in
the seventies. Jefferson also recorded for Inner City. When Schlitten and Fields parted company, Fields produced more Jefferson
records. But they didn't sell well.

By chance, Eddie sat in one night at a Greenwich Village club in
the early seventies. Horn player Richie Cole was working there.
They had a good time making music together. The next week Richie,
in his very early twenties, asked Eddie to go to work at a Washington, D.C., club.

"They were an odd couple," Joe Fields remembered. "But they
were soul brothers in bebop. Eddie was so much older than Richie
and didn't have the energy anymore, but Richie had the wheels and
took Eddie around. I don't know if Eddie's personality came across
in his music, but he was an old pro. He knew what was happening
to a T. He was responsible for Richie Cole's professional attitudes."
Cole agreed.

"Instrumentalists generally liked to work with Eddie," recalled trombonist Slide Hampton. "He actually had the same kind of drive and rhythmic intensity that an instrumentalist might have."

"Sometimes things happen around you, and you're not quite aware," said Joe Fields. "Eddie was aware, hip to whatever was going on. 'If you dig bebop, you'll dig it forever,' he said. 'But you can't do it forever.' He was as timely as tomorrow's news. He was therefore able to make proper suggestions to the Manhattan Transfer when it got too cute for words. Eddie put them back into the perspective of what had made them popular as beboppers in the first place. So they endeared themselves to jazz audiences again.

"About the music, Eddie never lost his sense of excitement. But there was trouble on the business end. If Eddie put a lyric to a song, the composer could sue. Eddie for the most part never got a dime for his work, because he didn't clear things the right way. But Eddie was sharp, with a great sense of humor for a guy caught in a certain kind of time lock. He and I always did business in a few minutes. He knew just what he wanted to do. Zap-zap. He got along with everybody. He was easygoing, smily, and, without overworking, he had a zest for life." Some other singers try to avoid talking to Fields on the phone, he said, preferring to deal with his secretary. "I think some of these guys can't hack it. I'm not the company. But they think I'm the boss. But Eddie wasn't like that. He was a normal human being."

Eddie and Yvonne, married April 17, 1969, by 1973 had separated, in a fashion, to stop fighting about money. Eddie moved into an apartment four blocks away. But when he went on the road, she kept his itinerary and picked him up at the airport.

Yvonne said, "He loved the music. In a word, he loved it. He didn't like to listen to his own albums. He would say, 'Oh, God, hear that note! I'm flat. Oh, the sound. Oh, the mix should be different.' He was a very nice man, easy to get along with. Though when he was formulating lyrics in his mind, he was moody. I could always tell when he was getting ready to compose—on napkins, paper bags, anything.

"He talked about being the first to put lyrics to the tunes. He wasn't a horn blower. About 'Moody's Mood for Love' and King Pleasure, Eddie just said, 'Well, he got it and I didn't.' I perceived there was nothing that could be done about it. He never once said that he himself was good. But he liked the lyrics he wrote. He was always comfortable about 'Moody's Mood' and liked to sing that one. I think he also liked his own version of 'Body and Soul' that starts off with Coleman Hawkins being king of the saxophone."

Eddie's fortunes in music picked up. He stopped driving a taxi. Yvonne said they talked about reconciling. He was honored at Carnegie Hall and went to California to work with Richie Cole. On the way back to New York, they stopped to play at Baker's Keyboard Lounge in Detroit. On May 9, 1979, as Jefferson was leaving the club, he was shot to death. One version of the murder is that Eddie was driving away from the club when someone drove up and fired four shotgun blasts, killed him and drove away. Another version says that Eddie, feeling nervous that night, wanted to get away from the club quickly. As he walked out the door, someone was waiting for him. Eddie's road manager identified a man, a tap dancer whom Eddie had known for years, in a police lineup (not Irv Taylor). The man went to trial and was acquitted. Rumor said that he had wanted to dance in Eddie's act. Yvonne remembered him; he had come to New York and, she felt, imposed upon Eddie, asking for a lot of help.

"The tragic part is that Eddie was cut down when things were starting to happen for him," Billy Mitchell remembered. "He was a very nice, personable, quiet, upright, upstanding man. He was an MP in the service. Out here on Long Island, he once made a citizen's arrest. He held a hit-and-run driver, who had hit an elderly man, until the police arrived. The guy who killed him was a nut. Eddie Jefferson didn't owe a nickel to anybody. I would bet my bottom dollar that Eddie Jefferson wouldn't gamble and have debts. We were going to start a band together the old-fashioned way, with uniforms. He was thrifty; he knew how hard it was to get a dollar. I saw him quite often. We used to have grand times together. We would sit around and talk about humorous little things. His death tore me up. I wasn't looking for that. It only hurts when I laugh."

Of the lyrics written for jazz solos and instrumentals, "Moody's Mood for Love" by Jefferson, " 'Round Midnight" by Bernard Hanighen, King Pleasure's lyric, "Jumping with Symphony Sid," disk jockey Sid Torin's theme song on WEVD Radio, and several by Hendricks are among the best known.

*   *   *

Which brings us to Lorraine Feather, born in 1954, daughter of *Los Angeles Times* jazz critic Leonard Feather. Lorraine sings with a new young trio, Swing, which has a record out on the Planet label distributed by Elektra and RCA. Lorraine wrote the lyrics for three jazz tunes on the record: Charlie Barnet's "The Right Idea"; "Big John's Special," a Horace Henderson composition originally played by Fletcher Henderson and then Benny Goodman; and Tommy Newsome's "La Boehm," also recorded by Goodman, which Lorraine has renamed "Trocadero Ballroom."

"Ever hear of Eddie Jefferson?" I asked her.

"Of course I know Eddie Jefferson [Billie Holiday was Lorraine's godmother]. I've been influenced by a lot of those musicians. I used to sing along with Lambert, Hendricks and Ross records, when I was tiny. I knew all the words. I've always known about Jefferson writing lyrics for jazz tunes. It was probably natural for me to try to put lyrics to tunes that are complicated in their phrasing and harmony. It was in my roots."

These fabulous inventions only become evident once they're done. Now it has come down to Lorraine Feather writing lyrics to instrumental jazz solos because it was the natural thing to do, once she got it from Leo Watson in a circuitous and fantastic example of how the races and generations keep cross-pollinating jazz from a black-created folk music into a sophisticated American art.

CHAPTER 14

A Coat of Many Colors for Jon Hendricks: Lyricist Laureate of Jazz

Other musicians call Jon Hendricks one of the most important people in jazz for his lyric writing and his conception of jazz singing. In the space of an hour's set in a club, he can go from a low-down, funky blues to an Italian ballad he has translated to a bebop song so fast you cannot understand the words. But you hear the horn solos, with their zest and, in the very vocalizing, their wit.

Hendricks wrote the jubilant lyric for Count Basie's "Jumpin' at the Woodside": "I gotta go, I wanna blow . . . a little room, a lotta fun . . . Betcha never heard of such a groovy hotel. Cop a room and then you can really tend to biz." But another tune, "Every Tub," also written for a Basie band tune, shows the blend of Jon Hendricks' deep wit and stout soul—motherwit with panache:

> Down among the people
> where the word is never writ
> They got a soulful, kind comment
> known as motherwit.
> For any event they got 'em
> Even 'bout a tub 'n how it's standin'
> on its bottom.
> So y' see,
> Oh, yeah, y' dig it

'n y' really gonna see
So if y' don't have eyes
t' really end up truly beat
Stand up on your two feet . . .
all the tubs I've ever known
Every tub is on its own
Need no help to stand alone . . .

There are days when Jon Hendricks, one of the two jazz singers on the board of the Kennedy Center honors committee in Washington, can barely talk at noontime. He may grunt and complain of a chronic sore throat. He may rest in a multicolored caftan made by Alexander Shields for Hendricks, whose mother told him he was blessed. But there are nighttimes when you would never guess about Jon Hendricks' midday throat malaise.

Jaw jutting, dressed formally, he and his present group Jon Hendricks and Company, patterned after Lambert, Hendricks and Ross, played to a standing-room-only crowd at the opening of Lush Life, a New York jazz club. The replica group, which made its first record in 1981, had been moving restlessly around the country and Europe, leading a typical jazz life. Hendricks runs a tight ship, putting his company, which does hair-trigger, synchronized ensemble work as well as solos, through its paces. His throat strain could be so bad that his voice cracked some nights. But in one Washington Square Park concert in 1982, Hendricks, in top form, close to a microphone, outblew a stageful of musicians, scatting like a horn, a loud, vital vocal acrobat. A lot depends upon whether the scene really inspires a musician. Once you have heard Hendricks scat as if he were a hot, screaming horn, you will wonder how he or anyone could make a noise again without resting for six months. And his swing is lordly. So Hendricks in 1982 could still do the three bs: blues, bebop and ballads.

At Lush Life he led off his group with a mannered "yeah-yeah" version of Count Basie's "Every Day," the old Basie arrangement exactly. Jon had assigned each member of his troupe an instrumental role to play—a sax, a trumpet, a trombone. Then on to "Caravan" by Duke Ellington as it was originally recorded. Jon started; then Judith, his soprano wife, did a "wawa" horn sound: someone did Rex Stewart's horn, then Barney Bigard's. (Sometimes Aria Hendricks, Jon and Judith's teenage daughter, with a high, strong voice, sits in, too.) Then Jon scatted the horn sound in Basie's "Whirlybird" arranged by Neal Hefti.

The human band, in 1982 composed of Judith, Michele Hendricks and Bob Gurland—whose trumpet imitation done totally by mouth would "traumatize the Mills Brothers," as Garry Giddins wrote in *The Village Voice*—then left the bandstand. Gurland has been praised by many notable critics for sounding as good as the Basie horn players. He also has a magnificent baritone when he sings straight. But he is unique. Hendricks knows it. And Gurland knows it. So most of his straight singing takes a back seat to his outrageous and beautiful horn scatting. He calls it a new form of singing; it is.

Hendricks sang his own songs, "Tell Me the Truth" and "No More," intellectual jazz anthems really, with a church-inspired quality, a shout at times. The lyrics are important things that Hendricks has to say about jive and truth, peace and war, life and death and living-death, drawing in Jesus and Christian principles, ending a tune on a bent and blue note—a gorgeous touch. He wrote one of these songs when he came back from several years' residence in England during the Nixon administration, which "wouldn't swing if you hung 'em," he used to say. And later he said it about the Reagan administration.

While jazz was commercially comatose in the 1960s, the instrumentalists and singers added new standards, premiered on Broadway or by the pop groups, to their repertoires. So Hendricks did Richard Rodgers' "The Sweetest Sounds I Ever Heard" in a soft voice. If anyone remained unaware that Jon Hendricks could transcend voice strain, he reminded the audience of his durable persona with his introductory monologue for the solo of his daughter Michele:

"I have children like people have mice. I have five children." (There was pathos in that remark, but relatively few people knew. Actually, he has seven children; but Dwight, the eldest, in his late thirties, and Jacques, in his early twenties—both by women Jon did not marry legally—are not musicians. Jon's five legitimate children have worked in music. One daughter, Colleen, a singer, died in 1981 from an accidental drug overdose at age twenty-five. But Jon, who believes in reincarnation, kept her in his act with the rest of his musical children.) "And all of them sing jazz. People ask me why? Is it genetic? Or en-viron-men*tal* . . . or is it hereditary?

No," he said, "I simply got them all together one day and told them that I ain't leaving them nothin'. And when I die, and my will is read, the lawyer will *intone* [and he said the word 'intone' with the resonance of a bell lick]: I, Jon Hendricks, being of sound mind and body, *spent it.* So all five of them are singing their buns off." A pause for audience laughter. "Ladies and gentlemen, the flower in my garden, Michele Hendricks."

And Michele, in her late twenties, who looked as if she would be old enough to vote in the next election, got up and gave "Daddy" a hug. Out of her dungarees and in one of her sleek evening gowns, Michele is the softly rounded siren, while Mother Judith, as lean as Gloria Vanderbilt, covers up in chiffons and silks.

In late 1981 Michele's solo number was a scat session with a bass-ist named Skip Cromby-Bey. "Get that?" Michele laughed at the elitist name. "He played substitutions [substitute chords for the chords that were written for tunes] and I tried to follow and sing the right scale over it. It was good ear training. But he went home to Milwaukee, because he didn't like life on the road." His duets with Michele were fun while they lasted; Michele crooned to him in contralto scat words, sounding like a bass herself.

In 1982, with Cromby-Bey gone Michele sang a torch song with the pianist, David Hazeltine, "Angel Eyes," her choice for her solo recording debut with Hendricks and Company. "Dad lets me choose my own material. I'm sure he wouldn't like it if I got up and sang 'Bad Moon Rising' [a rock song], but he likes what I choose. Mom [by whom Michele instinctively means Judith Hendricks, who is technically Michele's stepmother] used to sing 'Angel Eyes' to me when I was little. I think that's when I first fell in love with it."

In it she crooned one of the words so full of passion and angst that the word reverberated in memory long after she finished the tune. Sometimes she sounded exactly like her father, with the same tone and a comparable range. There were moments when you couldn't tell if Michele's sound belonged to a man or a woman, to Jon or herself. Each singer has a heady, haunting sound. And espe-cially Jon has a husky catch, the black frog-in-the-throat, which enriches a voice with warmth. In speech Jon has a slight lisp. It nearly evaporates when he performs.

"It's not the biggest voice in the world," he said. "I don't even have a real instrument. I say to Mel Torme, Tony Bennett and Joe Williams, 'I wish I had your big instrument.' They say, 'What are you talking about?' But what I have is feeling. My transcendence is my feeling.

"I'm always working and straining my voice. My instrument is weak. I'm a homemade singer. I made myself up and never understood how it was done. But I could sing in tune. I always had a rhythmic feeling. I had no lessons, no voice, no culture. Singing is a spiritual experience. The physical is a small part of it.

"In the beginning was the word, a sound, a creative force in the universe," said Hendricks, happy to rap about music, always with echoes of his religious background. His father was a minister of an African Methodist Episcopal Church, which adheres to a strict interpretation of the Bible. "And I think what I am is blessed with a vocal instrument that can move people. I don't know one note from the other. But I can hear anything. I know what musicians are talking about. That one chord fits and another doesn't. I know, because it doesn't fall right on my ear. I learned so quickly and proficiently by ear that I never bothered to learn to read or write music—that's mechanical. If you can hear it, you can sing it, and not to be able to play without music is not to be able to play.

"And enunciation of the words is so important. I got the first A in speech to be given in my class in five years. And I was the first in seven years to get an A in creative writing. You don't hear my lisp when I sing, because I had the spiritual desire to overcome it. Experience is the teacher, and you use your whole body to do the work. You practically have to stoop down to get the notes you want, the sound you want. I asked Louis Armstrong, 'How do you get those high notes?' And he said, 'I just look up, and there it is.' Did you ever see him looking up? It's a very spiritual thing to have faith in the gods. They're using your body."

It's a rare musician who doesn't credit the gods for dispensing the talent; all musicians disclaim responsibility for having received a gift; they feel mystically and religiously responsible only for managing the talent. Patti Bown, a singer-composer-pianist who accompanied Dinah Washington, has given an excellent explanation of the mystical attitude of musicians toward their music:

"I almost feel like a spirit takes over me as some kind of instrument, and after this body is gone, some other instrument will take over from me."

The religiosity of all musicians may buoy them up in the face of an omnipresent, awesome spectacle: the performance. Entertainers alone among all artists must overcome stage fright. Perhaps the most rational way for them to do it is by trusting their essence to God. But most of all, music, which is nonverbal, elicits emotions and excites the spirit—and becomes synonymous with the soul. Musicians, awestruck by music, become devout believers. Jon Hendricks believes wholeheartedly that he's a child of God, though, at the same time, he has always seen himself existing realistically in the thick of practical, secular matters. His other perception has involved him in the verbal art of lyric writing, a child of the iconoclastic intellect.

In his view he was raised at a crossroads of entertainment in this country: Toledo, Ohio, a bustling jazz town; he was born in nearby Newark.

"The trains traveling across the country stopped there. All the great entertainers and bootleggers were in Toledo all the time. It was so centrally located, on the way to Chicago, Louisville, St. Louis, Cleveland. At the Waiters and Bellmen [a Toledo club] I heard Ellington, Basie, Armstrong, Dorsey, Jimmy Lunceford. I heard Armstrong when I was fourteen years old. He told me I should stay at home as long as I could because the road life was tenuous for a kid. Ted Lewis offered me a job to be his shadow, but my mother said it lacked dignity. Fats Waller, a friend of the family, a sweet man from a religious family, wanted to take me on the road. But my father said he drank too much. Waller died early as a result of drinking."

Hendricks began working at age nine, supporting his large family, he said, earning about sixty dollars a night in Chateau La France, a local roadhouse run by gangsters. Some were running liquor; when they drove up to the club, they rubbed Jon's head. "You know, rub a nigger's head for luck. And they gave me ten- and twenty-dollar bills," he recalled. He needed the money. So instead of exploding with anger or humiliation, he transcended the insult, as though it were an ephemeral barrier in more limited minds—a wall for idiots, not the blessedly talented, to bang their heads against.

At age fourteen, he began singing in a high tenor voice at the Waiters and Bellmen, billed for two years as the sepia Bobby Breen. A neighbor, Art Tatum, who developed into the greatest jazz pianist who ever lived, also worked at the club. Jon sang with him for two years.

"When Tatum played piano, it was a different instrument. I learned to sing and scat the way he played. The way he ran chords was so beautiful and melodic." Pianists have marveled, listening to Tatum, saying to themselves, "What *is* he doing now?," trying to follow his hands. But for Jon it was a simpler matter: "You could always hear the melody no matter how much ad-libbing he did. The early years with Art Tatum remain the high point of my artistic life."

Jon's parents, strict church people, heard him sing only in church or at functions around town. Jon Hendricks' father, one can see in a framed portrait, was a straitlaced-looking man in a proper, high-collared white shirt, conservative jacket and metal-rimmed glasses. "I always keep that photograph out wherever I go," said Hendricks. Although the minister didn't go to clubs, musicians passing through town often visited the Hendricks' house, certain of being served good meals.

"There were twelve boys and three girls in the family. Two of my sisters were of age and very nice-looking. All the bands tried to get invited to dinner at our house. Mother was a fine cook," Jon related as his wife, Judith, set out platters of health salads, imaginatively spiced egg salad, cheeses, pâtés, dips and vegetables with all kinds of crackers on the living-room coffee table. "Andy Kirk and Harry 'Sweets' Edison, all their bands came to the house to eat dinner. They came for my sisters and the food. It was hard to find a place on the road where you could eat. Segregation, you know."

Pretty much fresh from Toledo, Jon was drafted in 1942, at age twenty-one, to spend 1942 to 1946 in Europe. He did some singing in Special Services, but by and large "was just a miserable soldier," a company clerk.

"We actually went to Europe to fight against anti-Semitism. But we found ourselves with two different armies, one for blacks, one for whites. Our black army had officers who were ignorant southerners. We had race riots in England." Hendricks is planning to write his own book about his Army experience, which led him, in a very unorthodox fashion, to live in France for a year. He learned French from a girlfriend, sang with a band and devised a crazy way to make a good living.

After his discharge, he majored in English at the University of Toledo and worked in jazz clubs at night; played drums, wrote lyrics and sang. He taught himself to play trombone, but put that down permanently before it ruined his embouchure (his mouth and control of what it must do for him to sing). Eventually he started law school. With eighteen months to go for a degree financed by the G.I. Bill, he met "Bird" (Charlie Parker) at a concert in Toledo.

"Due to Tatum, I was into bebop as a cultural flow; I scatted with Bird. Bird didn't let me leave the bandstand. He stopped me and asked who I was. I said, 'I'm a law student.' He said, 'You ain't no lawyer. You're a jazz singer.' I said, 'Yeah, what shall I do about that?' He said, 'Come to New York.' I said, 'I don't know anybody.' He said, 'You know me.' I said, 'Where will I find you?' He said, 'Just ask anybody. . . .' When my G.I. Bill ran out, I took the bus with my family to New York [Hendricks and his first wife had four children]. When we got into the Greyhound bus station, I called Joe Carroll [another jazz singer]. I knew him 'cause he worked with Dizzy in Toledo. I said, 'Where's Bird?' Carroll said, 'Seventh Avenue and 125th Street at the Apollo Bar.'

"So I went. Two years and four months previously, I had sung 'The Song Is You' with Bird. Now I looked as raggedy as a bowl of yakamein after traveling. As I walked past the bandstand, Bird called out after me, having seen me during a one-nighter two years and four months earlier, 'Hey, Jon, how you doing? Want to sing something?' He'd been telling everyone: this cat is mean.* My entrée everywhere was very easy because of him. I could sit in and become known. He changed my whole life. I became a bebop singer. My father was dead. My mother said I was blessed, no matter what I did. So I've led a magic life. I never went back to law school."

He had been writing songs for a long time. "I was always a philosophical soul, even at six and seven. I always thought I was a child of God and only here in this body to look around, an onlooker to take the lessons, so I'm never too influenced by all this madness. I always felt set apart from other kids. I wanted weightier talk. They wanted stars in movies; I was always into the unity and direction. To me, when the star spoke, it was someone who wrote the words. Writing was important to me.

"I started songwriting in Toledo. I had to write a different song every week [for his night job]. I wrote from an intuitive knowledge of life. I could be inspired by an Al Capp character, Lena the Hyena, the sight of whom was fatal. Capp had a contest to see who

---

* This guy can really sing jazz.

could draw this ugly character. And I wrote about 'Lena the Hyena,' with a face like a beat-up concertina, everyone has died who's seena . . ."

"I couldn't be the lyricist I am without an education. I'm able to call on various literary tricks, plots and character developments. I translate the instrumentals into an opera-like libretto. Like when I wrote 'Jumpin' at the Woodside.' There were no restrictions on the Woodside Hotel Guests [mostly jazz musicians in New York City] and from that I created the whole song and the horn solos. It's like in a novel when the character speaks. It's a musical literary form. A character speaks a song. Call it 'vocalese.' When I was with Lambert, Hendricks and Ross, Dave Lambert said, 'We're the Metropolitan Bopera Company.' That's what we were. Even to the music, we bring such life to the music."

Jon went to see Dave Lambert, who seemed skeptical about Jon in his three-piece suit. But when Lambert heard Jon's lyrics to "Four Brothers," he became excited and started working with Jon instantly, barely introduced. With some other singers they recorded "Four Brothers" for a small company, repeated the tune for Decca and remained obscure in the United States. But they decided to keep working together, using Count Basie's work primarily. Jon Hendricks told John Wilson, *New York Times* critic, about writing lyrics for "Blues Backstage," "Down for the Count," "Avenue C" and "Little Pony." Lambert arranged the work for the backup singers. Lambert and Hendricks went looking for a record company to produce their work.

Jon told the *Times:* " 'Everybody said, "We've got to hear how it sounds." We found it would cost $1,250 to get some singers to do the songs. At ABC-Paramount Records, we found a producer who was just getting started in the record business. Creed Taylor. He thought our songs were great and he agreed to record us. So Dave hired a bunch of singers, and we made the records. But the singers couldn't swing. They were terrible except for one of them—Annie Ross. . . .

" 'The records were so bad that everybody's job was on the line,' " Hendricks recalled. " 'We were in the hole for $1,250 and Creed was going to be fired. Then Dave asked Creed if we could get the studio at night, when nobody was around, and the three of us—Dave, Annie and me—would do the songs ourselves, overdubbing our voices to create the ensembles. It had never been done before and

Creed thought Dave was nuts. We had to hide what we were doing because Creed's bosses would have thought the same thing. So we went into a studio at midnight. We got out at six in the morning and we had recorded the album that became *Sing a Song of Basie*.'

"A few months after the album's release in 1958, the trio became the most sought-after singing group in jazz. For personal appearances, and on later recordings, they abandoned multitracking but they achieved similar effects with instrumental accompaniment. . . ."

The trio continued for six years, Jon's first marriage fell apart in 1959 as all his energy went into Lambert, Hendricks and Ross (L. H. & R.).

"I listened for what the band did. The closer we came to that, the better we were. Our songs were first recorded by Horace Silver, Basie and Ellington. Our group was supposed to play as much like the band as possible. So we could re-create. That's the only criterion I have for a group."

A critic in the 1980s, hearing the family group, said the old magic still worked.

"I know people who sing better than we do," said Hendricks. "The Manhattan Transfer and the new Hi-Los. But we'll swing all of them into bad health. I don't care if my voice is not as clear as a bell. I'm more interested in emotion than notes. If the feeling is groovy, I'll take that over the right notes. Jazz is feeling and emotion. The right notes are for the classical field. Guys may be more technically proficient than Louis Armstrong. But he could make you cry. That was his greatness."

During one 1959 L. H. & R. gig at Birdland, a young woman named Judith Dickstein was working as a photographer to earn money for tuition in design at Pratt Institute, for ballet lessons and courses in the occult. Not for singing, because she had never wanted to pursue that. But according to Jon, Judith thought to herself, "I want to sing Annie Ross's role. But I don't want to have anything to do with Jon Hendricks."

Judith recalled that through Jon's three-week gig, she wouldn't talk to him. "We gazed at each other, but I didn't want to get into trouble. But who can resist trouble? He was weird enough to suit me. At the end, I decided I could at least say 'Good-bye.' After I said 'Good-bye,' we never were apart again."

In its heyday and even after its demise, L. H. & R. had followers and students. Al Jarreau, a younger jazz singer, has named it as one of his chief influences. "Mark Murphy hung around us," Jon remembered about another, younger bebop-influenced singer whose special hero was Eddie Jefferson and who has since spent many years in Europe, made excellent records and starred in American clubs. "He was a devout student. He went through personal and professional changes and became a jazz singer and true to the culture. For that I salute him. He deserves the support of everyone who loves the idiom. My outlook toward him is paternal. And the same for Al Jarreau."

Lambert, Hendricks and Ross broke up in 1962 when Annie Ross, a very pretty, spirited redhead, with some connection with drug use, did not reenter the U.S. with the trio. Canadian-born Anne Marie Moss, who replaced Annie Ross for a while, recalled her first meeting with the trio:

"When I was with Maynard Ferguson, we did a 'Jazz for Moderns' tour. Ed Sarkesian and John Serabian organized it. On it was Chico Hamilton [a drummer] and his group; Chris Connor and a trio; Ferguson and me; and Lambert, Hendricks and Ross. We started off in a bus and ended in a plane or vice versa. Talk about exhaustion. I was the healthiest one on the bus and still got exhausted. One night we got stuck in a snowstorm and laid over in New York. It was freezing, but to save money on a hotel room, some of us decided to stay on the plane that was supposed to take us to our next gig. We wrapped ourselves in blankets. It was a dumb decision. There was no heat. You couldn't flush the toilet. One musician got off the plane to go to the bathroom. He was bonkers from tequila; he was drinking from our stop in Juárez. And he stepped out and fell from the whole height of the plane without even hurting himself. We helped him back up into this converted bomber.

"The pilot on that flight thought he was an opera star. The next day, as we were flying, I woke up from a nap and saw the pilot talking to someone on the plane. I went up to Sarkesian or Serabian and said, 'There's the pilot.' They said, 'Don't worry about it.' I was the junior cornball. I thought, 'Oh, God.' They said, 'Dave Lambert's flying the plane.' I was supposed to be relaxed by that because Dave had a commercial pilot's license. The pilot stood there, yelling 'Rosemarie.' I faked opera and kept making him say 'hi,' breathing out. I pretended it was an exercise for him, but I wanted to smell his breath and see where I was at."

One day on a bus on that tour, Annie Ross started singing. Anne Marie, sitting behind her, started scatting. Annie said, "I didn't know you did that." "Yes, I like to run changes," Anne Marie answered. So they sang together on the buses to pass the time. Annie Ross became sick with pneumonia in Washington, a day before a performance at the Howard Theater. The trio called Anne Marie to learn Annie's book and perform for her.

Later Anne Marie took over again temporarily. One night, she recalls, "Dave and Jon had gone out to dinner and eaten garlic. I was within shooting range onstage. Well, who has time to pull out the dental floss when you're running to perform? Annie used to warn me about onions for dinner. I saw a girl singer one time with a big piece of green in her tooth while she was singing 'Like Someone in Love.' Ha-ha. Annie was a super lady. She showed me how to store dresses on the road. She showed me the things you can do with your eyes because of the strong lights. She was a great cook. We were sort of pals to one another."

After Annie Ross left the trio permanently, Yolande Bavan, a bebopper born in Ceylon (now Sri Lanka), took over. Tiny, sometimes performing in saris, with only a trace of a Ceylonese accent, Miss Bavan brought off the miracle of singing jazz—of truly scatting like a funky, wailing horn—despite her most unlikely background. "I'm an outcast in Sri Lanka," she joked. The trio continued until 1964. Not long afterward, Dave Lambert, well-liked, a good Samaritan by reputation, got out of his car one night to help a stranger change a flat tire. A passing car hit and killed Lambert.

Jon Hendricks recalled the sixties: "It was a hard time for jazz musicians. If the country were more culturally oriented, recording companies would act responsibly and see that jazz artists recorded. But the companies have abrogated their responsibilities. The corporate duty is first to serve society and second make money. But the reality is that corporations get rid of the first part of that and just make money. And jazz musicians have been consigned to death. Ben Webster, Don Byas, so many. The average young American doesn't know anything about jazz. In Europe they think we're abject idiots and uncultured beasts for ignoring our own culture. Jazz is part of their curricula over there."

Jon went to work for thirty days in "Mother England," starting at Ronnie Scott's illustrious jazz club in London, as he has often recalled for nightclub audiences. "The English voted me the greatest singer in the world. So I stayed five years."

Michele remembered the L. H. & R. years leading to the English adventure. Very light-skinned, with closely cropped black hair on a perfectly shaped round head, Michele was four years old when Jon and his first wife were divorced. Jon, Jr., was the oldest; then came Michele, then Eric. Colleen was the infant. The kids lived with aunts and uncles, some of them avid churchgoers. When Michele was twelve, she and her brothers and sisters from Jon's first marriage went to live with Jon and Judith.

"So Judith is 'Mom,' " said Michele.

She first sang the Basie tune "Shiny Stockings," with Lambert, Hendricks and Ross when she was eight. "I was terrible. I had complete stage fright. I cried right onstage. It happened because I kept arguing with Dad that I was ready to sing. 'I'M READY I'M READY I'M READY!" He said, "YOU'RE NOT READY YOU'RE NOT READY, STUDY STUDY.' 'NO, I'M READY I'M READY.' 'YOU'RE NOT READY.' 'YES, I'M READY I'M READY!' So he said, 'Okay, you're singing tonight.' And I got up there and cried. I wasn't ready."

She arrived in London at age fourteen. "We were typical school kids, smoking pot. They didn't want to leave us alone and took us with them. That was a good thing, because they didn't come back for five years! He never discouraged any of us from becoming musicians. He would always let us get up and sing if we wanted to." She started singing with Jon in London professionally at age fifteen; she also remembered that Judith sang with him occasionally. But he worked primarily as a single performer.

Adjusting to England was not very hard for the family en masse. "At first in London, everyone looked so different to me. Mom and Colleen and I were on a subway tube, going to an interview for a school we were considering. We were just giggling at how different everyone looked to us. When we first started to watch TV, it was like a foreign language. We were just giggling and giggling."

Eventually the family went back to the United States in the 1970s and set up home base in San Francisco. Jon taught a history of jazz course at the University of California, which a family friend, Babs Gorman, remembered as chronologically chaotic but musically vital.

"He took us up through history instrument by instrument," she said. "He brought musicians in. We had about seventy-five people in the class. The next semester he taught a class in the pop-music business. He advertised it; and seven hundred fifty people showed up to take it. So we pared it down to four hundred people and got an auditorium. Musicians and managers brought their groups for a course on the business side of music. One singer gave a bitter account of rhythm-and-blues being a ghetto classification. But Jon was great. He held it all together. We became loyal fans."

Settled in Mill Valley, California, Jon wrote jazz criticism for the *San Francisco Chronicle* and worked mainly as a single performer. Then a show he had written, *Evolution of the Blues*, was produced in 1974. It needed an L. H. & R.-style group. Judith, with a very high, strong soprano voice, began listening to old L. H. & R. records to learn Annie Ross's book. The show, tracing the history of black music, ran for five years, then toured a few cities but got bogged down in litigation.

However, the reincarnation of L. H. & R. kept going with family members and some friendly baritones, Bobby McFerrin first, Bruce Scott second, then Bob Gurland. Gurland had been singing professionally since age seventeen and also became an entertainment lawyer. But a different kind of bar exam held greater allure. So he formed his own group "a minute" before meeting Jon Hendricks at the Bitter End in Greenwich Village.

Gurland was blowing his invisible trumpet hard with his lips and whole mouth and God knows what. He heard a string bass playing behind him. It was Jon Hendricks. They went off to a corner and scatted together for a while, unable to resist each other. Jon can scat a bass with a lip-popping sound that emulates the soft plucks and pungs of the bass strings exactly. Michele has a more human sound when she scats with a bass. But Jon *is* a bass or whatever other instrument he is scatting. Eventually Gurland joined the family group.

With her mellow sound, Michele came to like scatting with a bass; other singers, including Anne Marie Moss and Betty Carter, agree. "The bass plays one note—pung—and I have all this space to play around with," Michele said. "I like the guitar, too. They're quiet instruments. I can sing real soft and still be heard."

Michele has said that the typical Hendricks sound doesn't have a very romantic source. "I'm not a belter, I'm a crooner, because I got nodes trying to belt. I strain; I don't even talk right. There's too much pressure on my throat, especially if I get excited. My voice gets high; I get hoarse. If I sing without enough sleep or drink or smoke a lot, I get hoarse. There's a lot of tension in my throat. My nodes will be my saving grace. As long as I have them, I can't do anything in the extreme, if I want to sing.

"At one time I was so hoarse, I couldn't talk. I went to the doctor, and he told me that the shape of my vocal cords had grown into an hourglass. Instead of being parallel, straight up and down together, they had gotten swollen in one place and only met in that one place. That's why I was hoarse. Only one part of the vocal cords was being used. They were irritated. That's what nodes are. They're common to anyone who uses the voice a lot. My father has the same thing.

"But Sarah Vaughan SMOKES AND HAS THIS GOLDEN VOICE. She can sing through anything. When I strained my voice so much that I couldn't talk, I learned some things all over again. Now I breathe all right. Correctly. But if I wanted to get rid of the nodes, I would have to rest my vocal cords for a few months. Not even speak. Oh, throats are delicate little things! The doctor explained: 'If you were a piano player and constantly stubbed cigarettes out on your fingers and poured booze over them, what would all this do to your hands?' Of course! It makes sense. My throat is an instrument."

Her voice, somewhere between a contralto and soprano—though she started out as a soprano—improved after she gave up smoking. "It really makes a difference," she said, though she can sound slightly nasal and laryngitic in conversation, the way so many singers, including Betty Carter, do when not performing. "And no drinking either. I ate fresh vegetables and fruits all week," Michele said at the end of a week's gig at Lush Life. "I feel so much better"; a trace of soprano in contralto rising. When she was smoking she usually became hoarse by the third day of a week's gig. But no more.

Michele, the torch singer, even with nodes, was a tough act to follow when she soloed on "Angel Eyes." But Jon found the right contrasting formula to do it. Wisely, he selected a low-down blues about wanting to ramble and go home and stay away from women, but he knew himself better than to think he could give up loving in the morning, which was the hippest time of all. This song was fun. It had nothing to do with Hendricks' academic degrees or literacy. This one came from his roots, someplace before the hoopla, foreign awards, college teaching, the Kennedy Center board, before Lambert, Hendricks and Ross and Columbia and Bird; this tune came from a churchy place that Michele and the other children have visited only tangentially after their father's divorce. But Michele has clearly listened to him closely over the years.

"You have to have good ears, big ears, to sing jazz," Michele said. "Daddy nicknamed me 'Big Ears.' What I learned most from him is to listen to instrumentals and try to become an instrument."

That is approximately how Jon Hendricks, with special communion with instrumentalists, had explained his conception of jazz: "After I finished writing 'Goin' to Chicago' [a Basie tune] I told Buck Clayton, 'I just put words to what you played.' And he said, 'Did I play that? The lyric makes the tune more than it was—and changes it." Jon's smooth introduction and staccato interjection of the horn solos set to words gave the old blues song more punch and intensity where the tune used to pause for breath. The song became total sound, with star and chorus: Bopera.

And for the last eight bars of tenor saxophonist Lester Young's tune "Let Me See," Hendricks wrote about how you have to listen to the music if you wanted to "see," to understand what was going on. Hendricks went with pianist Randy Weston to visit Lester Young, who was ill in the Alvin Hotel in New York. (Hendricks has said that Young became an alcoholic because of his tremendous sensitivity in a world that pushed him around.) Young was sitting up, wearing pajamas. Hendricks was going to sing the lyrics when "Prez" said, "I don't use my eyes, I use my ears, and you gotta nice sound," Hendricks remembered. "That was exactly what I had written. When he said it, I didn't sing it for him. I didn't have to. He was always very psychic. When Randy and I left, we were both in tears, because Prez was so psychic. Sometimes musicians are so intuitive. He was a Virgo. I'm a Virgo. All the saxophone players are Virgos. Prez, Bird. That happened just before Prez died [in the late 1950s].

"It's true of a lot of artists; they operate by a sort of instinct. It's nature's instinct, not just an accidental thing. It's not involuntary but a gift given to those blessed. Some people have the faith to go with it. If you don't believe, you will certainly be subject to it, because those are the ones it attacks. Ha-ha-ha-ha. I believe in everything in self-defense."

Hendricks thought it would be "no problem" for him to write lyrics for the Free Jazz dissonances of Ornette Coleman or Sun Ra, even though the work would end up as it started: with no mass appeal. "You might just have screaming," said Hendricks. "If the instrument sings, you have a word; if the instrument screams, you have a sound. I would put lyrics to their music if I were asked to, because I respect them. As a writer you ought to be able to do everything. But my own interest wouldn't be there."

Jon's taste ordinarily takes precedence. "I could never sing a song that didn't make sense to me image-wise. There's a song with the words 'a steeple surrounded by people.' I asked: Are they on stilts? in balloons? How can people surround a steeple? I bought three different lead sheets of 'By the Time I Get to Phoenix.' I can never sing it. Anyone who can sneak out on a woman is the kind of guy I want to punch in the mouth. He's a shmuck. I've very subjective. You've got to be a hell of a guy to write my kind of lyrics. Johnny Mercer could do it. Lorenz Hart. J. Fred Coots. I can't sing songs that philosophically express sentiments I don't agree with. 'Help Me Make It Through the Night.' No. I need someone to help me through life. So to me that song is just a shallow, maudlin thought. Of course, Frank Sinatra liked it. But that was after he lost his taste. I couldn't put out an album called *She Shot Me Down*. Ha-ha."

For Jon bebop is intellectually inseparable from his religion. "Music is divided into melody, harmony and rhythm—concord produces peace, discord means disease, and rhythm is the emotions. Avant-garde and rock negate that." He nourishes his strong opinions about the unity of religion and music by his interests in the occult, philosophy, world events and music, which have made him the most *au courant*, didactic and informative of singers and lyricists.

Offstage and onstage at Lush Life's opening, as usual, there was a hint of intense concentration in the wiry, erect body, in the head often tilted slightly back confidently; of long and complex distances traveled in the alert glitter of the eyes. His tuxedo was unrippled, his hair perfectly trimmed. Hendricks had no clutter in his image, no more than in the essential words and notes he sings.

"You take up onto the stage your entire persona. So it behooves an artist to keep life as simple as possible. Don't take drugs with you on the stage. It's better to be simple. Once life was more complex and tortuous for me. Now life is simple—and the work easier," he said.

▲ Billie Holiday, the quintessential jazz singer, had an odd, heartrending and transcendent sound. Her style has touched every singer. (*The Institute of Jazz Studies, Rutgers University*)

▶ Ella Fitzgerald, with more commercial appeal than Billie Holiday, won her eleventh Grammy, more than any other female jazz singer, with her victory in 1981. (*The Institute of Jazz Studies, Rutgers University*)

▲ George Wein, producer of the Kool Jazz Festivals, hugs Mabel Mercer, a legendary singer whose interpretations of lyrics entranced other singers. (*The Institute of Jazz Studies, Rutgers University*)

Jazz singer Jackie Paris thought Fifty-second Street, Swing Street, in New York City in the 1940s was paradise on earth for a jazz musician. (*The Institute of Jazz Studies, Rutgers University*)

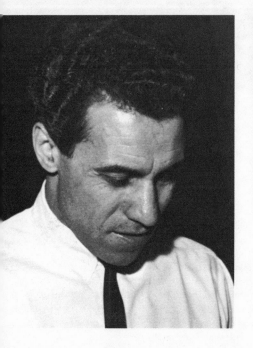

▲ Nat "King" Cole's unmistakable Sound still shows up regularly on the radio, long after his untimely death from cancer in 1965. His colossal popularity made him a pioneer for the acceptance of black entertainers. (*Fred Cole*)

◀ Jo Stafford's voice may have been as popular as Betty Grable's legs with the soldiers during World War II. (*Jo Stafford*)

▲ Sarah Vaughan, jazz diva. Hers is the most glorious female voice in jazz. (*CBS Records*)

▲ Her voice deepened with age, with an arresting baritone range, Sarah Vaughan won her first Grammy for a 1982 recording—after decades of being acclaimed as one of the greatest jazz singers. (*The Institute of Jazz Studies, Rutgers University*)

◀ A veritable Clark Gable of Jazz, Billy Eckstine went out on his own to become a great ballad singer after his jazz band folded in the late 1940s.

▼ Carmen McRae's feeling and control have made her one of the greatest jazz singers. She is called "The Teacher" by younger jazz singer Carol Sloane. (*The Institute of Jazz Studies, Rutgers University*)

▶ Mel Torme looks cuddly, but his style is swift and sophisticated. Other singers acknowledge him as one of the best singers of the genre.

▲ Mel Torme, *left,* and singer Harry Belafonte were very young but famous when this picture was taken. Call that era their Salade Niçoise days. (*The Institute of Jazz Studies, Rutgers University*)

◄ "Her Nibs, Miss Georgia Gibbs." Barney Josephson hired her to play in Café Society in the early 1940s. Audiences were apathetic. Josephson recalls: "She wore low-cut gowns with very narrow straps, high platform shoes, and had her hair and makeup done by experts. And she had a growth on her cheek: a wen. When the spotlight hit her face, the wen threw a shadow and looked larger than it was. She was bombing three times a night. But she was pushy and wanted to get somewhere. So she asked me: 'What's wrong?' " Josephson told her: "The whole goddam setup is wrong. Get rid of the heavy makeup. Be a nice, cute little Yiddishe girl. Go home and wash your face. Come in to work as if you're going out on a dinner date. Comb your hair down. None of this swirl going up to a bun. Wear regular, solid shoes. And wear a simple dress. Or even better, wear a suit." She looked at him as if he were crazy. But she went to work in a little blue suit and blue pumps. Then Josephson got a call. "She was screaming hysterically on the phone: 'Barney! It's great! Sensational! The suit! The suit!' She had done three songs, five encores and then begged off. And that's the way it was from then on. *Variety* picked it up. She bought more suits. Powder blue. Shocking pink. The headline called her The Suit Girl. So adorable. No one noticed the wen anymore. She sang the hell out of a song." (*The Institute of Jazz Studies, Rutgers University*)

◄ Etta Jones, an unpretentious woman, a formidable jazz singer, gets the vote as many jazz fans' favorite. (*Muse Records*)

► Helen Merrill says she gravitated naturally to bebop after listening to her mother sing Yugoslavian folk songs. Merrill spent so much time abroad that she became better known in Europe and Japan than in the United States. (*The Institute of Jazz Studies, Rutgers University*)

▲ Tony Bennett had an unerr-
ing sense about the songs that
he should sing. (*Tony Bennett*)

► Tony Bennett signs his self-
portrait "Benedetto," his real
name, with a suffix reminiscent of Tintoretto, who, as far
as we know, never sang a note.
In midlife, Bennett began putting as much energy into
painting as other musicians
sometimes put into a second
instrument. Bennett's colors
are as lush as his Sound. (*The
Institute of Jazz Studies,
Rutgers University*)

▲ Dinah Washington has been called a
pop singer, a blues singer and a jazz
singer. She called herself "Queen of the
Blues" at every possible opportunity. (*The
Institute of Jazz Studies, Rutgers University*)

► With a commanding presence and a
rich baritone, Joe Williams became an
international star during his years as
Count Basie's bandsinger and remained
a star ever afterward. Not long ago, a
New York City taxi driver looked as if
he were trying to back up over another
car when he turned his head and spotted Williams on the sidewalk hailing a
cab. (*Marty's supper club*)

Five Singers from Chicago: Introduction

Between 1918 and 1925 five of the greatest jazz singers were either born in Chicago or went to live there as young children with their families. Joe Williams, born in 1918 in Cordele, Georgia, was so young that he can't remember the trip from Georgia to Chicago. Nat "King" Cole, born in 1920, migrated there with his family as a small boy from Montgomery, Alabama. Dinah Washington, born in Tuscaloosa, Alabama, in 1924, was raised in Chicago. Mel Torme was born there in 1925. All were poor and grew up in black neighborhoods during the 1920s, when Chicago was the jazz mecca of the country. Anita O'Day was born in 1919 to parents who had migrated from Kansas City to Chicago; she, too, heard the music of the great black and white musicians who worked in Chicago clubs in those days. By the 1930s all were singing professionally.

CHAPTER 15

"You Are My Goddam Sunshine": Mel Torme

> You do like the horn does. You begin with the melody subliminally
> and interpret the chord structure. That's scat singing. All the great-
> est jazz singers can scat. Mel Torme is a fantastic scat singer . . .
> —JON HENDRICKS

Few claim there are no white jazz singers, but everyone says
that Mel Torme is one of the greatest jazz singers who has ever
lived. Why?

First there was the gift of the talent. Then there was his family's
need for money and his own drive to use the talent, to polish it as if
it were a dusty diamond covered with a film of "velvet fog." That
was Torme's nickname in his early years. And then there were the
roots. Melvin Howard Torme, born to a poor Jewish family, grew
up in a black neighborhood in Chicago. He began singing professionally at age four with the Coon-Sanders band at the Black Hawk
Restaurant near his house. "I saw very few white people until I was
six years old," he said.

There are times in the opening bars of a song when you cannot
tell if the tenor voice is coming from a man or a woman, a black or a
white. But from the gentle, precise sound—bell-true and in tune—

you know that you're hearing something special. Something elevated. The voice can sound like a bow drawn across strings. But then it's a sax, an oboe, a trombone or a trumpet.

Fifty-six years old and at the top of his profession in 1981, Torme looked perfect on the small stage at Marty's elegant Upper East Side supper club in Manhattan. A short man, he was the right size for Marty's boutique-scale stage. The lights glittered on his dark blond hair. His blazer with an emblem and gray slacks gave him a preppy look; there was a healthy glow to his cheeks; by stagelight he was dazzling.

"Lulu's back in town. Lululululu choooochooochooochatu."

He began building the medley.

"The repertoire itself is planned, but not the way I sing it. I want to kick people in the kneecaps who don't improvise. I sing differently every night. I never scat 'Lulu' the same way twice. It's never never never never never never never never the same," he has said.

To start "Autumn in New York," still building slowly, he flicked his hand at the piano and sang softly, pensively, with none of the big sound for which jazz is often erroneously known. Then his admiration for Fred Astaire got into the act; Torme, announcing that Astaire was his idol, glided into a song from the film *Swing Time:* "Pick yourself up, dust yourself off and start all over again." It was easy as pouring warm honey—or so it seemed—as intensity built behind a façade of the man's low-key élan. Gone was any trace of the prep-school kid. Jobim's "Meditation" made a fleeting appearance. And the medley became so convoluted you couldn't keep track of how he got from one song to another. He darted and spun around on a syllable, leaping from tune to tune. Sometimes the transitional words were his own. The intricate chord changes added to the swiftness: "STORMY WEATHER." Then Lena Horne was in his act: "It keeps raining all the time." Bam, and he was Fred Astaire again: "The way he wears his hat, the way he sings *ON* key." He tossed another petal from his bouquet of supersophisticated tunes at the audience: In "Let's Call the Whole Thing Off," he toyed with the different ways the lovers pronounced their vegetables. So, "Something's Gotta Give, Something's Gotta Give"; "My Shining Hour"; "The Way You Look Tonight"; "Flying Down to Rio." To the soda-pop tune—"He's the reeeal thing." He slid, behind the beat, into the melody of "Jesus Christ Superstar," substituting Fred Astaire's name for that of Jesus Christ.

It was so quick, you didn't know how he had managed to slip it all to you, eliding and gliding; then before you could reflect on that, he inserted another little medley, making a collage of medleys, with the Charles Aznavour tune "Yesterday When I Was Young" to wind up. Attention! Back to the Americans:

"They call her the first lady of song, I call her the high priestess, she can do no wrong, Oh, Ella be good." So much had happened in less than an hour; you had paid about thirty dollars to sit down for a Champagne bath of music. But it was not really froth, it was Montrachet. And then he was gone out the back door, upstairs to the dressing room.

Mel Torme was on a diet. Confronted by grapes, salad, lean meats, he sat on a sofa in his quietly upholstered St. Regis-Sheraton suite. The phone rang often—Gerry Mulligan, or Rex Reed, or Torme's longtime girlfriend, a West Coast lawyer, after three "bitter" divorces and child-custody suits (as the media always termed them) plus an occasional mistaken engagement announcement. Or his agent called from the West Coast to talk about money; there had been a loss of $30,000 in one enterprise, somehow. Torme was wrapped up in radio appearances, lunch dates, a TV special, concerts, clubs, composing; the phone jangle didn't disrupt him, but the street noises of cars, sirens and exploding buildings, which New Yorkers do not hear, sent him into a paroxysm of nerves. He shouted his pique: "God! Listen to that!" He waved a hand at a window and sat at a distance from his interviewer, offering the potato salad from his lunch of cold cuts. A tall, skinny drummer sat transfixed before a TV set, motionless except to answer the phone.

"I was born on September 13, 1925," Torme said, "and lived the first six years of my life in a black neighborhood. My mother played piano; during the Depression she also played sheet music in a dime store to demonstrate for the customers. A three-hundred-pound black lady named Alberta raised me. She played piano in a five-piece, all-girl orchestra on the weekends. I forget the name of the place, and I can't come up with her last name either. I've searched diligently. I was always around music.

"All my friends were black until I was six or seven. Colored people, we said in those days. During the Depression I sang pro for the first time at age four. I remember sitting on Carleton Coon's knee after I sang, while he played his drums. And then he hired me. It was a Monday-night gig for six months, fifteen dollars a night, with the Coon-Sanders band. From there I went to the Oriental Gardens on Wabash with Louis Panico, and then with Buddy Rogers and Frankie Masters. By the time that was all done, I was almost six. From age six to nine, I did kid vaudeville acts in Chicago."

By then the fair-haired little Jewish boy with an angelic smile began meeting more white people. But by then, too, the kind of music that Torme began singing for money for neighborhood audiences was what came naturally to his ear and indelibly trained it. He heard the same sounds that met Joe Williams, who was seven years older than Torme, every day in another black neighborhood of Chicago. Torme's earliest musical memories are the sounds of his playmates' voices—black voices, black speech—so natural to him that he did not hear the slightest hint of a southern accent in them. Torme said they had midwestern accents, though most had at least some underlying southern cadences. Torme lays claim to a flat midwestern *a* for himself. But the softness and huskiness, which Torme attributed to an imperfect tonsilectomy, come just as readily from his childhood ideal of how a man was supposed to sound.

"I wasn't doing anything different from anybody else," he said. "I wasn't consciously jazz oriented until age eleven or twelve. Then I started seriously collecting records. Bessie Smith. Louis Armstrong. King Oliver.

"Basie said I should have been black. Ethel Waters and I never met, but she said to someone, 'Is Mel Torme black?' 'No,' she was told. 'That's amazing,' she said. 'He sings with the soul of a black man.' So comparisons have been made. If there's any authenticity at all in my singing, the roots were there—what I listened to at an early age.

"My earliest toy was a radio. I got a musical education from my radio. It was a consuming passion. And going to theaters and nightclubs in Chicago to hear these great musicians who played. I used to go to the Club DeLisa in the heart of the black neighborhood on the South Side of Chicago.

"But I don't think jazz is a black art. Certainly it has black roots. That's the prime source. But when you think of Benny Goodman, it's unfair to say jazz is truly and simply a black art. God knows what would have happened to the jazz evolution if Goodman hadn't broken through and hired Teddy Wilson. Gerry Mulligan pioneered in jazz. It has melded into a single art form with many great jazz musicians, black and white, responsible. Everyone influences everyone else.

"I've felt prejudice, but never from a single black singer or musician. I've had a very happy acceptance. The prejudice comes mainly from white critics with the guilts. Jazz is purely subjective. If a critic thinks your skin must be black, I disagree.

"Joe Williams didn't influence me. [Although older than Torme, Williams didn't begin singing pro until after Torme.] He sang with the Basie band of the fifties and sixties, and I was starring at the Paramount in 1947. Now Williams is an influence in that I love to listen to him, that sweet, loving personality that comes through; especially when he sings the blues, I love him. And he sings in tune. Not too many people sing in tune. A lot of people who have very good reputations—females mainly—are not in tune and drive my ear crazy. Some men, too. But what is most important is their jazz conception, and I, as a listener, forgive them their poor intonation for their wonderful jazz conceptions.

"You get it all in one package marvelously with Joe Williams, Ella, Sarah, Billie Holiday; her voice did not have the commercially pleasing qualities of the other two, but for her time *and for all time* she's extraordinary.

"I don't think there's such a thing as a jazz singer, but I think there is the conception, if you've been exposed to bands and singers such as Jon Hendricks, he's superb, tremendously important. All have their individual sounds. Bing Crosby, June Richmond, Connee Boswell. Jackie Cain and Roy Kral: the best white singers. Sinatra within the framework. Jimmy Rushing, Buddy Rich. Bobby Sherwood, Harry Mills. The Andrews Sisters. Fred Astaire is probably my favorite singer. EDDIE JEFFERSON! You bet Eddie Jefferson!

"Jazz singing is extemporaneous, variations on a theme. There is a jazz conception of singing the popular song. You take in what you've been exposed to, you take it in by osmosis. And people like Connee Boswell and Bing Crosby had their feet planted in popular song with jazz influences and leanings, a jazz orientation.

"The jazz conception of singing has these elements. One, you stray far beyond the beat. Two, you anticipate a phrase, so you have total control. Three, your vibrato, the quiver of your voice. Four, your intonation; my frame of reference for intonation, for singing in tune, is the instruments. And five and six, your pronunciation and enunciation. The pronunciation is the accent. I've been accused of having a flat, midwestern *a* in my pronunciation, which immediately stamps a person. What part of the country he or she comes from. Stamps, stemps, stomps a person. Ha-ha. No, stomps a person is something different. And the enunciation is the articulation to make yourself understandable. Enunciation is especially important in an up, rhythm tune. There's more latitude in ballads. You have longer phrases, and the tempo is slower for pronouncing and enunciating.

"Oh, jazz and love are the hardest things to describe from rationale.

"Everything you do depends on the kind of song you're singing. With a ballad, I listen to myself [on tape or record later] to hear: did I read proper meaning and feeling into a love or torch song? With rhythm, with a jazz conception? Then I listen to the phrasing. And the intonation—am I singing in tune? It's harder to control the vibrato and intonation in jump and up jazz songs than in ballads. And with a scat song, I listen to see if I simulate the instrument I have in mind. When you scat, the voice is an extension of a horn. You make a voice into a surrogate horn to be on a par with the great jazz instrumentalists. Ella does sound like a horn. So do I. It's not conscious, though there are times I do a trumpet or a trombone, and in those instances I try to make myself sound like that instrument I have in mind.

"I've been influenced by instrumentalists and big bands: Duke Ellington, Count Basie, Jimmy Lunceford, Artie Shaw, Benny Goodman, Charlie Barnet, Fletcher Henderson, bands of that ilk.

"But primarily I've been influenced by arrangers: Neal Hefti, Billy May, Willie Moore, Jr., Duke, Marty Paich, Wally Stott, and I know damn well I could think of twenty more."

Torme didn't hear his voice on a record until he was twenty years old, in 1945, when he led a group of three singers as backup for Bing Crosby on Decca. For the next ten years, he worked "to break away from my bobby-sox, crooning, mellow voice. I wasn't born to do it, but my environment as a child and my taste as an adult got me to do a jazz-oriented conception of singing. I taught myself everything. In 1964 I started arranging for orchestras—now everything up to the symphony orchestra. It's been an aural experience."

Because his sound is so smooth, gentle and soft, his audiences at Marty's and others among the world's most expensive and elegant clubs do not always know they are hearing one of the preeminent jazz singers—a man who could bring all Art Tatum's spiritual heirs, all Bird's, all Duke's and Dizzy's to their feet, cheering.

"I'm not dealing [in Marty's] with people who are jazz fans. I can't get up there and do a performance of 'Sunny Gets Blue' or 'Blue Monday.' But I can go out there and sing 'You Are My Goddam Sunshine' and give it a jazz feeling. It's the way you do it, it's not the material. Take 'The Folks Who Live on the Hill,' because I'm most associated with that tune, as an example of my musical taste. First there's the choice of material, which has to have a basis of being five percent attractive musically and ninety-five percent attractive lyrically. Music is second. Lyric is the prime thing. Then there's the reading of the lyric. I have to have the ability to split a rhyme, if the splitting makes better sense.

"I was doing 'Blue Moon' for Richard Rodgers. I sang:

> You knew just what I was there for,
> You heard me saying a prayer,
> for someone I really could care for.

Not

> You heard me saying a prayer for,
> Someone I really could care for.

Richard Rodgers was a POP-U-LAR songwriter. Pompous. He gave me an argument about the way I split the lyric. He kept me from doing a David Frost show because of the way I split his lyric. Well, popular songs are open to interpretation. There isn't just one record of everything. And you don't have to sing on the beat. And not every singer sings the same way. The fact is that 'Blue Moon' can survive in rigid form and have Mel Torme do it his way—it's a great song.

"One day someone came to me and said Hugo Winterhalter had recorded my 'Christmas Song' as a cha-cha. That's a thirty-two-bar song. I was *happy* he heard it as a cha-cha. That's great. So I'm an antagonist of songwriters who think their songs are written in granite. When Sinatra sings, 'The Lady Is a Gas [Tramp],' I like that. Peggy Lee's record of 'Lover' at breakneck speed, and she's all over the place with it; it's her version. And that's what I believe in.

"My goal is to evolve. Excellence. There are singers who, if the room isn't jam-packed, take out their frustrations on the audience. But that half-full theater is paid for by people. I play each room as if it's full."

"It usually is," I said.

"Yes. But in Stamford, Connecticut, with Buddy Rich and his orchestra on a Saturday night in a two-thousand-seat house not long ago, only forty people showed up! I can't imagine why. But I sang my tail off. Afterwards we played the Waldorf, and that went beautifully.

"André Previn told me this story. Pierre Montreux was his mentor. André became conductor of the London Philharmonic and went on from there. But in London he had Pierre as guest conductor. It was a rainy night for the performance. And André saw only six hundred people sitting in a three-thousand-seat house, Festival Hall. 'How are we going to tell the maestro?' someone said. André said he would tell him, and he did. And Montreux said, 'Oh, twenty-four hundred people will miss a great concert!'

"To be a consummate pro under any circumstances, to comport oneself as a pro is part of what we're talking about. I've seen performers flip when something's wrong with the sound system or whatever. And once a tenor sax player, who was very good, was part of a Carnegie Hall performance. I was the host. He came dressed in white ducks rolled up, no socks, a white work shirt and cigarettes stuck in the cuff of his shirt. He was saying, 'Not only do I spit on the audience, but I spit on you, too, and you're all a bunch of jerks.' Just because we were willing to wear tuxedos. I call that extremely antisocial, improper behavior. I disdain it.

"When I sing, I concentrate. I never think as I'm singing: will lunch with Rex Reed tomorrow be canceled? But if I see a pretty girl, or a couple in love, I fantasize. Then it takes on a special flavor. I've never been so down—and I've been down!—that I've just gone through the motions, like a painter watching the World Series and painting your wall at the same time. I can't say that every night I put all my heart and soul into a performance, but on a scale of one to ten, I'm an eight and a half to nine. If I were bored, I wouldn't be doing this."

CHAPTER 16

Nat "King" Cole

... there was one guy who sang and played the piano in a way which changed my life. He influenced me above all others.... Musically I walked in his footsteps until I found a stride of my own. I stole many of his licks. And I got his vocal style down to a T. He was my idol: Talkin' 'bout Nat Cole.... I ... loved the way he sang, the way he phrased, the way his voice was deep and romantic and sexy. He caressed a ballad, got under it, and stroked it for all it was worth.

No one accompanied himself quite like Nat Cole—that was another thing. You might think playing the accompaniment is easy, but I'm here to tell you it ain't. No, sir; those little fills he ad-libbed behind himself were gems—always tasty, always clean, always inventive as hell....

So that was my first program—to become a junior Nat Cole. Many of those early tunes—"All for You" or "Straighten Up and Fly Right"—soon became part of my repertoire. His style wasn't my style—that would come years later—but it was one that put together so much of what I loved: jazz improvisation, pretty melodies, hot rhythms and an occasional taste of the blues.... I don't think anyone quite affected me like Nat Cole. I quickly learned that by being able to duplicate his popular hits, I could enjoy some recognition of my own....

—From *Brother Ray* by Ray Charles

195

I was sitting in my neighborhood beauty salon recently when I heard a familiar voice on the radio: Nat "King" Cole's. Immediately I called to mind the image of the sloe-eyed entertainer with a pompadour hairstyle leaning toward his piano and looking straight out at the audience, a slight smile playing on his lips. The shampoo beautician, born a few years before Cole died of lung cancer at age forty-five in February 1965, recognized the voice, too. It was the whisper of a seducer extraordinaire—one with the slyness and the warmth to promise that any falling tears would merely be part of that great American pastime, the romance game. He had a low-key style. But a rhythmic pulse made his songs sprint.

Billy Eckstine was quoted as saying that Cole took a style and made a voice out of it. Louis Armstrong had done the same thing. Eckstine had, on the other hand, taken a beautiful voice and made a romantic style of it. Cole said he wasn't thrilled with his own voice. He told his sister, Evelyn, "I can't sing. People are just crazy." But the late Milton Karle, Cole's press agent for record promotion from 1945 to 1953, said, "Nat knew he was great. He was just humble. But he knew that publishers wouldn't be rushing to him if he weren't great. And he never bragged." Cole had less than a two-octave range—nothing to write home about. So he emphasized his storytelling talent. "I'm an interpreter of stories," he was quoted as saying in *The New York Times*, "and when I perform it's like I'm just sitting down at my piano and telling fairy stories." There was a classiness in the perfect enunciation that he developed. His voice, however slight, had depth. His breathiness made the Sound heady, too; his musicianly gift for singing right on tune gave his delivery bite. "Unforgettable," one of his hit tunes, has come to be as much about the sound of his voice as it is a love song. Cole was one of the few singers who left a legacy of records popular long after his death.

Now and then the debate arises whether Nat "King" Cole was a pop or a jazz singer. In the forties he developed a straight commercial style for a long list of hit ballads. Then, in 1956 he made a peerless record of tunes called *After Midnight*—unmistakably swinging jazz with his trio and guest soloists. He played his deft piano to accompany himself. Critics welcomed him back to the jazz fold. But even the sensitively felt, idiomatically delivered folk-pop song "Nature Boy," a hit in a completely different groove from *After Midnight,* showed Cole's jazz background. And no less an authority than Dizzy Gillespie has said, "Nat 'King' Cole was a jazz singer." That ought to clear up the controversy.

November 1981. Fred Cole, fifty, the youngest of Nat's three brothers, was listening to the radio in a Fort Lauderdale hotel room, waiting for his show time to hit at a local club. He heard a special Thanksgiving Day broadcast begin. Three hours of Nat "King" Cole's records, with knowledgeable patter by Jack McDermott, a WKAT deejay in Miami, about Cole's life and music. Fred turned his tape recorder on and called McDermott to say thanks. McDermott invited Fred to the studio. Afterward Fred brought the tape back to Atlanta and replayed it, awakening memories of some of his favorite songs by Nat: "Got a Penny, Benny" is one; "My Lips Remember Your Kisses" is another. Not far behind are "I Like to Riff" and "The Sunny Side of the Street."

Eddie, Nat's oldest brother, who died in 1970, and Nat and their sister, Evelyn, were born in Montgomery, Alabama, and moved with their parents to Chicago when Nat was about four. Their father, the Reverend Edward J. Coles, had a Baptist Church congregation; their mother, Perlina, sang in her husband's choir. Isaac (Ike) and the baby, Fred, were born in Chicago. All the children gravitated to the proverbial piano in the poor black family's house. And all of them sang, sounding so much alike that you cannot tell easily when you hear a record if it's Nat or Fred, who has a minutely higher, lighter sound, or Eddie or Ike—all Nat's sound-alikes.

Many of the next Cole generation were musical, too. Natalie, Nat's daughter, became a star with a gospel feeling that Fred explained she learned from her maternal grandmother and great-grandmother. But she resembled the Cole family in her Sound. Ike's son, Eddie, became Natalie's music director. "He's the best musician in the family," said Fred. (At various times all the brothers have said that one or the other was the best. Evelyn, whom Nat nicknamed "Bay," recalled him saying about his brother Eddie, "He plays more piano than I do." "Ike's son, Eddie, plays piano," said Fred, "and sax and sings. He's a couple of years younger than Natalie. They live in California, around the corner from each other. That's her buddy." Fred's son, Lionel, an honor student, has talent for the piano.

Fred mused to himself about family matters, noodling on the attributes of each relative. "Natalie's little boy, who's four, has so much talent, it's a shame. He plays drums." In such a large and similarly talented family, there have been a lot of people to have opinions about. Fred murmured: "Eddie would talk to a lamp-post . . ." about his friendly, protective, elder brother. Said Evelyn, "The brothers loved and admired one another. The young ones idolized the older ones, without jealousy."

Eddie and Nat stocked the Coles' family apartment in Chicago with records by pianist Earl Hines, a Chicago-based star when Nat was growing up. Nat Cole said Hines guided him musically, while the Reverend Coles exerted the spiritual influence. The family owned records by Erskine Hawkins; Savannah Churchill, who had some big hits, among them "I Want to Be Loved by Only You"; Joe Liggins, a pianist and singer who had a big hit with "The Honey-dripper"; and Roosevelt Sykes, who called himself the original Honeydripper. Fred particularly liked a record he acquired from his older brothers: "I'm Walking by the River 'Cause I'm Meeting Someone There," sung by Una Mae Carlisle, Waller's onetime girl-friend. And Jay McShann's band, Illinois Jacquet, Coleman Haw-kins, Wardell Gray, and Fats Waller, too.

As a child in the 1930s, Nat Cole used to climb up the fire escape of the Indiana Theater to hear Jabbo Smith playing. Evelyn didn't climb with him, but since she and Nat were about the same age, they were buddies and confidants. In church she played the slow numbers for the choir; he played the fast ones. He was very quiet and shy, she recalled. "He had a way of covering it up, but he was very shy of girls when he was a teenager. If a girl liked him, she would have to go up and take over or get to him through me. He never had much to say, ha-ha, wouldn't have anything to say at all, until he was older; then he had more to say. But when he started out playing at dances, at about age sixteen, he used to tell me: 'Be sure to be there!' So he could tell the girls that he had to take his sister home afterwards. Even after he became famous, if he walked into a place, you wouldn't know he was there unless you recognized him. He never tried to call attention to himself."

He was so shy that he was "scared to death" of performing before "all those people," Evelyn also recalled. "But he did it anyway."

The only girl, right in the middle in age, she bridged the gap be-tween Nat and the younger boys when Eddie and Nat left home. She took Fred with her to the 308 Club on Thirty-ninth Street and

South Park, where she was working as a waitress; it was Fred's first visit to a nightclub. That visit gave him his most vivid impression of music. Lil Green, who sang "In the Dark," was performing there that night. Fred nursed a Coca-Cola. "The sight of the band up on the stand made a deep impression on me." He also recalled there were plenty of blues on the West Side and all over Chicago. On Mondays there were Blue Monday parties on Fifty-first Street and Indiana. The biggest took place at Club DeLisa, nearly an institution, with blues parties starting at 8:00 A.M. Monday and running till noon, and always packed. Chicago was full of music, a similar environment for Nat as well as for Fred a few years later.

"There were four-A.M. breakfast dances that lasted till eight A.M. Then we'd go home, sleep, and go out and jam. We used to hear Little Miss Cornshucks [who sang a popular tune called "So Long"]. She wore funny little costumes with bloomers and carried a little basket. When she sang, people threw money. There was Doctor Jo Jo [a blues singer and a master of ceremonies, who wore tails in all colors—orange, blue]. I was too young to be in the joints legally, but I had a fake draft card to get me into the Club DeLisa in the late forties and early fifties."

By that time Nat, twelve years older than Fred, had been gone for a long time. Eddie, who played bass with Noble Sissle, got Nat, at age seventeen, a job as a pianist with the road company of *Shuffle Along* in the 1930s. Nat still wasn't singing yet. He had only sung a bit of gospel, without enthusiasm, solely to please his father. That, plus a band Nat organized before he dropped out of high school, constituted music school.

When Nat went home to visit, Fred recalled: "Everyone was so glad to see him. One time he came back in a green '41 Buick. He drove me and Ike around. Nat loved clothes, so I did, too. He loved sweaters and brought some for us. He brought me a baseball glove. When Nat came along, things weren't plentiful in the family. But when I was coming up, things were more plentiful. Nat took care of the family."

In the late thirties, *Shuffle Along* folded. Nat was stranded in California. He had married Nadine Robinson, a dancer in the show. So he hustled gigs, playing anyplace for about five dollars a night. He found a gig at the Sewanee Inn for about seventy-five to eighty-five dollars a night with a trio: bass, guitar and piano. It would have been a quartet, but the drummer didn't show up for work. The year was 1937, big-band era. Club owners were not convinced that a small group could attract customers. However, Nat's trio was pleasing.

One night, Fred confirmed, a tipsy customer in a California joint insisted that Nat sing. He reluctantly obliged with "Sweet Lorraine"—the theme song of Jimmie Noone, another Cole favorite. Afterward, the customer was so happy that he said, "I crown you Nat 'King' Cole." (The man wasn't so drunk after all.) And that's how the Coles family lost its s, O best beloveds, and became American musical royalty.

In 1942 Nat and the trio, Wesley Prince on bass and Oscar Moore on guitar, moved to the 331 Club in Hollywood, an "in" spot. Songwriter Johnny Mercer and a friend, Glenn Wallichs, heard the Cole trio and offered them a recording contract with newly formed Capitol Records. The trio was a hit, first with a song that Nat had written, "Straighten Up and Fly Right." He had sold the rights for fifty dollars in his collard greens and salad days, so he didn't get royalties from the composition. But he made money from sales of his record. Other hits followed: "Gee, Baby Ain't I Good to You," "Frim Fram Sauce," "Route 66," "It's Only a Paper Moon," "Sweet Lorraine."

Fred remembered when people were playing "That Ain't Right," one of Nat's early hits, a lot around Chicago in the forties. Nat recorded "That Ain't Right" for Decca even before his Capitol days. "I remember when he played the Regal Theater in Chicago," said Fred. "When I was eleven or twelve, I went by train to meet him in New York. We stayed in a hotel on St. Nicholas Avenue. He took me to Madison Square Garden for fun. Then he played *The Kraft Music Hall* with Bing. We went to Yankee Stadium. All the guys yelled: 'Hi, Nat.' They gave me an autographed baseball. It was the only one I had until I met my idols, Larry Dobie and Jackie Robinson. Those days in New York with him I remember quite vividly."

Legend has it that a 1948-style, bearded hippie with bare feet, who had gone from Brooklyn to live on fruit and nuts in the western wilderness, slipped Cole a composition. It was called "Nature Boy." Cole bought it, recorded it and became far more famous than he had already been on radio, records and in clubs.

At about the same time, he divorced Nadine and married a beautiful woman, Maria Hawkins, who had taken the professional name of Ellington. Cole met Maria, a bright-eyed, light-skinned dancer, as she was rehearsing in a New York theater. By Maria's account in a book (*Nat "King" Cole: An Intimate Biography*, by Mrs. Cole with Louie Robinson), Nat approached her shyly, gave her rides home from the theater and didn't even kiss her. Finally he confided that he was married and getting a divorce. He took her away with him on a business trip, bought her a new wardrobe and married her in a $45,000 wedding—one of the biggest and splashiest ceremonies that Harlem had seen to date.

Not long afterward, the couple found themselves the centerpiece of a dispute. They had bought an elegant, English-style house in a fashionable section of Los Angeles. White neighbors protested the sale of the house to blacks. But the Supreme Court upheld the Coles' right to own and live on the property. The jarring racial incident died down until 1951 when the Internal Revenue Service, alleging that Cole owed $145,000 in back taxes, tried to appropriate the house.

"It was race that made the government go looking for Nat's tax problems," said Fred. A few months before his death in 1982, Milton Karle also recalled that, while Cole was making a lot of money at the time, "something was screwing up the funds." Cole was appearing at a Philadelphia theater when the story hit the headlines that his house had been attached by the government. Cole put great store by good money management after that. Said Fred: "He did a date for Norman Granz' 'Jazz at the Philharmonic' and got enough bread to pay off the tax bill. After that Nat was always telling me to learn the business end of the music. To go to school and learn as much as I could, he said."

Nat sent Fred to several schools, beginning with Juilliard in New York. But unable to concentrate on the work there, because of the happy diversions in town, Fred transferred to Boston's prestigious New England Conservatory of Music.

One morning as Fred was riding the bus, still half asleep, the newspaper headlines shocked him awake. A handful of white men in a Birmingham, Alabama, hall had assaulted Nat "King" Cole on stage. Cole was headlining a bill with singer June Christy, a petite blond singer with Stan Kenton, and Ted Heath before a segregated, all-white audience in early April 1956. Several men leaped to the stage and knocked Cole onto a piano bench. It shattered under him. They twisted his foot. Police broke the fight up fast and arrested the men. Others in the audience tried to apologize and convince Cole to finish the performance. But as *Time* magazine reported, Cole limped off the stage, saying that he loved show business but didn't want to die for it. He flew to Chicago for a checkup.

"I called my daddy right away," Fred said. "Nat flew up to his house and stayed a few days. Mother was dead by then." Cole went back down South, rejoining the tour, bucking criticism for playing before segregated audiences again. But he never went back to Birmingham. "Nat came up to Massachusetts a few weeks later and played Worcester. He never mentioned the Alabama incident to me, and I never mentioned it to him," said Fred. Later that month, Cole became a life member of the NAACP.

Milton Karle remembered other, quieter incidents. Although Cole was playing to a packed house in a Richmond, Virginia, theater, he had to sit "in the bus and eat lunch. He couldn't go into a restaurant and eat like a normal person," Karle recalled. Once Cole sat in the lobby of a New York hotel until 1:00 A.M., waiting for the hotel to honor his reservation, which, Karle said, was being denied because of race. Cole eventually got the room. But he was so well liked by everyone who knew him and worked with him that his influence cut deep. It once secured an apartment for a white friend in an area restricted to whites in New York City in the 1950s.

In the fifties the Coles adopted a child, Carol, his wife's niece, and had their own daughter, Natalie Maria. Karle recalled that Nat called her "Sweetie" and brought her to recording dates. Karle took her out of the studio, when the room had to come still for Cole to sing. After Natalie, Nat and Maria adopted Nat Kelly Cole and then had identical twins of their own. "Nat loved his kids," Fred recalled.

But even before Birmingham, *Look* magazine wrote a story calling Nat the "melancholy monarch." In the early fifties, he had collapsed while giving a concert at Carnegie Hall and was operated on for bleeding ulcers. The lean, six-foot-one entertainer had a portion of his stomach removed at the age of thirty-two.

"Things bothered him, but he kept them inside," said his sister, Evelyn, recalling his intensity.

The strains of tangling with the IRS and segregationists never showed in his low-key style. It was an era of wild success for Cole. He became one of the most popular entertainers in the country— and was increasingly called a pop singer by jazz purists for his hits, "Walking My Baby Back Home," "Too Young," "Answer Me, My

Love," "It's Only a Paper Moon," "Mona Lisa," "Ballerina," "Pretend," and hundreds more. His trio paved the way for the *nouvelle vague* of the small jazz groups. He began with a bass and a guitar, then discarded the guitar and added a drum, for a fashionably hard sound. Finally Cole stopped playing piano while he sang and added an orchestra with strings behind him.

By the late 1950s, he became one of the first blacks to have his own TV show broadcast on NBC, which unfortunately couldn't attract sponsors. The network made a big investment. Black entertainers waived large salaries to appear on the show. But it died.

The defeat did nothing to dim the brightness in his voice, or the luster of his bank accounts, or the warmth of his friendships. Tony Martin and Nat were once scheduled to go on *The Ed Sullivan Show*. Sullivan asked them, "Well, who goes first?" Milton Karle remembered. Tony Martin said, "Nat. He's the star." He lived well, reportedly enjoying a whale of a good time, with fine clothes, beautiful cars, legions of fans. Female fans loved him, as Karle recalled, and Cole loved females, fans and show people. Karle remembered Cole as fun-loving, not pretentious—a man who took care of his parents and was generous with his wife and family, providing them with a beautiful house and all the luxuries of life, including a chauffeured limousine for his wife, with whom he had a close relationship. Publicly he never expressed any bitterness or regrets.

"He was a person whose loves were, in this order," Maria Cole reminisced, "music—he could rap all night after working—with his musicians; then his family; then sports; then politics. He could argue politics more than anyone I ever saw in my life." Milton Karle recalled that Cole had personal relationships with several Presidents, including Truman and Kennedy, who liked him and his work. Maria Cole's father, a letter carrier in Boston, had been a rabid baseball fan, preparing her for married life with another one. She liked baseball, too, and still had her Dodgers box in California seventeen years after Cole died.

Milton Karle recalled Nat's enormous interest in sports, his friendships with Monty Irvin, who would become assistant to the baseball commissioner, and with Willie Mays and Sugar Ray Robinson, whom some people have called the classiest boxer who ever lived. "Sugar Ray and Nat were thick," said Karle. "Nat ran with the boys. He was popular with everybody. I was in *Billboard*'s list of the top five record promotion men because of my association with him. I made a fortune because of him. I had Peggy Lee, Tony Martin, Mel Torme, Nellie Lutcher, Johnny Desmond because of Cole's influence. He was a great artist. Everyone wanted to be on his team. I remember one recording session. Nat had Sugar with him and was teaching him how to sing in between takes. Nat had the cigarette dangling out of the side of his mouth; he always had that. That's what gave him a fast death."

By 1964 Cole, who had spent most of his adult life on the road, had still not managed to quit chain smoking. Sometimes he had three cigarettes going at once; he wielded the pitifully inadequate weapon of a trademark filter against his habit. He began having severe back pains, from which he finally collapsed. In December 1964 he checked into a hospital and had his left lung removed because of cancer. It had spread throughout his body.

As he lay dying in the hospital, he nagged Fred to stop smoking. One day, after visiting Nat, Fred and Natalie Cole, then fifteen, left the hospital and got into Fred's car. Immediately Fred lit up a cigarette.

Natalie said, "I thought you promised Daddy you were going to give up smoking."

"So I threw the cigarettes out," Fred said, "and have smoked only two cigarettes since then."

Too weak to sing or even to walk, Nat Cole went home for a few days during the holidays. The weekend before he died, he insisted he wanted to go for a ride. So Maria took him out in the car. When she got him back to the hospital, he went to sleep forever.

There was only room at the top for one singer with a voice with the Nat "King" Cole Sound. Nat told another pianist once, chatting backstage, that any one of his brothers could have been the star. "He said he was simply lucky," said the pianist. "But I think it might not have been luck. I think Nat had a special sensitivity that made his thing superb. Anyway, all of the Coles seem to have found happiness. They grew up in a happy atmosphere and didn't have chips on their shoulders."

Family loyalties, mutual admiration and affection seemed to have overridden other considerations in the Cole family. Nat Cole and all his brothers have called Evelyn from the road and confided their difficulties, whatever they were at the time, and asked her to pray for them. "Natalie still calls me from the road. She tells me

I've got a straight line. Even now, they say, 'Pray for me.' That's the first thing we were ever taught, and it works," said Evelyn, who settled in Los Angeles, a widow and the mother of one daughter.

At one time the family wanted Fred to move to Los Angeles, to be close to relatives. But he liked the look and feel of Atlanta for his wife and kids. Nevertheless, he said:

"Sometimes I hear my father and my brother talking to me."

"Which brother?"

"Nat! My father and Nat!" he said.

"I suppose it hasn't been a plus that Fred sounds like Nat," I said to Margaret Cole, Fred's wife.

"It sure hasn't!" she said.

"I could write a book about the injustices," said Fred. "People would rather knock me for being Nat's brother." Not Joe Williams, however, to whom Fred is especially thankful for his promotion and backing with club owners in the United States.

However, it's a different soccer game for Fred in Brazil. "I was playing in Indianapolis. A cat called me from Brazil. I thought it was to do some promotion. Unbeknownst to me, I was in a big soap opera down there in prime-time TV. In December 1978, one of my songs was going like wildfire. After I closed at Michael's Pub in December of that year, my wife and I flew down to Rio. A huge crowd with TV cameras was standing there, giving someone a tremendous greeting. I thought there must be a diplomat on the plane. It was me!

"I was dumbfounded. I had never had a hit record. But one of my records has sold over a million down there. It's called 'For Once in My Life,' or, translated from the Portuguese title for it, 'I Loved You,' 'Ameu Voce,'" he said, pronouncing it amayvosay, smiling sweetly. "I'm a household word down there, with five albums out. I can't go into a restaurant there without them taking pictures. I can't pick up a check. They loved my brother to death down there."

"And they love you."

"Oh, yes, but I don't believe anybody was better than Nat 'King' Cole in Brazil. Nat jammed a stadium with more people than any other singer ever did."

Fred makes frequent trips to Brazil's major cities for gigs and then flies back to the suburban area of Atlanta, with Georgia pines around his ranch-style house. The mail often brings requests for public appearances and many other things in connection with his late brother, years after Nat's death. Fred and Margaret have talked about moving to Brazil, where Fred, along with so many other jazz musicians, thinks the music is ideal—and the people gorgeous and the lifestyle one great honeypot. But Margaret hasn't wanted to take Lionel, their thirteen-year-old, musically gifted honor student out of his school, nor their daughter, Crystal, who needs special help with dyslexia, out of hers. Fred won't move to Brazil without them, although he grins at the notion of what it would be like to live and star in paradise.

Maria Ellington Cole remarried for a while, but then divorced to live quietly in a house in western Massachusetts in the summers, attending to the problems of the swimming pool, sometimes traveling to her house in her native Boston. "I'm prejudiced, because I was in love with him. I was married to him for seventeen years. We're not people who go around tooting our own horns, but Bing thought that no one else touched Nat as a singer. With all due respect to Frank [Sinatra], whom I'm personally fond of, he's not up to Nat. Nat was a very special person. I still get fan mail; some people come to see me. A lot is nostalgia, but what else do we have? He's gone."

CHAPTER 17

"Ice Was a Three-Note Thing": Joe Williams

By all rights, the success story of Count Basie's orchestra with Joe Williams should never have happened as late as it did: in 1956, a decade after the big-band era died and the singers went their own ways. But the hits of the Basie-Williams team had a loud swing that made your heart beat faster and your skin tingle—a resilient Sound with which Basie and Williams competed against pop music for the limelight and won.

At Carnegie Hall, in the Kool Jazz Festival of 1982, Joe Williams relived his Basie days, singing some of the repertoire that made him famous: "Shake, Rattle and Roll," "Cherry Red," "Every Day I've Got the Blues," "Who She Do." The audience stood up for Williams long before the reviews called him "commanding" in the next day's papers. And on the same stage the next year, Williams outdid himself by singing a cappella Duke Ellington's "Come Sunday," a prayer for his people, proving he has the most gorgeous voice, dramatic presence and lovable sensibility of any man in entertainment outside of opera.

At midnight in the 1950s, you could turn on your radio to Symphony Sid's show on WEVD, New York. It started with the Lester Young-King Pleasure tune: "Jumping with Symphony Sid." Then

207

Sid's gravelly voice, as deep as a cello tinged with a southern accent, laid back on the words as he murmured, wheezed and growled about jazz and played records. Pianist Ray Bryant heard the show, as he traveled the lonesome roads of America, touring on jazz gigs: "When I could pick up the show, Sid kept me company many nights." Sid talked about Miles, Sarah, Ella and Joe Williams. You could depend upon hearing Joe Williams on this show, Williams singing all kinds of tunes, not just the hits he had with Basie, which the other stations played, too. I was certain Symphony Sid was black.

Actually Sid Torin was a New York Jew who, by radio, brought the rich jazz scene to New Yorkers. During college I listened many nights. Sid's show, which showcased his favorites repeatedly, lasted until 5:00 A.M. and precluded my attending an 11:15 A.M. French class. I flunked the course, but I knew Sid's voice anywhere—and the sounds of the instrumentalists and singers—Nina Simone's atmospheric huskiness; Ella's bell; Sarah's felinity; Joe Williams' clear baritone rarely blaring out all its force.

Williams coddled you with his virile, gentle sound, so polished that a rough, aggressive blues song, such as "Cherry Red," written and belted by Big Joe Turner, would never be his best material. Joe's were the love songs—the ones with a ribald and risqué joie de vivre, the laments of betrayed lovers, the sensitive invitations to intimacy. He could sing without a trace of the husky tear of the black voice. Or he could get down into the bluesy black idiom and tell you: "It ain't no use, I put you down . . . ain't no use, there ain't no more for you to say, just take your love and go away; when you leave, please don't return, it ain't no use, baby, it ain't no use." Or he could abandon cynicism to the wind and jump those rousing tunes most associated with him: "Roll 'Em, Pete," "Smack Dab in the Middle," "Every Day" and "All Right, Okay, You Win" with Count Basie, his mentor and surrogate father. The big bandleader had invited Williams to join the band in 1954; with Basie, Williams leaped to international fame.

Basie was the reason that I heard Joe Williams on WEVD during his first years as a star, and Williams was the reason I listened with exceptional attentiveness to Basie. Of all Basie's band-singers—Billie Holiday, Helen Humes, Thelma Carpenter, Jimmy Rushing—Williams' voice seemed the most influenced by pop singers. He could pronounce a word any which way—to make it get down in Birdland's basement or prance blithely into the Waldorf. It was during his years with Basie that the band played the Waldorf's Starlight Roof—the first time a black band appeared in that elegant and expensive room.

Twenty years after Williams and Basie parted company, Williams, starring at Caesar's Palace in Atlantic City, reminisced about the Basie years. An imposing six-footer with a craggy face, still clear-voiced after sixty, Williams found a quiet nook in the casino, away from the crowds, and, wearing shorts and a T-shirt, told of the Count's influence on his destiny.

"Basie was looking for a bandsinger in 1954. He sent for me to come to his hotel room. Basie wanted me to come all over the country and see what people elsewhere thought of my work, not just the people in the Middle West. Exactly he said to me, 'Right now you're the premier singer in Chicago, Cleveland, Milwaukee, and you can do very well in that area alone. But sooner or later, someone will come along and catch the imagination of the public, and you won't be quite as popular.' I could relate to that. I was never away from the band from the day after Christmas 1954 until June 1961. By 1956, we made some hit records for Norman Granz. So people in Europe knew my work with Basie. Those things are still selling. They are like wow.

"Basie was the leader. That's who he was. He called the tunes. He set the tempos, the pacing. Actually he was the catalyst of the presentation, and I was just one part of it, just one of eighteen voices. That's what that was."

Williams had the voice at the time Basie presented him with a risk, a challenge and artistic support. When they had first met in 1942, there wasn't any special chemistry between them. "The men had heard me singing around Chicago and recommended me to Basie," Williams recalled. And so through the network of fellow musicians—the usual way jazz musicians have risen—Williams went to work in 1942 with the Basie septet for ten weeks at the Brass Rail in Chicago. Sitting in unofficially at first, Williams became a regular on that gig, getting fifty dollars a week out of Basie's pocket. Otherwise Williams was not fully into the music business then, working part time as a Fuller Brush Company cosmetics salesman. But while scuffling, Williams found gigs at the Regal Theater with such people as the legendary Fats Waller. "A genius," Williams remembered. "Basie was just one of the people I met then. I worked with Andy Kirk, Calloway, Buddy Rich, Lionel Hampton, Coleman Hawkins—he was one of the first international people who wanted me to sing ballads. I worked with Fletcher Henderson, for God's sake, he was one of the orchestras, and Basie was one of those big, big stars that I met," said Williams.

About fifteen years younger than Basie, Williams learned from the leader "to take care of the instrument, which is the body." Although Williams smoked heavily for a while, he cut it out whenever he thought it was affecting his voice. Primarily, "I stopped screaming at baseball-hockey-basketball games. I rarely raise my voice now except to holler 'Fore' on a golf course. I learned control. Rather than scream at someone, I'll whistle.

"I told Basie once that my throat was terrible, just awful! He told me [Williams hunched over and imitated a pianist fingering his instrument], 'Don't tell me, kid. I play piano.' I got to the bottom of that. He took care of his hands, and I had to take care of my voice. At first I was hurt that he didn't care. He was supposed to care. But I learned from it. Here's the philosophy I learned: Now tell me, how did you get into this miserable condition? Tell me how you got to it, so I can avoid it. I can say, 'Oooops, I heard about that, good-bye.' "

Williams chose his own songs and sometimes fought with Basie to try out new music. Basie had a reputation for wanting to keep playing the same music. But Williams also recalled, "He taught me that I should fight for anything I believed in musically. It's like with your parents. You have to fight for what you believe in."

Some experts say that Basie made Joe Williams famous, others that Williams gave Basie's band the commercial boost. In any case, together the men enjoyed such a success that Williams has said: "I haven't had to think about money since Basie told me I was ahead of the game in the late fifties. We both were able to touch the public. We enjoyed what we were doing, and, if it found favor, marvelous. If anything, we're extensions of each other in our experiences of each other."

Another day, another dollar for Williams at Caesar's, where he sat down at two in the afternoon for breakfast in a casino coffee shop and ordered fried eggs, bacon, orange juice and coffee. The waitress served the coffee first.

"Ooooh, that's good," Williams said. Steam rose from the black coffee around his roughhewn jaw. The sweet, light smell of his cologne and the coffee aroma made his table a fine place in which to breathe. The waitress took her time about bringing the orange juice.

"I generally like to have the juice first," he said to me and a photographer with us, and improvised a little song softly, a melodic jazz phrase never heard before, sharps and flats rising. "Where's the juice, honey?," the regionless diction impeccable, the spare baritone still as clear as it had been thirty years before, perhaps better.

I chuckled. "If you sang that to me, I'd come running with the juice."

Joe Williams responded with a smile and reached out for the breast pocket of my raw silk jacket, brushing my breast as he removed a pack of cigarettes. Startled, I held the jacket away from my body as he put the cigarettes back in.

A small smile tugged at his mouth. "I left my pipe upstairs," he said in his warm, matter-of-fact voice.

It's better for his health; he tries to pay attention to that, with a touch of high blood pressure.

However, when he has his sense of fun up, he decides not to think about how old he is—"it's a state of mind," he says—and mooches cigarettes and spends twenty to thirty weeks a year on the road, earning $3,000 to $7,000 a night usually. Still sexy after sixty. He makes it to the best jazz spots in the world: Marty's and Sweet Basil and St. Peter's and Lincoln Center in New York; Blues Alley in Washington; Rick's Café Americain in Chicago; the Meridien in Paris; Ronnie Scott's in London; and everything nice in Japan, Egypt, India, Iran, Turkey, everyplace. All roads lead to Las Vegas, home for him and his fourth wife, Jillean, a British fan he met in 1957 after a Waldorf performance.

At the time, Joe was unhappily married to his third wife, the mother of his two children. She named their son for Joe and their daughter for Joe's mother, Anne. "My third wife loved my mother. I guess she loved me, too, in her lucid moments. She didn't have many lucid moments," he said. Seeing Jillean, he thought: "Gee, there's a nice girl. Who needs it?" After they had been seeing each other for a year, she said to him, "You really can't stand to be trapped." It took him another year to make up his mind. "But what do you do with the pleasantest person you've ever known? You'd have to be a little sick not to want to spend your time with that kind

of person. And it can just go on forever and ever and ever." They
were married in 1959 and set up house in Las Vegas with their cats
and dogs and a window that blows out bang in a stormy night and
is fixed fast. "Just fix it, there must be some insurance," he told Jillean by phone in that baritone redolent of sweet talk.

Still awaiting the orange juice, he philosophized: "Feeding.
That's women's old trick. Feed 'em and fuck 'em."

I groped for something to say, but couldn't think suddenly. If I
said, "Good-bye," my "hot minute" (musician's slang for business)
would be over. I said, "I suppose you're rather shy sometimes."

"I'm not aggressive, period," he said. "When people are nice, I
respond. And feeding a man—that's the way a woman has to loosen
up a man."

Two perfect eggs arrived, sunny-side up with small yolks and
four strips of ruddy bacon strewn across their pristine whites.

"So gorgeous," Williams said. "I want to get in bed with it."

I finally laughed. Half an hour earlier, I had awakened him for
the interview. I said, "You must want to go back to sleep. You've
been dreaming."

"No, I'm just thinking of all the different ruses a woman uses on
a man," he persisted.

I asked if, while he ate, I could proceed.

He said, "Yes, but you will never find out anything."

Williams was born in Cordele, Georgia, on December 12, 1918,
and raised, without his father in the house, by his mother and
grandmother. When he was three, the family moved to Chicago.
"My mother, who was a domestic, played piano. I used to sing and
entertain myself, being an only child. I had a whole choir singing in
my head with me. I could hear all the parts. My mother took me to
church, where she sang in the choir and played the organ." He
looked into space abstractedly. "I always heard the music. I could
have played an instrument as well as I sing, whichever one called to
me. But singing isn't something you do. It's really more something
that comes through you." The gift that comes mysteriously from the
"outside," as any singer will tell you.

No one gave him special encouragement to sing. "I think the ten-
dency was not to flatter or encourage when I was a kid. In grammar
school when you sang or performed, it was for the enjoyment of the
class per se. If you said something funny, and you thought it was

funny, that was it. I enjoyed what I was doing and continued to do it. It was a long time until I heard what I was doing objectively. When I did, I wasn't pleased. I've been trying to make it better ever since. That was some years ago. I'm not going to use energy to remember one hundred years ago when I first heard myself. I'm on my day off today [his first day off in a several-months-long tour of the East and Midwest—time he would normally spend, jazz-musician-fashion, between performances, lying in bed, snoozing, half watching TV, half planning, with intensity bordering on worry, for opening night, conserving energy, and being lonesome for home]."

When he listens to himself as he performs, he said, "I hear myself in harmony with the background. Before the show, I listen to the orchestra to make sure the music is right. I'll get my part right later." Afterward, on tape or records, "I always wonder why I couldn't make it better. Sometimes I hear something awfully good, though. Timbre I've heard that I've liked. Or the feeling—what I've improvised over what is being played as support." And his phrasing and diction—those of an urban rather than a country blues singer. "Some of the itinerant blues singers couldn't be understood. They had a good feeling. But to decode what they were saying, you had to guess. They had regional accents. The difference in my background is a reason I do a thing differently."

So Big Joe Turner does a witty but raw "Cherry Red," inviting a woman to rock him in her big brass bed. Williams softens the call and plays with the melody, leaving out the brass bed altogether, with a sophisticated orchestra arrangement as support. The blues feeling—the vibrato and the voice moving all over the place—is there. But Williams tells the woman he has to hurry, he can't be late, he'll come back to let her squeeze him till his face turns cherry red. Turner, however, is in no hurry; he is hunkered down on that big brass bed, all business, to the point.

Williams started working at age sixteen in a downtown Chicago place called Kitty Davis', dropping out of high school to bring in the lion's share of a small family income, doubling as a singer and a latrine cleaner. He made twenty to thirty dollars a night in tips, in a family that had been living on twenty dollars a week. "I suddenly felt that I was helping out. Until that point, they had supported me. I had done a little fruit and vegetable selling at age ten and carried ice to the third floor for an ice man, who paid me about fifty cents. I had energy. Besides, it was a musical experience," he recalled. "Everything is a musical experience, if you listen." (The iceman's call was "Ice Man Here"—three notes, one high, two low and the same, and Williams sang them with a lilt.) "I don't think in my whole life I had ever saved more than fifty-five dollars. But thirty dollars a night! It was fun to bring it home. In fact, my mother said that my grandmother had told her: 'He's such a good boy, I hope when he grows up that he has a lot of money.' "

He gave his money to his mother. "It was part of dealing with the spirit of those who love us. You have to have someone who wishes you well. Then I asked my mother for seven cents to go to work the next night." (She died in 1968—the day after Dr. King's assassination. Williams was in Dallas, having a tour of Dealey Plaza at the time.) "Three sad things all at once. The African and the Indian in me feel that we do deal with the spirit of those we love and what they want and what they meant"—referring perhaps to the tradition of ancestor worship in the African culture.

After his mother, his first teacher was his radio. He heard Duke Ellington and Ethel Waters broadcast from the Cotton Club in New York City in the thirties. Unlike so many other musicians, he didn't sit up all night with the radio, listening long after lights out, but instead shut it off on cue. "Got a kiss and went to sleep. I also remember listening to the Metropolitan Opera, Milton Cross. His speaking voice, as he read from the libretto, was unforgettable—*La Bohème, Butterfly; Carmen* was very popular; *Aida* and all those goodies. And there were the Marian Anderson junkies, of course. Roland Hayes, Paul Robeson, Lawrence Tibbett. Everything from Waters to Marian Anderson. By the time gospel came around, I was already singing pop songs. I missed that thing. I was already out of the church and into the pop world. The gospel influence is very strong with other singers—Aretha Franklin, Nat 'King' Cole—and now the young men, too, are gospel oriented. But I'm not. My orientation did not come from that. The music of those singers is a child of the Negro spiritual."

He was also influenced early by singers whom the larger public had never heard of—Pha Terrell, for one.

"He touched people with his versions of 'Until the Real Thing Comes Along,' 'Just Fooling Myself' and 'What Will I Tell My Heart?' June Richmond was a fine singer with the Jimmy Dorsey band and with Andy Kirk before that. Armstrong was written about because he was recording. But other people were singing at the same time. And I know there must have been others before them, though I don't know who they were. I didn't hear Bessie Smith until quite late; perhaps after she died, I heard her records. I was lucky to hear some of the people who sang without mikes. Mae Ellis was one. The writers missed a lot of great singers. I was overpowered by them. I just took it in. The mikes in some instances ruined careers [picking up every wart and blemish in a voice]. The instrumentalists influenced me, too; Pete Johnson, Albert Ammons, Art Tatum. And I heard the blues singers: Roosevelt Sykes, Bill Broonzy, Memphis Slim, Jimmy Rushing, Joe Turner. Some of them were a part of the South that I wasn't supposed to deal with. My mother wanted to know how I heard 'Cherry Red.' She came to the club and heard me sing it. I was simply all ears, listening to the overall performance—the vocalist and the support. And from the very beginning, I was influenced by Ethel Waters. She sang with much feeling, with sophisticated phrasing."

The traumas of her life never showed in her face or work. "I wonder if it isn't better to have had some of that, and beatings, and go on to be recognized all over the world as a supertalent, a gifted person," Joe Williams said. He had just been recognized around Caesar's Boardwalk Regency Hotel-Casino by personnel as young as twenty-one; and in the sixties and seventies he had been recognized in *Down Beat*'s Critics' Poll as a jazz singer for several years. "I wonder if that is part of her talent," he said, "and if she put some of those experiences into her work." His dark eyes were canny; despite a bit of coffee, he was still speaking slowly, as if the caffeine had not roused him yet. "Anything but an ordinary life." The waitress poured more coffee. I put my cigarettes on the table; he helped himself.

"Some people go through life without any real sunshine or storm. And she did have them and was able to express them. Some women have only to outrun Big Brother and fight off Father. They don't even know why they're having someone jumping on their bones." He laughed softly. "The thing about experiences is you learn from them and know what to avoid. A man has that quite early in life because he has to survive in the street. Work takes him out of the house."

Purists have accused Williams of having gone all the way pop as the years have gone by. But Joe Williams liked versatility from the start and found instruction in other famed singers who are viewed similarly—as pop by some, jazz by others, or as a mixture of the two. Long before joining Basie, Williams was singing ballads with big bands in Chicago. It wasn't until he joined Basie, bringing along a few blues songs, both written and head arrangements, that Williams became known as an urban blues artist, combining elements of a pop, nonethnic style with street argot.

"Nat 'King' Cole was an elegant performer to watch. I learned a lot from his easy-mannered delivery. And also Frank Sinatra, when he was singing with Dorsey. I recognized the quality of his work from listening to him on the radio. I enjoyed him, though I never consciously or unconsciously tried to imitate him, because we were doing such different things. But I had to go to see him. I went to the Palace Theater. Other people you watch to know what not to do. Ha-ha-ha. In general, in singing it behooves you to do as little as possible to distract from the singing, especially if you're singing well. How many gestures are there anyway?"

Therefore in some settings, such as Marty's on Manhattan's Upper East Side, you can almost see Joe Williams holding still. He becomes an instrument: a still body in a chic dinner jacket, a hand holding a microphone, an intense and large-boned face. His pose, which exemplifies the naturalness of doing very little, is as much a part of his performance as his supple voice, which can and will do anything; dance an octave away from the melody and back, become dramatic, heavy and seductive with vibrato, or clear and innocent as a blue sky on a sunny morning. He may blow on the changes for most of a song and improvise the melody, or he may answer the instrumental support. The bell-sharp baritone and the lyrics lead his performance, which he aims at the entire room. "If you get hung up on showing only one side to an audience because you think it's your good side, your one good dimension, you become one-dimensional. You have to live with all of it. Jo Jones [the famous drummer, once in the Basie band] said, 'Don't ignore people in the balcony or the corner so they don't feel you don't even know they're there,' " Williams said.

He first communicated to a national audience by radio, which, far more than TV, influenced his style. In 1938 and 1939 he broadcast regularly on CBS and NBC and later from Birdland with Basie in 1955. "Radio was old hat to me. It helped me not to be visual but to sound good. When you do a lot of live radio coast to coast, you get that experience."

Television requires a performer to be more diffuse, less concentrated than radio does. So TV is not Williams' favorite gig—except for its publicity value. Perhaps because he holds so still on TV, he never seems to throw his voice around with the casual abandon he can reach while singing, for example, at an outdoor concert in the rain or in a nightclub. Also he has an almost trademark trace of nervousness at the opening of some performances; that moment's intensity is picked up by the TV cameras—an endearing but uncool trait. And in the 1980s, as he waits his turn to go on the Johnny Carson show, "my hands still get moist," he has said. Carson has shaken those moist hands before air time and said, "Oh, you're okay."

Fame itself has influenced Williams' style. Within one year, from 1955 to 1956, he went from local celebrity in Chicago to globetrotting Basie protégé.

"Norman Granz deserves a great deal of credit for getting the records out, and we made personal appearances all over the world through a lot of people. They did a lot of promotion and—ha-ha— they made a lot of money. We ate and drank our way around the world and, like George Shearing, who said he couldn't see the places, so he must taste them, well, we tasted them all."

He has had the experience of appearing often on TV—exposure which he has said modestly was solely responsible for making him a star. "Exposure is what you're dealing with. I had something to expose, and the doing was up to me. I was fortunate to be presented in the media, through the John Wilsons, Leonard Feathers, Nat Hentoffs. They've been writing about me. When I left Basie, I had six months' advance booking. The public relations for Rick's and Marty's are excellent. My new manager has an excellent reputation. And all these things are probably responsible for my recognition. Johnny Carson, Merv Griffin, Mike Douglas at one time. So people call out to me in the street. Prior to these years, Steve Allen and— prior to all of them, in 1955—Jackie Gleason put me on coast to coast with Sarah Vaughan, and from that to Dinah Shore three or four times."

The critics' boosts for his ripe voice and superb showmanship have run to almost uniform raves. A dozen years after Williams left Basie, John Wilson wrote: "Williams has grown slowly but steadily from the powerful blues singer he was . . . to an extremely perceptive and convincing singer of ballads and unusual pop songs and, eventually, to a relaxed, witty and debonair monologist. . . . He has a personal warmth that communicates particularly well in a small room. . . . The blues he sang with Basie are still the strong backbone of his repertoire, but he has become so skillful . . . that he could bring a sparkle to any bit of musical dross."

Robert Palmer has written that Joe Williams has been unfairly typecast as a blues singer. And Ira Gitler, another jazz critic and producer, writer and enterpreneur, has said, "Joe does everything. He has total recall of lyrics and tunes. When he sings Ellington, he'll throw in a vocalized version of Ellington band parts. I recently heard him sing 'Everything Must Change,' and end it with uncanny imitations of growl, trumpet and trombone. . . . When he does a tune associated with Lester [Young], he often scats one of Lester's recorded solos."

As both Basie and Williams grew older, Wilson wrote: "Williams is a dominant, vitalizing force" with the Basie orchestra. And John J. O'Connor, *Times* TV critic, caught the drift of Williams' "mellow side" on a PBS broadcast.

Ellis Larkins, a onetime Williams accompanist, has said succinctly, "Joe's the only one I know who doesn't have to strain. He can do it in any key."

I heard Williams on radio before I saw his live act. ("Act! It's not an act!" he said. It's what he does—and is.) His impressive build adds to the effect of his spellbinding voice, his articulation and phrasing, and his meticulous control of his improvisations. The first moment I heard him, he was singing a moody ballad; I was captivated by the warmth and sexiness of the voice and the no-nonsense delivery. However, perhaps directly because of his controlled intensity, there was a loftiness, a remoteness to his artistry; I envisaged him, romantically, singing alone on a street corner, wearing a trench coat, on a dark night. He made me feel that he was singing directly to me—a quality that comes through in few other singers. That Mona Lisa smile in his voice—a sensation of intimacy suddenly arriving on the scene—comes through whether I have heard him on records or in person. And that has been the secret of his greatness.

Which is not to say the cat is dead serious. In "Just the Way You Are," he asks someone not to do anything special to please him because she never pleased him before anyway. No no no, not dead serious at all. He also has an interesting, double-entendre throwaway line: "Catch me on the fly."

Williams, thinking of all the ways he has touched the public, said, "You realize the impact of it when you get to a place like Yugoslavia and people are standing in line with a stack of your LPs. You sit there at the end of the bar and autograph each one."

"It's a high point in their lives," said a bearded photographer, who had joined Williams at the table for breakfast, snapping pictures and sipping cold coffee.

"And mine!" Williams added, picking up still another cigarette, his third or fourth, from the pack I had left on the table, and using my lighter; he doesn't carry matches since he has given up cigarettes when he doesn't see them. "You still have the responsibility to the gift that comes through you."

His firsthand observations of the great variety of people and governments in the world touched his emotions, enlarged his comprehension and affected his professionalism. "Every day, every day," he says about how he came by his savvy. His ease and repertoire grew to give him stardom as a popular, blues and jazz singer, one of the few singers to achieve stardom in so many categories—and one of the few who can seem sometimes to be singing in all three genres at once. Which role does he like best? The sophisticated interpreter of a Cole Porter-Noel Coward idiom? Or the funky blues wailer, resplendent in a pink dinner jacket, cracking jokes about his son driving a "hog" (BMW)? "I love it all. It's exhilarating," he said. "It's fun."

Since he underwent such satisfying professional growth and achieved such financial success during his Basie years, why did he decide to go out on his own? At the time, in 1961, Williams was forty-two, had been married a bare couple of years to Jillean, happily. "When one grows up, it's time to leave home," he explained.

It was not an easy break to make. Basie had led everyone, assuming the ultimate responsibility, even though "Basie had never told anyone how to sing or play an instrument," Williams recalled. "Can you imagine all the entertaining that must have gone on all those years? All the musical surprises he must have had. It isn't dull. If something went down very, very well, he would just give a slow nod." And Williams moved his head up and down a few times in ultra-slow motion. "When things went wrong, he would lose his temper just like anyone else. But ninety-nine percent of the time, he was in control."

Williams learned from watching Basie lead. "Someone should try to compute the cost of what it's been for Basie to take musicians around the world with their salaries, clothes, food, accommodations, debts and problems for forty years." So Williams decided to try to do the same. He left without any rancor between himself and Basie. "I gave him six months' notice that I was leaving. And on the night I opened at Storyville in Boston, Basie and I rode up together on the train, ate and drank together, and, on the marquee it said: 'Count Basie Presents Joe Williams.' And he introduced me to the audience," Williams recalled exactly. "I worked forty-six weeks that year," first with the Andy Kirk quintet, and, since the midsixties, with groups Williams has put together in each city during his twenty- to thirty-week tours each year. He has reunited with Basie for special events—concerts and awards ceremonies, primarily.

"I think people do a lot of things between thirty-five and forty, and between forty and fifty, toward growth; one could very easily become stagnant. I was one of the fortunate ones. We managed to be busy in that period when I went from salaried employee to paying the salaries and making all the arrangements for everyone. So I missed much of the trauma that people go through as they're getting older. I'm sure I didn't do it all so gracefully. I remember being out of sorts about things not really so important. I'm not perfect. I said things I wish that I'd handled more diplomatically. I love what Kennedy said: 'I'd like to reserve judgment.' I wish I'd said that more often. You can find better solutions than making a hotheaded snap judgment. But anyway Basie and I are still together in a lot of ways and a lot of times.

"For the six years I worked with Basie, I don't think he and I ever shook hands. But the night I left the band, after the last note, we stood there in each other's arms. And from that point on, we never see each other without kissing and hugging. So I guess we haven't shook hands yet." And he chortled happily, with unselfconscious wit—so much a part of his singing and performing charm.

With the same give-the-young-a-chance attitude that Basie showed toward him, Williams invited the newest Basie bandsinger, Dennis Rowland, to the stage to sit in at Sweet Basil. Rowland made a big hit with his dramatic, Broadway-style voice, calling, "I want to be here on the street where you live" repeatedly. "I want to be here, I want to be here." Afterward Williams got up and joked, "I want to be here! I want to be here! Don't you *never* come on my job and do that again!" He followed with a nicely contrasting, intricately improvised blues.

Williams is skeptical of anyone who says that jazz singing springs directly from any one form or source. "The first instrument was the human voice. Drums were probably the second," he said, struggling to make his explanation of the art simple. "The Indians, when they were chanting, were singing. The shepherds in Spain singing gypsy songs were expressing their feelings. The produce man selling baskets of peaches had his call. That's part of folklore. The human voice has always been expressing itself. There's just human expression. Mostly, I think jazz singing is improvisation.

"There's always all these noises around us. I use them all the time. I draw on them for improv. For example, I just heard a colored fellow somewhere in this room. I heard him telling someone near us [Williams sang on descending notes, as clear as a violin, as bright as a voice can be]:

     'I

        heard

              that.'

"For the blacks the need to improvise was born when African slaves were told they had to speak the language of their masters. And they played games with the things that were taken so formally and seriously. Like the word 'evening.' E'nen. Eeeenen. E'nen. Ellington would write all these noises around us all the time. [Softly] E-e-e-e-e-e-e-e-e-e-e-e. [Fortissimo, from the diaphragm]: Ha-ha-ha-ha-ha-ha-hah-ha-ha-ha-ha-ha-ha. Writers say jazz singing began with Louis Armstrong and Ethel Waters. But there were always improvisers. Music is conversation. Maybe that's why it isn't more popular. Ha-ha-ha."

But it is a popular art with Williams, who by the 1980s no longer has to focus totally on his craft and can have a gay old time rapping about anything that interests him. One of the highlights for him of playing Caesar's Boardwalk Regency Hotel-Casino was Bill Cosby, who was appearing there, too. After the show he and Cosby liked to go out on the town, the way jazzmen had done thirty years earlier. "On the South Side of Chicago, we used to hang out, stars and cops together having a good time. It was all after hours, all totally illegal. I remember a cop arresting a guy for putting a coin in a jukebox, while Art Tatum was just sitting at a piano. Just *sitting*. We asked the cop what the guy was being charged with, and it was disturbing the peace. Ha-ha. The cop probably saved the guy's life. Other people might have killed him. It's different now. You don't have people making the rounds the way they used to. They've all become Establishment."

His eyes take on a less abstracted light when he talks about the world outside of music: his observations of world tensions during his travels—the travels that have been the university education for so many jazz musicians—and his consciousness of race, which is rarely far from his thoughts. He believes, despite his long marriage to an Englishwoman, that white people don't like blacks. "Period. And it's documented in the Kerner Commission report," he said, referring to the late President Johnson's blue-ribbon-panel findings. "But it's like the lady who comes through everything. You have to deal with anything corrosive so that it doesn't mar life. You don't ever forget, and you don't ever let them forget. I don't like it one little bit that someone can get away with something like slavery in the United States, genocide in Nazi Germany.

"God says vengeance is His, but I'm sure He would rather we be very vigilant. There's no need to let someone cut in and chop off your nuts, pardon my French. We must be vigilant and not be used for someone else's pleasure."

I asked, "Don't you think that it's a good idea to try to forget about the past and go on from there? Not to keep reminding the children about what happened, because they're the ones who suffer? The older people who did it don't care. It's the young people who catch it."

"No! I think we should never let anyone forget. I hate unfairness. That's my religion. I grew up with a sense of fair play. Never hitting a fellow when he's down. Look at Nixon. We shouldn't have hit him when he was down, when his credibility was down and he was out of office, out of power. It doesn't matter if he wanted to be king. It should have prepared us for other people. But not to keep hitting Nixon." He straighted my jacket for me and folded it carefully over my arm, then bummed another cigarette. "Will you think about that? So it will never happen again."

"Yes, I'll think about it," I said. "It will never happen again in this country."

Returning my cigarette pack to me, he picked up my hand, kissed it gallantly and said he was in no hurry, had time to chat more. Williams, as so many singers are, is comfortable talking.

"If the story makes sense to me, and I like the harmonic structure, I sing the song. I sing if I can't help it. Listen to these lyrics: 'Time goes by so fast. It seems we're never really free. Some things shouldn't matter quite so much. And some will never be. . . . Keep me close to where you run to hide, I'm never hard to find. Take your time. Save that time for me.' Isn't that the most WHIMSICAL lyric?" he asked, his eyes taking on a faraway look, his face softening, his hands fluttering for a minute, giving him an almost ethereal quality.

"I just sing. The phrasing comes from putting things together that make sense."

CHAPTER 18

Dinah Washington's Love Stories

When I went to work with Dinah Washington, I learned what the blues were all about.—JUNIOR MANCE, her piano accompanist for two years

Dinah Washington ... pop singer ... —*The New York Times*

Dinah was a jazz singer. She sang everything.—EDDIE HEY-WOOD, JR.

Dinah taught me her exquisite phrasing, to create something original with an already written melody that enhanced it and yet still never lost the original melody. She wasn't analytical, but she sharply focused on the tune. Sometimes after a record date, she'd have a few drinks and cry, listening to her own records and reminiscing. You know, that's how things had been, how poor they had been. She always liked to listen to herself. She was such an artist. She was a "one-take" or "two-take" person. No "twenty-takes" to make a record. She'd focus right in on what was necessary. She had a church and rhythm-and-blues background, but she could sing everything right across the board. She was a mixture of all, she transcended labels. So many singers imitate her. You can hear her influence in Nancy Wilson and Lu Elliott.
—PATTI BOWN, pianist, singer and accompanist to Dinah Washington

This is a love story about a singer who died young, age thirty-nine, a few days before Christmas 1963—mainly because she didn't know where she belonged in her personal life. Musically she was just as confusing to the critics because she was uncategorizable. But she found her way in the maze of her music with ease; there she was perfectly clear. A friend remembers her as the most convinced singer, who enjoyed positive statements in her music. One of her biggest hits, "What a Diff'rence a Day Makes," gave her a thrilling dream to work with.

"She could sing everything with conviction," said her friend Robert Richards, a New York City illustrator. "She used to say: 'Just bring me the bitch who could do what I can do—and do it all well.' "

She made at least twenty-four albums for Mercury and Roulette records; her recording, with strings and her natural funk, of "What a Diff'rence a Day Makes" topped a million dollars in sales. She may have earned $150,000 a year.

Some critics said she sang pop; others said blues. She began by singing gospel in her mother's Baptist church in Chicago, and that was evident in Dinah's powerful, praise-loud delivery. And if you didn't know you were SUPPOSED to be listening to a pop or blues singer who began in a black church, you could swear she was a jazz singer, other influences notwithstanding. What she did to "Blue Skies" no jazz singer has ever outjazzed, outimprovised, or phrased more feelingly, according to my ear, which heard the swing and the improv just as sure as Billie Holiday's—though with a more popular approach and a more accessible, commercial sound. Dinah bent the notes, improvised above and below the original melody line, phrased the lines and even emphasized the syllables uniquely. And the rhythm swung. She took trips on the tunes. Try to sing along with her, and you quickly lose her in the improv. She was a popular singer mainly in her popularity. Incorporating all types of singing styles, she was, in short, a singer's singer who absorbed Billie, then went on to influence a whole generation of pop and jazz singers. Nancy Wilson took Dinah for a bluesy jazz master. It's no secret that Wilson, especially in her softer-voiced, round-figured early years launched her career based on a gorgeous emulation of Dinah Washington. And on the song she is most associated with, "Guess Who I Saw Today," she has achieved her own sound, transcending the powerful and magnetic influence of Dinah lurking just beneath the surface. Bette Midler, a struggling actress in New York City, heard one of Dinah's records, fell in love and worked from then on to become a jazz-influenced pop singer instead of an actress.

Jazz musicians loved and admired Dinah musically. In her personal life, there were also some people who loved her, "though Dinah didn't think so," recalled Eddie Chamblee, a delicate, soft-spoken tenor saxophonist who was, by his count, her fourth or fifth husband.

They went to high school together in Chicago. "I was playing horn, because the girls hung around the band," said Eddie. "And Dinah sang in my first band. She was the best singer, the only singer in the school. Even then she was singing. She had been married very young, in her teens; then she was divorced. She ran with the bad girls in the school, the rougher element. They didn't play hooky; school was the only place to go, and who would hire a thirteen-year-old kid? But she ran with a rough crowd, while I stayed with the band.

"We had a normal, poor, black kids' childhood. Welfare would have been riches. I was making fifteen cents a night playing in a band and worked up to a dollar and a quarter a night. Lil Green [the singer who made such an impression on Fred Cole in Chicago's 308 Club] had a hit record on a race recording and made a dollar a night with my trio. So she got us fired for making a dollar and a quarter.

"I had no idea that I would marry Dinah. She was not a raving beauty as a teenager. I just didn't want to be bothered with girls. You know, get those girls out of here. The high school attitude. So she didn't appeal to me. And in the band we were on our personal ego trips. We just grabbed music as a way to go. I was twenty-eight years old before I made music a career."

After they graduated in 1940, Eddie and Dinah didn't meet again for fifteen years. Eddie went into the Army, married, divorced twice—and remet Dinah in Los Angeles. She was singing with the Hampton band, which hired Eddie to play saxophone.

"A year later we were married. You've got to lay it on charisma. People fell in love with her voice. And she had her womanly wiles. She was warm and kind to me. I respected her musicianship. I had nobody. I was just divorced at the time. She evinced an interest in me. Under certain circumstances, she was a beautiful woman. On stage, emoting, she could tear your heart out.

"Dinah was deeper than most people could see. At first you saw only the harsh side. She had a shell around her."

Eddie Chamblee was wearing a pink-colored shirt to cheer himself up. He had the day off because he had just been sick and missed a few gigs with his own band. Now he would not be able to drink whiskey anymore, none of that gin that had kept him going from one gig to another all winter. On Saturdays it was a five-hour gig for brunch at Sweet Basil, then a nighttime gig uptown. The gin had finally conflicted with his pills for high blood pressure and given him a brief fit—not something easy to imagine in this mild-mannered man with the measured voice, who sometimes goes to work in banker's gray suits. By this time, sipping a Perrier, he had outlived Dinah by nearly twenty years. But she seemed fresh in his mind.

"She was not naïve," he said. "You couldn't take her. Although she knew that she was making less money in some places because she was black, not white. Yes, that's true. But all her life she wanted her mother to love her. In a man Dinah was looking for love, for total complete acceptance that she never got from her mother. The mother was dominating. Dinah resisted. The conflict was: who's going to rule the roost? Dinah was not a complicated woman, if you knew the bottom line. She had a warmth and basic honesty and love for children. She had two: George Jenkins, a drummer, has had problems; the other, Bobby Grayson, went to live with his grandmother, Dinah's mother, and won't sing a note, though he looks just like Dinah and sings just as good as she does. It's a complete waste. He won't sing a note because his mother's life was sordid to him.

"She had a group of conflicting emotions that had the most to do with how she presented her songs. She sang a ballad better sometimes if she was hurt. Not necessarily because of a man but maybe because of her sons or her mother. She would curse you out, or she would curse out a club owner, then put a girl in the hospital to have a baby—and pay all the expenses.

"Dinah was like Judy Garland. She drew all the whores, pimps and losers. Certain entertainers draw a certain element in audiences and in friends. If a singer sings a loser's love song, the audience identifies. 'Somewhere Over the Rainbow' is a loser's lament. 'Blue Skies' is another. 'Look to the Rainbow' is another. Dinah sang those. I'll win somewhere, she sang. Dinah figured that somewhere over the rainbow she would find a man who loved her. She sang songs of losers. She sang happy blues, too, and drew all kinds of people. But she would get in a crap game in two seconds, and she would lose. To anyone who was in the game! She was cautious about money, but she blew quite a little."

"She was always the actress," remembered Patti Bown, an ample, Seattle-born pianist with a penchant for bright muumuus and ponchos, who can play anything from bebop to far-out Free Jazz, some her own compositions. Patti worked as Dinah's musical director in the early sixties. "She called me to go to work for her. She said, 'Bitch?' I knew her voice. I hung up. She called back and said, 'This is Dinah Washington, Queen of the Blues.' She always called herself that. Rehearsal took place in a car on our way to Asbury Park. She told me the keys and the songs she wanted to sing. That was the whole rehearsal. Then she jumped around from key to key during the show; I followed her. I have perfect pitch. Then, onstage she asked me to play a tune. Because the trio was at one end of a big, wide stage and she was at the other end, I couldn't hear her. So I said, 'Excuse me, Miss Washington,' and she said, "Play so-and-so, bitch.' I said, 'I'm still trying to be a lady.' She said it again. I got up and apologized to the audience, which could hear her, and I said, 'Play it yourself, bitch. You're supposed to be a piano player.' So she played, and I sang. The audience loved it. They thought it was part of the act!

"Afterwards, she said, 'Let's stay together.' I pulled out a contract on her, saying, 'I like to emanate as a lady. If you want to get raunchy, I can get there, too. But I don't want that. Also I hear you're death on other piano players. So if you say rehearsal is at one, you pay from then for me and my trio. And you *pay* me. I've got a son to support!' There were three copies of the contract. So we started to work.

"Funny, psychic things used to happen. I'd be in one room, she in another. She would make a list of songs she wanted to sing. I would make up my list for her, and it was the same list. I'm sure we were friends from some other life. In Atlantic City she told a bellhop to wake me up at seven A.M. to go to work. I had just left her at five A.M. She was on diet pills and couldn't go to sleep. I would find her noodling downstairs on the hotel piano, grinning from ear to ear that she had woke me up. She called me a two-bit piano player, so I called her a two-bit singer. We both laughed. In any city where we performed, I used to try to stay on the other side of town from her. The gig was beautiful. It was before and after the job.

"She would hold on to my salary for fear I would leave her. She would run some games on me about my salary. But when she finally decided I was her friend, she would call me in the middle of the night and say she was sending her car, the Blue Beetle, with her chauffeur for me. He would really come for me and lean on the bell until I got up. I loved her. She knew it and took advantage of that, which is okay. When I left her, I told her she could call me if she ever got stuck. And she did! Ha-ha. She called me in to play a gig at the Apollo with her in the mornings. It lasted all day. Then afterwards I would go downtown to work with Quincy Jones at Basin Street East and then play a record date with him all night until ten A.M. Then I had to be at the Apollo at eleven A.M. I did that for a few days, with no sleep, until I collapsed of exhaustion."

Another singer recalled that Dinah had wanted to give her a nice mink coat. But Dinah had given still another singer a dress and then told everyone that the singer was wearing her old clothes. So the second singer refused the mink coat, because, she said, "I didn't want to go out like that. She sold sandwiches to a pop group she had picked up for her show. Every time they sat down to eat, she told them what the food cost out of the contract she hadn't paid them." But she loaned expensive clothes and hairpieces and props to many singers. At least half a dozen have said that despite her reputation for mercurial behavior, she showed them kindness and warmth. In short, her colleagues liked her.

Gladys and Lionel Hampton discovered her singing at a dance in Chicago and asked her to join them. Then Gladys taught her how to dress stylishly. Dinah scored a big hit with the band. Eventually, rumor has it, the Hamptons fired her during a fight. Said Eddie Chamblee, who simply heard about the fight, "Dinah was always on the defensive. The fight was probably over an inconsequential matter. We always considered Dinah two people. Her real name was Ruth Jones. At times she was still Ruth Jones; her stage name was Dinah Washington. Ruth was a warm, beautiful person. She had two sisters and a brother. Her mother taught music. Dinah taught, too, before moving out to jazz. And her mother would never compromise. She hated that Dinah sang jazz. It was the Mahalia Jackson attitude.

"She was a split personality. There was a medical problem involved. Like Bridey Murphy. That will explain exactly what I mean. There was another person there. You could see the change. It was visible. As I was looking at her, her expression, even her choice of words, would change. Dinah Washington would call you all kinds of dirty names, and Ruth Jones would apologize. But Dinah had the ego of an ox. That's where the Queen of the Blues came in. Ruth Jones was a sweet little girl who came out of the church. I preferred Ruth because I'm a softy. But I could see the Dinah Washington, too. At times they were probably together. When she was asleep. Sibling rivalry and mother-daughter rivalry caused it all."

She formed her own group after leaving the Hamptons—with great success.

Junior Mance went to work for her after his discharge from the Army in 1954. He got a call to sit in on rehearsal at her house because her regular pianist was absent. "I thought it would be serious business," Mance said. "But I arrived to find fantastic smells from the soul food. We did a song, then had a drink, ate, did another song, more drinks, more food. After one tune Dinah asked me did I want a job? The rehearsal was really a party. I said to myself, 'This is the job I've been looking for all my life.' Rehearsal really relaxed me."

"She was an accomplished musician," Eddie Chamblee said, "a teacher and a pianist. If any musician in her band hit a wrong note, she would stop them. She had a perfect ear. I sang duets with her. Brook Benton, too. She made me sound like a rose. But I didn't *dare* hit a wrong note. We did the Fats Waller album on Mercury and another one. We had a beautiful partnership. But we had a little tiff, and my ego was hurt. It destroyed the marriage. I blame myself for that. She was always in love with me. Maybe that's my ego again. But we were very close. We almost got married again in Bermuda, then once again in New York. In my heart of hearts, I knew something would go wrong again. But I loved her."

After the divorce Eddie stayed on with her group for two years as her musical director. Her next husband used to go to Eddie and ask, "How do you handle her?"

"Did I ever tell you about my wedding night?" Eddie said. "In Washington, D.C.? When we got back to the hotel room, there was a girl in the bed. We knew her. I didn't care. Men were attracted to Dinah. Women were attracted to her, too. I wouldn't say anything. That would be interfering in someone's life. And of course, ha-ha, I'm a voyeur. I was a dynamo in those days anyway. I had seven girlfriends in Cleveland. They were fighting to see who would be the last one out of the car.

"People in show business lived like that. It wasn't anything much. A girl one night in a club was sticking her tongue out at Dinah and me. She wanted to go home with Dinah."

The strains of the road did nothing to settle or organize Dinah. Travel itself was arduous, and the destination could be dangerous.

"Remember the incident where Nat 'King' Cole got beaten up on-stage in Alabama?" Junior Mance said. "Well, we played in the same place shortly afterward. Dinah dressed flamboyantly. She had a fur stole over her arm; underneath the stole she had a pistol. Ann Little, her hairdresser, was standing in the wings with a pistol under her stole, too. Now that I think of it, if anything had broken loose, we would have been in a world of trouble. They had a rope down the middle of the hall, with us on one side and y'all on the other."

Robert Richards, a country boy from Sanford, Maine, who became friends with many jazz singers, was working as an illustrator in Boston when he met Dinah Washington in about 1960. She was doing a gig in that city.

"I was saved from banality by Dinah. She told me to come on the road with her because there was nothing happening in Boston. I closed up my modest apartment and went on the road. I was in my late teens, just a kid; she was in her midthirties. Basically she supported me because I left my job to go with her. We were just friends. Later I lived with her in Harlem.

"It was the most incredible experience for me. Dinah was unique. She had one lover right after another. Her house was like a depot. There was always something going on, people dealing and trading in God knows what all, and hot merchandise. It was hard to get her to go to work. But once you got her there, it was fine. And she was always on the road."

* * *

Once, while maintaining a house in the heart of Harlem, Dinah was arrested. A woman claimed that Dinah hadn't paid some money she owed, so Dinah pulled a gun, probably unloaded, on her. Dinah occasionally pulled a gun on people to intimidate them, said a friend, who thinks the gun was never loaded. "But the sight of a gun is enough to scare you!" Eddie Chamblee pointed out. The woman who claimed Dinah owed her money called the police. Other people in the house, who were playing Tonk, a card game, sneaked away. Dinah waited alone, dressed in Herbert Levine shoes, a full-length mink coat and a green boa, she later told friends. When she let the police in, she was eating collard greens and cornbread. They took her to the Women's House of Detention, where she spent the night. The next day, free again, she told friends that the prostitutes she had met in jail looked at her rich clothes and said, "You must work the East Side."

Stories about Dinah, probably the most colorful figure in jazz, abound—from the raunchy to the ribald. Sylvia Syms recalled: "Dinah was a wonderful jazz singer—and had such a sense of humor. Easter Sunday was a big day at Birdland and Smalls' Paradise uptown. Everybody got dressed to kill. One Easter, Count Basie and Joe Williams were playing at Birdland. Dinah walked down the stairs, dressed to the nines, with diamonds in the high heels of her shoes. She came to my table and said, 'I'm the Queen.'

"I said, 'Dinah, you are not the Queen. I'm the Queen, and I'm still living.' She thought that was the funniest thing."

Said Robert Richards: "I didn't stay very long in Harlem. That was a wild experience. And she didn't live very long after that."

Patti Bown: "Doctors gave her diet pills because she tended to put on weight. It was hard for her to diet on the road, and she was vain. She had beautiful arms and hands and legs. But she didn't know how to take the weight off any other way, so she took the pills and was up for nights in a row. She had a purse that looked like a pocketbook, but it held pills of every color of the rainbow, some to pick you up, some to knock you out."

Eddie Chamblee: "The doctor gave her a lot of pills. He made a lot of money off her. She would take pills, drink and forget she had taken her pills. Valium is the worst thing ever invented. Her death was a pure and simple accident. If anybody had been with her who knew what to do when she overdosed, it wouldn't have happened. We all knew what to do. Walk her, slap her, walk it off. That was what Marilyn Monroe needed, too."

Patti Bown: "She was happy a few days before she died. We talked on the phone. It was early December. She invited me out for Christmas to her house [in Detroit]. I was planning to go. Her death was an accident. She was planning to start the Dinah Washington Scholarship Fund to benefit young singers. She had already started a booking agency. Queen Artists or something like that. They booked Sammy Davis, Muhammad Ali, Aretha Franklin, and Sheila and Gordon McCrae for a while, famous artists, black and white. I believe she was happy with 'Night-Train' Lane."*

Dinah and Dick "Night Train" Lane went to the airport to pick up Dinah's sons, coming home from a private school in the East for the Christmas holidays. "Night Train" Lane, a star halfback for the Detroit Lions, had been married to Dinah for about six months at the time. He fell asleep in one room and didn't know that Dinah had overdosed. He discovered the body when he woke up.

"That Christmas is a blank to me now. I can't remember it," said Patti Bown.

Eddie Chamblee: "When she died, I cried for the second time in my life. It was a horrible waste. All the musicians she knew. All the music she knew. It took me a long time to get over that. Even now, we don't have a singer in her category. She was just one of a kind.

"I think she sang from the heart. An unconscious outpouring of feeling, of happiness and torment. She loved Billie Holiday. And her favorite singer was Tony Bennett. For his feeling. Not Frank Sinatra. Not too many people know that. When Dinah was singing, she was talking to her public. All of her songs were conversations with her audience. I think that was her goal." And Eddie sang a lyric about asking for love, "Am I Asking Too Much?," with vibrato on the word "love." He sings himself, mainly exciting scat tunes that he likes to do with a loud drum. "And that was the story and beauty of her singing."

* Dinah married one man twice, so her marriage to Lane was her eighth.

CHAPTER 19

Lady O'Day: The Case of the Missing Uvula

In her book *High Times, Hard Times,* an autobiography written with George Eells, Anita O'Day detailed a life totally steered by her talent. Music was the sturdy rudder of her otherwise frail boat—through an impersonal first marriage with an isolated mama's boy, whose drumming Anita loved, to a long and deep relationship with her second husband. But that marriage foundered, too. She embarked on an affair with heroin, to which her longtime friend, drummer John Poole, had introduced her reluctantly when they were young.

Eventually Poole married, stopped taking heroin and went to live in Hawaii with his wife. Anita stayed on the West Coast, where she nearly died from an overdose. After that she, too, quit drugs and went to Hawaii to begin recuperating from a fourteen-year habit. Poole kept a solicitous eye on her. The cure worked. But Poole's marriage didn't. Anita and Poole remained friends, rebuilt drug-free lives and decided to live close to each other in separate mobile homes, in what a friend describes as a lovely wooded area of San Jacinto in southern California, nurturing each other through life's vicissitudes and gigs. That has been their personal story, a kind of triumph. Many people, including some musicians, have assumed that John Poole and Anita O'Day married. But they didn't.

234

Instead they have served each other as surrogate families and confidants.

Freeman Gunther, an occasional music critic and a friend of Miss
O'Day's, says she told him that she likes California "because you
can sleep in your car there." And she likes a mobile home because
she can take it on the road whenever she likes.

Anita O'Day began singing professionally as a teenager, when
her mother let her go out to make her own way in the Depresson
era's danceathons. Anita had a remote relationship with her
mother, whom she has portrayed as withdrawn and depressed. But
her mother liked music. And Anita thought her own greatest asset
was her singing ability. She had a different sound and a stylized
swing. Eventually she found out that part of her style was due to
her missing uvula. A doctor had snipped it off carelessly during a
childhood tonsillectomy. Ever afterward, Anita sang ah-ah-ah-ah
instead of aaaaaahhhhhhh. She could never hold notes.

But she could get off, for example, by scatting the word "clear"
from "On a Clear Day You Can See Forever" and sail into the great
forever on pure scat. No matter what she has sung or with whom,
from the days she started getting gigs in Chicago clubs to her band-
singing stints with Gene Krupa and Stan Kenton, and her special
appeal with trumpeter Roy Eldridge (despite their ego conflicts),
she has been able to swing a whole band, so strong and quick is her
rhythmic sense.

(Interestingly, she heard comedian Martha Raye and claimed
her as an early influence. As a teenage amateur, Martha Raye used
to sit in with Earl Hines' band in Chicago. At a Sacramento jazz
festival in 1981, hearing she was in the audience, Hines called Raye
to sing with his band for old times' sake).

Once upon a time, in 1956, Anita O'Day began a recording of
"Sweet Georgia Brown," dissonant, running changes in a duet with
a drum, and then changed tempos. She's a wizard with jazz
rhythms, doing anything she wants to with the time. She deals out
of hand with the harmonies, the lyrics, always doing the unexpected with the melodies, the syllables and the vowels. Because of
an intuitive mastery of rhythm, she is greased lightning with a
tune. Her special talents led her to tell a former accompanist, Norman Simmons, that she has considered herself a stylist, not a
singer.

Getting ready for a gig in New York City on a night when things were not going smoothly for her, Anita O'Day let John Poole speak for her. Poole, who said that Anita O'Day is a genius, added that he did most of the talking for her to the co-writer of her book. Afterward Anita took a four-month vacation.

"The book was psychologically upsetting. How would you like to relive your life for two and a half years?" he said.

Subsequently, as she considered selling her book to make a film, she wanted to retain control of the script and sound track. Most people wanted to play up her drug use and hard times. But, Poole pointed out, she was the first white woman to record a scat tune, "That's What You Think," in 1942. She wanted to stress her music in any work based on her book.

Since its publication, complete with a discography, she also put out a total of seven records on her own label: Emily, Box 123, North Haven, Conn. 06473. Although she had become most famous for her up-tempo singing, she wanted to do an album of straight ballads with violins and music by Tiny Kahn, a bebop-era drummer-arranger-composer in Chicago.

She also wanted to do "An Evening with Anita O'Day" at Carnegie Hall or Lincoln Center to show her concept of jazz.

What is her concept of jazz?

"Hmmmm," Poole said. "I don't know. She didn't even say that in her book, did she?" He called out: "Anita, what's your concept of your music?"

Anita O'Day walked up to him, looked him straight in the eye and said quietly, "It's according to how good or bad the coffee is."

Yes, it was a jive answer. But it also sounded as if she meant her approach depends upon her moods; jazz is a feeling.

"She's moody," said Freeman Gunther (and others agree). "She's about as moody as anyone you've ever known. She can be very friendly, and she can be very cool even to people she has known for a long time. But she's a genius."

Anita O'Day has a legendary attitude: the quick-tongued delivery of a street-smart, dime-store clerk coupled with a patrician musical gift. Emphasis on the latter if you've ever witnessed the way she walks to a bandstand, tall, long-legged, big-breasted and slender, with the proudest posture in jazz singing.

In a more bucolic setting, poolside in a small town in Connecticut where she stays on the East Coast, she once told another friend about how she approached at least one tune, "On the Trail," the

Roy Rogers song. She said that for her interpretation, she saw a lonely figure walking beside a horse or a donkey, with only one more curve until they got to a place where it would be okay, and they had to keep going. Her friend didn't understand the frame of reference. But "that's the subtext that lets her sing it the way she does. That's the immediacy," he said.

So O'Day's conception of a tune—its proper jazz interpretation—combines her initial visualization with the quality of the coffee.

CHAPTER 20

Mabel Mercer,
Boîte Star

The singer's true mission is to reveal the soul in sound. A great singer has a radiance which puts a spell on an audience—at least sometimes.—from *Great Singers* by Kurt Pahlens

In one of those entrepreneurial moves that Americans occasionally do with a *succès fou,* freckle-faced, reddish-haired, light-skinned Ada Smith, a West Virginian born in 1895, made a tiny name for herself as a cabaret singer in Chicago, then in 1924 went to sing at Le Grand Duc, on rue Montmartre in Paris, and decided to stay there. "Wouldn't you?" she said.

She opened a club at 26 rue Pigalle and called it Bricktop's after her own nickname. There Cab Calloway once got into a fracas with his first wife over a pretty French girl he was dallying with in *la toilette.* Bricktop's and, for all we know, her toilet—became one of the regular stops for musicians in Paris. In the early 1930s, Bricktop asked Mabel Mercer, a British-born singer, also particularly light-skinned and with an English music-hall background, to go to work.

"I liked Mabel," Bricktop reminisced half a century later.

"That's how I hired my entertainers. If I liked them personally. And she used to have a beautiful soprano. She used to sing 'Night and Day,' 'Love for Sale.' She sang Cole Porter songs before anyone did."

Miss Mercer recalled those days for Whitney Balliett in a *New Yorker* interview. "The British and American elite patronized Bricktop's. . . . It was a Champagne world. The Duke and Duchess of Windsor used to come in, and I got to know them. And later, when the Duke was governor of the Bahamas, and I was passing through on my way to America, I sang at Government House. . . ."

Jimmy Lyons, Mabel Mercer's last accompanist before her retirement at the end of 1978, believes that Cole Porter, who was living in Paris for a while, used to stop into Bricktop's and ask Mabel to sing his songs, so he could hear how they sounded. If she couldn't make it fly, it wasn't a flag. When World War II broke out, she decided to go to America. Herbert Jacoby, owner of Le Ruban Bleu in New York City, invited her to sing at his chic club on Fifth Avenue and Fifty-sixth Street.

If, as Joe Williams has said, singing is conversation, then Mabel Mercer more than any other singer demonstrated it. She has always seemed to half talk, half sing. Critics call the style "parlando" and say she used it increasingly as she grew older. One had the impression that she might be talking because she did that better than she sang. But Jimmy Lyons has said she never really talked at all and always sang, with marvelous timing and very good intonation. She also sang at the Onyx Club, a jazz club on Fifty-second Street, even though she could never be considered a member of the jazz family.

For her, the more likely element was Le Ruban Bleu. Technically on the West Side of Manhattan, it had the feeling of being on the other side of Fifth Avenue, in effect, on the Upper East Side. Eventually, Herbert Jacoby left the club and, in partnership with Max Gordon, owned the Blue Angel on the East Side, where Jimmy Lyons worked regularly in the 1950s. It was just a short step for Mercer to go across the street from her room at R.S.V.P. to hear Lyons. He did the same to listen to her. She also worked at Tony's on Fifty-second Street, Upstairs at the Downstairs, the St. Regis Hotel, where she opened the Astor Bar, and the Roundtable: places where if you were the star, you not only had a following, you ruled a cult that adored your every inflection. She had all her inflections in the right places.

She was small, with Caucasian features, and had a regal bearing in her bright-colored gowns and shawls; she wore nothing daring, had no sexpot image. Mercer's mother had been a white English music-hall star and her father, a black acrobat and dancer—an American, Miss Mercer told Whitney Balliett. And her voice was a triumph of charm and sensitivity; with her rolled r's and restrained accent, she sounded like a mischievous dowager, not seeking an audience but granting one. The royalty motif is not foreign to her own thoughts. She told Whitney Balliett about her bucolic country house: "I have more here in the country than royalty has."

Great singers paid attention to her: Frank Sinatra, Nat "King" Cole, Billie Holiday and soul-stylist Lena Horne.

Long known as a *grande dame* of song, by the late 1960s she had recorded with Bobby Short, another reigning monarch of the boîtes of café society after it was renamed the Jet Set and was going into another incarnation as the Beautiful People. She sang in a packed Town Hall: ". . . seeducative mood . . . I am not stuck on you, lover, I am glued." Such little touches.

"She put everything she had into her lyrics," said Jimmy Lyons. "And she rehearsed it until she had it down infallibly. Every word had to mean something. That's why rehearsals were so monotonous. She had to get it the way she wanted it. Mabel's the only one I knew who could make you laugh or cry at her will. I saw Mel Torme really cry with tears in his eyes. 'Send in the Clowns' made people cry. And 'These Foolish Things.' She could put a spell on you. She made people howl with laughter, too. Our shows were never planned. We got onstage with a three-hundred-song repertoire. We knew what we were going to do for an opener. After that we would wing it. Sometimes she would draw a blank and ask me what to sing. If she didn't agree with me, she would shrug it off."

Lyons and Mercer made an album together called *Merely Marvelous* for Atlantic in the fifties and then didn't play together again until 1968. Her piano player, Buddy Barnes, on his honeymoon in Paris, was grounded by a strike and couldn't make it back in time for her Town Hall concert with Bobby Short. So she called Jimmy Lyons, with the concert six days away.

"I said to her, 'You've got to be kidding.' She did strange, off-the-wall tunes. I didn't know more than six songs in her repertoire. She was going to sing thirty to forty tunes in a concert. I insisted we rehearse day and night. When Bobby Short was onstage at

Town Hall, she and I were still upstairs rehearsing. Then I found
out that they were recording the concert live. I lost weight. Fifty
people sat on the stage, it was so packed. But once again the gods
were with us . . . ," said the slender, pale, mild-mannered pianist.

She decorated songs. For that reason, songwriters were "mad" to
have her introduce their lyrics. She performed the debuts of "Fly
Me to the Moon" and "While We're Young." She liked Bert
Howard songs. She nicknamed her tunes. One she used to call
"Wrinkles" because it was about someone growing old. The real
title was "It Was Worth It." She sang many Cy Coleman and Cole
Porter tunes; one Porter tune she fancied especially was "Where,
Oh Where?" Another she did since its inception was by Lerner and
Loewe: "When You're Sixty-five" from *On a Clear Day You Can
See Forever.*

"It was an honor if she sang your song because she wouldn't sing
it unless it was very strong. She had a strong, good soprano voice,"
said Lyons.

Miss Mercer explained her style, for which she had no formal
singing lessons. "It's just a matter of reading a book out loud and
with sense, with full stops and commas and the sense of what you're
singing about. And more reading and elocution and enunciation.
And it's experience, too.

"Then there's the choice of songs. Don't sing anything you can't
make sense out of. Some people use sound more than sense. I don't.
But if you've got a good voice, use it. I can't do jazz songs, and I
can't do the freak songs that the youngsters do. I suppose I'm a
square. But Billie Holiday used to come into a place where I was
working and learned from me by listening. I myself listened to
everybody and learned what to do and what not to do. Even the
opera singers taught me something. I liked Louis Armstrong; he
had to be a very good musician to do what he did. I liked the blues,
too, though I don't understand too much."

Bricktop recalled that, during World War II, Mercer went to the
Bahamas and married an American, Chelsea Farr, who sang with
the Delta Rhythm Boys, a quartet along the lines of the Ink Spots
and the Mills Brothers. Miss Mercer and Mr. Farr, who was younger than she, married out of friendship rather than romance,
friends say, who add that the marriage enabled her to pass muster
with the United States immigration authorities during wartime.

She lived on 110th Street and Central Park, then moved to upstate New York to Red Rock near East Chatham. From there, though officially retired, she ventured out after the late 1970s for occasional performances. During the 1982 Kool Jazz Festival, she appeared at Carnegie Hall with the beautiful, even softer-voiced Marlene Verplanck to honor songwriter Alec Wilder. He had been a special friend of Miss Mercer's and used to visit her in the country, she told Balliett, to recover from his exhausting life in New York. She regarded her country house as a balm for her soul. Even when working in clubs, she commuted from her house to New York City.

She also starred at Lincoln Center in the 1982 Kool New York Jazz Festival with the powerful singer Eileen Farrell. They focused on the importance of lyrics. In the packed hall, singer Sylvia Syms, in a glittering dress, hung out on the stairs snuggled against a wall, and watched Miss Mercer raptly. Pianist Tommy Flanagan turned out after his own rave review for his own concert a few days previously. And Whitney Balliett spotted singer Anita Ellis in the audience.

Dressed in black with a royal-blue cape, Miss Mercer took a corny, tired lyric and imbued it with high wit, holding the audience in thrall and making it laugh with her arch delivery of the tune "You Came a Long Way from St. Louis." Her interpretation, in a very assured voice, sheared about forty years off her age and stripped the whole genre of laughably pretentious lovers to their shorts. With her rich, round tones, she puts you in a "seeeeducative mood," so you will not be "stuck on her, lover, you will be glued."

CHAPTER 21

A Great Critic
Says a Few Words About
the Legendary Frank Sinatra

Singers heard his technique from the start. Not Betty Carter, who says he doesn't sing jazz. But Jeri Southern, Rosemary Clooney, Jo Stafford and so many others say Frank Sinatra does the most masterful phrasing of lyrics in the jazz idiom—and always did. Joe Williams heard something special in the early Sinatra. Anne Marie Moss, as a kid sneaking into clubs and listening at home, heard "the pure interpretative reading of a lyric—that's Sinatra," she said.

"There wasn't anything piercing or superficial in the early Sinatra. When he sang about the snow melting in 'Violets for Your Furs,' you could almost see the sleet for miles. I don't care about technique; I don't care if a voice squeaks; I'm talking about intestines, singing with feeling," she said.

Whitney Balliett didn't hear what the singers did. The eminent *New Yorker* critic didn't cotton to Sinatra until his later years. Then Balliett caught the essence of Sinatra's style on paper, against the background of the immense legend and the influence Sinatra has exerted over other singers and wielded in the music industry:

"All eighty-three of the vocals that he did with Dorsey between February 1, 1940 and July 2, 1942 . . . are, with a few celebrated exceptions, vapid and inert," Balliett wrote. "Sinatra had broken with the bouncy, gingham style of Bing Crosby . . . and by virtue of his simplicity and straightforwardness, he projected a kind of modernity. But his sense of phrasing was unfinished and his diction was unsteady—he tended to let his words drift away open-ended. There was a slight nasal quality to his singing, he was not always in tune, and he had little sense of dynamics. His vibrato was skinny. . . . The best things Sinatra recorded with Dorsey were done with the Pied Pipers, who seemed to make him work hard. Four of these numbers, 'I'll Never Smile Again,' 'Stardust,' 'I Guess I'll Have to Dream the Rest' and 'The One I Love,' still have a hymning, bas-relief quality," wrote Balliett, skimming over Sinatra's career, until a September 1982 concert at Carnegie Hall in New York.

Of that show, Balliett wrote:

Sinatra's new strengths were brilliantly displayed. . . . His voice, close to a tenor in his Dorsey days, has become a true baritone, and it has taken on thickness and timbre and resilience. He can growl and sound hoarse. He can shout. His vibrato is tight and controlled. He has a fine sense of dynamics. He has mentioned his admiration for Billie Holiday, and she seems at this late date to have subtly possessed him. He uses her exhilarating rhythmic devices (her mysterious way of enhancing her accompaniment by slowing down and speeding up her own tempo) and her sometimes staccato, rocking diction. Occasionally, his voice resembles the heavy, robed one she developed in the forties. Also evident are the definitive phrasing of Mabel Mercer and, in small pinches, the abandon of Ray Charles. The early Sinatra sang with veiled emotion; the present one was clearly moved by much of what he did the other night at Carnegie Hall, and his transports were passed on to the audience. He did a slow, slightly husky "Come Rain or Come Shine," using Billie Holiday's legato pacing, his face brimming with emotion. . . . All his unexcelled showmanship was in place. There were the searchlight blue eyes that give the impression they are looking into every pair of eyes in the hall; the ineffable cool and skill that make his singing appear effortless; the flashing smiles that dispel the emotion of the last song and light the way for the next one; the easy stage motions, even including the seemingly ostentatious sipping of a glass of red wine.

Sinatra and his backup musicians took Balliett's breath away. And the critique ended.

CHAPTER 22

The Glorious Voice
of Sarah Vaughan

By 1982 Sarah Vaughan, daughter of a carpenter and a laundress in Newark, New Jersey, was very, very busy being a star—with a musical reputation that made her tantamount to an American icon—a favorite with the best musicians, a musician herself, and a commercial success. She rose early, went to work doing publicity on TV and by afternoon had been known to tell someone to whom she didn't feel like talking: "I don't know nothing about it." Called to a restaurant telephone by her manager, who was trying to steer her from lunch toward yet another interview, she sauntered reluctantly to the receiver with a cheerless pout, said a few words, and, when finished talking, handed the receiver to anyone around her who cared to take it—a maître d', a prospective interviewer, *n'importe qui,* above her head, over her shoulder, back turned on all.

That's one image of Sarah Vaughan.

Another came from former accompanists, who remembered a convivial Sarah, who liked to go out on the town, drink, tell stories, reminisce and listen to music with friends. Sometimes Carmen McRae and Sarah got together when they were in the same town at the same time, and went to discos or other places where they wouldn't be instantly recognized. Sometimes Miss Vaughan has

246

been mobbed. It's also true that she could sit quietly in the corner of a dining room of a posh East Side Manhattan hotel, dressed in shirt and slacks, wearing glasses, her hair in a by-now classic Italian artichoke cut popular in the late 1950s; a neat, quiet woman, she could mind her own business and have few people bother her or perhaps even recognize her.

But Sarah Vaughan is one of the biggest stars, with the most glorious female voice in jazz, who admires opera singer Leontyne Price's voice more than anyone else's. Miss Vaughan probably could have sung opera, too. "The instrument was there. But the knowledge, the legitimacy of that whole world were not for her," said Bob James, her accompanist and musical director in the late 1960s. "Nor for Streisand. But if the aria were in Sarah's range, she could bring something to it that a classically trained singer could not." Miss Vaughan chose to stay a very big star in jazz. And the 1980 anniversary of her fortieth year as a jazz superstar underscored her tenure and found her busier than ever.

Columbia Records had just released an album of Sarah Vaughan singing Gershwin tunes and scheduled a week of promotional appearances on New York television and news shows. Miss Vaughan managed to fit a dinner at Sardi's and an evening at the Lena Horne show into her schedule. Primarily the docket was full of media interviews, rehearsals, sessions of all kinds, parties. And her entourage, musicians and friends, danced around the stardom during the week that they were thrown together in a charged, work-with-party situation at the Drake Hotel.

"Some days everything is 'yes,' some days everything is 'no,' " her manager explained about her attitude toward the pressures.

"So nice but rather mercurial," says Bob James. "Sometimes she was treated well, sometimes not, and in this business one becomes self-protective."

On TV Miss Vaughan told an interviewer that she hates having nothing to do on the one hand. But when she's working she has on occasion told noisy audiences to shut up. She noticed that it puts them off to have her say that, exactly as it had put her mother off many years ago. For a long time, the star has had the nickname "Sassy."

Musicians laud her influence. Billy Taylor, the pianist, worked with her on some record dates in the 1950s. About thirty years later he was still playing "If You Could See Me Now," which she had taught him, in her key. "She's as adventurous as an instrumental-ist," said Mr. Taylor. "She takes the same kind of liberties in play-ing around the melodies. She's demanding of her accompanists, as Carmen McRae is—two of the most adventurous singers, primarily because they're both pianists and know exactly what those intervals are [the note relationships; the distances between two notes; the spaces between the notes in a chord]."

Patti Bown, who accompanied Sarah for a brief time after work-ing for Dinah Washington, recalled Sarah "as a lady." So did a nonmusician friend illustrator Robert Richards, the same jazz-singing fan who was also Dinah Washington's friend and confi-dant. In the 1940s, when Richards was growing up in a small town in Maine, Sarah Vaughan was the first jazz singer he ever heard.

"I was eight years old," he recalled. "A neighbor took me to his house and played some records for me. I heard Dizzy Gillespie, then Charlie Parker and then Sarah. She was singing 'Black Coffee.' The minute I heard that, I knew I was getting out of Sanford, Maine. I didn't know if she was black or white or what. Those things didn't occur to me. But I knew I could start to do whatever it was that I was thinking, whatever that process was in a child. Later, when I told her that story, she said:

" 'Don't tell me that. It's such a responsibility.'

"It was just a little to the left, but I had only heard things to the right, where they were supposed to be," he said, adding, "Sarah is completely secure in what she does and looks forward to it. She gen-uinely enjoys it. She's as likely to break into song for you as not."

Asked to sing one night when she had dropped into Birdland, she wanted to do "The Sweetest Sounds I Ever Heard." Bob James was playing that night, knew the tune and did it with her. She seemed to like the way he played with her, he thought. A few months later, he got a call from Quincy Jones, a friend, as a go-between for Sarah. She needed a piano player.

"So I joined her," Bob James said. "Buster Williams, her bassist, stayed for a while to teach me her tunes. Then he left, and I hired a new drummer and bass player. It was a phenomenal experience. She's a great musician, a great singer and a superb piano player. She could push me aside and show me how to do it. I hadn't had much experience working with singers.

"The first thing she taught me was that a singer makes strong de-mands with tempo. Every singer has a favorite tempo for every song. I was used to playing with instrumentalists and doing a variety of tempos for the same song. She liked to do it one way for her breathing and comfort. It was hard for me to remember about the tempo, but it was an invaluable lesson. Subsequently I've been in a position to select a tempo and remember it. And she could improvise. If you fed her something new and different, like a chord, she could take it—and so far that none of us could keep up with it."

Robert Richards has noticed that she takes a Fender-Rhodes piano with her on the road. "The joy of jazz singing is undiminished for her. Not that she doesn't get nervous. I've seen her so nervous before a show that she makes countless trips to the bathroom and says, 'I can't do it. I just can't do it.' But then she does it. What a totally sweet lady."

Several people have noted that she gets frightened, especially at the thought of accompanying herself and singing at the same time. Even contemplating performances of pure singing flusters her, particularly if she will be singing tunes she hasn't done before. "There's a certain shy quality about her on the stage," Richards has noticed.

Said Bob James: "She never liked to talk or announce between the tunes. I've heard anxiety in her voice, definitely, when she talks. But when she sings, she's 'home free.' She would relax eventually during a long run in one place, when the people became familiar. But I have seen her panic to the degree that she would forget our names when it came time to announce the trio. She thought of herself as an instrumentalist. She would forget lyrics sometimes, partially because she was thinking of the notes, the lines, the phrasings more like a horn player. The lyrics are not that important to her.

"It was a great experience for her to play at the White House when Lyndon Johnson was President," James recalled. "It was a state dinner for Prime Minister Sato of Japan. And she was really nervous—extremely—in the afternoon before the performance, which was to be in the East Room. For me it was a chance to play the famous Steinway made with ornate legs shaped like eagles designed for the White House. But the East Room is not like being in a theater or a club or a concert hall. It is fairly lit up, with all the famous political people and guests sitting in chairs only three or four feet away from the performers. It's like working in a living room.

"Afterwards, we had our pictures taken with President and Mrs.

Johnson. A dance band played. Dean Rusk and his wife and all those people were there. We were invited to the dance after the show, too, Sarah, myself, Larry Rockwell, the bassist, and Omar Clay, the drummer. So we're standing around, not knowing what to do. President Johnson asked Sarah to dance. She was thrilled. So I decided to make the evening meaningful for us. I asked Mrs. Johnson to dance. We chitchatted about how she liked Washington. Omar asked her to dance. He didn't want to be left out. Maybe Larry did, too. It was a great experience, especially for Sarah. She and Lyndon seemed to get along well."

She was in midcareer at that milestone performance. Her greatest influences had been horn players—Miles Davis, Dizzy Gillespie, Charlie Parker—and singer Billy Eckstine, who had become her personal friend and professional mentor at the start of her career. Together they had sung "Dedicated to You" and Cole Porter's "I Love You" in the 1940s when they were exploratory singers in bebop.

Jabbo Smith, who was playing in Newark where Sarah grew up, said he encouraged her to try out for the Apollo Theater amateur contest. Born in 1929, with a background as a choir singer in her local Mt. Zion Baptist Church, Sarah Vaughan entered the contest at age fifteen, singing "Body and Soul" on April 3, 1942. She won a gig paying forty dollars for a week's engagement at the theater. When Earl Hines heard her, he reportedly said, "Is that child singing or am I dreaming?" Ella Fitzgerald, a previous winner at the Apollo, was on hand for Miss Vaughan's victory and stopped her from "signing myself away to all the agents hanging around," she said. Hines hired her.

In 1945 Sarah Vaughan remet George Treadwell, a trumpeter who, it was reported in the media, had heard her win the Apollo contest. He worked with her at Café Society Downtown three years later. Treadwell decided that she needed some glamorous grooming. According to newspaper reports of the time, he withdrew his $8,000 savings from a bank, bought a two-dollar marriage license, and married her on September 17, 1946. He invested the rest of the money in gowns, special arrangements, elocution lessons and other accoutrements of a show-business career.

"He can count good, and he likes chili and so do I," Sarah said then to a journalist.

Her first hit record, "It's Magic," sold over two million copies.

"Don't Blame Me" and "I Cover the Waterfront" became jazz classics. She began winning polls as a top woman song stylist. In 1949 she earned $2,500 for a week at the Apollo. In the 1950s her gross yearly income was estimated at wildly varying but high figures of a quarter of a million to a million dollars, without record royalties, which were said to bring in another $50,000 a year. She sold about a million records a year.

In 1956, she and Treadwell, her business manager, were divorced. Then she married Clyde Atkins, a former football player with the San Francisco Forty-niners and the Green Bay Packers. Atkins, too, became her manager for the duration of their marriage. Her closest men friends or her husbands have always become involved in managing her career. At times she has recorded little, because of some confusion about what to do for the recording end of her career, observers have said, adding that some managers may not always have known what was best to do for her career and have made decisions counter to her best interests. But Sarah has liked to involve her nearest and dearest in the mechanics of her career, riveting their interest upon it.

In 1950 *Time* magazine wrote that some jazz critics claimed Sarah glided around her two-octave range with the confident swoop of a chicken hawk and could stop not only at quarter tones en route, but even at eighths. Her beat could be as steady as a bass fiddle's or as unpredictable as an African drum's. And she could play her voice with the ease of a trombonist or sing as straight as a church soloist. For her version of the Lord's Prayer, she received a congratulatory wire from Marian Anderson.

By the mid-1950s she was singing in a style categorized as pop as well as jazz, for financial and aesthetic reasons. She said she wanted to prove that she could sing popular songs and make all the money that popular stylings would bring. In one 1957 anthology, she listed her hobbies as cooking, golfing, shopping for clothes and reading comic books—"especially the weird kind that feature witches and vampires." Earlier she had also told the *Sunday News Magazine* the same thing for May 22, 1955, publication. A decade later, Bob James remembered, Sarah still relaxed by reading comics and watching soap operas. "Her daytime life was not complicated. I was amazed at that. She liked to sing and hang out and not much else."

Her marriage to Atkins lasted until 1966, at about the time that

Bob James went to work for Sarah. Her marital résumé had a gap, which was filled by a friendship with Preacher Wells, with whom she had "a close relationship of some kind," said James. "I dealt with him for most of my four years. We spent a lot of time in Las Vegas. They had a real nice apartment there for about three months of the year. Preacher stayed there when we were on the road or in New York or Newark [where Sarah Vaughan's mother continued to live]."

However, Bob James recalled, "I thought Sarah had really simple values. She wanted to be comfortable, but mainly she wanted to get into the music and live there. She was always hanging out, often till sunup. When I worked for her, I found out that I was really not a night person. She and Carmen were close friends and liked to hang out. And other musicians, too. Sinatra loved Sarah and came to the Riviera in Las Vegas to hear her and hang out afterwards. She would tell us about the parties and the pranks. For example, one night they went by the room of Jilly, the New York nightclub owner, in the wee hours and got him out of bed with some outrageous prank. Sarah thought that was so funny. She liked being part of that behind-the-scenes world, where Sinatra wasn't being famous but just hanging out and doing silly, fun things."

In 1971 she married Marshall Fisher, a Las Vegas restaurant owner, and divorced him in 1977. In 1978 she married another musician, Waymon Reed, from the Basie band. That marriage also folded after a long run, as show seasons go, but it was her briefest marriage. All her husbands have been, in effect, "Mr. Sarah Vaughan," subsidiary to the career, Robert Richards surmised. Her mind has simply been primarily cn the music, some colleagues agree.

The pressures and demands of stardom and its lifestyle never seemed to bear down on Miss Vaughan musically. Bob James recalled that she was always determined to keep her performing and singing pure. Basically she just wanted to sing with a trio and give herself the most room to improvise; occasionally she liked to sing with a large orchestra if there were a super arranger whom she respected. She understood enough arranging to know."

Miss Vaughan has an adopted daughter, Deborah, who has studied dance and attends college in Santa Barbara, California.

So the "Divine Sarah's" career soared through it all. She didn't quibble with that nickname and even called her management office

Devine One, with a little improv on the spelling. She has worked with just about every jazz musician from Earl Hines to Dizzy Gillespie to Clark Terry. Critics have done a bit of nit-picking, saying that her records have not reflected the true glory of her voice, that her lyric interpretations have not equaled her magnificent vocal instrument. But in 1957 John Wilson of *The New York Times* wrote a few words, which have held true throughout Sarah Vaughan's career: "She has what may well be the finest voice ever applied to jazz. She is now using it to drive home the dramatic sense of her songs rather than fight it. She is, as she always has been, completely at home in the jazz idiom, swinging with a jazz feeling through everything she sings. And rounding out the picture, she has become an assured performer with an elfin charm that can be quite infectious . . . she [can] breathe needed life into a concert . . . sinking . . . into the doldrums. . . ."

In his review of a record, "Tenderly," which she did for MGM, Wilson wrote: "Sarah Vaughan had one of the finest voices with which a singer of popular songs has ever been blessed. Not content with this, however, she became a determined stylist with a fondness for tonsil-rattling vibrato and for sudden swoops from her normal soprano to low register contralto, which gave the impression that she had jumped down a well."

Said Bob James: "Sarah wanted to show off her instrument. Pop songs don't allow that. But she would show off by going way above and way below the pop song."

The determined stylizations were quite different from her early recordings, such as the classic "If You Could See Me Now," best described as *gorgeous*, sung by a young Sarah backed by famous jazz musicians.

But reviews and comparisons between the young and the older Sarah barely matter. In 1982, frequently shuttling between New York City and her California home in the San Fernando Valley, she capped a promotional week for her newest Columbia record with a concert celebrating her forty years in show business. She appeared in a flowing, chiffon-like dress the color of a melting peppermint candy cane. Considerably heavier than when she started out at about 125 pounds, she sang in a truly magnificent voice with superb theatrics. She followed that concert with another one during the Kool Jazz Festival—a performance lauded as one of the best in her life.

So never mind her girlish hand-fluttering as she stutters her way courageously through chitchat with the audience between tunes. She has a dark, rich range that goes normally from about C below middle C to D above middle C, "though she could go up to A flat or A, or maybe even higher than that on a good night," said Bob James—at least a two-and-a-half- to three-octave range. It sounds like more. The voice and the powerful stylings transcend everything. And if, as she grew older, she seemed to find the lower register more her métier, it was ridiculous to quibble about any blurrings. She has been just so good.

CHAPTER 23

The Time of
Ella Fitzgerald

Ella Fitzgerald has combined it all in one package, a peerless sense of rhythm that allows her to move like quicksilver over the notes, with perfect intonation, her voice full of ease and musical inventiveness—altogether a joyful noise. She can sound like a bell or a trumpet or a lioness at will. "No one in the world can beat Ella as a riff singer," said Ethel Waters long ago, at a time when Ethel was primarily acting instead of singing. And Ella Fitzgerald propels all of her assets with an intensely rhythmic undercurrent, sometimes only a subtle ripple, other times an awesome wave—an inexorable natural force with which she engulfs and sweeps away the audience.

She won the Apollo contest in 1934 at about age sixteen, which makes her the most senior of the two living female jazz icons, herself and Sarah Vaughan. Ella Fitzgerald's passport gives her birth date as April 25, 1918. Legend has it that Ella, a shy young woman, thought she would dance in the Apollo contest. But something changed her mind onstage; perhaps her knees turned to jelly. She still shakes with fright during performances after nearly fifty years as a performer. At the Apollo she decided to sing a tune called "Judy," several sources said, though someone else said it was "The

Object of My Affection." Others noodle about the possibility of yet another tune. In any case, the audience demanded encores.

An entertainer named Bardu Ali, fronting the band for tiny, hunchbacked drummer Chick Webb at the Apollo that night, was so astounded at the girl's voice that he introduced her to Webb. He and his wife took her under their wings and into the Webb band, becoming her guardians. Her mother had died when she was fourteen, or younger, according to the most repeated version of her childhood. Very little has been written about this stage of her life.

"I thought my singing was pretty much hollering," she said, "but Webb didn't." In 1935 she made her first records with the Webb band—"Are You Here to Stay?" and "Love and Kisses"; and then three years later, "A-Tisket, A-Tasket," adapted, it was said, by Ella from an old nursery rhyme. It became a national hit and launched her as a star. She was depicted at the time in Earl Wilson's newspaper column as a fun-loving girl who liked to play cute games with pennies backstage.

Subsequently she won *Down Beat* magazine's award as Best Female Singer for eighteen consecutive years, and eleven Grammy awards, the highest awards of the National Academy of Recording Arts and Sciences, more than any other female jazz singer. She made more than 250 albums and sold over 50 million, according to one source; 100 million said another. Chick Webb died at age twenty-nine of spinal tuberculosis in 1939, after a career in which he often played in excruciating pain. Ella took over his band for three years, until the Army dismantled it. After that she went out with the Four Keys. Jay McShann recalled appearing in a show with Ella in those days. Asked to introduce her group, he got mixed up somehow and said, "Ella Keys and the Four Fitzgeralds." He also recalled the funny look she gave him. The Army eventually reduced the Keys to a skeleton. And Ella went solo.

In this period, too, she was married for the first time to Benny Kornegay, a shipyard worker. But a newspaper account of the young couple suggested that Ella's mind was more on music than ménage. While she was away on the road, Benny played her records at home, Sidney Fields wrote in his column, "Only Human," then went out to listen to more of his wife's singing on a jukebox.

"When I clown, he don't mind," Ella Fitzgerald was quoted as saying at the end of 1942. "And I'm always clowning. He understands when people like to do something it's better not to try and stop them. But I have to learn to cook. We just started our apartment and I want to get into the kitchen. We've been eating in restaurants, and he's getting tired of it. What more do I want? Please say I want to be a star like Ethel Waters with a Broadway show. I doubt it, though. Maybe I got an inferiority complex. Maybe I'm saying I doubt it because I'm hoping it will be just the opposite."

It was. It was all music, no dialogue. The girl who had come from Newport News, Virginia, to grow up in Nyack, New York, under the care of a relative, ended that marriage after two years and tried a second time with bassist Ray Brown, Sr., in 1948, when she was thirty years old. They met when they traveled with Dizzy Gillespie's band in the 1940s. "That's when she started scatting," Brown recalls. In 1950 the Browns had a son, Ray, Jr.—who became a drummer—and were divorced in 1952. She told Fields, who wrote for the *Mirror*, in 1957: "I guess I pick them wrong. But I want to get married again. I'm still looking. Everybody wants companionship." However, she never married again.

Her career as a solo recording artist for Victor, and then from 1935 to 1955 for Decca, had gone along well enough. She filled the years with albums of solid tunes with orchestras, strings and all, backing her clear, nimble voice with its brilliant, rhythmic drive. In the 1940s she had a big hit with "How High the Moon," just to toss off the name of one of her many hits. She made a few films, including *St. Louis Blues* and *Pete Kelly's Blues*, in which she sang "Hard-Hearted Hannah." In 1950 she earned $3,250 a week during an engagement at New York's Paramount Theater.

In 1955 she went under someone's wing again, this time Norman Granz'. He was producing "Jazz at the Philharmonic" tours, in which Ella had already been involved, and records on the Verve label.

Granz started her on a career of recording albums of songbooks of the most famous American composers—Cole Porter, and more Cole Porter; Jerome Kern; Johnny Mercer; Rodgers and Hart; Harold Arlen; Irving Berlin; Duke Ellington; W. C. Handy; a grab bag of "Misty," "Angel Eyes," "September Song," "Let No Man Write My Epitaph" and others; a reissue of "A-Tisket, A-Tasket," "A Sunday Kind of Love," and other Fitzgerald hits; Ella with Benny Goodman in 1936, and Ella in Hollywood. In Granz she found exquisite career organization. And her career soared above almost everyone else's, prompting so many musicians to say she has been the best that ever lived.

With Granz' management she played the world—all the great music houses in the United States, with the best jazz musicians. She toured Latin America, Europe and Asia. She was the first jazz singer to appear at the Flamingo in Las Vegas and in the Venetian Room of the Fairmont Hotel in San Francisco. With Louis Armstrong, she made classic jazz recordings—another boost to her stardom.

At the height of the rock craze in the 1960s, Ella Fitzgerald thought she would like to do "Goin' Out of My Head," "Sunny," and an album of Beatles songs like "Yesterday" and "Michelle." To satisfy a fan, she learned "Ode to Billie Joe" and performed it with written notes—an effective touch by a woman whose career centered almost totally on old standards. But her greatest appeal for everyone always lay in the classics, such as "Mack the Knife" and "How High the Moon." There was never anything zany about her work to put her into the running for a piece of the rock-audience pie. Her career has been remarkably consistent—scat tunes, ballads and up-tempo numbers, with one of the most unmistakable, best-loved sounds in jazz. After so many years, she still sounded fresh, bringing people to their feet, clapping and calling for more, when she sang "Teach Me Tonight" straightforwardly, with an almost Broadway-musical bounce, at Carnegie Hall in 1982. She did a varied repertoire: "Deep Purple," "Let's Do It," "God Bless the Child," "Lullaby of Birdland," " 'Round Midnight," "Honeysuckle Rose," which she really swung with a trombone and tenor sax, showing, as usual, that she could do it all. And "Take the 'A' Train," which she scatted and from which she darted off on a chord to "Heat Wave." At one time, so successful was she with "A-Tisket, A-Tasket," she adapted another childhood classic, "Old MacDonald Had a Farm." It has remained in her repertoire for decades, beloved of this eminent scatter and her public for the *ee-i-os*, the chick-chicks, quack-quacks, oink-oinks and moo-moos, as she keeps going up a half-tone: "Old MacDonald had a farm, what a swinging farm . . . How you going to keep them down on the farm? . . ." And she did that, too.

Norman Granz has had the ideal person to manage to superstardom. "She has no bad habits, doesn't smoke, doesn't drink, though she enjoys her food," said Jimmy Rowles, a former accompanist. "She takes good care of herself. Gets enough rest. Except when she gets bothered for interviews. People bother her. So she leaps into limos and disappears. She has things on her mind to do. And as a legend, her life doesn't belong to her. So it's hard for her to escape when she's going through a hotel lobby filled with autograph seekers. But sincerity is the first word that pops into my head when I think of what she's like. You can hear it when she sings. She likes to sing the tunes. The only time she scats is when the song requires it. Otherwise she likes to sing straight."

It's legend in the music business that Norman Granz has done all the talking for Ella Fitzgerald to her public when she's offstage. She lives very privately and self-protectively in a large house in Beverly Hills. Intrusions by the press fluster her to pique. In 1965 Leonard Feather wrote in the *New York Post:* "Ella's wafer-thin skin against criticism is a second source of insecurity. When Frank Sinatra impugned her phrasing and breathing in a recent magazine article, she says, 'I was so upset I could hardly sing for a week.' She had looked forward to [a European tour she was undertaking at the time] as a desperately needed morale-booster: 'I was beginning to be afraid. I felt maybe I just didn't have it, and I had no hit record. It took a lot of people to convince me there are more important things.' "

Feather reported in the same column that Ella Fitzgerald felt lonely at the top, so removed from the milieu in which she had grown to stardom. Her reunions with musicians from the old days took place at recording sessions and in concerts. She kept working hard—on the road a great deal of the year, with little leisure time most of her life.

When her accompanist-pianist Tommy Flanagan had a heart attack and decided to withdraw from the arduous life on the road after more than fifteen years of musical association with Fitzgerald, he and the singer had little further contact. Norman Granz continued to do the talking, while Ella continued to sing "just this side of the angels," as a headline described her work.

But in 1974 when he was still her accompanist, Tommy Flanagan, a slender man with a fringe of white hair, told writer Ernest Dunbar about her way of working:

"Sometimes Ella comes up with a tune that she's heard somewhere, or I may send her a song that I feel is especially for her.

Then we get together to find the key she's comfortable in. She tells me how she feels this piece should be done—serious or playful and humorous—the kind of mood it communicates to her. I then work up an orchestration that embodies her ideas and my own and we try it together. But an arrangement for Ella is only a framework within which to move. She will still do all kinds of things within that framework. Often, she'll add a new twist or improvisation, even when we're actually onstage performing. She may lag behind the beat a bit or move ahead of it, but she always knows exactly what she is doing. What would be musically risky for some singers, she pulls off easily. She rarely sings a song exactly the same way she did it last. But we've all played together for so long that no matter what she does, we are all right there together."

Sy Oliver, who has done arrangements for Ella, implies she is a musician's dream come true to work with. "Poor little Ella," the joke goes, can't play piano, as Sarah Vaughan and Carmen McRae can. All Ella can do is sing everything right on the first take. She can play "scat" with Jon Hendricks off the cuff at parties—one of the highlights of any party I've ever heard about.

But she was and is rarely reported in any social whirl; instead, one reporter wrote, although she got along with musicians well, she lived privately. She numbered among her friends some women whom she knew for years. With close friends, she opens up and talks about music and cooking—two of her passions. She raised a niece, who was a fan of the Motown stars, as well as her own son, Ray Jr., now a rock musician, in her Beverly Hills home. "Despite her celebrity, she's notoriously shy. She's uncomfortable with strangers after all these years," notes George Wein, producer of the Kool Jazz Festivals. "A lot of black kids are shy, dealing in a white world. She was a gawky kid. When people pay her compliments, they mean something to her."

And she has fond memories of the magnificent musicians she has worked with. Dunbar wrote of her sorrow at Duke Ellington's funeral at St. John's Cathedral in New York City, where she sang a dirgelike version of Ellington's "In My Solitude" and the spiritual "Just a Closer Walk with Thee." People cried when they heard her. Later she told Dunbar:

"I didn't know what I was singing. I have the feeling I was singing the wrong words, but all I knew was that from where I was standing, I could look right across at his body, and I was sort of frozen. You knew his death had to come sometime, I guess, but I'd known him ever since I was a girl. He used to tell me a lot of things that made a lot of sense. Once I had a big problem with a love affair when he and I were working in the same theater and I turned to him for advice. He told me, 'Ella; it's like a toothache. If it hurts bad enough, you get rid of it. You miss it for a while, but you feel better afterwards.' Some musicians put other performers down, but Duke never had anything bad to say about anyone. I don't think people realized even yet how great the man was."

George Wein recalled, "When Louis Armstrong died, everyone came looking to perform. Ella flew in from Chicago, sat in a pew dressed as a mourner in front of me, and flew back out right away. She wasn't looking for publicity. She's that kind of person."

She has sung all her tunes, a vast repertoire, with unflagging vivacity. She can go from little-girl sweetness to a driving, rasping noise. She can make any sound that she wants to, including a saxophone, with all stops and mutes out and a full, rich timbre. Musicians have vacillated between calling her the greatest who ever lived and, still mindful of Billie, the greatest living. Once in a while someone says Carmen McRae is the greatest. But most say it's a draw between Ella and Sarah.

CHAPTER 24

Noodling with Norman Simmons About Carmen McRae

Slim, with a medium-sized smile, of medium height and "moderately intense," he said, Norman Simmons in middle age (born in Chicago in 1929) looked back on a thirty-year career of playing piano for some of the best jazz singers in the United States. He has received two National Endowment for the Arts grants for composing. But he has been particularly respected for his arranging and accompanying—for Dakota Staton, Ernestine Anderson, Anita O'Day, Betty Carter, Billy Daniels, Helen Forrest, Barbara Lea, Helen Humes, Jimmy Rushing, Al Hibbler, Maxine Sullivan, Chris Connor, Johnny Hartman, David Allyn, Joe Williams—and, during eight years in the sixties, for Carmen McRae.

"In about 1961, I went to work for Carmen McRae. FEARFULLY. I went looking for work with Johnny and Jaws [Johnny Griffin and Eddie "Lockjaw" Davis] at the Apollo Theater—and met Carmen there. I wanted to play for her, but she had a fearful reputation. Jaws was my mentor; he has always called me 'son.' He said, 'You and Carmen will be perfect together.' He could foresee it. So that started eight and a half years of various experiences.

"One of our first gigs took place in Hartford, Connecticut. I was wearing garters to hold my stockings up. And as I'm playing, high on a stage where everyone could see my feet, Carmen suddenly

points down at my foot and says aloud, 'What's that on your leg?'
My garter had dropped down. It was a very embarrassing moment.

"Soon afterwards, she joined Columbia Records. For her first
recording, they told her that she could do anything she wanted to.
So she decided on a tribute to Billie Holiday and told me she
wanted it loosely arranged. I did a few charts. When she looked at
them, she said, 'Do the whole thing.'

"That record went smoothly." (Released several times, the record
has had a recent incarnation as *Carmen-Billie,* and includes
"Strange Fruit," a song that almost no one has touched since Billie
Holiday won international acclaim for it—almost no one but Carmen, who sings it in a spellbinding, quiet voice.)

"She knew me instinctively, and I knew her. It was never discussed. Our friendship came from the music. That's how it first has
to come. She was never difficult with me. I did my work and was responsible. We collaborated. I took criticism, but I never got up-
tight. Other musicians did when they fell short of her musical
expectations. She requires a high level of proficiency and inspiration. She offers strong leadership and requires musicians who can
add their own creativity to the music. She seems very arranged, but
the performance must be fresh every time. You can't just play the
job with Carmen.

"She's a great singer, from my standpoint as an accompanist. I
can feel the singers under my fingers. I can feel the way they sing,
if they really mean something, by the songs they choose and the
way they choose to sing. Carmen's a leader in that sense. She offers
you the material, and she's strong enough for you to hold on to.

"Carmen taught me that it was my responsibility to be in charge
onstage during the performance. One time, at the Village Gate, the
rhythm section [piano, drums and bass make up the usual rhythm
section] was not coming together. We had two musicians who
weren't jelling, the drummer and myself. So I decided to lay out
[not play] and let her go with bass and drums. Afterwards she told
me that she had been listening for me.

"Don't you *ever* drop out again," she said. Because if anything
went wrong on the stage, she would be looking for me to specify
where we should all be. I had already been doing the job about five
years when that surfaced. My concept of accompanying matured. I
needed to understand that the responsibility never shifted off me,
no matter who was playing with us. I became more positive about

my job, not by pounding but by pulsating. That's the key to accompanying a singer: supply the beat. A piano can play time and harmony and imply them for the bass, the drum and the singer. The piano gives direction; other musicians follow a piano more than they do a singer. So you don't end up with three different interpretations. The piano player follows the singer, who leads, and the other musicians follow the piano. It relates to the concept of the piano having the possibility to be an orchestra. When I started playing, I used to listen to Duke Ellington; he was orchestrating while someone else played the lead. I've always been interested in the orchestration. And I always orchestrate as well as pulsate.

"Carmen taught me what accompaniment was about:

"Every singer is different, but the basis for playing with each one is the same. Pianists have the problem of how much to play. They shouldn't play too much. And there are questions of taste and how much to hold back. Holding back is especially important. But how much? Carmen's a musician herself and can tell you what it is that she's doing or wants. Many other singers can't say. She taught me that all singers can put the chords in the right place for themselves; any singer can do it better for him- or herself than any accompanist. The singer knows exactly what he or she is feeling.

"So she told me to listen to singers who play for themselves. I listened to that and got a wonderful foundation for accompanying. You realize how little they're doing—and what's actually needed and what's superfluous. They give themselves exactly what they need to sing on with a minimum of embellishments. You may hear pianists play and shine; yet what they are playing may not be appropriately helpful to the vocalist.

"Carmen's a member of the musicians' union. Stand-up singers are not usually members of the musicians' union, only of AGVA [the American Guild of Variety Artists]. The only singers in the musician's union are listed as instrumentalists. Carmen started out playing and singing for herself. So, at the final encore she would always sit down at the piano. I would get a chance to go in the back and listen. She played for herself on a Japanese album. I read that she was nervous about accompanying herself on that album. But she's good; her soloing style is like Thelonious Monk's.

"When she sings ballads, she sticks to the foundational accompaniment. Most pianists embellish rather than orchestrate. Those two words are the key. Soloists embellish; they take liberties. Orchestration is not liberty. If it moves a lot, it does it for a definite meaning. Up-tempo things don't require the same support. And there's not that much space [silence] for an accompanist to fill.

"Carmen taught me about suspense. The space belongs to the singer. Carmen communicates with her music through space, too. If a pianist elaborates in a singer's space, the singer has to wait, and maybe the train of phrasing is broken. That's where taste, sensitivity come in; knowing where it's appropriate to elaborate. The audience should be able to hear what the singer's going to say next and not be diverted by a great piano embellishment.

"Also, if the pianist moves around a lot, if his notes cross over the vocalist's notes, conflict can develop, because the voice is a sensory type of instrument. It's linear. The piano mustn't be linear, too. Instead a pianist must play the chords vertically.

"Anita O'Day is a little different. She likes some linear suggestions from the piano. She improvises; so does the pianist. But still it can be overdone. So she says it's a horse race, which she always loses.

"If you run across the vocalist's lines or fill in all the space, you can ruin the suspense. Suspense has to do with the drama of the phrasing of the lyric. The space is there not just for the singer to take a breath, but as a pause before the delivery of the next line. The pulse is there all the time, but the linear part, the vocal, has breathing spaces, pauses. When the linear part stops, you have to wait for it. The silence becomes a part of the music. So you leave it. Some singers like you to fill in more than others. You must be sensitive about that. Carmen is capable of utilizing the accompaniment at its barest essentials.

"Carmen can sing so soft and so slow, she's so effective that when she comes still, the house is still. That's suspense. She can hypnotize you with one word every fifteen minutes. Ha-ha-ha. She knows how to deliver and use that space.

"In other words, she has a story to tell. She's a great storyteller. She has acting ability to. Others do, too. But she's torchy. Others may dramatize, but not as heartrendingly as she can. She can really draw you in. I think the key to it is her romance with words and syllables and her understanding of lyrics. She breaks it down to small portions and syllabizes. She can slow a word down to make sure you hear what she said. So she implies emotions. Jerome Kern and other great writers had to restrict themselves in writing the lyrics; they couldn't put in very little nuance of feeling. Carmen can bring out the implication in the thing, even a sense of profanity, just by the way she says it.

"In 'Lover Man,' she says, 'I *don't* know why ...'" She picks a negative for emphasis; that stops it. Then *'something'* in the next line. And *'lover'* in the next. She practically bites her lip to sing *'lover.'* Her improv is used to bring out the enunciation in whatever she's saying. *'The thrthrthrill...'* See how she did it!"

We were listening to a recording of "Lover Man" that Norman had arranged for Carmen twenty years earlier.

"It was thrthrthrilling," I said.

"And 'no one.' She slowed that word down. And then it gets really strong, until she finally whiles off into the word 'dream.' And 'I go to bed with a prayer that you'll make love to me....' And 'Someday we'll meet and you'll dry all my tears—then whis*pah* sweet little things....' She doesn't push places that are meaningless to pause at. Many singers do not spend time and milk each word. And at the end, 'a heavenly—dream [with the word 'heavenly' soaring upward to the word 'dream']. And afterward, she sings, 'Again and again and again' to emphasize the hugging and kissing in the lyrics. She'll hit a high note at the end and sustain it for a long time with no vibrato. She shows absolute control that way; then she will bring in the vibrato. And she's not in a hurry. It's exactly what it should be."

Some critics have said that she did not deliver lyrics sincerely until the 1980s. But Norman thinks the critics may have simply taken that long to realize her understanding of lyrics. "She knew the lyrics sincerely when we recorded 'Lover Man' on the Billie Holiday tribute album," he says. Critics have also said Carmen's voice is not pretty. "She doesn't have a soft, gentle voice, that's true," Norman says. "You wouldn't say at first that she has a pretty voice. It's coarser than Ella's or Sarah's voice. Guttier. But she has control.

"It all comes together in her emotion, control and knowledge of the story of the song. All the singers say that the words are most important, that the story is, but they don't come out with the result. And the song is singing them. To sing the song, they must pick up high points within even a syllable to get across, not just the high point of the story idea. They must isolate a syllable, or a strong word, in some kind of way to get an audience reaction.

"They have to plan ahead for that. Pros of all kinds do. When a tennis pro has just made a good shot, he has the next three already planned. There are climactic parts for a word, for a line and for a whole song. And a singer has to plan that for the whole game.

"Carmen does not supply the black church element in her music that we hear in other black singers. That used to concern her when she played black clubs until she found that black audiences ate her up. But she's not a funky-type singer. Neither is Sarah. Nor Billie. However, they had hits. Carmen's record of "Skyliner" was popular, and so was "Take Five," which she did with Dave Brubeck, but it was not a big hit. She has existed in her category, one of the greatest jazz singers who ever lived, without a major hit once in her life. Carmen's bookings are not for hot records. People go to hear her sing consistently the way she does.

"And she sings the way she feels. If she's happy or angry, then you get a happy or angry set. She works from feeling and doesn't put on a routine thing. Her intensity comes from that. If she gets up there and finds out you came to see her, she puts her heart and soul into it. But if you didn't come to see her, she is not inspired, and she will take her heart and soul and go home. If she takes her intensity home, you know it; you miss something.

"The musicians can feel it when she hits the stage. Music is her therapy. If she's down, the better the music has to be. If she's not bubbly, we'd better be damn good tonight to give her the lift. I got trained by that. Bob Cranshaw, her bassist when I went to work for her, was on top of that; I saw him make it work. If she didn't feel good, she would come in and start going through the book [reviewing the songs she would sing for the show]. She would pull out songs you hadn't played in a hundred years and throw out songs from the night before. Then Cranshaw didn't let her have any chance to find fault with us. He filled in. She's a perfectionist. As Dakota Staton's ex-husband, Haggi Talib Dawud used to say, 'Every night is Carnegie Hall.' There are no unimportant nights or sets. That's how Carmen is, too.

"You don't think in terms of an easy night. You can't lay back and just do the job. If you think you're short that night, you have to find some way to come up with it or hope somebody will bring you up.

"Psychologically, if Carmen was involved in a romance, she was more lenient on us musically. But if she had been all alone in a hotel room, it was all on the stage.

"One guy really softened Carmen. Carmen liked Frank Severino, the drummer, right from the start; she liked the way he played, and she liked him. He was not the kind of musician Carmen would usually hire. For one thing, his reading wasn't so good at that time. So she had to compromise all her standards. My love for Carmen was in duty and music. When we stayed in a place, the trio was in one hotel, and she was in another. She was the *boss*. But Frankie would go to her. He walked with her and brought her presents.

"One time we were playing the hungry i in California. Joan Rivers, the comedian, had her first engagement there at the time. The owner did not like her. She was broken-hearted. Frankie didn't know her, but he felt for her and bought her some candy. Carmen could sense that quality in him from the start. He had been afraid to go out on the road with a star as strong as Carmen. But she wooed him. She even hired his best friend, a bassist, to make Frank comfortable. Ha-ha. That was a big change for the group, right in there. We put in three or four years together, he and I. When I left, he continued. Sometimes it was just Frankie and me in her car, driving across country, while Carmen flew. We would pick up a bass player in the cities where we played.

"It was not a love affair. It was strictly friendship. More maternal love.

"Frankie was a feeling person. He was sweet; his personality applied, appealed, to a sweet side in her that you never saw. She didn't do anything different herself. Except the most DIFFERENT thing was to hire him. Ha-ha. She had to compromise some of her ABSOLUTE CRITERIA to let him get it together. And she did it. And he did it—got it together.

"Of all the singers, Carmen was my sweetheart, because of her artistry and her elegance. And because she passed it on to me. She's very together, a very strong woman. Strong is a funny word. We use it to mean resistance. In reference to Carmen, I mean she's together, straight-ahead and honest with herself, not penetrated and not going to be pushed around or let you impose on her. She's very down-to-earth. Her character and personality are very strong. Things you might criticize her for—being hard on musicians—she knows those things about herself. She *is* demanding.

"Something in Carmen's character and carriage carries over to the music. She doesn't let anyone stomp around in her life. People don't stomp around in my life, either, though I don't walk around puffed up. I'm compliant, and yet I have the capability to handle leadership; I'm straight-ahead. I think she saw these things in me.

"When I did 'Lover Man' in the tribute album to Billie Holiday, Carmen could see that I was inside of her. I didn't just do some charts. In the long run, I guess we worked so closely together that I lost my own identity. After a while, other job offers didn't come. It was a marriage. And the most important growth period of my musicianship. I was close enough to a great artist to have her transfer to me. She took time training me. I don't think she took as much time to train pianists after me. She may have just expected them to know. A lot of my musical direction was constructed while I played with her.

▶ Annie Ross had an especially intense way of hitting the high notes with the bebop singing group, Lambert, Hendricks and Ross, in the late 1950s and early 1960s. (*Annie Ross*)

▲ Dave Lambert, Jon Hendricks and Annie Ross became one of the foremost bebop singing groups in the late 1950s with their album *Sing a Song of Basie.* (*CBS Records*)

▼ Jon Hendricks, wearing the cap, with his wife, Judith, *left,* his daughter Michele and an exciting young baritone, Bob Gurland, performed and recorded the Lambert, Hendricks and Ross repertoire in the early 1980s. (*Lush Life jazz club*)

◄ A fine, sensuous stylist, an exceptional composer, Peggy Lee sang with Benny Goodman in the early 1940s. (*The Institute of Jazz Studies, Rutgers University*)

▼ The adorable June Christy followed
Anita O'Day as Stan Kenton's bandsinger.
Popular through the 1950s, Christy later
dropped out of sight, reportedly living in
California. (*The Institute of Jazz Studies,
Rutgers University*)

▲ Rosemary Clooney, who skyrocketed to
fame with "Come On-a My House," later
wrote a book about how tumultuous a
ménage it had been for the jazz-influenced
singer and her husband, actor José Ferrer.
(*The Institute of Jazz Studies, Rutgers
University*)

▲ Chris Connor was popular with jazz audiences and record
buyers in the 1950s and, fervently singing some of the standards of that era, earned good reviews in the 1980s. By then she
was living quietly on Long Island, shielded by her manager.
(*The Institute of Jazz Studies, Rutgers University*)

▲ Trumpet and flugelhorn player Clark Terry thinks of himself as an instrumentalist first, but critics are mad for his "mumbles"—a form of scat singing that can sound like a parody of the way politicians speak when running for the Senate. When Terry teaches jazz, he gets his students to scat first to help them play instruments. He was awarded a gold key for his contributions to Quinnipiac College. (*The Institute of Jazz Studies, Rutgers University*)

Clark Terry, *above*, in 1965. (*The Institute of Jazz Studies, Rutgers University*)

▲ Bob Dorough, pianist, singer and composer, got the idea that an instrumentalist could also sing a little sometimes, and went to Paris to hone his style. (*Alan C. Ross*)

▶ Dave Frishberg, pianist, singer and composer, studied journalism, which influenced his lyric writing; he calls it "a three-minute art form." Like Bob Dorough, Frishberg's a jazz boîte performer. (*Dave Frishberg*)

▲ Betty Carter, who began with the beboppers, became the most *au courant* jazz singer of the late 1970s and early 1980s, admired for her style and daring. Her performing charm can rivet an audience.

As a young woman, Betty Carter began scatting with Lionel Hampton's band and finding her way to become, several decades later, a kinetic vocal improviser. Although hardly a household word, she's the only avant-garde jazz singer who can draw very big audiences. (*Photo Files*)

◀ Sylvia Syms, who became a jazz singer despite her father's disapproval, radiates a special warmth to audiences, confiding her lyrics in them. (*Nancy Elliott*)

▶ Musicians love to work with Andy Bey, singer, composer, pianist and National Endowment for the Arts award winner because of his beautiful voice and musical agility. (*Andy Bey*)

▼ By the 1980s critics stopped saying there were no great young jazz singers because they had heard Bobby McFerrin, an innovator who can sound as much like the instrument as the instrument itself. He has collected the most eclectic group of major influences ever cited by a singer: Keith Jarrett, a pianist, who inspires McFerrin with a vision of an a cappella concert; Charles Ives, the composer; and Fred Astaire—"It's not so much his singing but the rhythmic thing he did with his feet. The way he jumps around on furniture and makes things fly through the air," says McFerrin, a lithe, slender man who literally jumps with energy in performance.

▲ Ernestine Anderson left Seattle to sing with a big band, and lived the typical gypsy life of a jazz musician on the road. Eventually she made Seattle her home base. By the early eighties she was associated with a Seattle club named for her.

▲ Janet Lawson takes fascinating musical risks, scatting works by Tadd Dameron, Charles Mingus, Thelonious Monk and original compositions by musicians in her quintet. The quintet backed her in her first album as leader, for which she was nominated for a Grammy in 1981. (*Jay Livingston*)

▲ Brazilian-born rhythm singer and pianist Tania Maria makes you very aware of the percussive power of the piano and the human voice. (*Eric Kressman*)

▲ One of the best-known jazz-influenced younger singers, Al Jarreau has gotten the *de rigueur* exposure of TV, most notably on the Johnny Carson show.

◄ Carmen Lundy is one of the fine jazz singers to have emerged recently, singing her own very interesting compositions. (*Scott Sternbach*)

CHAPTER 25

The Feeling
of Carmen McRae

The summer of 1982, in a kinetic performance at the Henry Street Settlement House on the Lower East Side in New York City, Carmen McRae showed up to work in purple pants and a bright red sweatshirt with a gigantic white flower embossed across her chest. She looked like someone's mother just in from umpiring a Little League game. She displayed no nerves; long ago she became famous for having no opening-night jitters.

At age sixty, Carmen McRae had a chiseled, Levantine face. Nothing had lowered the eyebrows peaking over the bridge of her Nefertiti-like nose; no scowl had left a rivulet in her brow. She opened her five-dollar-a-ticket show for the folks who couldn't afford uptown prices with something to give Betty Carter a scare: "Linger Awhile" à la Honneger, Stravinsky, Berg. Bizzare. Out. But swinging. It was the latest thing in jazz singing. Carmen McRae was totally with it—one of the most *au courant* and authentic jazz singers in the country.

"All my inspiration really came from Billie. She is still the best, the greatest," she has said, in interviews and onstage. You can hear it better in Carmen McRae than in Sarah Vaughan, because McRae is much less elaborate, more idiomatic and pared down. She can hold as still as the sphinx. Singing or silent, she keeps her mannerisms and gestures to a minimum to match her lean, strong interpretations.

For "Sophisticated Lady," her aristocratic nose pointed somewhere toward Mecca, transcending her sweatshirt. "Do Nothing Till You Hear from Me" followed, with its tag line assuring you that she would not be in touch; the target of her tune has ruined someone's dream, so he may sit there and wait for *nada*, said Carmen. A very fast "Foggy Day" in London town; it's the age of the Concorde jet in her interpretation.

Then she sat down on a stool: "I have a fact of life . . . 'Everything must end—nothing stays the same—everyone will change—no one stays the same—the young become the old—mysteries dooooooooooo unfold. . . .'" On another night a few weeks later, in a different mood, she sang a very embellished interpretation of "everything must change . . . sun lights uhuhuhuhuhup . . . humingbirds have to fly yeah yeah yeah . . . and music makes me cryyyyyyyy [and she was really crying]."

Carmen McRae, too, changes. From early rave reviews, to charges by the critics that she had a hard style, to counterclaims that she had a soft, light, bebop style, to further kudos that she was intently hip, which meant she was not commercially appealing. Carmen McRae has kept changing in the perceptions of the critics. They have kept hearing her differently from performance to performance, though they have kept saying she stands on the top rung of the professional ladder. The more McRae changes, the more she seems to stay with it.

Toward the end of the Henry Street set, she did a very fast "Thou Swell" with some of the best vocal improvisation ever heard. When she tried to get offstage, people yelled their encore choices at her. She said, "Get it out, or you'll get gas." And she sang her own choice.

With her very closely cropped hair, she has the least demure expression of any singer. There is no hesitancy in her delivery. When she was young, she had a Marlene Dietrich air. Now that she's an older woman, the siren mask has solidified, with a touch of arrogance, to make her look like a retired spy.

Born on April 8, 1922, in Harlem, the daughter of a Manhattan health club manager, Oscar McRae, and his wife, Evadne, who had three other children, Carmen grew up in Brooklyn and attended Julia Richman High School. She had no formal voice training, but studied piano for about five years. Her parents hoped she would become a classical pianist. "But I'd keep sheet music for pop tunes in among the classical stuff on the piano," she reminisced to the *New York Sunday News* when she was forty. "As soon as everyone was out of earshot, I let go with the pops."

One Wednesday she won as a pianist-singer at the Apollo Theater amateur night. Teddy Wilson's first wife, Irene Wilson Kitchings, also a singer, pianist and composer, tried to give Miss McRae's career an early boost. Miss McRae got an audition with Benny Goodman, who told her to come back after she had gotten some experience.

Her parents opposed a show-business career and persuaded her to take a secretarial course. She spent two years in Washington, D.C., working for the government during the war. But she had already met Billie Holiday, and the instinct to sing and play jazz won out. Back in Brooklyn by 1943, Miss McRae started working by day in a clerical job and by night in clubs. She even spent one summer as a chorus girl in Atlantic City.

From about 1944 to 1947, she worked as a singer with the big bands of alto saxophonist Benny Carter, then Count Basie, and finally Mercer Ellington, Duke's son, with whom she recorded. When Mercer's band broke up in Chicago, she decided to stay there and went out as a single act, singing and playing piano in about 1948. On a tip from a girlfriend, she auditioned for a club job as a pianist-singer, started with a two-week contract and stayed for seventeen weeks. At one time she was so broke, she told *Time* magazine, that she had to borrow money from a club owner to join the local union. A girlfriend of comedian George Kirby, who later became ill from drug addiction, McRae stayed in Chicago, "playing and singing for three and a half years," she told the *News*. "I would have stayed longer, but my parents were bugging me about coming home. So I did. I was playing a small club in Brooklyn, when I was offered a contract with a small recording company [Bethlehem]. And then things really started happening," she told *The New York Times*.

That recording contract in the early fifties helped bring her out of relative obscurity. In 1952 she began working as the intermission pianist at Minton's, a Harlem jazz club where musicians loved to jam. Then Miss McRae decided to get up from the piano bench and sing solo—not an easy move.

"Sitting at the piano and singing had been a helpful experience, but it made standing up seem pretty awkward at first," she later recalled.

Her success as a stand-up singer convinced her to forgo accompanying herself on the piano regularly in performance. The Bethlehem record led to a recording contract with a larger company, Decca. In 1954 she won the *Down Beat* magazine poll as the Best New Female Singer. In 1955 she tied with Ella Fitzgerald for the lead in the *Metronome* magazine poll.

She has commented publicly on her aesthetics, which have produced unique and elaborate melodies to support her intensely kinetic narrative of lyrics. "Every word is very important to me." Lyrics come first, then the melody. "The lyrics of a song I might decide to sing must have something that I can convince you with. It's like an actress who selects a role that contains something she wants to portray. If I don't have something new to offer in a song, well, I just won't sing it." She avoided singing "Send in the Clowns" until she learned what the title was all about. Clowns are always rushed in to distract the crowd's attention from disasters at a circus.

She has told interviewers that she's jazz oriented and has wanted only to be categorized as a good or bad singer, not necessarily a jazz singer.

She decided bravely at one time to take on the challenge of doing an album of tunes associated with Billie Holiday. It was Norman Simmons' arrangement of "Lover Man" for his boss that prompted the late Ralph Gleason, a highly respected critic, to write in the *New York Post* in 1966: "I heard her recently do 'Lover Man' with an exquisite passion I had thought never to hear in the song again." He further remarked on a longer-haired Miss McRae's sparkling eyes, lovely smile and arrogant stance, which made him think of "Lolita, not the girl next door." By that year she had been married and divorced from drummer Kenny Clarke and later from pianist Ike Isaacs, who had led the instrumental trio for Lambert, Hendricks and Ross. She was living alone in a Lincoln Towers apartment on the West Side of Manhattan. She never remarried.

She has done few interviews with the media, avoiding invitations from deejays as well as print writers, despite commercial considerations, keeping a low profile in a business where superstardom demands exposure. She did tell drummer Arthur Taylor for his book of interviews, *Notes and Tones,* about the value she places upon a singer knowing how to play piano. "Without it, I would perhaps not even be singing, or if I had become a singer, it might not be as impressive as whatever it is I do now. It is important, if you want to be a lasting artist. Any artist who really knows what he or she is doing musically will last."

That interview with Taylor contained many of Miss McRae's impassioned views on race, jazz and her love-hate affair with traveling—the chore of travel disappears each time she steps on a stage and the music goes well. With Taylor she aired issues and feelings that she does not present generally to the media. She recently told a friend that she could not deal with an interview and put off a prospective interviewer by saying that she was busy being interviewed. She graciously meets and greets people, does some natural bantering, asks a few pithy questions herself—but can draw the line brusquely at answering any.

CHAPTER 26

"We Should Have Gone More Places": Annie Ross

In the late 1950s and early 1960s, a very pretty little red-headed singer cut a deep, brief swath across the American jazz scene with the bebop trio of Lambert, Hendricks and Ross. The effervescence and genius of the trio were caught on records and films as the two men and a woman starred in the clubs—and were gone. Annie Ross retreated into the country where she had been born: England. Her repatriation was total.

At age fifty-two, she sat in her dressing room backstage at the Drury Lane's Theatre Royal, Catherine Street, London's West End, where she was costarring in *The Pirates of Penzance,* a world away from jazz. She was singing and acting the role of a rebel: Ruth, the pirate. And she contemplated a week's visit to New York City. Someone wanted to produce a concert with her, Bob Dorough and Blossom Dearie at Town Hall. "A week in New York. I'd love it!" Her eyes took on a faraway, dreamy look. But not guilelessly dreamy. They fastened upon a point she saw with surety. The eyes of a George Bernard Shaw heroine, an actress.

"Oh, I just love New York so much. It's my favorite city in the world. I was there in January and March for three weeks. I was getting ready to go back to New York and do a big number. But I went to see my agent, and I found out that I had this show. Then I

283

got a film to do, *Superman III*. That wouldn't have happened if I were in the States. Oh, I have such a good time in New York. There's someplace to go every night. The Lower East Side. The Turkish and Russian baths on Tenth Street. They have pickled herring and vodka. I love the energy and vitality of New York. I feel at home in England. I have friends, my apartment. I know the shopkeeper on the corner. But New York is where it's really at."

Annie Ross is still one of the trimmest, most attractive women to sing jazz. She arrived at the theater wearing leather slacks, a fancy belt that looked as if it were made of gold leaf and a cream-colored silk shirt. POW! She put on rimless granny glasses for a minute to examine the face, with its perfect complexion, upon which she would have to do a makeup job. She has a large makeup mirror with eight bright bulbs in a large gray and white dressing room, with four chairs, a gray telephone and a fine closet, in one of the oldest theaters in London.

She disappeared for a few minutes to do her warm-up vocal exercises, which she never used to do for jazz singing. But for eight shows a week in a play, she needs to treat her voice with particular care. "I use a real high part of my voice. I don't usually use it. Also, there's a song that falls in the middle of my range. I go from chest to head voice. The idea is to get the break out so there isn't an audible difference. The exercises make a difference. And I don't smoke until halfway through the show. And I don't drink, except for Red Zinger herbal tea, until after work."

Annie was born, one of five children, on July 26, 1930 in Mitcham, Surrey, England, to a music-hall family—right after a matinee. Her father, preoccupied with a football game that day, mistakenly registered the date as July 25. For many years she celebrated her birthday on the wrong day. Eventually she questioned her father, who said he had registered it wrong. "In fact, my whole life has been wrong," she said. But after she went back to live in England, a lot of things eventually got straightened out. "My father died in 1982. We had a wonderful New Year's together. I got to know him well and told him I loved him. I have no regrets about that." But she and her mother, who died in 1976, never became close. "I never got that one together," she said.

She began performing at age three. "It was nothing unusual in my family. All the kids did." The family, which was Scottish, lived most of the time in Glasgow and worked there and in Ireland, on bandstands and in small theaters. When Annie was four, her parents took her to New York, where she won a talent competition with Paul Whiteman's orchestra on a radio show. She wore a kilt and sang a song, which her father had written, in a thick Scottish accent. The prize was a six-month contract with MGM. Then her parents had to go back to England and look after the other children.

So Annie went to Hollywood to visit her mother's sister, singer Ella Logan, who was established in the United States. "And I just stayed out there," Annie said. "She raised me as her daughter."

While in New York City, Annie had already heard a record of Ella Fitzgerald's "A-Tisket, A-Tasket," loved it and memorized it so she could sing it. "The musicality of Ella Fitzgerald appealed to me and has never diminished one bit." In California she made a film, *The Little Rascals*, with "Our Gang," in which she sang a swing version of "Loch Lomond." But her aunt Ella didn't allow her to see it for fear Annie would become conceited. Years later, when she did see it, she thought she looked like a "terribly precocious midget."

The film contract was rather a joke. "In actual fact, they had Shirley Temple. They didn't need me." Ella Logan was against exploitation of children anyway. So Annie simply lived with her— and met wonderful musicians who often visited the house: Lena Horne, Roy Eldridge, Duke Ellington and his band, Erroll Garner. Also Annie, at age fourteen, sneaked out of the house, wearing high heels and makeup, smoking an obligatory stage-prop cigarette to make her look older, to see Slim Gaillard at Billy Berg's.

That year, too, her aunt's husband, a screenwriter, bought a record collection. "Luckily for me, it contained Lady's 'Strange Fruit'." And she learned "I Didn't Know About You," one of Duke Ellington's lesser-known tunes, which she sang for him. "He was amazed that a fourteen-year-old could sing it. Dixieland was out of the question. It was old-fashioned. I could relate much more to modern jazz. I loved the harmonies and the chords. Tunes like 'Laura.'"

"My aunt Ella was very advanced for her era, because she loved jazz. Unusual, but not so much so because Scots have moor music, which is how they communicated on the moors when the clans were fighting. It sounds like tobacco auctioneering. Like scatting. There would always be a fiddler and ad-lib scat things. So it's not hard for me to see how the Celts are very musical and attracted to jazz. Also, we had oppression. We were put down by the English, forbidden to wear a kilt. And we wanted to communicate without speaking. So we sang.

"My aunt made records in the United States with Perry Botkin, Manny Klein—a great session trumpet player. It was natural for me to gravitate to jazz. Jazz is my home, and it always will be.

"I really hated school by the time I got to the tenth grade and didn't want to continue. I was really bored. So I headed for the American Academy of Dramatic Arts in New York when I was sixteen. The next year I went back to Scotland at the request of my parents—to remeet my family," said Annie. The faraway look came back into her steady eyes. "But we didn't have anything in common. We were strangers." Dramatic pause. "So I came to London and got a job with a band in a nightclub for twenty-five dollars a week. The Orchid Room. It was a terribly snobbish, private club. When I wasn't singing, I had to sit in the ladies' room."

She went to understudy the lead in a London show starring well-known British performers. When the show closed, she went to Paris to join a vocal trio with Hugh Martin—who had written "The Trolley Song" and "Have Yourself a Merry Little Christmas"—"a trio ahead of its time," she recalled. It played a few gigs. Then Hugh got an offer to write for the *Ziegfeld Follies* and headed for New York. Annie had no thought of going back to live with her aunt.

"My aunt didn't really want me to come back. [By that time] I didn't get along with her."

"Essentially you've been on your own since you were sixteen years old?" went the question.

The head raised; the eyes focused on empty space, as if it were filled. She could have been acting in a scene out of *Barrymore Remembers*. Any Barrymore. Remembering those kinds of things that Barrymores could remember and glimpse ardently. "Yeeeeeeeessssssss." Dramatic pause, as she ambled across the room. "So I went to Paris when I was eighteen. There's nothing like being eighteen in Paris." Neither a smile nor a frown, only a controlled and lovely voice glancing the words. "I got a job with a French band, toured Europe and landed in Paris. At the time there was a great exodus of black musicians from the States. And they made Paris great."

She made her first record, "Le Vent Vert," with James Moody, the reeds player, who had gone to Paris to recuperate from the pain of it all for a few weeks and stayed three years. "I learned a lot from him. He used to have me sing down the chords. He would play a chord. I would then sing down my own chord, which was what I heard. Coleman Hawkins and Don Byas and loads and loads of musicians were there." So was Kenny Clarke, with whom Annie had a love affair—and a child, a son, who has become a drummer in the United States, as his father still is in Paris.

In many ways Paris was idyllic, personally and professionally. "I can remember in Paris the first time that someone played a record of Dizzy's, 'Things to Come.' It was as if a tornado had just whipped by. And the first time I heard Sarah Vaughan, and Lady, and 'B,' and Bird. I had been looking for something unconsciously, and suddenly there was something so breathtaking. It was a great time of discovery. Like the first time I heard the multitracking played back [on the record *Sing a Song of Basie,* which would place Lambert, Hendricks and Ross into the forefront of bebop]. It was incredible. We knew we had something. A magic moment.

"In Paris, one day, it was a hot summer day. I was in a little hotel with the windows open. Someone had gotten a record of Sarah singing 'I Cover the Waterfront.' Normally in France they bang on the wall and ask you to turn it down. And someone called out to us in part French, part English, to turn the music up. We looked out. And there was this little black face. It was Louis of the great black tap-dance team, Pops and Louis."

In Paris Annie did many things that she wanted to do because she wanted to do them, whether they were healthy or not, whether they would have long-run repercussions or not. In Paris she used drugs. "I wanted to do it," she says. She no longer does. To do the film *Superman III* while working in *Pirates,* she got up at 5:30 A.M., went to the studio until 1:00 P.M., then, on matinee days, did two shows—for one and a half months. "That's hell," she said. "The adrenaline is going at the end of the day. So I have a few drinks, watch video, sleep, get up and do my gig. I take a lot of vitamins. I hate to go to bed. I hang out far more than the kids in my show do. They ask me: 'How do you do it?' I say: 'It's years of rehearsal.' I do have terrific energy." The complexities of her once convoluted lifestyle have left no visible trace; neither are they topics she wants to dwell on publicly.

"Certain aspects of my life, I'm not ready to talk about. I don't want to hurt my kid [who, of course, has two exceptionally gifted parents]. If I do tell the truth one day, I'll involve a lot of people and private moments."

The Paris adventure lasted five musically educational, socially inhibited years. "We were writing songs every night, either at work or afterwards, hanging out. I had been writing from a very early age. My first song with any acclaim was 'Twisted' [to the Wardell Gray tune]."

That happened in New York. "I just got on a boat and went to New York." Arriving, she did a Patrice Munsel show, one of four singers behind the star, with Hugh Martin as the musical director. "I was doing great. I had an apartment and nearly a year's work. One day I was at a friend's house, Bob Bach, who was married to Jean Bach. We were in the living room when the phone rang. It was Dave Lambert. Bob was friendly with Dorothy Kilgallen. They had started a little record company. Actually they had simply put out one record of someone they liked. And Dave said he had a great idea to do this thing of Basie. 'Okay,' Bob said. So over came Jon Hendricks and Dave. They wanted to do it with six session singers, and they rang me to coach the other women on the Basie feeling. That was it. The singers didn't have the feeling."

Eventually to keep the whole idea from going down the drain, Dave and Jon went into the studio for an all-night recording session and came out with the brilliant *Sing a Song of Basie*.

"In the beginning of Lambert, Hendricks and Ross, it was good times. It was thrilling. And there was always one moment when everything jelled and swung. I had never had voice lessons. I can't read music. I can do a little solfeggio. But at that time, training wasn't done. My aunt didn't want me to have a trained voice. It would have been a great advantage. Not essential, but it would be nice."

The faraway look came again. "I left Lambert, Hendricks and Ross because it wasn't fun anymore. It was no fun. And I had always wanted to go back to England. We were over here in town, and I had personality disagreements with Jon."

"Not Dave?"

"No."

"How do I handle that?"

"People just drift apart," said Annie.

"Right in the middle of a set?"

"That's right," she said swiftly with ineffable pleasantness. (Dramatic pause.) "He's tremendously talented." (There have been long-lived difficulties in straightening out the royalties from the Lambert, Hendricks and Ross enterprises.) Says Jon: "Annie's a great lyric writer." It jibes with Annie Ross' idea that Jon gives the impression of running a tight ship, while Annie has always had her own instinctive approach to life and music. She approaches everything emotionally, she says. That was what made her a fine jazz singer. "Jazz is emotional. It's feeling. I can either pat my feet and laugh out loud—or cry. I think that if something or somebody can make you feel these two emotions, that's genius maybe. That's what great singers and actors do to me. I think it's fundamental." By the time she teamed up with Hendricks, she had already been making decisions for herself, for better or worse, since her midteens, and had written lyrics when she was fresh in New York and incredibly prescient.

Annie met Bob Weinstock, head of Prestige Records, in the early fifties. "Bob played 'Moody's Mood' for me. Then I did a wonderful promotion job on myself. So Bob handed me a list of records and said that if I heard anything I liked, I should write the words and get back to him. Times were hard. I was back the next day with the lyrics to 'Twisted.' I admired Wardell Gray certainly. And the title of his tune suggested something to me."

Years before shrinks came completely into vogue, and before the wisdom of analyzing your analyst became clear, too, Annie wrote a tune about a rebel, who as a child heard that little children were supposed to sleep tight and drank a bottle of vodka. When she grew up, her analyst told her that she went out of her mind when she left his sight. That rap was not for our heroine. She split. The upshot was a tongue-twisting ditty about how dotty a shrink can be, too.

"My concept of jazz is that it should make you feel good and smile. No deep, complicated concept. I never went to a shrink, though I knew some. I knew people who got into the black box. Maybe it's my Scottish background, but I don't go for a lot of bullshit. I have to find out the truth. And I've seen friends get so concerned with who they were. And the money and the dependency that goes along with analysis. I know a Park Avenue shrink, who is bright and makes plenty of money, but he couldn't talk to his own son. He couldn't deal with his own problems.

"I also had a friend married to Dave Garroway. I remet her. And she said, 'You must go to this shrink.' I said that I felt good. She said, 'You'll feel better.' So I went for two months. And he never said anything. I was ready to do a 'lady in the dark'* thing on the couch. Then I said, 'How do you remember what I say?' He answered, 'It's my job.' So I tape-recorded myself. It was junk. A load of garbage. And I didn't go back. Psychiatry is invaluable in some cases. But people get so intensely into themselves. There's a saying in England: you get so intense that you disappear up your own ass. And that's where, I feel, it's at.

"Also, I'm an optimist. I've always been one in the most dire moments. I always thought that as low as I was, that's as high as I'd be later on. Things balance out. If you're that low, that's how good you'll feel later.

"I've made mistakes. I wanted to do the things I did. If I decide to do a thing, I don't do it halfway."

There was, of course, more to her leaving Lambert, Hendricks and Ross than friction with Jon Hendricks. Her untamed lifestyle, including a love affair with Tony Bennett and then especially a three-year affair with Lenny Bruce, contributed to her separation from the trio and the United States. In summary, she preferred to critique certain adventures in her life as having become "no fun anymore." Apropos of drugs, she said, "I got to the very bottom and got very bored. I smoke grass now, but I don't do the other. Drugs were lethal. It had ceased to be fun, as Lambert, Hendricks and Ross had ceased to be fun."

Back in London, she went on TV as a single. "On your own, it's frightening in the beginning," with nobody singing on either side of you. But in England she began to build a new life, starting a club called Annie's Room in the West End, a few steps from the stage door of the Theatre Royal. A popular club, Annie's Room lasted only nine months "because nobody connected with it had ever run a club before. That was the problem."

Some people still ask if the club is open and add they would love to see Annie again. She knew hundreds of musicians. Man and woman, they say how much they liked her. And club owners, too.

"She's a nice lady, really great," said Anne Marie Moss, remembering many poignant and hilarious incidents from the days of Annie's Swath—the swath she cut across the United States jazz

---

* Reference is to a 1940s musical play, *Lady in the Dark*.

scene. For a while, Annie, who loved to cook and who has published a cookbook, moved into Anne Marie's Brooklyn apartment. It had been the usual thing for Annie Ross to give parties. People remember her as full of fun. Anne Marie sang at the Brooklyn Academy of Music one night and came home to find a party in full swing; Annie had cooked pasta. But as Anne Marie tasted it, she said to herself, "Mr. Clean." She went to the kitchen and found a big yellow pail that Annie had used to mix the pasta in. Normally Anne Marie used the pail to mix disinfectants with water and wash the floors. No doubt Annie had liked that shiny pot so clean from all the disinfectants. But pasta was not all that the guests were enjoying at the party. So, a little high, they didn't notice a funny taste.

In England there came a great notion to Annie Ross to settle down. An English-Irish actor, Sean Lynch, met Annie in a nightclub and elected himself. "He asked me if I were Annie Ross. I said, 'Yes.' He said, 'I love you' and left. Later, I was introduced to him by Michael Caine. Sean moved in with me. We got married and spent twelve years together." They were divorced. Then he died in a car crash. For the past seven years, Peter Jeffrey, an actor, has been Annie's "fella."

They don't live together and have no plans to marry. "I need my own space, and he needs his. It seems to last longer when you don't live with someone. I think so. And I can have my freedom and feel I can say I have two weeks off, I'm going to New York to see some shows. And he wants me to come back. He gets all the benefits of being married. I did marriage and don't think it's for me as a working woman.

"I think there are people that I've loved and will always love. And they know who they are. Lenny Bruce. I was with him for three years. I adored Tony Bennett. We always say we'll get together when we're both around eighty. We're ace friends. I'm a loyal friend. I help people. If I know someone's not doing good, I don't brag. And if I commit myself to you, I'll go through draggy hospital scenes with you. And there are people who will do the same for me.

"I've acted in some heavy, straight dramatic roles. In *Kennedy's Children.* I don't sing in *Superman III.* I think Carmen and Sarah are actresses, the way they deliver lyrics. I've been doing more acting in the past ten years. And I enjoy singing everything.

"Music is the best passport in the world. You can go to any country and bring your music to it. Lambert, Hendricks and Ross never got to Japan, where our records were well received. I've been many more places on my own than with the group. We should have gone more places."

CHAPTER 27

Tony Bennett:
"A Rhythmic Rapport"

"Boulevard of Broken Dreams" was the first hit. Then over the years came "Because of You," "Rags to Riches," "Stranger in Paradise," "I Left My Heart in San Francisco," "Put On a Happy Face," "Once Upon a Time," "Shadow of Your Smile," "I Wanna Be Loved," "I Wanna Be Around," "Here in My Heart," "The Good Life," "In the Middle of an Island," "Just in Time," "Till," "Climb Every Mountain," "Firefly," "A Time for Love," "Our Lady of Fatima" and "Blue Velvet." And another three dozen songs that he introduced.

Tony Bennett realized every singer's dream many times, turning out hit records that have sold over a million copies before, during and after the rock era, which he didn't have to lick and didn't have to join to stay popular. He just kept singing with vivacious consistency. His voice, a raspy, potent baritone that can lace a ballad with a dash of "jump," became part of the American landscape. When you hear the first few bars of any song he sings, you never have to ask, "Is that Tony Bennett?" As with Nat Cole, Bing Crosby, Frank Sinatra and a handful of others, you always recognize Bennett's Sound. He owns a few songs: "I Left My Heart in San Francisco," for one, just as Cole owned "Unforgettable," Jolson owned "Swanee," Billie Holiday "Strange Fruit," Peggy Lee

"Lover," Armstrong "Hello, Dolly," Bing Crosby "White Christmas ..." and "Sam," the piano player in *Casablanca*, "As Time Goes By."

Only one question comes to mind about Bennett's singing. What kind of singer is he? Critics call him a popular singer, though he fits fairly neatly into the jazz family. As that eminent jazz critic John Wilson said in a review: "Bennett [did] his own special thing—[built] a rhythmic rapport with his audience through his use of an emphatic, swinging beat in all his songs, both those that were essentially rhythm tunes and the ballads." Then Wilson called Bennett "pop." But drummer Kenny Clarke defined jazz as syncopated music. If it's syncopated, it's jazz, he said. Eddie Heywood, Duke Ellington and scores more agree with that simple test. Anyone can quibble subtly and brilliantly. So if Betty Carter says Bennett is a popular singer because his voice isn't soft enough, she's offering a qualification to think about. But Bennett swings. As Frank Sinatra has done so much for phrasing for a lot of singers, Tony Bennett has stood for apropos rhythmic feeling. If there were any precedent for him, perhaps it was Al Jolson.

"Are you a pop singer? a jazz singer? or a jazz-influenced popular singer who digs jazz?" I asked, sinking onto the huge, L-shaped beige-colored couch in his huge, monochromatic living room—an exceptionally soothing room enlivened by bright canvases: a street scene in progress, a lush view of a Mediterranean village and a few portraits Bennett paints. Some of his canvases sell for $10,000, his upbeat secretary, Diana Parker, seated on an angle of the L, said. She supplied more color to the interior with her bright pink- and turquoise-colored jeans and T-shirt.

"I'm a pop singer who sings jazz," Bennett, dressed mutedly, said in a whispery voice, pleasantly low key, without pretension—and with his nice nose intact. He never had it straightened, though in his early years some promoters once suggested plastic surgery. Before Bennett, only comedians such as Jimmy Durante could get away with having big noses. Bennett recalled how tough his nose made it to get singing jobs as a youngster. "I auditioned and really did good sometimes, and I lost jobs because of my nose. And everything." He smiled. "But now that I'm established, I look like the deep prototype of a singer."

I said that I didn't understand how he could define himself as a pop singer who sang jazz. He said the problem lay in the phenomenon of labels—the same problem that annoyed his old friend, Billy Eckstine. "I've always been a popular singer," Bennett said. "That's what I'll always be, God willing, if I have my health. I came from humble beginnings, so I'm a people's singer. Labels stop individualism; they stop inventiveness, expressiveness. In the music there's not enough creative feeling today.

"Outside of Louis Armstrong, Billie Holiday, Jimmy Rushing and Joe Williams, there are very few jazz singers whose whole statement was jazz. I'm a popular singer, socially speaking, who sings jazz, musically speaking."

He has recorded eighty-eight albums, created ten standard songs and had about three dozen hit records, about one a year, mathematically speaking, in the thirty years he's been "going strong"—as many hits as any singer in history. The *Los Angeles Times Calendar* magazine took a poll of the public's twenty favorite songs in 1982. Bennett's music director spotted it and noticed that Bennett was doing seventeen of the hits in his current repertoire and had recorded all of them. He has made "upwards of fifty million dollars, less than a hundred million," he said, in his career.

After his talent, two things made him a superstar; both sprang from fine judgment: "I've unconsciously migrated to where the public is at. I gravitated toward good music. After I had ten hits at CBS [Columbia Records] I decided not to compromise and just go toward good music. I worked with Ellington, Basie, Neal Hefti, Woody Herman, Earl Hines, Stan Getz, Tommy Flanagan, Bernie Leighton. And this summer my sons have booked me to work with symphony orchestras."

And he has accepted good advice, along any boulevards of broken and realized dreams he may have traveled. One of his first mentors, Pearl Bailey, told him to beware of helium on the brain—a spiritual gas that begins to make some people, as they earn a lot of money, leave the ground in an ego balloon. Judy Garland, whom Bennett has called the greatest singer of the century, advised him never to open his act anyplace without including three new songs in it. Sophie Tucker told him to have a new act whenever he played a city. "This is the healthy aspect to being a good performer," he has said. "Don't become complacent. Always take the challenge of the next three songs no matter how many sure-fire hits you have. At least you know you are going somewhere. You're moving, not standing still and riding on your last hit." Goddard Lieberson at Columbia Records told him, "Don't ever sing anything that you don't feel."

"That's why I don't like to sing a bad song," Bennett has said. "I've discovered if you really mean what you are saying in a song, it can be communicated to an audience." Attracted by the needlework and fine artistry in songs, he gave up clowning self-consciously and came out singing with natural feeling for his first singing job at age sixteen, in a Queens club, for fifteen dollars a weekend plus tips. He was basically self-taught. Public school music classes were "boring," because "bored teachers" gave their students an uninspired surfeit of Gilbert and Sullivan. But Tony met one hip teacher named Sonberg. He had a fine phonograph—"a mindblower in those days," Bennett reminisced, "and I played an Art Tatum record. It exploded my mind. Tatum was one of a kind, a musical monster. I still warm up and do scales with him. I phrase like he plays. He does a production on a song. He'll do eight bars out of tempo, go into the tempo, change a key, go back out of tempo again. Where it becomes predictable, he stops it. You're forced to listen all the time. He always does the right tempo, the right production.

"Everyone's afraid of jazz. The record companies are afraid that people won't buy jazz. So you can go so far into it, and then it's taboo. But actually the best talent comes out of it. It's like nature, nothing to be afraid of, it's just here, and great, to have fun with. I was influenced by Mel Torme, Billy Eckstine and Sarah Vaughan. 'If You Could See Me Now'—that song by Eckstine and also by Vaughan comes to mind. 'B' and Sarah were spearheads of popular singing. They started a whole new way of singing when they were with Earl Hines. Later 'B' had his own band, with Dizzy and Fats Navarro and all those great musicians in one band. It was a tremendous musical era, with complex music, serious math. A whole new music came out of it.

" 'B,' who's my good buddy, is ten years my elder. He taught me about how things go down and what to expect. When I was going to do my first European tour, he told me about the promoters, what to expect from them, from the audiences, what to expect in general. It happened exactly the way he said it would."

Previous to his first European tour as a singer in the fifties, Bennett had spent about two months with the 63rd Infantry Division

in combat in Europe. "Not long, but it was combat," he said succinctly. Afterward, still in Europe, somewhere near Mannheim,
Germany, news columnist Sidney Fields reported that Bennett
remet a black high school buddy, Frank Smith. Corporal Smith, a
music lover and a Protestant, invited music lover Corporal Benedetto, a Catholic, to go to church to hear the music. Afterward, they
had dinner together.

"A mess sergeant with a southern accent came over and told me
Frank would have to eat in the kitchen," Bennett told Fields. "I
guess I blew my top because next day I was busted down to private." "And shipped off to the detail of digging soldiers' bodies
from mass graves and putting them in individual coffins," Fields
wrote.

"But that didn't last long," Bennett recalled, "because a Major
Leftkoff got me out of it and put me in as a music librarian with the
Special Services, American Forces Network, in Germany. I sang,
too, in 1945 or 1946." After a few art courses at the University of
Heidelberg, he returned to New York to go to school on the G.I. Bill
at the American Theater Wing, where he studied singing with
Miriam Spier on Fifty-second Street, across from the Three Deuces.
Spier taught him to imitate the instrumentalists: Getz, Garner,
Tatum. Bennett liked Bing Crosby, too. "He knew just what to do."
Bennett studied dramatics, diction—and tried to get work, without
much luck, and listened to his mother encourage him to keep study-
ing. She kept at her dressmaking job.

"I was gambling on myself in those days," Bennett has said. An
old friend, Fred Katz, who was working as Lena Horne's accompanist, got theatrical manager Ray Muscarella to listen to Tony sing.
Muscarella put Bennett on the payroll at fifty dollars a week for
three years. "He bought me clothes and instruction," Bennett said.

Eventually he won second prize, runner-up to Rosemary
Clooney, on Arthur Godfrey's *Talent Scouts* show. Comedian Jan
Murray hired Bennett and Clooney for his TV show *Songs for Sale*.
The next break came through Pearl Bailey, who was singing at a
Greenwich Village club. By chance, she heard Bennett audition
and called out: "Hire that kid."

Bob Hope caught his act, changed Bennett's name from Benedetto (and even from Joe Bari, a briefly used stage name) and took
him touring. By 1950 Bennett had a short-lived hit with a demon-

stration record of "Boulevard of Broken Dreams." Mitch Miller heard it and signed Bennett for Columbia. Next came a million seller, "Because of You."

In Cleveland in 1951, Bennett, a star, met Patricia Ann Beech, a nineteen-year-old fan from Galion, Ohio, in a club where he was working. On the wedding license the next year, Bennett gave a River Edge, New Jersey, address, the house he had bought for his mother as soon as his fortunes rose. That ended a seventeen-year stint for his mother in a factory. Bennett and his wife were next reported living in a modern apartment house on a cliff in Riverdale, the Bronx, with a glass wall through which to view a frieze of the Hudson River and the George Washington Bridge. Tony and "Sandy," his wife's nickname, had one son, D'Andrea (Danny), and were awaiting the birth of another child, who would turn out to be a son, Daegal, in the early 1950s. With only one child, Sandy had been traveling with her husband, estimating that their baby, Danny, had logged 50,000 miles. But Sandy said she thought she might quit traveling when the second child was born.

Eventually the Bennetts bought a house in Englewood, New Jersey. Family life had its light moments. Bennett recalled how Dizzy Gillespie once came to the door, which one son opened. Dizzy, who can be the most gently witty man, said, "I'm Dizzy." The boy, thinking the stranger felt faint, "told him to sit down," Bennett recalled, laughing heartily.

Bennett said he was always "moving around," on the road as a singer in those years—and ever after. That constant drain on a musician and his family added to whatever strains the Bennett family may have had. By 1960 Bennett and Sandy had a trial separation that lasted thirty months. Despite his friendships and associations with musicians and his own career, which kept him occupied, Bennett suffered from his family's breakup. He asked Sandy to try again. She agreed. He tried to spend more time at the house in Englewood. But in the long run, the marriage didn't survive the decade. By mid-1970 Bennett and his second wife-to-be, Sandy Grant, had a daughter, Joanna.

Distressed by his situation, still only legally separated from his first wife, Bennett told Kay Gardella of the New York *Daily News;* "I'm the kind of person who dislikes scandal of any kind. My situation with Sandy may seem unnatural to some. My own consolation is to look back at some of the masters like Frank Sinatra and Char-

lie Chaplin and other great performers whose style of life clashed
with society because of their intense concentration on their work."
He added that he was "convinced the average person can't understand an artist" and insisted "the real sin in this world is not love
but gossip. It's a very vicious thing, and I'm not a vicious person. I
know I'm a good person, who loves people and loves to entertain,
which is why any reference to my private life is very confusing to
me. All I want to do is sing and make people happy."

The press in his hometown did not portray Bennett's new family
as scandalous, having always regarded him as an engaging, amiable
personality, devoid of hype, deserving of fame—the most cuddly of
stars.

He and his second wife had two daughters, Joanna and Antonia,
who were twelve and eight respectively in 1982. That marriage
ended in the late seventies. Bennett's mother died in 1977. He still
shies away from talking about his family life, saying only, "I like
my ex-wives very much." His sons, Danny and Daegal, began singing in a rock group called Neon.

"They have great voices and do a lot of work. The kids were always around music. They were around the stand when I went out
with Basie in the summers. They were around in a position to meet
the Beatles and Dizzy Gillespie and others." So the kids learned
without Bennett giving them formal lessons. "I'm blessed with nice
children that sing well. I can't ask for more," he said. At one time as
part of their act, which has played at CBGB's and Trax, two New
York clubs attracting young crowds, one son dyed his hair blue, the
other went pink-colored; each son had a chemical assignation. It
amused Bennett in retrospect to think about the colors temporarily
on his kids' heads as much as the same colors cheered him up, when
he noticed them on his tanned secretary, Diana Parker. "I like those
colors," he noted.

Color constitutes a great deal of where it's at for Bennett, who
went through "a dramatic transition," he said, in the early 1980s.
He was spending as much time painting as he did singing. Johnny
Carson displayed some Bennett canvases on the *Tonight* show, one
of the greatest forums in the country for spreading the word about
anything. Afterward Bennett found his canvases in demand. Wally
Findlay, a prestigious gallery in New York City, suggested that
Bennett hang a show there.

"Would that be good?" he asked his secretary offhandedly.

"It's intimate," she said.

"And a good address," Bennett mused practically.

"The public loves that," Diana mused. "They get to see the private Tony. What he does with his time when he's not out front singing for them. It's an insight into the man."

Bennett has been one of the few musicians to branch out to another art instead of another instrument. Astoundingly, he's a good painter. Astoundingly, because painting has no technical relationship to music. Both arts usually demand total concentration. But the lushness of his music, the emphatic beat have shown up again in the bluntly drawn, lush greenery of his landscapes.

CHAPTER 28

Rosemary Clooney: Interpretations from the Labyrinth

Ample, dressed regally in bright red, Rosemary Clooney inspired a Carnegie Hall audience to give her a special ovation for some of the best singing of the 1983 Kool Jazz Festival. A series of little miracles brought her to that point. First of all, Rosemary Clooney says she has always had bad judgment for picking tunes that will be hits. " 'Come On-a My House.' I really hated the song and the whole idea." She told Mitch Miller at Columbia Records, to which she was signed, that she didn't want to do the tune. He threatened to fire her.

"We had quite a few takes before Mitch was satisfied with the recording.... I ended up with an Italian accent for an Armenian song ... it was the only kind of accent I knew. Thanks to all the guys in Tony's [Pastor's] band who had always taken me to meet their families on the road.

"With 'Come On-a My House' recorded, I went on to other things with hardly a thought that anything good would come of that session. Too many things had gone wrong, plus which I still didn't like the song," she wrote in her autobiography.

The song made her a star. In the summer of 1950, she had been making only $150 a week, "doing all sorts of odd engagements." Then the song started blaring from every Broadway store. Nobody

ever again had to announce her as "Rosemary Clooney, the singer."
It was ROSEMARY CLOONEY. She made the cover of *Time* mag-
azine; other major magazines and newspapers did stories about her.
By Christmas 1950, she had become a household word. Eventually
"Rosemary Clooney" was shortened to "Rosie"; she joined the con-
stellation of stars known by their first names.

Rosie followed a tortuous route through the complications of a
poor, unstable family life to fame and fortune. In her autobiography *This for Remembrance,* she documented her father's drinking
problem, her broken home, her mother's "desertion," when she went
to California to make a new life for herself with a new husband, a
sailor. Rosemary and her sister, Betty, lived with their father quite
happily while he worked in a defense plant in Cincinnati, temporarily on the wagon. Then he went on a binge in April 1945.

Betty arranged for the sisters to audition for a radio show—and
even negotiated an advance payment for carfare home. So the teenage Clooney sisters, Rosemary in high school, Betty in junior high,
began taking care of themselves totally.

The big-band era had been their music school. In a Cincinnati
drugstore, the sisters had put their nickels in a jukebox and
listened to Harry James records—"Velvet Moon," "I Had the
Craziest Dream," "It Seems to Me I've Heard That Song Before"—
while their father bought them butterscotch sundaes. Bandsingers
were among Rosemary's greatest influences, she recalled: "Helen
Forrest was a big favorite of mine. Doris Day. Sinatra was my favorite. I once called him long distance from Cincinnati. The poor
girl who answered the phone asked me whatever gave me the idea
that he'd be at that number. I said that I had seen his number in a
fan magazine. I never got over that bobby-soxer feeling about him.
He made you think and feel a little more. Bing Crosby I loved for
other reasons. He was more subtle. He trod lightly in your life. So
he was always there."

So Rosie has trod a fine line musically. That is, some say she's a
popular singer. A few say she's a jazz singer. She doesn't claim to
be more than jazz influenced—but that markedly, and made all the
more impressive for her particularly lovely voice.

"It's hard for me to characterize my own voice. Earthy. Round.
Sultry," she said recently. "There's a sense of humor with what I
do; it's subtle. And I sing in time." She once spent a day with Billie
Holiday, drinking Orange Blossoms in Rosie's California house.

Billie talked about things not in her book. For example, Tony Pastor had found a doctor who would treat her (Billie) for an illness when she was touring in the South. "I loved her so much," Rosemary Clooney said. "I think her ability to show pain was something that I identified very strongly with. I don't know if I do that, but I certainly recognized her honesty."

Other notable influences came from jazz. "Mildred Bailey's easy swing. Bing got so much from her, and I through Bing. I never met her but I knew how Bing worked; I could almost see the pulse more than in a hard, swinging singer.

"And Ethel Waters' attention to lyrics. The words meant so much to her. Her performance as an actress comes across. Ella Fitzgerald for the just damn good professional doing it all the time. With her tremendous intonation, she sings in the center of a note. She sounds like a tiny girl, with innocence and a new approach each time she sings."

Rosie worked and recorded with some of the greatest jazz musicians in the world: Crosby, Frank, and Ellington, and Billy Strayhorn. In her autobiography she tells of a "highlight": working with Billy Strayhorn.

"Billy had such symbolism," she recalled; he instructed her in the proper interpretation of "Blue Rose," telling her to become a girl combing her hair for a date, listening to Duke Ellington on the radio, so Rosie would sound spontaneous, not orchestrated. "I think that came across. Such imagery you wouldn't believe. He did that every time," said Miss Clooney by phone, the warmth and enthusiasm in her voice undiminished by long distance.

"I listened to Johnny Hodges slide to the edge of being out of tune. Strayhorn told me, 'Don't do it as much as Johnny. He's a master.' We fixed chicken soup together. I never saw the haunted side that must have been there," she said about Strayhorn, who wrote the haunting jazz classic "Chelsea Bridge."

"I have an interpretive sense that's good. I'm not inventive," said Miss Clooney, "but I'm inspired by jazz musicians. They listen to the way you're feeling in a minute in a four-bar phrase. They're much more sensitive to what I do. Scott Hamilton, Warren Vaché, Cal Tjader would respond to humor faster than anything.

"In myself I listen for overall feeling. I don't pull it apart. It could always be better. If the feeling's okay, I leave it alone."

The feeling's okay, now, spiritually and musically. But in a fine biography of a show-business personality, Miss Clooney with Raymond Strait tells graphically of a nightmarish mental collapse abetted with pills. The story has a candor and naturalness that also come through when she nurtures a song huskily, almost maternally.

From obscurity she traveled to stardom, quickly followed by a love affair with a great actor, José Ferrer, many years her senior, who revealed on their honeymoon that his idea of a husband-wife relationship was a joust.

She wrote of hearing him tell another man about a raunchy, casual sexual encounter with a woman who went backstage to see him, the great José Ferrer. "I was crushed," Miss Clooney wrote. "Just crushed. . . . All of that had happened while I was rushing to finish 'White Christmas' in California. So I could be with my husband in New York. I started to cry and was still crying when he came up to bed. . . . He asked me, 'What's the matter?' I said, 'I heard your conversation, Joe. All of it.' I'll never forget the look of dismissal in his expression when he said to me, 'Maybe we should call it off right now.' It wasn't ever going to be that easy. I wouldn't allow it. . . . I found myself saying, 'No, no, let's try.' "

The marriage went on; five children were born. The couple divorced, remarried and finally abandoned the cruel relationship. But it died hard for Miss Clooney, who had maintained a curiously maternal attitude toward it. Another relationship, an affair with a young married man, foundered on his unavailability and precipitated a pill-popping period in Miss Clooney's life and her nightmarish mental breakdown.

She seems to have looked into an abyss, sighted an angel of death and finally sung, charmed or soothed it into submission. She rebuilt her career and developed a relationship with a man she had known and almost married when they were young and she was dating José Ferrer. She took the path with Ferrer, built a life with him, dismantled it to begin again, as she wrote in her autobiography. (So we are all strange children, groping around in the dark.)

CHAPTER 29

One of Billie's Children: Sylvia Syms

In the 1930s, Fifty-second Street in New York City was swinging with a lot of little clubs through which so many of the best musicians passed. The clubs were the Three Deuces, the Onyx, the Downbeat, Tony's, Club 18, Kelly's Stables, the Famous Door— and, headquarters of the Street, Birdland; Bebop City around the corner at 1619 Broadway in the Brill Building (Tin Pan Alley); the Royal Roost at Broadway and Forty-ninth Street. Hundreds played in these clubs until the street gave way to strip joints in 1948. Birdland closed its doors in the midsixties. Then the street got its official name, Swing Street, enshrining its history.

Famous singers worked here: Billie Holiday, Billy Eckstine, Sarah Vaughan, Ella Fitzgerald, Maxine Sullivan, Al Hibbler among them. And a young hopeful, Sylvia Syms, showed up in the clubs, looking for inspiration.

At age fifteen, in the summer of 1939, she began sneaking out of her family's apartment, took a subway to Fifty-second Street, and stood outside one of the clubs, listening to Billie Holiday. And, Sylvia says, one night Billie hid her in the checkroom and took Sylvia to Harlem, where she met wonderful musicians who would become her friends.

Sylvia's father, a Russian immigrant, was alarmed. He had seen a sign in a mid-Manhattan hotel: ENTERTAINERS NOT WELCOME. Despite his opposition, she pressed on to become a singer. "I wasn't good-looking, so I couldn't get a band job. But I was darling, bright and honest, and I wanted to sing so bad. Ha. I probably sang so bad, too."

Her first pro job, for twenty-five dollars a night, was with a group at Kelly's Stables in 1942—"nobody special," she said. "I was good enough. An amateur. Benny Carter's band was there. He was my friend. Nat Cole had an intermission trio. That was a wonderful time. I tried to imitate Billie. It was a bad imitation. Then I found my own feeling, time, and my own ferocious tenderness. I wasn't polished until I went to work at the Little Casino in the Village. I worked every night; I started to grow."

Mike Lerner, of *Down Beat* magazine wrote a rave review: "He said I was better than Lee Wiley and Ella Fitzgerald and Billie Holiday and Mildred Bailey all wrapped into one. That was the kiss of death. People came looking for that. How can you live up to that? Nobody could recognize me. After that I worked in little joints."

Reminiscing in 1982, having outlived Billie Holiday by several decades, Sylvia Syms gave a funny description of her career, which has included praised performances in Broadway hits and clubs. "I never did much but work in clubs. I did a 1949 revival with Mae West on Broadway. I played a shoplifter, sang a terrible song called 'Yipayeddiaya," shook my skirt from side to side and waved feathers. My first record burned down before it was released." (A fire destroyed it just after it had been produced.) "I did it with Stan Kenton and Shelly Manne; Neal Hefti wrote the arrangements. A few years later I made a record for Atlantic with Barbara Carroll; that was my first release."

The way it has really been: Sylvia never got by on looks and a good figure. Her stage presence gave her success on Broadway. And her easy, swinging style, both personally and professionally, and her sense of humor earned her the respect of jazz musicians and club owners, though she calls herself jazz influenced, not a jazz singer. At age 59, about five feet tall (or less) and plump in the Jimmy Rushing tradition, with straight, reddish-blond hair, she was showing up for nightly performances at the chic Café Carlyle in bright-colored, loose-fitting dresses, looking like the mother of the bride. One night, two men were smoking cigars. The men wouldn't extinguish them, though the maître d' made a request. Sylvia glared at them for a long time, tsk-tsking to herself—"Isn't that awful?"—waiting in the back of the café while her trio warmed up. The smoke made her gasp; she has only one lung and suffers from emphysema. But blanketed in perfume, as if it would insulate her against the smoke, she cued herself and went onstage.

Her voice was strong; the way she took possession of the lyrics— Billie's biggest influence on her—made her style venerable; her charming patter engaged the audience as she told apocryphal tales about tunes in her repertoire. She confided her plans to make an album with her friend Sinatra as conductor. She mentioned her weight. (One afternoon, in rehearsal at another club, she walked to the open-hearth kitchen and boomed: "Where's the cook? Hi. You're the important one here. You're the one I want to see. You're going to keep me looking the way I do!") She said she was no longer young. The audience became comfortable with her candor. She has the knack of making people feel like confidants.

She tailored her repertoire to her age, opening with a salute to her first romance . . . long ago. In "That Old Devil Moon," the pronunciation held a trace of New York in the short *a*'s in "can't" and "candor." Miss Syms was herself. Her voice at fifty-nine sounded lower, louder and rougher at times, with more vibrato than in her younger days. On records it was clear, on-key, full of musicality— and sexy; qualities that all singers dream of having in one package. Though Sylvia's voice grew thicker with age, it also ripened. She has remained Little Miss Totally Tuneful. As the smoke evaporated, her breathing became less audible, her delivery smoother, reminiscent of her youth, when her voice sounded silken.

Early in the show, she did the polished jazz musician's trick of gliding into a song that came out of the chord changes of the previous song. ("No chantoosey should do a show without Porter . . . he even wrote the Yale song," she confided.) She started the verse to Cole Porter's "Night and Day"—"Like the beat-beat-beat of the tomtom . . ." Then she took the last word of the verse, "You you you," and alighted onto a pedestal of "You'd Be So Nice to Come Home To," which led quickly to: "I've Got You Under My Skin." The word "you" operated as a pivot.

"That makes it fun and interesting," she said another night, preparing in her Carlyle suite for another show. "Medleys are dumb unless they're meaningful. If you have five different tunes that are disjointed, that's no good. They have to have an attachment to each other. They can be a medley of spring songs or all the seasons, but they have to have a relationship. And you shouldn't do more than one medley in a show. People want to hear the totality. How it begins, evolves and resolves."

That's her taste, for a simple, earthy showmanship, with a line of patter to add interest. Mel Torme may do two medleys.

There's richness, too, in Miss Syms' phrasing and emphasis on certain words; you remember "Dream Dancing with You" as the aura of her singing long after the show ends. What she has given over to age has been replaced by direct regard for the audience. She can deliver a torch song to illuminate the sensibilities of a mature woman in love with a married man; she explains her rationale for sharing him rather than giving him up. Syms is an articulate singer with the knack of singing a song as if she had composed it herself.

While she joked about her own résumé, she viewed her future with high seriousness. "I'm toying with the idea of doing 'Love for Sale.' I did it years go." Her eyes narrowed. "But now the problem is that the song advertises young love." Sylvia Syms was analyzing that. "I've been trying to contemplate how. Has anyone ever considered what happens to a hooker when she gets old? So there's this old hooker standing there, still trying to make a living. It's the visual of a song that makes it work for me.

"Some material is ageless, some pointless. I've always sung standards—songs that can be written tomorrow. Anytime. And I still do torch songs. I do one that's walk-in-front-of-a-truck-time. 'Time Heals Everything' by Jerry Herman. It says: yes, I'm going to forget you, I'll forget everything about you one day, I'll forget how you look and everything we meant to each other, but goddam it, when is that day going to come?

"I couldn't sing 'The Boy Next Door,' because the boy next door is a grandfather. You must choose what you're best for. What makes an individual? Ninety thousand people sing a song. But each time, it's my musk, attitude and relationship. I never studied music or acting. I have an animal sense. It comes with time, with learning your craft, something you must never stop learning. Then you take the lessons to heaven or hell and start a class there."

When she had learned enough to be considered established professionally, at age twenty-six in 1949, she married Brett Morrison, who played The Shadow on radio. "A wonderful man. He died about two years ago. We were long since divorced and remarried. But he was always special to me; he goes with me everyplace." She showed a green ring that he had given her. "The marriage broke up because I was young and dumb and didn't know how to be married. A marriage was a partnership. I didn't understand that. I still don't, really. I tried it again with a very important man. I won't tell you who. He doesn't need the publicity." (It was the late actor, Ed Begley, from whom she was divorced.) "I would live in sin with a musician but never marry one. By the very nature of their job and travels, musicians are made for polygamy. It's natural. How can a guy go on the road and not fool around? You have a better crack at marriage if you don't expect a long-term love affair. A relationship or a friendship is much better."

A mechanical voice interrupted her. A talking clock on her makeup table gave a few beeps and announced the time nasally. She smiled. "I live my life by that. It wakes me up every morning. It plays the 'War of 1812 Overture.' And if in five minutes you don't get up, it yells, GET UP! GET UP! GET UP! AND THE MUSIC GETS LOUDER AND LOUDER! It's a fabulous thing." She popped a piece of Aspergum into her mouth to feed the frogs in her throat.

She said, "Now where were we?"

I said, "Talking about love. But we really should talk about music."

Her wide smile came with lightning speed. "It's the same thing. Without anger, lust, agony, ecstasy, there would be no music."

CHAPTER 30

The Lure of Birdland
and Environs, Leading
to a Night in El Paso

It was probably the best-known jazz club the country ever knew. In 1959, ten years after it opened on Broadway between Fifty-second and Fifty-third streets, Birdland enticed Anne Marie Moss to leave her quiet home in Toronto. Maynard Ferguson invited her to sing with his band at Birdland. She expected elegance, because of Birdland's reputation. Instead she found a cellar. "But it was fancy musically," said Anne Marie, a stately blonde with a robust, healthy smile. She can swing with such production, in no hurry, that her work sometimes sounds like jazz *lieder*.

Eventually, through her own work and her marriage to Jackie Paris, a premier jazz singer on Fifty-second Street in the forties, she became a fixture on Manhattan's jazz scene. But her finances were less stellar. She paid about $300 rent while earning $125 weekly. She recalled visiting a higher-paid musician's apartment. He told her to take some ham in the kitchen. "So I went in and saw so many roaches on the ham, I thought the cloves were moving."

Long before then, Jackie Paris, who trained by listening to Ella Fitzgerald on radio, crossed the Hudson River from Nutley, New Jersey. By the late forties, he had worked for twenty-three weeks at the Onyx Club, recorded with Dizzy Gillespie and sung with Art Tatum.

310

" 'You've got something,' Tatum said to me. I nearly flipped. I grew up in the bebop era, with all the best musicians. That experience you can't buy. The great moments of learning something every day," Paris reminisced.

Jeri Southern felt the lure of Birdland, too. At home in Royal, Nebraska, she learned—via records and radio—from Nat Cole, Sarah Vaughan, Mary Ann McCall, Mel Torme and Frank Sinatra. "Sinatra above all," Jeri said recently in Hollywood, where she teaches piano and orchestrates for films. "He considered a lyric above all, with a sensitivity to the individual words, phrases and the total song."

By the end of the forties, she had made her way to the Hi-Note Club in Chicago, where her warm, intimate style touched Anita O'Day. She called Jeri "a wonderful jazz singer." Monte Kay, Birdland's manager, stopped at the Hi-Note and asked Jeri:

"Would you like to work at Birdland?"

"That excited me tremendously. I asked about money," she recalled. "He said, 'You'll be playing intermission. A hundred and fifty dollars.'

"I said, 'A hundred and fifty dollars isn't much on the road.'

"He said, 'You call New York the road?'

"Ha-ha. Birdland wasn't the road, of course."

The money barely covered her living expenses. But she stuck it out, meeting Fitzgerald, McRae, Vaughan, Sinatra and Peggy Lee. Then she recorded for Decca and had a hit with "When I Fall in Love." Eventually the itinerant life of a singer palled; she settled in California, drifting away from her early jazz influence.

About the same time, Ernestine Anderson came off the road with Lionel Hampton and decided to try her luck in New York. She was quick to make friends, find her way, learn what was happening. But it was never easy going, as almost every jazz singer's life story has suggested. Pianist Norman Simmons, who has worked with Ernestine, can remember meeting many musicians through her in New York and nearly starving to death in her apartment. Friends don't necessarily equal enough work. He went back to Chicago to join Dakota Staton, then a newly risen star with *The Late Late Show*, an album, and concert and TV dates.

Ella Fitzgerald and Sarah Vaughan may have earned astronomical fees and royalties. Ella earns as much as twenty-five thousand dollars for singing at concerts and corporate functions, where she is treated royally with all the trimmings and pomp that big corporations can afford to lavish on stars. And she reportedly earned fifty thousand dollars for singing her heart out on a Continental Airlines flight in 1983. Such is not the case with scores of fine singers. Ernestine, nominated for a Grammy award for her 1981 album, has devised another method for economic survival. She has established home base in her parents' house in Seattle, Washington, where she became involved in a club, Ernestine's; she travels to gigs all over the world.

Anne Marie Moss teaches in her apartment and sings in clubs. She lives in one of the loveliest neighborhoods in New York: the Upper East Side in the Sixties, in, to all appearances, a charming brownstone. The bathtub is in the kitchen, the toilet in the hallway—typical, old-fashioned design. She lived there with Jackie Paris during their marriage and remembers when they had no rent money because they had cleaned their clothes for the next performance. Sometimes they found no dressing room at a club and had messed their clothes in the kitchen. Anne Marie cracks jokes, in performance, about peeling carrots in her kitchen and spattering the living room couch because the apartment is so small.

Financial logistics for wonderful singers who have not become top stars are bone-wearying and frustrating. Prickly wit becomes a *modus operandi* and *vivendi*.

Carol Sloane, one of the finest of the post-Fitzgerald generation of singers and a special admirer of Carmen McRae, whom Carol calls "The Teacher," tried living in New York with all the financial and professional pressures that the city entails. She arrived as rock began ruling. Eventually she moved to Chapel Hill, North Carolina, where she books entertainers for a jazz club, at which she sings too, and travels half the year to sing jazz in other clubs.

In 1958 at age twenty-one, Carol sang in New York with Les and Larry Elgart; at the Village Vanguard with Coleman Hawkins; with Ben Webster and many others. She sang at the Newport Jazz Festival, recorded with Columbia, and went on the Johnny Carson show. "Awards in themselves," she said. "I'm always eager to do it—and humble. I hope it just goes on, 'cause I love to sing."

Ernestine Anderson's parents moved from Houston to Seattle to get their teenage daughter away from clubs. Right away she found work in Seattle. "But I had a one-track mind," Ernestine recalled.

"I could only think of music." Once, as a child, she had gone "wrong" singing in church and stopped. Someone told her never to stop. With that in mind, she kept going during a contest to win her first professional job for twenty-five dollars, improvising around the melody of a pop song after she had told the band to play in the wrong key. Later a musician said she was a jazz singer. "I was just trying to save my neck," she recalled.

Begin with her cascading Afro or her brightly decorated, long corn rows, her high, round cheeks, her perfect snub nose, her slightly protruding two front teeth. In profile she looks like a teeny-bopping cheerleader, except for long false eyelashes, which she sometimes wears to breakfast. Even then she looks like fun, full of life.

Definitely one of the most emotional singers, in performance she seduces an audience and the piano player, and convinces herself with a sensual, chanting rendition of "Teach Me Tonight," prowling the stage, chanting, "Tonight ... mmmmmtonight ... heh-heh-heh ... tonight is all right, you can reach me tonight." She looks high. Her normally alert eyes are half closed. Her speech slurs. The piano player has all he can do to keep playing as she leans toward him and signifies (teases) with a few "tonights." Ernestine flirts outrageously, playfully and kittenishly. Ella Fitzgerald, on this tune which is so popular with female jazz singers (each with her own idea of what she would like to learn and teach), swings it straightforwardly, with musical-theater finesse. Every singer puts the imprint of her own emotions and goals on the songs. Ernestine is churchy, with something else up her sleeve. She sermonizes "tonight" for a long time, never quitting, with her early lesson made manifest.

It has kept her going through the loneliness of touring, the failures of several marriages, and the disappointments of showing up for gigs and finding them canceled. All of that and more has happened, making the jazz life arduous. "But I can say a lot more musically than one-on-one. Singing's an outlet for me. As far back as I can remember, I wanted to sing," she said.

Carol Sloane recently arrived at a New York club to find no dressing room. "It's so important. A place to recharge. A gig is not a jam session. And if you have any sense, you don't party all night," she said. She sat at tables with musicians who had come to hear her—and got the shock of her life when she touched a railing next to the piano as she sang; she thought she was being electrocuted. "About club conditions, the piano, air-conditioning, sound system, you find out the truth when you get there. We've all been through it many times."

Sometimes a singer must compete with ringing telephones and noisy cash registers. The conditions are high-tension, not to mention the excitement of the backup trio and the singing itself. Carol takes classical music tapes on the road to calm herself down later in her hotel room.

Sometimes there's absolutely nothing a singer can do but weep or laugh, even years later. Anne Marie Moss recalls a night in El Paso, Texas, with Maynard Ferguson's band. A praying mantis flew into her mouth. "I was singing 'The Song Is You.' Then I took a deep breath. The praying mantis flew in. I was singing so fast that I was chomping him to death. I was spitting all over the audience. They started clapping. I told them, 'I'm not scatting. I'm spitting!' "

CHAPTER 31

Jazz-Boîte Singing

If you have ever thought of a boîte singer as a special breed with ineffable charm and an aura of lightness and worldly wisdom, you'd be right about veterans of the boîtes—musicians such as Dave Frishberg, who appears in intimate clubs and sings his own tunes, among them "Van Lingle Mungo," a recitation of a list of 1940s baseball players. The song would be zany were it not for its melancholy melody and Frishberg's interpretation, by turns light-toned on some syllables, drawled out thoughtfully on others. When his niece heard it, she said, "I like that song about your childhood friends."

Frishberg has also written "Sweet Kentucky Ham": "It's ten P.M. They're rolling up the sidewalks in Milwaukee and the only place to eat is just across the street. So you sit there with a bowl of navy bean. And you turn the pages of your magazine. You feel you want to quit while you're behind. 'Cause you've got Sweet Kentucky Ham on your mind." And he has written "I'm Hip," with a wry lyric about a naïve man who tries to dress himself up in *au courant*, trendy activities and calls himself a sophisticate. He wrote the tune with Bob Dorough, a jazz singer, pianist, composer and occasional arranger. Dorough and Frishberg met in New York City, where anybody in the music business can expect to meet everybody else, no matter where a musician comes from originally. Frishberg came from St. Paul, Minnesota. Dorough, who developed musically in a hit-and-miss way, was born in Arkansas on December 12, 1923, with the Depression ahead—a talented boy from a poor white family in the South. To hear him tell it, it sounds like the kind of trap you almost never get out of.

Occasionally the family had a piano in the house—but no phonograph. Now and then the family moved, "since my father was always looking for a deal," Dorough recalled. Dorough's high school bandmaster in Plainview, Texas, discovered Dorough's musical aptitude. After that, Dorough thought about music, analyzing intervals and harmonies. He stayed with his bandmaster for a postgraduate year, heard the white swing bands and got a job playing simple chord changes on piano with a hillbilly band—"beginning to come alive," he recalled.

"It didn't happen that I became integrated until I went to Camp Stoneman [in the Army] near San Francisco and played in a mixed band. Special Services. Everybody was either crazy or impaired [Dorough had a punctured eardrum]. Also I first heard Basie and Lunceford in Sweet's Auditorium in Oakland. And I began to write more arrangements for a jazz band."

He married, majored in composition at North Texas State College and "was very serious," he said. He played bebop and listened to Charlie Parker and Dizzy Gillespie by night and still attended his eight o'clock classes. The Doroughs moved to New York City, where Bob spent two years at Columbia, taking math, history, Greek, theater courses, until he ran out of G.I. money and "went berserk," digging the New York scene. "I went wild and lived a wild life, living high, after seven years of marriage. So the academic world went down the drain." During this period he wrote his favorite among his own tunes: "Devil may care, no cares for me, I'm as happy as I can be, I've learned to love and to live, Devil may care."

"What made 'Devil May Care' work is that it has a nice philosophy married to the swing of it," said Dorough. "It's a happy swinging song, man, it's a happy, swinging song."

He began singing and playing professionally at Trude Heller's when it was a boîte. The influences had been Nat "King" Cole, Louis Jordan and Joe Mooney, a blind organist, accordion player and singer whom Dorough first heard on records. He noted that Trummy Young, Lunceford's trombonist, sang with the band.

Lionel Hampton sang now and then. "The idea hit me that now and then a jazz musician would sing a song. That was the essence. You didn't have to be a singer out in front."

Eventually he landed in Paris, as Sugar Ray Robinson's musical director, and decided to stay there and work at the Mars Club, a hangout for English-speaking show people. Dorough met Blossom Dearie and accompanied Maya Angelou, a singer and dancer as well as a writer, in 1954 and 1955.

"I was in between marriages. Paris is a great place to be when you're like that. I learned good songs and how to entertain, to communicate. It was every night. So I learned to do my thing. It's hard to make people listen. I learned jazz and the tunes and worked them out. But I was homesick. I missed the bass and drums."

Back in the United States, Dorough recorded an album, *Devil May Care,* on the Bethlehem label in New York, and wrote lyrics to "Yardbird Suite" as a memorial to Charlie Parker. In 1958 he went to Los Angeles, sang and played piano—"I got more jobs than I had ever gotten in my life." But he came back East because he missed it. In 1960 he married his second wife, Corine, and had a daughter. He worked in commercial music—and kept singing and playing.

"I spent a lot of years just trying to make them listen to me, working in bars. They want a piano player who can sing some songs, and they couldn't care less. I tried to get through to them. It was a great effort to communicate with an audience that didn't want to hear you. I would dream of a time when I could sing a thing my way. I tried so hard to get through. Just kept trying and trying to make my voice sound better. To make its tone better, to sing the kind of things I should sing. My repertoire is overweight on the up-beat side [with a driving interpretation of "Baltimore Oriole"; if you want to hear a cat seducing a bird, hear this]. I ask their indulgence to sing a slow, sad song. Figuratively I do.

"How do I get the song the way I want it? I try, I try. I just try, and try, and try. I just try. When performing, a lot is unconscious. I listen for good diction, a good pitch, a good tune. That means the rhythm. That's a perfect combination. I think if all three are good, you'll get over to your audience and get communication. You can probably make it with just two. Good pitch is more sophisticated than the other two. It's hard to stay in tune.

"Good lyrics are more important than a bad melody. I can sing a song and sell it, if the words are good. Jazz instrumentalists would find that disgusting, but they don't have the words to rely on. And not everyone would agree. Sarah and Ella are always singing asinine songs, and, by using their musical voices, they can make the songs beautiful. But a good lyric can really sound lousy without music. It's dull without music. It's the rhythm that it's put into that supports a song, brightens it and brings it to life. You gotta have music or it ain't a song.

"Marrying the lyric to the music is the jazz thing. And I'm going to do it differently, according to my mood and audience. A straighter singer may have things more worked out. We have things worked out but have minute variations, subtle ones, that keep us from having rules. We have an open line to the situation. Who am I singing to? How much am I in love? That's very important. I sing a lot of love songs. And all kinds of things affect the jazz singer. There's apt to be a lot of flexibility in jazz."

PART IV

The B-Natural Generation: "They Reflect the Times They Live In"

"Instead of singing this"—and Eddie Heywood, Jr., sang middle C, E, G and high C—"or this"—and he sang middle C, E, G and B flat—"they sing this: middle C, E, G and B natural. They never let the audience relax. They reflect the times they live in."

"So they're the B-natural generation," I said.

"Yes, something like that. I know what you mean," he said, talking about certain of the most *au courant* jazz singers and the Free Jazz singers. Some say they're rooted in bebop; others say that, as their instrumental counterparts do, they sound at times totally uprooted.

Then I discussed them with a bebop drummer, gigging around town, with a college degree and a consuming passion for jazz in his background:

"They got it from Dizzy and Bird. At least that's what I think," he said. "Ornette Coleman got it from Dizzy and Bird, too. Personally I don't like it when it's too far out. It doesn't swing. It isn't jazz. Some of the figures that Ornette Coleman is playing swing; I can see some of it. Not much. But some of them doing it, singing and playing Out—it just doesn't swing.

"I remember one matinee in the 1960s at the Five Spot on Third Avenue. Charles Mingus was there. He announced to the audience that he was presenting the greatest jazz musicians in the world. He had a sign up saying: 'The Greatest Jazz Musicians in the World.' Behind this sign the musicians were hidden. And they were playing Out. Out. Out. Afterwards, the audience clapped like crazy. Mingus took down the sign and showed the musicians. A bunch of kids were standing there, the kids of a friend of mine, a bassist. They were banging and blowing any damn thing. The greatest jazz musicians in the world! A bunch of kids! You might as well stick your horn up your ass and fart."

Why did the singers go from the pretty melodies of Louis Armstrong, Billie Holiday and Sarah Vaughan to the dissonances, sometimes dissonant fragments, of Betty Carter's tunes; to the art songs of jazz-based Jay Clayton, who, with her gorgeous soprano voice, leaves you with the impression that you have heard her in recital, not in a jazz set? Why have critics sometimes said that Susannah McCorkle sings popular music on records and in clubs in the 1980s, when she surely would have been called a jazz singer on the Waters axis in the 1930s?

In the beginning of jazz, horn players tried to imitate the human voice. By the 1920s, as the horn grew in stature, some singers had started trying to return the compliment, taking it as an accolade that they sounded like horns. Furthermore, they wanted to sing the bebop horn solos. Eventually some creative singers wanted to write their own solos, improvising off the horns. Then a few Free Jazz singers wanted to improvise not only off the horns, not only off the chords, but off the rhythms and textures and volume of the music—off silence, off the walls, off anything that moved or made a sound or even anything that held still. They started a Dada-like movement* (which had existed in the art world), while bebop purists, their predecessors and the majority of jazz fans thought Dada obliterated "Jada" (a simple, early jazz tune).

Each new era in jazz has brought singers who have not wanted to sound like their predecessors—because you've got to make progress, catch the attention and respect of your peers, your producers, your critics and, if possible, the banks. If you don't have something fresh about you, it doesn't matter what you do.

Becoming progressive in the forties, the beboppers enriched the

---

* The Dada-like movement was the abolition of traditional cultural and aesthetic forms by a technique of comic derision in which irrationality, chance and intuition were the guiding principles.

music and overtook swing quickly, weaning jazz fans away from the older-fashioned music in about a decade.

By the 1980s the Free Jazz instrumentalists and singers, who extended the innovations of the beboppers, were still attracting a limited audience. But the number of fans was growing, as some became more receptive to dissonance, while some Free Jazz musicians lightened, sweetened and streamlined their sounds.

Changes in society have given the new jazz musicians an added push. In the 1960s the Equal Opportunity Act passed in Congress. Many colleges—liberal arts and established music schools, such as the New England Conservatory of Music—started jazz programs and hired well-known jazz experts and musicians as teachers, people such as Gunther Schuller and Jaki Byard. The schools drew in talented youngsters, primarily instrumentalists, with scholarships to study jazz, arranging, classical techniques, performing. And in the sixties, the government started giving National Endowment for the Arts grants to instrumentalists and singers to compose and perform. Prestige unheard of for jazz in earlier eras. Musicians began incorporating all the music they studied into their work. For example, Dennis Rowland, Count Basie's bandsinger beginning in the late 1970s, with a beautiful, schooled baritone, got a B.S. degree in music education and taught music in Detroit public schools before auditioning and turning professional full time with Basie. Rowland has an underpinning of blues and a panache of Broadway musical theater à la Alfred Drake, with the classic Basie repertoire holding his act together in the middle. Rowland has entertained notions of Broadway theater as a goal.

Unfortunately, very few schools have offered improvisational singing classes—and no degrees in improvisation. Singers have always been considered second-class musicians—in part because they carried no visible instruments, in part because many do not have an instrumentalist's knowledge of the basics of music and cannot discuss the music technically. However, some jazz instrumentalists and singers—Clark Terry, Joe Williams, Bobby McFerrin, Janet Lawson, Jay Clayton, Sheila Jordan, Jeanne Lee, Anne Marie Moss—have been teaching regular courses or visiting schools to give clinics. Terry starts his instrumental students by making them sing improv. Lawson makes them improvise their names first.

For the women jazz singers and instrumentalists, the Equal Opportunity Act meant they could risk more if they had the courage and inclination to try. Some women picked up horns instead of singing. Others decided to sound more like horns. Both the singers and instrumentalists, men and women, belonged to the first generation to grow up under the threat of a mushroom cloud. So they looked to their own anxious and self-protectively narcissistic psyches to make palpable in sound their emotional reactions to an increasingly complex society. Paralleling literature, too, the Free Jazz singers could be said to have started doing "stream-of-consciousness" tunes. Fiction writers had left a straightforward story line in the 1920s and delved into a character's head to present someone's sensory perception of the world as the story. Painters became abstract in their art long ago. So it was the singers' perceptions of the tunes that led them to sing Out, seemingly to scrap the proscribed musical clues for tunes.

Bebop musicians said the Free Jazz players left the chords and stopped swinging. Stopped singing jazz. But Free Jazz tenor saxophonist Chico Freeman, rooted in bebop, with a master's degree in music, tried to explain all free, bebop-rooted jazz musicians when he said he left the chords for a loftier perch—the twenty-third floor of a building, for example, from which vantage point he really appreciated the strength of the blues foundation of his music.

Free Jazz may not be the future of jazz. But the chord dropouts have formed a movement of adventuresome, jazz-derived musicians. Even the most popular of the new jazz singers, Al Jarreau, has paid attention to Far-Out developments in music and incorporated elements of tension into his commercial jazz sound. So has bebop-rooted Andy Bey with a magnificent voice. So it's hard to tell where, or if, jazz ends and art song begins in the blues-based work of nubile-voiced Bobby McFerrin and of honey-voiced Jeanne Lee; in the plaintive laments of Sheila Jordan, who likes to work with a bass; in the reverberating aria for murdered Atlanta children written by mainstream jazz singer Joe Lee Wilson; in the arresting work of the gifted Betty Carter; and in the pure scat of Janet Lawson. All claim that bebop inspired them; Jarreau and Lawson name Jon Hendricks as one of their particular influences.

Ask the public who the most popular jazz singers are. Most people will answer Fitzgerald, Vaughan, Sinatra, Bennett and a few others whose jazz classification the critics sometimes debate. But these popular stars have come to symbolize jazz to the public. A new wave of jazz singers was headed off and becalmed for over a decade by the crosscurrent of rock. Whether the singers were singing dissonances or commercial tunes, they couldn't find audiences. Singers like Hendricks' protégé, Mark Murphy, a swinging bebopper who sang the tunes recognizably, headed for Europe in search of appreciation.

Only in the late 1970s and early 1980s did young jazz singers begin riding in on what seemed to be a wave of new popularity for jazz in the United States. The renewed interest was spawned in part by Fusion—jazz popularized—with the help of charismatic trumpeter Miles Davis and his album *Bitches Brew**—by amplified electronic instruments that related to the accoutrements of rock's massive sound. Some rock fans switched to more complex music— old or mainstream jazz from the swing and bebop eras. And purists of those eras notwithstanding, a few new musicians and singers gained some leverage in the 1980s. Tuned into the complexities of their audiences, the singers serenaded them with the sounds of their culture-shocked psyches—sometimes tempered and melodic, sometimes chaotic, sometimes fiery and poetic, sometimes with the dash of Latin rhythms supplied by the country's growing Spanish-speaking population. Brazil's instrumentalists and singers increasingly impressed and influenced American singers, too.

The goal of jazz singing, the young musicians said, remained the same: to entertain the people and communicate feelings and ideas—even if some Free Jazz players were criticized as bebop's urchins, without stories to tell.

---

* Clark Terry has said it sounded like Australian foo birds flying around, and kangaroos making love. Otherwise it was fine.

CHAPTER 32

Betty Carter:
Guru of "Out"

Betty Carter, who has been singing extremely stylized, increasingly Out jazz since the 1960s, was still not a household word by the 1980s. However, by the late 1970s, if ever a jazz singer were having her day, it was Betty Carter. Because she was doing something new. Or was she?

She was singing, *without any vibrato, in between the chord changes, and above and below the notes of a tune. And she was usually singing there only.* She could go through a whole set and never sing one melodic line of a tune the way it was written. Billie Holiday sang between the chord changes, hitting the blue notes for improvisation, for shading, changing the feeling of the tune as it was written, giving it pathos and swing, and *always returning* to the tune as it was written. Betty Carter decided to be different—extreme—by singing *only* the notes that the accompanist's chords suggested. She took Billie's "idea," which was Louis Armstrong's "idea," before that, and ran all the way with it, circumscribing her own diamond—or, more accurately, her own outfield. But Billie and Betty have a similar steady quality and horn purity in the tone, and, nearly unique with these two female singers, a whine instead of a growl. (Eddie Jefferson had a great whine, too.)

324

Carter's Modified-Out version of "My Favorite Things" can stir up more excitement than the original, certainly, which was intended as a ballad and not as Carter's rhythmic tour de force. Once you've heard her fast tempo and charged phrasing, you can't go home again to any previous interpretation. But her Way-Out "Body and Soul" is so dissonant that, if you don't know the words, you will never detect that she is singing "Body and Soul." Coleman Hawkins' classic, honeyed version is a balm compared with Betty Carter's version, which, to my ear, sounds inappropriate. *New York Times* critic John S. Wilson finds almost no fault with Carter's idiosyncratic singing, however. He finds her "the most exciting jazz singer of the day," praising her "flexible voice" with rich bottom notes and her stretched phrasing with its accents and pauses, which "give her delivery the intensity that has always marked her singing." But something else disturbs him: her 1980s penchant for singing one slow song after another so that, in the aggregate, they're repetitious. Perhaps that's the answer. But when Betty Carter does the right tune with the right dissonances at the right tempo, she hits the jackpot. (Pro jazz singers tell students to vary their tempos, because a nightclub audience won't sit still for a diet of ballads only. And by Christmas 1982, Betty Carter, dressed in a black crepe jump suit and a bejeweled belt, in a club gave a classic performance of exactly how everything should be done—a perfectly balanced set by an enchanting entertainer, who is also one of the best-dressed female singers of jazz.)

Betty Carter has done fast, intensely swinging jobs on tunes that she has kept recognizable, dazzling with her emphases, hitting Out notes meaningfully, to revitalize the emotional habits we have developed from listening to standards done pretty straight by everyone. Her work can excite even if sometimes, because it seems so cerebrally devised, it can make you nervous, reminding you that you live in a tense, modern world.

At the same time as vintage swing and bebop jazz were coming back into vogue, Betty Carter was getting high cover charges in the best jazz clubs, zooming upward toward concert-artist status for singing Free Jazz—Out-and-Out jazz. If you say that phrase aloud, you will get an inkling of Miss Betty Carter's style if you have. never heard her. She is the only jazz singer who can swing while giving you intimations of Honegger and a flying saucer accident.

When Lionel Hampton went to the White House for a tribute to himself in 1981, he invited Miss Carter to go with him, not the blues-and-Dinah-influenced Nancy Wilson.

By 1982 at the Bottom Line in New York, Betty Carter had added something new to her newness: strings. They tempered her dissonance. Furthermore, she seemed to like the tempering—or at least she loved the audience's reception of it. This is what happened:

Her trio did a very exciting warm-up, as it usually did for her gigs. A polyrhythmic drum solo especially incited the audience. One heard more of Brazil, Cuba and the Orient than New Orleans in her drummer.

You could hear Louis, as the breathiness and softness of her voice suddenly became funneled into a clear, horn sound. (Ernestine Anderson said she would hate to be a young singer trying to analyze what Betty Carter is doing. Ernestine takes Carter out of the category of singer and calls her a horn.) But with the tune completely gone, Betty sounded arrestingly fresh, nervous, humorless, blue, cold. Her voice can move as fast and unreflectively as a zoom lens over a mysterious landscape.

Her performance was a bravura affair of sound and rhythm: abstractions that sometimes had nothing to do with a melody—"What a Little Moonlight Can Do" as viewed from a space capsule. Her torch song "Good-bye" sounded similar: "I'll never forget how we promised to LOVE ONE ANOTHER ... we *said* we'd never *say goodbyyyy.*" The word "good-bye" held a long time was the key to the story. A classic emphasis. "Sigh" was emphasized next, and "let's let love diiiieeeeeee," falling down. (She sang vertically, picking chords and moving around them.) "And please kiss me as you go and then—good-bye," barely resolved, low and almost blue. The audience did not relax. Following that, a trademark, original song of short, choppy phrases had the same aura.

Other singers sing about "icy silence" in overheated voices that could melt it, but Betty Carter's sound can be icy silence personified. She can unsettle an audience, when she makes life's complications palpable in sound. People can hear the craziness, or chaos, of a changing world synthesized by her craft, daring and a gem of sensibility—by her ear for an attention-getting gimmick. Her dynamism never lets an audience's mind wander. But I sometimes miss the

tunes. Without them, I lose track of the stories. Betty Carter can affect me like the sight of books burning in the film *Fahrenheit 451*.

She finished the set with the trio, singing a standard nearly Totally Out: "Every Time We Say Good-bye"—an interpretation
light years away from her moving and traditional one on a classic
old recording with Ray Charles. Then she scatted a song, facing
down and challenging the loud polyrhythms of the drums. There is
no question that her voice is an instrument, a force that the other
instruments must contend with—by turns a horn, or its echo, or
merely a soft, sexy murmur; her voice is whatever she wants it to be.

After a break, strings, a lot of them, assembled on the stage.
David Amram's orchestra dominated, while Betty Carter's trio sat
to one side. Betty materialized again, this time wearing a high-
necked, lacy sky-blue gown. If you were sitting close to the brightly
lit stage, you could see her beautiful dark eyes brimming with intense light. They can startle and fix you forever with the impression
that they have just seen Lazarus rise.

But something went haywire with the strings for a moment. It
was only the second time in her life that Betty had sung with them.
The first time had been the previous summer, 1981, in Prospect
Park, Brooklyn, with the Brooklyn Philharmonia. A girlfriend recalled that everyone in the large crowd came still. One of the
owners of the Bottom Line heard Betty's performance and wanted
to repeat it indoors. But something went wrong with the strings. So
Betty stopped the music and carried on theatrically, nattering at
the musicians briefly. Mainly her brilliant eyes fixed them. *Les
yeux brûlent.** Somehow the music got under way again. And she
sang about feeling the breeze steal across her pillow, like a will-of-
the-wisp. Her voice sounded like the breeze: "And there is sadness,
because there's no you," the breeze crooned.

The strings were lush and feminine; Betty Carter was singing a
tuneful tune with them, slower and less individualistically than she
had delivered her previous set, without the "fireworks" of her version of "My Favorite Things." But she was singing beautifully. The
strings—so linear and leaving her no space—softened her. Perhaps
because they were so new to her, she didn't know yet how to challenge or use them to augment her concept. So the strings exerted a
melodic influence on her choice of notes; she lengthened and

* The eyes burn.

smoothed her phrasing. She was singing 'for the audience and not for God. Against this background she sang with a ripe, feminine attitude "Cocktails for Two." And I was able to tell the difference between the songs. However, she did manage to end dramatically by taking a step forward, pausing, then pushing out a few notes counter to the serenity of the strings. She stole the show.

So Betty Carter finishes as a star. She has made a place for herself, coming along a circuitous route, the outside track. She ran with her concept so long, insistently and vibrantly that she has made it work seamlessly, convinced you with her drive, charisma and control. She has outlasted a once-resistant (or perhaps merely indifferent) public and cast a spell, as the years passed, over audiences and critics. Whether her route is a permanent one for jazz singing remains to be seen. But she is the only Out singer who can attract a huge crowd.

Betty Carter stated definitely that she drew her inspiration from the beboppers, especially from Bird and Dizzy.

"I sing a few phrases," she said with a chuckle, slightly nasal and laryngitic in conversation. "Otherwise I destroy the tunes. I was influenced by players, not singers. I have never before heard anyone say that I sound like Louis or Billie. If so, it's unbeknownst—UNBEKNOWST—to me. On a concept level, Billie and I may be similar. But my music is more intricate, because I delay more and do more music than she did. She did the melody pretty straight, and I change it totally. I had to.

"In black jazz there's only room for one Ella, Dinah, one Bessie. In white jazz Anita O'Day was the beginning. She influenced Chris Connor, who, by the way, didn't have Anita's musical ability. But most of the white singers sound too close for comfort. Blacks who sound that close together couldn't make it.

"I had to do something different to survive," Betty continued. "I was faster on 'Lady Be Good' than Ella. Plus I put in my own passage. It was taboo for any black singer to be like anybody else. No way I could get anyplace if I imitated anybody. There's a white singer, Marilyn Moore; I heard her on the radio a little while ago. She sounds like Billie Holiday, but she never got past first base. However, if she were black, she wouldn't have even gotten on the radio. Aside from the beboppers, I don't know what made me go the way I did. I just did it."

So, in part it was a survival instinct that led her to take the innovations of the beboppers and go all the way Out. "Also sometimes the lyrics really get away [lost] when you sing them straight, because you really don't talk that way. You *do* hesitate. And that has more of an impact."

Born in Flint, Michigan, on May 16, 1930, which made her about fifty years old when she became commercially established, Betty Carter was written up *very* sparingly in the normally rather sparing 1970s *Jazz Encyclopedia* by *Los Angeles Times* critic Leonard Feather. He did call her one of the "few genuine jazz singers," said she breathed new life into the music, mentioned that she did club and college dates and had done two albums on her own label, Bet-Car. But this seemed little attention to pay to a woman who has been around as long as several hundred other far better-known and less genuine jazz singers. The notice in the encyclopedia was as much as most publications gave Betty Carter until she was about to go into her fabulous fifties. She has over the years also made records for ABC, Paramount, Roulette, Atco, Epic, United Artists and Columbia. But the Columbia record went into the can, she said, for about twenty-five years and was not released until she had already made a name for herself in the eighties by attracting—FANS. To understate the case, Betty Carter was not a product of media hype.

"I first heard Charlie Parker in 1946 in Detroit when I was in high school. I was influenced by him and just by plain music, not any one kind. I had a good ear. I had a few piano lessons and charisma. My voice was not that great. Sarah Vaughan was on the scene at the same time with that beautiful voice. But the bebop music of the Parker era was challenging. It gave me a chance as a singer to bend a note and spread out.

"I joined the high school band. My parents didn't influence or encourage me. But I decided in high school to become a singer. Everyone else knew I would do it, too. I had some charisma. Maybe I wasn't going to be a great singer; nobody could say that. But I had some charisma and ideas. I had a way about me that people liked. My music teacher in the a cappella [choir] liked what I did. I wish I had had a little training outside. But experience lets you do it. You get the talent, and it's up to you what to do with it.

"I joined the Lionel Hampton band in 1948 to go on the road. He heard me singing at a dance and was looking for a singer. So I stayed with him for two years. We fought like cats and dogs because I was a bebopper, and he was a swingster."

Her real name was Lillie Mae Jones, but by the time she played with Hampton, she had adopted the name Lorraine Carter for the stage. Hampton, who Betty says was piqued by her passion for bebop, started introducing her as Betty Bebop, a name so catchy that she buried her pique about it along with "Lorraine" forever.

"I liked Dizzy's band better. Also I wanted to sing songs with words, and Lionel had me scatting all the time. Now I'm glad I was scatting. It was on-the-job training. It taught me what to hear, how to listen to what's going on behind you and how to make it work for you. Come and take a course in here in the band to sound like a horn.

"Hampton wanted my feeling for bebop. He resented it, but still he wanted it. So he had Jeanette Franklin and Irma Curry, who are out of the business now, to sing the tunes, the beautiful melodies. I was the other kid."

Betty Carter came to New York alone, "beating the boards, hitting all the places, in Brooklyn, anyplace for work." Trumpeter Buck Clayton remembered her in Harlem in the fifties; she wore a cap as a trademark. "I did the Apollo quite a bit. Philly. Washington. Boston. I did my best to see if I could do it on my own. It was secure with the band. Now what do you do? While I was with the band, I had made a little name for doing my bebop thing. And that got me over. You don't give up what you're known for. But I added on by myself to get the feeling of the words.

"I worked with musicians all over the place. I couldn't afford my own group. You have to really shine to get your own group. I sang with everybody as they were growing up, too. We were all contemporaries and all trying to do the same thing. There were a lot of places to work. If you were good, you could get a job. The music companies hadn't made us all into robots as they have today. You didn't have to have an album to get work. You just had to be good. Or if a club owner thought you had potential, he'd give you a job.

"There was a gradual evolution in my style, too. I tried to stay away from the routine. I figured the only ones who could be mad at me were the composers for changing their songs and not singing them the right way. But you've got thousands of singers who can sing the melodies straight. So, as I worked and became more informed, my style evolved.

"I worked in a club with one group one night and sang 'Body and Soul,' and the next night with another trio with another approach.

If you have ears, and if you care, you hear the differences. I used what the piano players gave me. It's something that you have to really work at. No one can really write a jazz song. It's an interpretation, a feeling. It can't be taught. You can learn all the changes and chords, but if the feeling isn't there, you're just a player. Everyone who changes a note or scats is not spontaneous. Leontyne Price and Sarah Vaughan and I are going to sing a song differently. On " 'Round Midnight," the classicals can't do what we do. You've got to want it and do it and go out and get it. You're not going to do it alone in a room.

"I went Out.

"No one told me to do it. I never thought about what Billie did. I'm Betty Carter. I've been singing 'What a Little Moonlight Can Do' in five [5/4 time, a popular meter in Eastern Europe, India and the Middle East] for a long time. I can do it. Not everyone can do it. And I've tried to keep on top of the music. Maybe I was able to do it because I didn't become famous thirty years ago with what I was doing then. If I had become famous, maybe I would still be doing that today. But as things worked out, I stayed sharp and on my toes, gigging around and in touch with a lot of different musicians. The more in touch you are with them, the more you're going to think. Some enhance you. Some are not adequate; you have to lift them up. So I've gotten this way from contact with people."

It also seemed from her meditations on race relations and music that Betty Carter, in middle age, came into more contact with white people, who respected her music enormously, than she had ever done as a young woman. She mused on the systems and prejudices, clearly stating that she thought there was a black jazz and a white jazz, that all white tenor saxophonists sound alike, and that musicians were unequally credited on a race basis long after race records officially stopped being produced. Bebop, in her opinion, with scatting being done by Dizzy Gillespie and others, including herself, was "just a new music for black people. They didn't stop making race records until the Beatles. In 1964 the barrier for white people to go out and buy black music was lifted, when the Beatles said their influence came from the blacks. Elvis Presley had been around long before that, and he never said a word about his music coming from the blacks. The music was still really segregated. WEVD in the fifties in New York City played black jazz, while WNEW did Frank Sinatra and Peggy Lee. It was a long time before Nat 'King' Cole got on WNEW. He broke the Las Vegas barrier.

"Black entertainers couldn't stay in the Las Vegas hotels where they were working. Dinah Washington had to build a tent outside a Las Vegas hotel. Sammy Davis had his problems there. The Beatles came along and said the music came from the blacks and freed them up. Now more white people are listening to me than blacks. B. B. King has more white people now."

Betty Carter, who seemed enchanted, amused and enlivened by her own steadily expanding vistas, greeted a girlfriend, Carol, an accountant, who dropped by, bringing flowers, looking to while away some time in conversation. Betty said it was her second bouquet of the day. The first one had come from a little white girl from Intermediate School 93 in Betty's neighboorhood of neat row houses on a quiet and quaint-looking Brooklyn street near Flatbush Avenue. The girl was assigned to do a school composition on a famous black person. All her classmates chose Martin Luther King. So her mother suggested: "Why not do Betty Carter?" "Who?" the kid said.

The mother called Betty Carter, who is hospitable and agreed to an interview. The child came by. "She learned so much in a few minutes," Betty said, the light gleaming in her eyes. Actually the child stayed an hour.

And from that subject, Betty went to the strings—and her own impression that the blue dress she wore to sing with them was "conservative." But she knew intuitively that no matter how much trouble she had because of lack of rehearsals with the strings, their part of her gig at the Bottom Line went sensationally well. So she was happy that she had recorded the gig; that it was videotaped, too, and done on a digital record. "The Man volunteered to do that." All went smoothly. "Nobody knew it was being recorded. And they took care of the sound checks! And they took care of the light checks before I got there! It was just perfect. In a studio you say: 'What's wrong with that??? What? What's that? What's that? I can't hear you! It's no good! WHAT? I DON'T HEAR I DON'T HEAR I DIDN'T HEAR.' " And she scatted studio noises of complexity and confusion. "You waste time and money in a studio!"

About the review of her show: *"The New York Times* called me iconoclastic. An iconoclastic singer. Ha-ha. I pull the tunes apart. I get so much embarrassment, so I said, 'Let me just do the real melody here,' so I did six bars straight, so they know I know the melody, and then I went Out again. All my own tunes are different. No words and no tunes. That's why I did 'Jumps' [her own composition, which she did with her trio, not the strings]." She has also written such Out tunes as "Open the Door," "Tight," "Happy," "So," "Fake." The abruptness of the titles intimates the tunes' oddities. "It's hard to get the feeling of 'Jumps.' Anyway, the trio was really good that night. The strings had a lot wrong with them."

"But it didn't matter," I said. And when I said, too, that her blue dress was just right with "Cocktails for Two," her eyes lit up, engulfed her entire face and became her persona. She looked back at her girlfriend, Carol, and said emphatically:

"That's what I'm going to do next. Go into Carnegie Hall with a big orchestra and STRINGS."

And to me:

"I've always gotten along with audiences. It has been one of those things that has gotten me over. No problem. I get the same reactions in Europe as I do here. Other musicians tell me that they get nothing here and over there they get tremendous applause. I don't know why I haven't had that difference in reception.

"In Japan, though, it's different than here. The Japanese audience is a sea of faces. No smiles, no glowing eyes. You don't see those things in Japan. And when you finish, they suddenly let out with applause like crazy." And she raised one hand in a fist over her head, rather like the Statue of Liberty, and let out a whoop with *banzai* feeling. "And you say, 'They *liked* it!' It's a surprise. Then they go back to their . . ." (She slumped down into a pose of blank-faced grimness. Somebody should offer this woman an acting role.) "They seem to be on automatic. No 'ooooooh, Betty, sing it!' which really inspires you. But then"—clapping fast—"that's the Japanese. Then they line up for blocks to get your autograph with neat cards and markers all ready for you, and they keep bowing like they love love love. But just watching their faces, you would never know it. Ha-ha, they can imitate Helen Merrill and Abbey Lincoln, but they can't copy me. AND I'M SO GLAD!" The eyes lit up again, those dazzling dark eyes. "Have you heard them copy Pops? The Japanese. They copy Pops."

I said, "I heard them copy him down in New Orleans," forgetting for a minute that musicians in New Orleans are usually black, occasionally white, always American and never Japanese.

"I'M NOT TALKING ABOUT NEW ORLEANS. I'M NOT *SURPRISED* THEY CAN DO IT IN NEW ORLEANS. I MEAN JAPAN. THE JAPANESE CAN COPY POPS!"

Race is a constant: the politics of race, and race and politics, in the music business; and pure politics or pure race keep coming up. About her gig at the White House in the tribute to Lionel Hampton during the Reagan administration: "Hampton has always been a Republican. Reagan is doing something for Hampton's foundation," she mused, pondering the political overtones of her appearance there. Then she proudly and appreciatively showed her invitaton, complete with a souvenir drawing of the White House. "That's the Oval Office lit up," she said, beaming about one illuminated window.

So the improv that Betty Carter hummed, so full of the complications of race, was intriguing. She said: "If I had been a white female, I would have been a big star years earlier. If I were white, with my drive and concept, I'd have had a contract with Columbia. Chris Connor couldn't sing her way out of a paper bag in the 1950s, but she got a PR job and became a star. Peggy Lee wanted to be like Billie Holiday, and she has plenty of money now from that. The whole concept of the business is that LaVern Baker sang 'Tweedle Dee,' and then Georgia Gibbs sang the same tune and covered it, got it sewed up [as the hit version], because Baker was black and Gibbs was white. OH, IF I WAS WHITE YOU'D HAVE TO GO THROUGH TEN PEOPLE TO SEE ME!" A smile went with that. But she was convinced that if Motown hadn't held on to Gladys Knight and Stevie Wonder, "whites would have taken that over, too. Motown didn't do a thing for jazz, of course. But they did okay by some black music." And "blacks must sell to white audiences," she noted, "to get over, while whites don't have to sell to black audiences." An industry estimate is that 55 percent of all the buyers of jazz records are blacks, who make up approximately 15 percent of the population.

"Now Mel Torme. NOW YOU DIDN'T HEAR ME SAY ANYTHING BAD ABOUT MEL TORME!" Her opinions of other singers, always favoring the black ones, ranged from praise for one, although he's pop, to criticism for another, because he's pop. Essentially, though, her eclectic tastes run toward the best, transcending labels. "Johnny Mathis. He's the boss. He's in control of it."

"He's pop," I said.

"Never mind that. He's the boss. Nobody breathes or phrases like he does."

Girlfriend Carol said that she had seen Al Jarreau on TV that day. He was asked his advice to jazz singers starting out. "And he said, 'Do it because you love it, not because you want to be famous.'"

Betty: "Hmmmm. Like him. He's not a jazz singer. He's pop. Manufactured."

Carol: "He said, 'Sing in dives,' and I thought about Betty. She sang in all kinds of places and not just exclusive ones. She sang in Slugs . . ." a notorious, long-closed Lower East Side club with wonderful music, where musicians were underpaid and everyone endangered because of the grim neighborhood.

Through it all, Betty held on to a center: her pretty house, the brightest, richest red one on her prim-looking block, where she raised two sons. In 1961 at age thirty-one, she married for the first and only time to a nonmusician whose name she will not disclose. By the time she was singing with strings, son Kagle, seventeen, was a student at Friends Academy, and Myles, twenty-one, was studying communications at C. W. Post College.

"I was mature when I married, and the kids didn't go wrong because I was away. My friends and their father helped me raise them. Having my kids was the most dramatic thing that's ever happened to me. They're mine, and I did it. I pushed them out by myself, and they turned out pretty good. And they can carry on for me. I don't need to do much else."

Divorced in 1971, she never remarried "because I didn't fall in love." (Dramatic pause.) "I was in love with a musician once." (Pause.) "One time. After the marriage."

"Who?"

"I'm not going to tell you who. But it was a new, young experience. Of course, he was younger than me. You can't get a new experience with old head. He influenced my music. He was very instrumental in the new spirit I have now. It's the young level that gives you that. But that's over now.

"I go out on dates. But that's not very interesting. My husband didn't believe in my thing." (He had urged her to sing in a commercial style until she had a hit, and then go back to her own style.) "He's a private person, doing his thing, and I'm doing mine. He's my kids' father, so I just let it lay.

"You either love each other or not [whether you're both musicians or creative or not.] It depends on how much respect you have for another person, not whether he's in the business or not. But when you're dealing with careers of this magnitude, you're straining your ability to hang in there. It's not easy for a spouse to watch someone going up. It takes a great person to survive that."

"And you must be completely involved with your career," I said.

"I'm afraid so," Betty said. "From the beginning you are. People remind me of things I did years ago. And I don't remember at all, if it wasn't to do with music. I'm so busy concentrating on the music, I forget people or things I should have remembered."

"Do you believe in the love lyrics you sing?" I asked her.

"If you've got any feeling at all, there's NO WAY you can get up and sing those lyrics if you don't feel them, believe in them. You've got to!"

"But some are love songs that you can't believe in after you get some experience in life."

"I LOVE LOVE! Don't you?"

"I mean, some are silly songs. Didn't you ever sing a silly song?" I asked.

She was pacing around the kitchen, which was filled with plants. A glass door led to a garden. We could see it from the big, round kitchen table where we were sitting in her high-ceilinged house with the woodsy ambience of a Cape Cod cottage. She alighted at the table again. "Oh, sure. If I were singing a corny, silly song, you can bet the music will be so hip that the music will compensate. What's that corny song I sing? 'By the Bend in the River.' It's the arrangement that I like. The music. Musically you can do it in such a way that the lyrics don't sound corny. And you can still put your love in there. You love the music, and you can do a job on the corny lyrics. And then you can still make love to the music.

"It's the concept of jazz that makes you unique. Jazz is special. The people who are leading it are special. You don't have to guess about the leaders. Pops. Count. Duke. Dizzy. Billie. Sarah. Ella."
Betty.

CHAPTER 33

Andy Bey's Subtlety;
Joe Lee Wilson's
Reverberations

Andy Bey is one of the best-kept secrets in jazz. Media rarely mention him. He can look at unfamiliar, avant-garde music and, in a few minutes, stand up and sing it in a group led by such people as the dynamic, driving horn player Hannibal Peterson. Or Bey can go it alone. He can stand in the shadows and sing "Take The 'A' Train," improvising a great deal on the chords, with a bass or a cappella, holding you with his soft, slow interpretation.

He has worked with scores of brilliant jazz musicians—Charles Mingus, Max Roach, Dakota Staton, Mel Lewis and Thad Jones, to name a few. In 1975 he received an NEA grant to compose.

He has a broad face with an easy smile, along with an affable manner and a youthful build. He can wax voluble and intense. Somehow he has never found the right manager.

"I was born in Newark, New Jersey, on October 28, 1939. There was always music in the house. By age five I was playing gigs [on piano] at church and in bars. I might have made twenty-five dollars a day on Sundays. My father was a window cleaner. My mother was a housewife. Sometimes she did housework for a day. She lives in a house in North Newark. The family was as stable as it could be. Everyone had their problems. My family was poor, yes, they were. I

337

was the youngest of nine kids. Three of us went into music professionally.

"I can remember playing when I was five, six, going into people's homes with my little money bracelet. My father took me to in-laws and friends. I'd play for them. They'd say, 'Look at the child prodigy.' It was the same time as Sugar Child Robinson. He played boogie-woogie with his elbows, made movies and worked at the Apollo, and also at the Adams Theater in Newark. I was the Newark version. People called me another Sugar Child Robinson.

"I played boogie-woogie or anything on the radio that I could pick up. Eddie Heywood's 'Begin the Beguine.' Many musicians passed through Newark, or I heard them on radio or records. Betty Carter, Dinah Washington, Wynone Harris, Buddy and Ella Johnson, Ella Fitzgerald, Sarah Vaughan, Billy Eckstine, Nat 'King' Cole, B. B. King, Ruth Brown.

"I left high school in my senior year, got my diploma later and went to do a gig in Miami with my sisters. I met Billy Eckstine. He sang 'All the Way' while I accompanied him. I was in seventh heaven. He was my idol. Before I started to sing with my sisters, I was doing TV shows, performing all the records Billy Eckstine had made: 'Jealousy' and 'Caravan.' He was every black singer's idol. I was touched by 'B.'

"I was touched by quite a few of the singers. Most of my life I have loved music. It was my world. Music was my *only* world. Jazz is more sophisticated, with more harmonics, than the blues. But you don't have to improvise or scat or change the melody to sing jazz. Jazz is basically a feeling, which is the blues. I ain't going to argue with nobody, but the blues make jazz stronger. They have people with great voices who feel they have to scat or improvise. But sometimes it takes away from the tune. Sometimes I hardly do any improv with a tune. Other times I feel I want to do something with it. But if you just try to show your technique on every line, you're boring. Everything you do sounds the same. I love to scat. But I don't always do it.

"When you sing the blues, you're totally naked. If you cannot sing the blues, it's going to come out. People in a shanty don't care about how sophisticated your harmonics are. They want to hear a good voice with good range. If you can get down to the human level, you can commmunicate.

"You can't just get out there and be slick. You can't just change the notes. People should groove with that sound. Your style is there naturally. Your sound is your style. Billie and Judy Garland communicated feelings with their natural sounds. Billie compromised the least."

Why is he not better known when so many people say he's a great singer?

"I'm hard to know," he said. "That's my personality and my karma. A lot of critics and club owners and I don't speak. I've been introduced to critics and don't do more than say hello. Recently a manager wanted to handle me exclusively for concert and record dates. The manager seemed bossy. I'll have to think about it. Maybe I'll do it. I don't want anyone telling me how to sing. I'm thinking about going to college. It could help me in some ways. Or course, I know a lot of musicians with degrees are not working, and some are very busy and have no degrees.

"To be famous, you have to go through so much. For what? I never wanted to set the world on fire. I just wanted to burn it a little. The main thing is to get yourself together. Yeah. Musically. I'd like to get away from power singing and combine head [falsetto], like Bobby McFerrin can do, with chest [forte] voice. Sometimes your voice goes if a rhythm section is playing louder than you're singing. Professionally I'm subtle. And that's all I can do."

Joe Lee Wilson's Reverberations

Samuel Taylor Coleridge, a British Romantic poet, fell asleep after using opium and dreamed some stanzas of "Kubla Khan": "In Xanadu did Kubla Khan/A stately pleasure-dome decree:/Where Alph, the sacred river ran/Through caverns measureless to man/Down to a sunless sea. . . ." Awakened by a visitor, Coleridge quickly wrote down the words of the first stanza. But after the intrusion of the visit, he couldn't remember the second stanza.

In 1981 the opiate gripping the mind was a stream of reports about Atlanta's murdered children. Joe Lee Wilson, an Oklahoma-born black married to an Englishwoman and living in Europe, knew about the killings. One day, as he was flying with his group to a gig in Beirut, Lebanon, his pianist, Micky Taylor, said, "They're trying to kill us off in America."

"I didn't know how serious it was until then," Joe Lee recalled.

His concentration deepened suddenly. When he got to Beirut, he went to a hotel, fell asleep and woke up in a cold sweat to put down the lyrics he had dreamed. For a reason he has never understood, he called the song by its title in the dream: "R. R. Metalworks."

"I knew the dream was about the kids. I put it down on tape and then, a few months later, in Camden, England, when I had to sing at a festival, I said to myself, 'I know. I'll sing this song!' The title had nothing to do with the song. It's like a city cry. The way they called the news before there were newspapers. It starts with a moan:

> Mothers are crying,
> Babies are dying,
> Stone writing on the wall,
> People of Atlanta
> Better beware.
> A big burly wolf
> With white curly hair.
> Is it really a wolf? A wolf?
> Or maybe a spy, a man in disguise,
> Black children better take care.

In 1981 in St. Peter's Lutheran Church at Citicorp in New York City, at a rally for the children, Joe Lee sang this song, the most powerfully felt moments of the rally—not only for his huge voice but for the haunting lyric married to an eerie tune. It was a song that in future could always remind people viscerally of the terror of the child-murder epidemic.

Heavily blues oriented, Joe Lee has a voice so powerful that he adjusts sound systems in clubs to make sure he doesn't reverberate and transform a room into a canyon. He belongs to a generation with many formally educated jazz musicians. When he wrote "R. R. Metalworks," he was in his early forties, a traditional singer who had majored in singing at Los Angeles City College. Once he dubbed his bald voice teacher "Martian Head." His lyrics are usually less jive but exactly as imagistic. His gift as an imagist elevated his most serious song, "R. R. Metalworks," into a song of social commentary that Paul Robeson would have felt at home with.

CHAPTER 34

Janet Lawson's
Scat Songs

Essentially Carol Sloane, Anne Marie Moss, the churchy, seductive Ernestine Anderson, who was nominated for a Grammy for her album in 1981, and, usually, Andy Bey sing jazz in the Billie-Ella tradition. They and many more fine jazz singers matured as rock began dominating the scene (with the exception of Ernestine, who started singing professionally before then). But Janet Lawson, their contemporary, primarily scats complex compositions by Mingus, Monk, Tadd Dameron. She does her work with amazing pyrotechnics; she knows how to make microtones work for her—inflections, tones that fall in the cracks between the notes. She is fine and perseverant at what she does; she gets criticized by other singers and club owners. But she keeps scatting. She gets praised, of course, too. Her first album as leader was nominated for a Grammy in 1981.

Dizzy Gillespie has noticed that some lyrics "don't jell with the music." Gillespie has the musical subtlety to divine that some lyrics can conflict with music, while a nonmusical audience might not even notice the clash. Dizzy has also said that lyrics can lift music.

Janet Lawson, who recorded the words on "Moody's Mood for Love" with Eddie Jefferson for Inner City, agrees about the lift of scat.

She has stretched her very pretty voice with exercises to a range of three and a half, sometimes nearly four, octaves—more than Sarah Vaughan's—and in a split second can swoop from the flute's high register to the low notes of a bass. Even when she is singing so Far Out that she gets quite dissonant, she can sound sweet, partly because her choice of scat sounds contributes to the sweetness. It's inherent in her tone, which can have a "moon" and "June" sound. She can also scream with a driving horn sound, as forcefully as any avant-garde saxophonist.

Janet has the long, black flowing hair of a ballet dancer, a fine complexion, delicate features and brown eyes that can project a keen sense of mischief, or benevolent curiosity, or an aesthete's dreaminess.

In the late seventies, she organized her own quintet with a pianist, a bassist, a drummer and reeds player Roger Rosenberg—all very contemporary players. Janet has led them in gigs at the Bottom Line, Sweet Basil, Seventh Avenue South, Greene Street and other New York City clubs. Sometimes she has jumped in a van and driven them to Connecticut, Washington, D.C.—wherever the bookings exist.

"We're going to do a song called 'Bill's Tune' by Bill O'Connell, the pianist," she told a Sweet Basil audience. "But there are so many tunes called 'Bill's Tune' that we had to give it another title. A tentative title. It's called 'Identity Crisis.' "

"Bill's Other Tune," the drummer, Jimmy Madison, called out.

"Ha-ha." Janet laughed. "Identity Crisis. You get it? It's in E flat, and then it's in E. Like that."

Afterward the group did "Reflections." "It's one of Thelonious Monk's more obscure tunes," she said. "You can't hum it. You have to listen."

"If you can hum it, join in," the bassist, Ratzo Harris, called out.

"Ha-ha." Janet laughed—and started out pretty straightforwardly in her lower range, then suddenly did some high little spastic, hornlike riffs. ("Lawson uses a provocative variety of devices to carry out her vocalizing," John Wilson wrote in 1979. "Humming murmurs, staccato shouts, broad, sweeping lines that rise from gorgeously rich low notes and explode like roman candles in a scattering of previously placed highs." He has also given her rave reviews for her "dream-jazz voice" and generally exquisite technique.)

Says Janet, who can make scat sound torchy: "The music is about change. People say it's always differently. We do the same tunes for months and months. Each time we do it differently. The music is always evolving. It gets freer. Sometimes we open it up in the middle of a tune. We break away from the structure, create a free form, and somewhere along the line go back to the tune. Bill will play a cluster of chords. I'll pick out harmonies and sing that. And then he'll play off me. And I play off what he has improvised. It's like a party. We come up with new colors.

"Until recently you couldn't sing Out in some rooms. You had to stay within confines. Other rooms are strictly for instrumentalists. And it's very hard for a singer to get booked. I called Beefsteak Charlie for a gig. The boss said, 'No, this room is for horn players.' I said, 'I sing like a horn.' He agreed to listen to my tape. He said, 'You do.' He hired me."

At age forty-one, Janet was living, as she has for a long time, on the Upper West Side of Manhattan near Riverside Park, where she teaches improvisational jazz singing. She also operates as a visiting teacher to schools and colleges. She recently organized Improvised Music Collective, a nonprofit musicians' corporation, to teach and perform all kinds of music improvisation in schools. She composed music with lyricist Diane Snow for a show called "Jass Is a Lady," about women in jazz, for which she received a grant from the National Endowment for the Arts.

A vegetarian, she has banned cigarettes from the apartment and has stocked it with books on music and philosophy. A small music room is cluttered with the artifacts of Janet's professional life—a piano, an answering machine, a tape recorder, a stereo, a radio, scores, lead sheets, records.

"My mother was a singer, my dad was a drummer; they took me to their gigs. So I grew up in music and learned by osmosis. It was a headstart on learning. When I was three, I sang on a Saturday morning radio show for kids and at the Hippodrome Theater. My mother taught me 'Paper Doll' and 'Don't Fence Me In.' Sonny Rollins [a saxophone player] plays that; it tickles me.

"My mother was a traditional and emotional singer and lyricist. She was from the 'I can't do math' generation. That fear that women have inculcated and that is ingrained. A lot of women say they sing by feeling. 'I don't know a key, I just do it.' They're afraid to know the math of the music. That attitude kills your musical instrument. My mother would sing out of the measures all the time and whisper to my father, 'Where are we?' My father sang the melody in her ear. She was pre-feminine mystique. But my environment was richly musical.

"I studied piano, knew some Chopin and the Circle of the Fourths. I understood chords, II, V^7, I's [twos, fives, ones], the chord progressions. I knew solfeggio. And I think I always had an instinct for improvising. My mother would call out, 'Janet, I can hear you're not reading.' So I squelched improvisational skills, got into technical work and got bored. Eventually I went back to improvising, because I couldn't find that free, creative chord otherwise."

As a teenager, she started singing with bands for training and for pleasure. "Something intrinsic in my spirit makes a connection with the music. I learned a lot of tunes. You've got to know the tunes and the melodies."

In 1959, at age nineteen, she went from Baltimore to New York, and for fifteen years she typed either at regular office jobs or for temporary secretarial agencies. "I wouldn't want anyone to think it has been easy for me and a drag for him or her. That would discourage a kid. So, yeah, I typed. At the same time, I was gigging like crazy." She did all sorts of jobs and demos and sang in joints in Brooklyn, the Bronx, Staten Island. Singing straight at the time. "And I traveled around the world as a singer. An agent asked me to sing in Spanish. So I said, 'Sí'. I boned up on my high school Spanish and learned songs in Spanish. I borrowed gowns, a wedding gown once. And I went to these gigs.

"I probably did see myself as the slinky chick on occasion, when men who heard me singing asked me out to dinner. I probably lived that fantasy. Yes. It was exciting, traveling in El Salvador, singing and talking in Spanish. It was all very romantic. I met a Chilean man. I was in the movie reel. I don't know that much of me believed it. I guess not, because I left it and came back.

"When I was new in New York, I would go to a club and sit and listen to a piano player who was a singer, too. He was well known. And I had a crush on him. I was so naïve. I didn't know he was married, but I used to wait for him to come in. And the musicians who worked with him were beautiful. It was like out of a movie. He had that certain class of suave—charm! I was into that. If I had to really say what my feeling is about that, or in general, I think I wasn't clear. I think I was in a state of fog. You meet someone and you say: maybe this is it. I'm curious and adventuresome to some degree."

The married piano player-singer, who is black, returned the romantic interest, though his marriage felled it. Many years later he looked back on his side of the innocent crush wistfully. It had hurt him to realize his limitations. "I wish she would find someone good enough for her," he added.

The issue of race does not even come up in either of the reminiscences. It goes without saying that the possibility for interracial friendships, affairs and marriages exists, and has existed, with little or no controversy in the jazz world long before the number of interracial marriages began creeping up in society in general.

As a young white singer new on the scene, Janet found professional acceptance common by the 1960s. "Chris White, Curtis Boyd, Harold Mabern, Ron Carter, Pete La Rocca, Ben Riley [all black instrumentalists] were wonderfully helpful on my early gigs. They really gave me their support. As my musicianship grew, only white and black men musicians with ego problems gave me trouble. Otherwise the black-white, man-woman situation is fine."

Some of the younger musicians agree that integration has spawned a greater social and racial freedom in the music world; some disagree. Helen Forrest wrote that a few black musicians on the road with her in the Benny Goodman band didn't talk to her. Forty years later, Janet has little idea of what that kind of segregated race relations must have been like.

"I come from a Czech Catholic, Russian Jewish background. A rich heritage. I dig my own roots. Then, if you can get past the narrow vision of your roots, you can get into what other people are doing. All music is someone's roots. But you don't stop there at your own roots. They're all connected. I can understand someone else's experience."

For about ten years Janet did gigs around the world and in New York City. In 1969 Janet's mother died. "I was so symbiotically attached, I couldn't sing for two years. Because all my life I had been trying to live for her, through her, and her for me and through me. In a way her death was a breath of fresh air. I could finally let go. So I was able to get some space."

But not right away. As her mother lay dying, she told Janet, who was twenty-nine, to go to a particular man. "He'll take care of you," her mother said. Janet went to live with him for several years. "It was the first time I really seriously tried to deal with commitment."

An amateur musician, he managed her career for a while. But that aspect of the relationship created conflicts. The couple broke up. After her mother's death, too, Janet discovered improvisational theater out West. "It was free-spirited and drew on a lot of improvisational spaces. I got involved."

Then a musician, Bill Whited, called her to do a gig in New Jersey. Janet said, "I don't sing anymore."

He said, "You'll have fun."

She said, "That got me. So I went Out. Out. I started improvising. Everything changed in my life then. I supported the meat boycott, stopped eating meat, started Yoga and meditating.

"My main influence has been horns. Dizzy influenced Sarah. Prez influenced Billie Holiday. Any major singer has been influenced by horns. And Armstrong was the first scat singer. The horn influence began when I was fifteen. I was a traditional bandsinger who got up at letter D and sat down at letter E. But I was enveloped in the saxes, trombones, trumpets. I was hearing things that way. When I was singing with Dad's drums, I heard horns. With a trio, I heard horn sounds. I don't know why. I feel like an instrument, not that I sound like one; I feel I *am* one, and I have an affinity with all horns from flutes to saxes.

"When I was little, I looked up to contemporary singers of the day. There were things I wanted to do. Jeri Southern had a frosty, soft voice." Dakota Staton had a big voice, which Janet particularly wished for. She wanted Ella Fitzgerald's easy swing, too. "She didn't have to push. I listened to Nat 'King' Cole—and Frank Sinatra because of his phrasing. I listened to his songs over and over until I could lip-sync them. Then when you deviate, you find your own voice. I got into Peggy Lee, who came from Billie Holiday. I listened to Ray Charles' phrasing. I love that church thing. I lip-synced Ray Charles to feel the black way of saying things. So it's a blending of black and white music. Then I went into instruments. Bird. There are no grooves left on my recordings of the Savoy releases. I got into Sonny Rollins, Monk, Bud Powell, Duke, Mingus, Max Roach and Miles.

"I hear as if the total orchestra is trying to come through [the way piano players often say they hear]. Scat singing is total improv." (Bobby McFerrin added that improvisation is abandonment to feelings.) "It's jazz in the same way that any other instrumentalist makes up melodies. I don't live every moment of every day as total improv. But I try to.

"If I had to label myself, I'd call myself an improvisational musician who uses her voice as an instrument to travel across the bar lines. 'Ain't Misbehavin'' is in four-four time. Four beats to a measure. But instead I'm stretching my phrasing across. Time is an illusion. It expands, it contracts. In improvising you create your own time. So I play with it and feel no restriction. We can agree we're coming from four-four time. But we don't have to live with it."

In her music room, she teaches vocal improvisation privately—a type of sophisticated class you find primarily on the West or East coasts in this bicoastal American entertainment world. She asks students to sing melodies based on technical information from chords and scales. She coaches them in improvising, taking clues from all kinds of instrumentals and even from each other's improvisations—a test of wit, instinct and musicality.

"If you're singing with a band," she tells students, "you can't be in your own little world. You have to pick up on what's going on."

Recently she formed a nonprofit corporation to take vocal improvisation into schools, and got a job to teach this relatively rare course at William Paterson College in Wayne, New Jersey. "We've got to get into the system," she says, to earn money and keep the art alive.

"I feel passionate about the music. I love it. It's the key to my freedom. If I can be true to the music, I can be true in the rest of my life. I know of no other experience that gives me myself and that spirit of improvisation that comes to me through music.

"But the gift isn't mine. If I thought it was mine, I would worry if I could do it again. I would be depressed. I'm not scared, because the music isn't mine; it's coming through me, and I dedicate the evening to the oneness we're all part of. Otherwise the music is prevented from coming out. When I open up my mouth, the music comes out. But I don't claim it. No more than I can claim the sunset I see every day."

CHAPTER 35

The Beat of Tania Maria: "A Piano Is Not Like a Man"

It was Carnegie Hall, the Kool Jazz Festival. Tania Maria walked out to her piano to join her trio, wearing a plain knitted dress with stripes going around and around, emphasizing her roundness. "Now, no talk, let's go to Brazil," she said in her throaty voice with a heavy accent, curiously more like Greta Garbo's in *Ninotchka* than a Brazilian's. Both feet in black pumps socked the floor. The whole body got into the act. She sometimes half stood and danced the samba as she played. Her head danced, independent of her body. She scatted: "Yetsasasasbubabboobu." Something like that, with Portuguese flavor. She kept it up, perpetual rhythm, playing, singing, piano-bench dancing, for an hour. Sometimes the audience roared and rocked in the seats—not something jazz fans at concerts in the great music halls of New York usually do.

Tania Maria is a far cry from Astrud Gilberto, a pretty girl with a facility for singing the samba beat in a soft voice lightly. Tania Maria is outrageous.

From Carmen McRae to the musical Coles to Dave Frishberg, the Brazilians have it. Frishberg, traveling with tapes of Brazilian singers for company, has said the future sounds like Brazilian music, second in popularity around the world to music from the United States.

348

Latin rhythms aren't suddenly entering gringo jazz. The African beat with a Latin tempering came from the islands and mainland South America into New Orleans long before jazz was jazz. The Latin beat came from the Africans taken by the French and Spanish as slaves into the Southern Hemisphere. Dizzy Gillespie has often favored Latin drummers; Chano Pozo from Cuba played with Dizzy in his early years. In 1981 another Cuban, Ignacio Beroa, joined Dizzy's group. And Daniel Ponce, a newly arrived Cuban conga player, has been stirring some excitement in jazz circles.

An influx of Spanish-speaking immigrants from Cuba, Puerto Rico, Panama, Mexico, Colombia, Venezuela, plus the French-speaking black Haitians, are spreading Latin accents further and deeper into the United States, most especially into the music. Brazil, even though it is so far away, has along with nearby but isolated Cuba sent some formidable musicians to the States. Paquito D'Rivera, one of the most touted tenor saxophonists in this country, escaped from Cuba during the last great exodus. He first sought asylum in Spain, then worked his way to New York, where he had a recording contract with Columbia ever since Gillespie first heard him. Drummer Ignacio Beroa left Cuba at the same time. Both were nurtured on old American jazz records that remained in Cuba after the revolution and on daily broadcasts of jazz via the Voice of America. Some singers have come from Cuba, too. Lupe Joli Garcia reigned for a while as the Queen of Latin Soul, singing at hurricane velocity.

From Brazil the political journey to the United States is easier, though the physical distance is far greater. But the musical climate in the States lures some fine Brazilian musicians away from Copacabaña. Along with the samba, Tania Maria plays plenty of licks learned from the bebop jazz pianists, dissonances and all. And the United States musical community has especially welcomed the Brazilians because of the beat.

Tania Maria looks exotic, even with plastic-rimmed eyeglasses, against her *café au lait* complexion. She wears glasses sometimes while performing, with her hair flying; it seems to stand out on end like Little Orphan Annie's, when it is not trimmed short. Her French-born manager-husband, Eric Kressman, who was a successful businessman in France, fell in love with Tania Maria in Paris.

"I had a business and quit three years ago to manage Tania

Maria. Sometimes it's difficult to find a manager, especially for a lady in France, where everything is sometimes like this, sometimes like that, everything," Eric Kressman said. And he waved his hand back and forth. "In France managers are not really serious. I didn't know what is management of an artist. But I said to myself: I will try it. Also, I suppose she had a big talent, but, I said to myself, ha-ha, maybe not for this work. But I'll try to work seriously; I have to learn. And she was ready to accept some mistakes. Before this, I was obliged to manage and conduct a big company in France and to know money. But show business is another thing. And I made some mistakes in the beginning, I am sure. But I said to me that she could make a good career."

Eric, a tall and boyishly lean, pink-and-white-complexioned Frenchman with a strong jaw, talked with an irresistible French accent as he drove along the streets of Port Washington, New York, taking me to meet Tania Maria. He stopped to look at a car for sale in the street; he wanted to replace the one he had been renting for months, ever since he and his wife and daughter arrived to keep building Tania's career in the United States. They settled on Long Island in a rented house—new immigrants, without much English at first.

While still in France, he reminisced: "I decided to see what the progress had been after six months. And I say, 'Oh, my God, terrible.' But then after ten months in Europe, she played the Olympia Theater, the Théâtre de la Ville, with a very big success there, and the Palais de Glace. She played only in theaters in Paris and made only concerts. That is the way of Tania. She played Fat Tuesday's in New York, yes, but it's too small for her." (Tania Maria made a great and stirring rhythmic noise in that small, low-ceilinged club, with her piano, her voice, her drummer, her conga player—and a bassist who sometimes was nearly drowned out in the Brazilian revelry.) "A lot of energy goes into singing and playing instruments together, in a club, with smoke. She is obliged not to stop. It's a little hard to play three sets a night. It's too much. She must be very careful with her voice. She would like to play in a big club. Maybe the Bottom Line. But that's like a concert hall."

At the house, where strong French coffee is kept on tap, Tania Maria sat on the floor of her basement studio. An upright piano stood against one wall; her husband's desk faced it. The centerpiece was a blond-wood coffee table with an old roach, left by a friend, lying in an ashtray. She thrummed some remarkable, fast rhythms breathtakingly transcendent to our half-halting English conversation laced with French about love and music.

In 1975 she came to New York to play in the Kool Jazz Festival, then still called the Newport Jazz Festival, and opened Sarah Vaughan's program. George Wein's representative, Simon Genebra, had heard Tania playing in the Via Brazil club in Paris and invited her to the United States festival. "But I didn't understand nothing in English. It seems that people wanted me to stay. But I didn't because I didn't understand. And George Wein, who invited me, was angry because he thinks I said to him no. He was upset because I wouldn't stay. He wanted me to work in Michael's Pub in February 1976. But I said I cannot stay because I have contract to go to Tunisia. Can you imagine? I changed from United States to Tunisia? He could not understand. But this is my history. Today I understand. He wanted to make a record at that time. Ha-ha. Can you believe?" And her laughter got lusty, low in her throat and powerful, the way her singing does. "Tunisia. I went to Tunisia!

"My real feelings about music started when I was twenty-two or twenty-three, because I decided to live this kind of life of a musician. A strange life, because you don't belong to you anymore. I always had impression that Brazilian music was something very strong. And in Brazilian music the most important is the rhythm. And in my music, I keep this. My harmony and melody are influenced by Ravel and Stravinsky and Americans. But the rhythm is Brazilian."

While she is proud that the jazz family has accepted her, she doesn't feel she really belongs—though her acceptance is based on her own analysis of her sound. "My music is not like notes, it's pure emotion," while "jazz is free emotion and makes a big contribution to liberty," she said.

"Of Latin music, I cannot say enough. The Brazilians, who were colonized by the Portuguese, don't like to mix their music with that of other Latin countries. In Argentina, and in the rest of South America, it's difficult to find a black man. The rest of South America is very little black. And so in Brazil there is another feeling. In Brazil we had Indians, whites and blacks. So I believe in many colors mixed. This is the difference; it reflects in music.

"In Brazil you have, in each region, folk music. In Rio de Janeiro the samba is the folk music. The rhythm came from Africa, and the samba made progress. Samba cançao [slow] or very fast, or bossa nova, from samba but more sophisticated—a music from aspiration." And she breathed and banged on the table to show the rhythm of breathing, or the breathing of the rhythm.

"Always jazz puts you against the wall, but samba makes you go back and forth, ahead and behind. Normally you play jazz for two hours; you become depressed, because it's all here in your head. But Latin music is throughout your body. And this is the big mystery of Latin music. So we absorb the thing of jazz totally for the whole body, and it's very sensual." (She turned her head from side to side.)

"Music is something you begin when you are small." She was born in the north of Brazil on May 9, 1948, and grew up in the south, near Rio. The eldest of five children, she began studying the piano in a conservatory when she was seven. She didn't know if she had any talent and didn't begin to play in her mature style until she left the classical conservatory. "There I never felt I could be an artist. Nobody told me. I was obliged to do the lessons. I studied solfeggio two days a week but never worked at it. I went to school, also. In my little town, having a piano was very important. And my mother was hot to have her first daughter in piano.

"I think my big problem in life was that I was a girl. A child prodigy at age twelve. I won a piano contest against people twice my age, playing samba, not classical, in Rio de Janeiro. It wasn't good, because you're not well understood by other people. Because by your age, you cannot be adult. You can make like, but you cannot."

At age thirteen, she started playing at dances around her home base, in little towns, even in Rio. But she wasn't serious about music at that time. "Sometimes I preferred to play with friends rather than play piano. But one day when I was twenty-three, I wake up and say: 'What do you want to do?' I answer to myself: 'Music.' I left all my problems behind me. My family and ego problems behind me. And even some friends. And I put myself in the musical artists' life. A good life, but a hard life, because if you want to live in very good health, you must dedicate your life to this. Three quarters of your life must go to this. Only one quarter for your husband, child, mother. Music is a mistress very possessive. If you say to her, 'Ciãou,' she can say, 'Ciãou' and forever. So it's very dangerous.

"Music is like life. Every day she can change. And you must be prepared. It can change both outside yourself and also inside yourself. Normally you make music both places.

"There are two categories. Musicians who are loved and others who say they are the best and have big security. I don't have big security. And I don't want. If you are perfect, life is not intelligent for you.

"Comte Guy de Casteja of Paris heard me in the Club Twenty-one in Rio de Janeiro. If someone hear me, he will find something. He wanted to make a Brazilian club in Paris and tried to find a group to import. He invited me to Paris.

"I have two big musical influences in my life: Luis Eça and Johnny Alf. They both play piano and compose. Alf is a singer, too. Eça is the best piano player in Brazil. The influences on these people were American and European. Of the Americans, Eça liked Art Tatum, but Johnny liked Nat 'King' Cole. Eça studied in Switzerland and won first prize. He plays our music like magic with a new inspiration because of the classical background. More of a pianist-arranger-composer. He has incredible technique. Johnny is more sensitive; he'll never be well understood. He has only two songs that are popular, but thousands of others. He is like Bill Evans; he plays very happy and romantic music, and romantic is not always jazz."

With these influences, at age twenty-six she went to Paris to play for three months and stayed for seven years.

"Europe for me was seven years of good time. My father was happy when I went to Europe. But my mother was never happy. She wanted me to play piano and make a good marriage. My mother thinks still today that her children belong to her. But now she starts to wake up and know children are for the world. I am glad to make a contribution. And she starts to be happy for me now. But my father was always happy. My father is more open.

"Paris was the first place that I felt really good about my music. The audience made me feel strong and confident. I first lived near Métro Glacière, before Place d'Italie, in the thirteenth *arrondissement*. Later I moved to Rambouillet, near Versailles, to a house, because I liked to work at night—to one A.M, two A. M. I don't have good feelings in the day to work. I worked very good in Rambouillet. I played a lot, not exercises, just played. I don't practice. I would like very much to be a right person and have some discipline, but I'm not like that. I can leave the piano for one week.

"It's like love. I can stay one week without, but when you make, you make very well. It's like a man to me. But it's the piano that gives me this sensation. Not like a man who gives me when he wants to give me.

"I played in Via Brasil in Montparnasse in the Tour de Montparnasse. For the first time in my life, I heard people say I make good jazz music. In Brazil it's embarrassing to be jazz." In Brazil if she wanted a job and someone told the boss she played jazz, she wouldn't get the work. "Because it's American. They want real Brazilian. In France the same word opens all the doors for me. It was like a dream. In Brazil I was closed up. In Paris I could start to love me. When you are not loved by people, you cannot love yourself. So I felt good.

"Eric—I met him—he met me. He listened once when I was on radio. He was in his house and heard me. And he heard I will be in concert at Palais de Chaillot. And he came to the concert. And he don't talk with me first time. 'Do you know where this girl plays?' he asks someone. 'Bilboquet, a club in Saint-Germain-des-Prés.' I started a career in this jazz family. And Eric came to hear me and started a wonderful love story. I can't tell you, very personal. Like everybody. But for me it was special. And for me he's very special.

"He was always a jazz fan. He had a classical education. His father was a composer in church. Hymns. Eric came from Calvinist and Prussian background. And he likes very much jazz and good music. He has a good taste. I like very much my music, but I don't like the show-business ambience. These things make me feel depressed. I don't like business. But Eric does."

They married in 1978 when Tania was thirty. "After five years I said, 'I would like to go to America.'

" 'Why?' he said.

"I said, 'Because I was in good stage in Europe. Because I had enough work for a normal life. Because I was starting to have less emotions than I wanted to have. I had already been married three years.'

"And he said to me, 'If you feel like this, we're going to go.' But he didn't say when. But we started to work, our minds and spirit. We did not know how to come here. We didn't know anybody. And it's very difficult to make a deal with people. And also Europe takes Americans, but America doesn't take Europeans." (Europe has traditionally welcomed American jazz musicians as heroes, but the

United States, which created the music, hasn't often honored European jazz musicians.)

"I had to go to India for a festival and then to Australia. And in Australia I met Cleo Laine's manager. She had seen me in the festival and told her manager that I'm wonderful. So he introduced me to Charlie Byrd, the guitar player, who has a jazz club in Washington. And he invited me to play in his club and told the owner of Concord Jazz Records that I'm a good musician. The owner listened to my tape and invited me from Europe." She made two records for Concord in late 1981 and early 1982, and was planning a third, as she faced a busy itinerary for the summer of 1982.

"Now her music is a mélange," said Eric. "I will be surprised if I don't hear something of George Benson and Al Jarreau in the third record. She wants to be popular. I like to play in concerts and jazz festivals, but she has many ideas. Too many ideas, I think. Ha-ha. But she wants to 'konkreteeze' [concretize] the ideas. For that you must have a little money. For money you must be popular.

"She likes to listen to Chick Corea [the Free Jazz pianist] but also to Al Jarreau and Quincy Jones—he's jazz but he's not jazz. She would like to work with him and with Aretha Franklin and Stevie Wonder [both commercially successful as well as admired musicians, bearing the pop label]. Of course, she would also like to play with Ron Carter [a jazz bassist]."

During their first summer with a United States headquarters, they were heading for Seattle, Washington; Portland, Oregon; Los Angeles, for a "Concert by the Sea"; then would go to Vancouver, Canada. From there to Berlin and Essen, Germany; then France to a club in Montmartre; then to Geneva's New Morning Club; and back to Paris to the New Morning Club on the Grand Boulevard, near Porte Saint-Martin. "In Germany she plays with a big orchestra, forty people with strings. We will know after how it works," said Eric, smiling.

Then to the Kool Jazz Festival, the Concord Festival in California. In November, Cuba. "Yes, I think it's very interesting, Cuba," Eric said. "Not for the money, there's no dollars. But it's interesting to see the music."

For the European trip she was taking her own musicians, all Americans. "It's silly to go to Europe with American musicians," Eric mused. "But if you arrive with American musicians, they say she's great. It's terrible! They have very good musicians in Europe.

We can hire them there. But if she doesn't come with American musicians, they think she has no money, she's not very good. I don't understand. It's crazy. We have very bad musicians in the United States, too. But America is the church of jazz musicians."

A List of Singers

A *representative* listing of jazz-influenced singers is as follows:
Nellie Lutcher; Martha Raye; Herb Jeffries; Bob Eberly and Ray
Eberle; Velma Middleton; Ella Logan; Lee Wiley; Jo Stafford;
Betty Roche; Billie Holiday; Ruth Etting; Frank Sinatra; Savan-
nah Churchill; Vi Redd; Ella Fitzgerald; *les belles* Helenes Ward,
O'Connell, Forrest, Humes and, later, Merrill.

And Ivie Anderson; June Richmond; Henry Wells; Hoagy Carmichael; Leo Watson; Nat "King" Cole and his brothers, Ike, Eddie
and Fred; Slim Gaillard; Cab Calloway; Babs Gonzalez, who could
imitate all the others; and Eddie Jefferson (also, Luba Rashiek,
who sounds exactly like Jefferson).

And Jimmy Rushing; Big Joe Turner; Pha Terrell; Bon Bon; Mel
Torme; Frances Faye; Joe Williams; Thelma Carpenter; Rose
Murphy, the "chee-chee" girl; Buddy Stewart; Dave Lambert;
Annie Ross; Jon Hendricks; Maxine Sullivan; Buddy Greco;
Johnny Hartman; Joe Carroll; Anita O'Day; Teddi King; Kay
Arman; Georgia Brown; Ketty Lester; Sarah Vaughan; Carmen
McRae; Frances Wayne; Billy Eckstine; Les McCann; Taj Mahal;
Doris Day; Billy Daniels; David Allyn; Dick Haymes; Buddy
Greco; Sylvia Syms; Pearl Bailey; Della Reese; Leon Thomas; Joe
Mooney; Lou Rawls; Esther Phillips; Eddie "Cleanhead" Vinson;

Gloria Lynn; Al Hibbler; Dan Grissom; King Pleasure; Ray Charles; Kenny Hagood; Earl Coleman; Ruth Brown; Nina Simone; Carrie Smith; Jeri Southern; Etta Jones, who can do an uncanny mime of Billie Holiday.

And Cleo Laine; Jackie Cain and Roy Kral; Irene Kral; the Hi-Los; Mose Allison; the Manhattan Transfer; Arthur Prysock; Dakota Staton; Steve Lawrence and Eydie Gorme; Blossom Dearie; Perry Como; Barbara Lea; Peggy Lee; Tony Bennett; Shirley Horn; Anita Ellis; Joya Sherrill; Margaret Whiting; Dinah Washington; the swinging Beverly Kenney, who could make a jazz song even out of "Mairzy Doats," but who died very young; Bob Dorough; Dave Frishberg; Nancy Wilson; Maxine Brown; Jackie Paris; Anne Marie Moss; Bill Henderson; Ethel Ennis; Morgana King; Chris Connor; Damita Jo; Cleo Laine; June Christy; Miriam Klein (who lives in Europe); Teresa Brewer; Kay Starr; Lena Horne; Rosemary Clooney; Bobby Troup; Georgia Gibbs; Andy Bey, and Salome and Geraldine Bey; Norman Mapp; Lonnie Satin; Rita Reys; Emmy Kemp; Lee Richardson; Ann Burton; Carol Ventura; Ernestine Anderson; Stella Marrs; Louis Jordan; Sue Raney; Yolande Bavan; Sheila Jordan; Abbey Lincoln; Judy Garland (controversial in this list but loved by jazz musicians); Pat Kirby; Elis Regina, a marvelous Brazilian singer; Astrud Gilberto; Bobby Short; Roberta Flack; and many others—all jazz or jazz-influenced singers.

And Betty Carter; Al Jarreau; Carmen Lundy; Monica Zetterling; Mark Murphy; Bobby McFerrin; Urszula Dudziak; João Gilberto; Chaka Khan; Tania Maria; Jane Harvey; Natalie Cole; Aretha Franklin; Vocal Jazz, Inc.; Kathleen Adair; Jon Lucien; Flora Purim; Karen Krog (another singer in Europe); Carol Sloane; Stevie Wonder; Michael Franks; Joe Lee Wilson; Chris Calloway; the New Hi-Los; Trish Turner; Susannah McCorkle; Marlene Verplanck; Evelyn Blakey; Maria Muldaur; Judy Niemack; Diane Reeves; Jay Clayton; Deedee Bridgewater; Janet Lawson; Roberta Davis, a slightly known jazz singing treasure living in the country's heartland.

And Joanne Norris; Jeanne Lee; Marion Cowings; Roseanna Vitro; Emilie Long; Carol Fredette; Marva Josie; Grace Testani; Carla White; Carmen Barnes; Jean Carn; Keisha St. Joan; Dennis Rowland; Birdie Greene; Cathy Rich, who is Buddy Rich's daughter; Kim Shaw; Jane Blackstone; Laurie Antonioli; Donna Lee;

Esther Phillips; Marilyn Moore; Lorraine Feather, who is Leonard Feather's daughter; and Steve March, who is Mel Torme's son . . .

And the instrumentalists who have sung, too—among them:

Jimmy Rowles, a pianist who was nominated for a Grammy singing award; Jelly Roll Morton; Jabbo Smith; Hot Lips Page; Roy Eldridge; Lionel Hampton; Chet Baker; Doc Cheatham; Jonah Jones; Eddie Chamblee; Oscar Peterson, who sounds as much like Nat "King" Cole as Cole's brothers do.

And George Benson, the jazz guitarist and popular singing superstar; Hazel Scott; Slam Stewart; Clark Terry; Major Holley; Ray Nance; Dizzy Gillespie; Little Joe Turner, who lives in Paris; Jack Teagarden; Woody Herman; Carline Ray; James Moody; Nina Sheldon; Arvel Shaw; Barbara London; Amina Claudine Myers; Joe Muranyi; and a hundred others.

Bibliography

Albertson, Chris. *Bessie.* New York: Stein & Day, 1972.

Astaire, Fred. *Steps in Time, An Autobiography.* New York: Da Capo Press, 1979. (Originally published by Harper & Row, New York, 1959.)

Balliett, Whitney. *Dinosaurs in the Morning.* Philadelphia and New York: J. B. Lippincott Co., 1962.

———. *Ecstasy at the Onion.* New York: The Bobbs-Merrill Co., Inc., 1971.

———. *New York Notes—A Journal of Jazz in the '70s.* Boston: Houghton Mifflin Co., 1976.

———. Article in *The New Yorker* magazine, September 1982.

Blesh, Rudi. *Shining Trumpets: A History of Jazz.* New York: Da Capo Press, 1975.

Calloway, Cab, and Bryant Rollins. *Of Minnie the Moocher and Me.* New York: Thomas Y. Crowell Co., 1976.

Charles, Ray, and David Ritz. *Brother Ray.* New York: Dial Press, 1978.

Chilton, John, with foreword by Buck Clayton. *"Billie's Blues," The Billie Holiday Story.* New York: Day Books (Stein & Day), 1975. Also, Quartet Books, London.

Clooney, Rosemary, and Raymond Strait. *This for Remembrance.* New York: Playboy Press Paperbacks, 1977–1979.

Coker, Jerry. *Listening to Jazz*. Englewood Cliffs, N.J.: Prentice-Hall, 1978.

Cole, Maria, and Louis Robinson. *Nat King Cole, An Intimate Biography*. New York: William Morrow & Co., Inc., 1971.

Crosby, Kathryn. *Bing and Other Things*. New York: Meredith Press, 1967.

Feather, Leonard. *The Encyclopedias of Jazz in the '60s and '70s*. New York: Horizon Press, 1966 and 1976.

———. *Inside Jazz*. New York: Da Capo Press, 1977.

———. "James Joyce of Jazz," *Esquire* magazine, New York City, 1945.

Forrest, Helen, and Bill Libby. *I Had the Craziest Dream*. New York: Coward, McCann & Geoghegan, 1981.

Goffin, Robert. *Horn of Plenty: The Story of Louis Armstrong*. New York: Allen, Towne & Heath, 1947.

Haskins, James, and Kathleen Benson. *Scott Joplin*. New York: Doubleday & Co., 1978.

Hentoff, Nat. *The Jazz Life*. New York: Da Capo Press, 1978; Dial Press, 1961.

Holiday, Billie, and William Dufty. *Lady Sings the Blues*. New York: Doubleday, 1956.

Horne, Lena, and Richard Schickel. *Lena*. New York: Doubleday & Co., 1965.

Jones, LeRoi. *Blues People*. New York: William Morrow & Co., 1963.

Jones, Max, and John Chilton. *Louis—The Armstrong Story*. Boston: Little, Brown & Co., 1971.

Kirkeby, Ed, and Duncan P. Schiett with Sinclair Traill. *Ain't Misbehavin'—The Story of Fats Waller*. New York: Dodd, Mead & Co., 1966.

Liska, A. James. "Sarah Vaughan: I'm Not a Jazz Singer," *Down Beat*, May 1982.

Lyons, Len. *The 101 Great Jazz Albums*. New York: William Morrow & Co., 1980.

Meryman, Richard. *Louis Armstrong: A Self-Portrait*. New York: Eakins Press, 1971.

Morgenstern, Dan. *The Jazz Story*. New York: Jazz Museum, 1973.

The New York Times. Morgue clips, including clips on various singers from *Newsweek*, *Time*, the *New York Post*, the *New York Daily News*, the *Saturday Review*.

O'Day, Anita, and George Eells. *High Times, Hard Times*. New York: G. P. Putnam's Sons, 1981.

Ostransky, Leroy. *Jazz City.* Englewood Cliffs, N.J.: Prentice-Hall, 1978.

Pahlens, Kurt. *Great Singers.* New York: Stein & Day, 1974; and W. H. Allen & Co., Ltd., London, England.

Panassié, Hugues. *Louis Armstrong.* New York: Da Capo Press, 1980.

Pavarotti, Luciano, and William Wright. *My Own Story.* New York: Doubleday & Co., 1981.

Pleasants, Henry. *Great American Popular Singers.* New York: Simon & Schuster, 1974.

Purim, Flora, and Edward Bunker. *Freedom Song.* New York: Berkley Books, 1982.

Reisner, Robert George. *Jazz Titans.* New York: Doubleday & Co., 1960.

Rose, Al. *Eubie Blake.* New York: Schirmer Books, 1979.

Schuller, Gunther. *Early Jazz.* New York: Oxford University Press, 1968.

Shaw, Arnold. *The Street That Never Slept.* New York: Coward, McCann & Geoghegan, 1971.

Southern, Eileen. *The Music of Black Americans, A History.* New York: W. W. Norton & Co., 1971.

Stearns, Marshall. *The Story of Jazz.* New York: Oxford University Press, 1978.

———, and Jean Stearns. *Jazz Dance, New York and London.* New York: Macmillan; London: Collier-Macmillan, 1968.

Taylor, Arthur. *Notes and Tones.* New York: Perigee Books, G. P. Putnam's Sons, 1982.

Thompson, Charles. *Bing—The Authorized Biography.* New York: David McKay Co., Inc., 1975.

Tucker, Sophie. *Some of These Days.* New York: David McKay Co., Inc., 1975.

Ulanov, Barry. *A History of Jazz in America.* New York: Viking Press, 1952.

Ullman, Michael. *Jazz Lives.* Washington, D.C.: New Republic Books, 1980.

Waller, Maurice, and Anthony Calabrese. *Fats Waller.* New York: Schirmer Books, 1977.

Waters, Ethel, and Charles Samuels. *His Eye Is on the Sparrow.* New York: Doubleday & Co., 1950.

Wilmer, Valerie. *As Serious As Your Life.* London: Alison & Busby, 1977.

Wilson, Earl. *Sinatra—An Unauthorized Biography.* New York: Signet/New American Library, 1976.

Index

364 Index

Tex Medly

- Squeeze Me
- Lazy River
- Sugar Blues
- Others Tune?
- Sister Kate
- New Orleans